THE NOTWITHSTANDING CLAUSE
AND THE CANADIAN CHARTER

The Notwithstanding Clause and the Canadian Charter

Rights, Reforms, and Controversies

Edited by Peter L. Biro

McGill-Queen's University Press
Montreal & Kingston • London • Chicago

ISBN 978-0-2280-2019-6 (cloth)
ISBN 978-0-2280-2020-2 (paper)
ISBN 978-0-2280-2021-9 (ePDF)
ISBN 978-0-2280-2022-6 (ePUB)

Legal deposit second quarter 2024
Bibliothèque nationale du Québec

Printed in Canada on acid-free paper that is 100% ancient forest free
(100% post-consumer recycled), processed chlorine free

This book has been published with the help of a grant from the Canadian Federation
for the Humanities and Social Sciences, through the Awards to Scholarly Publications
Program, using funds provided by the Social Sciences and Humanities Research
Council of Canada.

Funded by the   Financé par le
Government   gouvernement   Canada Council   Conseil des arts
of Canada   du Canada   for the Arts   du Canada

We acknowledge the support of the Canada Council for the Arts.
Nous remercions le Conseil des arts du Canada de son soutien.

Mcgill-Queen's University Press in Montreal is on land which long served
as a site of meeting and exchange amongst Indigenous Peoples, including the
Haudenosaunee and Anishinabeg nations. In Kingston it is situated on the territory
of the Haudenosaunee and Anishinaabek. We acknowledge and thank the diverse
Indigenous Peoples whose footsteps have marked these territories on which peoples
of the world now gather.

Library and Archives Canada Cataloguing in Publication

Title: The notwithstanding clause and the Canadian charter :
rights, reforms, and controversies / edited by Peter L. Biro.
Names: Biro, Peter L., 1960– editor.
Description: Includes bibliographical references and index.
Identifiers: Canadiana (print) 2023057873X | Canadiana (ebook) 20230578780
| ISBN 9780228020196 (hardcover) | ISBN 9780228020202 (softcover) | ISBN
9780228020219 (PDF) | ISBN 9780228020226 (ePUB)
Subjects: LCSH: Canada. Canadian Charter of Rights and Freedoms. | LCSH:
Derogation (Law)—Canada.
Classification: LCC KE4381.5 N68 2024 | LCC KF4483.C519 N68 2024
kfmod | DDC 342.7108/5—dc23

This book was typeset in 10.5/13 Sabon.

Contents

Acknowledgments

The contributors to this volume gathered at Massey College in Toronto in April 2022 for two days of intensive presentations and discussions about the nature, significance, operation, and impact on Canada's law and politics, of section 33 of the Charter, the notwithstanding clause. All understood that the object of our inquiry was important and of consequence for the country and all were committed to an open-minded, if also occasionally passionate, engagement with one another on a subject that has divided scholars, politicians, and citizens alike. The result of that engagement is contained in the pages of this volume. It is to the contributors, first and foremost, that I give thanks, to their willingness to consider each other's arguments, critiques, and insights, and to their generosity in making well-considered revisions to their respective chapters in light of those arguments, critiques, and insights. In this connection, it must also be acknowledged that the peer review process resulted in considerable improvements to this volume and, while the identities of the readers in that process remain unknown to me, I would be remiss not to thank and acknowledge them nonetheless for their meticulous reading, commentary, and critiques.

I am thankful to Nathalie Des Rosiers who, as principal of Massey College, both graciously welcomed us and allowed us to convene at Massey, and also contributed substantively in our proceedings and discussions.

I am especially grateful to Emily Andrew who, as editor at McGill-Queen's University Press, believed in the project and shepherded it from inception to completion. Without Emily's invaluable guidance, expertise, and encouragement, this volume would not have come to fruition. Thanks also go to MQUP editorial assistant Joanne Pisano and the entire MQUP team, including managing editor Kathleen Fraser, publicist Jacqueline Davis, and copy editor Jared Toney, for supporting the project, Emily Bradley for her technical and editorial assistance, Michael Biro and Erika Biro for proofreading the manuscript, and indexer, Judy Dunlop.

Finally, I wish to acknowledge the Federation for the Humanities and Social Sciences Awards to Scholarly Publications Program, and Section 1, whose financial support made publication of this volume possible.

THE NOTWITHSTANDING CLAUSE
AND THE CANADIAN CHARTER

Setting the Stage: Chekhov's Gun Inverted

Peter L. Biro

Over four decades ago, Queen Elizabeth II visited Canada to affirm the coming into force of the Constitution Act, 1982, including, of course, Part 1 thereof, the Canadian Charter of Rights and Freedoms (the "Charter"). In her speech on the occasion of the proclamation of our new Constitution, the Queen stated, "Constitutional revision is really a matter of adapting to changing needs and circumstances while safeguarding stability and providing protection for guaranteed rights. Change and movement are essential signs of life. The Constitution, which so splendidly met the needs of the very young Canada of the late nineteenth century, could not have been anticipated in the conditions of national life in 1982 and beyond. It is fitting, therefore, that the main feature of Canada's new Constitution should be that it strengthens the rights of its people while establishing a process of amendment which will make needed changes easier to accomplish than they were in the past."[1]

At the time of the Charter's enactment in 1982, liberal constitutional democracy seemed very much in the ascendant throughout the West and beyond. But by the time a group of Canada's leading constitutional and public policy scholars, jurists, and democracy advocates convened some forty years later in the library of Massey College for an intensive colloquium on the significance, meaning, impact, operation, and (de)merits of section 33 of the Charter, the notwithstanding clause (NWC), also known as the override clause[2] NWC, the tide had turned. Liberal constitutionalism was everywhere under siege and in retreat, democratic backsliding was rampant and the independence, influence, and legitimacy of the judiciary that had been elevated and fortified in the course of the human rights and

civil liberties reforms of the previous decades were now being recon-
sidered and challenged in all quarters, from Budapest to Brasilia,
and from Washington, DC, to Jerusalem.

Canadians heralded the advent of the Charter as a constitutional
bulwark against state-imposed constraints on human rights and
civil liberties, but no liberal democracy, including Canada, can be
entirely shielded from the winds of democratic backsliding blow-
ing elsewhere.

After four decades of Canadian politics and jurisprudence in the
Charter era, we have occasion, in this volume of essays arising
out of that extraordinary gathering at Massey College, to take the
measure of Her Majesty's assessment of Canada's new Constitution
and in light of the purposes, effects, uses, and operation of the NWC
to date.

The NWC allows Parliament or a provincial legislature to pass an act
that expressly declares that such legislation or any of its provisions
"shall operate notwithstanding a provision included in section 2
or sections 7 to 15 [the fundamental freedoms, legal and equality
rights provisions] of this Charter."[3] Its invocation and promulgation
must comply with certain formalities, most notably those pertaining
to the term of its effectiveness and its possible renewal. Whether
this provision constitutes an outright override of Charter rights and
freedoms barring all judicial review or a limited and contextually
specific suspension, subject to judicial review, of those rights and
freedoms, or whether it does not actually suspend or override rights
and freedoms whatsoever, but instead resituates – from the courts
to the legislatures – the forum in which such rights and freedoms
are to be defined and protected, are central questions and themes
explored in this volume of essays. The inclusion of the NWC in the
Charter has generated a fair amount of debate and controversy on
these basic questions – questions which require an inquiry into the
nature of, and distinctions between, constitutionality, constitutional
validity, consistency, effect, operability, and legitimacy – and, on the
question of whether the NWC is a good thing or a bad thing to have
in the constitution of a mature, liberal democratic society or, more
properly, whether it has both genuinely salutary and deleterious
implications for Canadian civic culture.

Given the complexity of the subject matter and the diversity of
available perspectives – political, scholarly, geographic, lay, and

expert – on the nature, purpose, and merits of the NWC, we should not expect to resolve and dispose of these basic questions with one-dimensional answers and incontrovertible judgments and conclusions. Indeed, this volume bears out the complex, nuanced, still controversial and ever-evolving interpretations and uses of the NWC. This nuance and complexity is well represented by Eric Adams and Erin Bower in a recent article in which they observe that, "It is striking just how many of its conceptual proponents foregrounded the protection of rights – not their override, derogation, or denial – as the rationale for the existence of the notwithstanding clause."[4] The following essays do not shy away from controversies or the adoption of particular interpretations of the NWC. But rather than promoting any particular agenda, the contributors aim to advance and deepen our understanding of the NWC and to get at the true nature of the provision, from the mechanics, operation, and effect of the clause to its significance for Canadian politics and culture and the future of civil liberties and liberal constitutionalism in Canada.

"If in Act 1 you have a pistol hanging on the wall, then it must fire in the last act. Otherwise, don't put it there."[5] The Russian playwright and short story writer Anton Chekhov was articulating a dramatic principle standing for the proposition that every element in a story must be necessary and all irrelevant elements must be removed. This was not, it should be noted, a matter of a story's internal logic or integrity, but rather, it was a matter of audience psychology. Chekhov was concerned that playwrights and stage directors occasionally make false promises with the result that audiences leave disappointed and unsatisfied. If the pistol is in the scene, the audience expects that it will be used in the manner that firearms generally are. The dramatic tension created by the presence of the weapon in the scene cries out for catharsis.

Of course, constitutions are not scripts or plays; constitution drafters are neither playwrights nor directors, and governments are not audience members. But in the political arena, as in the theatre, the psychology of the participants, and not the script alone, influences how a text will be interpreted and, indeed, applied.

In the forty years since the Canadian Charter of Rights and Freedoms was enacted, provincial and territorial governments have fired the NWC pistol some twenty-five times in legislation, although they apparently used blanks on eight of those occasions, as the clause's invocation was promulgated and made effective in only sixteen of those twenty-five instances.[6]

Speaking in the House of Commons in November 1981 as he announced agreement between the first ministers on the inclusion in the Charter of the NWC, also known as the "override clause," then Justice Minister Chretien said of its purpose: "What the Premiers and Prime Minister agreed to is a safety valve which is unlikely ever to be used except in non-controversial circumstances by Parliament to override certain sections of the Charter. The purpose of an override clause is to provide the flexibility that is required to ensure that legislatures rather than judges have the final say on important matters of public policy."[7] It would be used, he explained, as a last resort to "correct absurd situations."[8]

Reflecting on the purpose of the NWC some thirty years after the Charter's enactment – in which he had played an instrumental role – former Saskatchewan premier Allan Blakeney explained that section 33 was intended as an instrument "to mediate the clash of Charter and non-Charter rights," all of which, he contended, were equally important to both the moral and legal interests at play in Canadian society and politics. Blakeney was adamant that the Charter was never intended to establish a hierarchy that would privilege the constitutionally enumerated rights and freedoms – such as freedom of expression, religion, assembly – over various unenumerated, moral rights which he understood principally as being social and economic rights – such as the right to food, shelter, and health care. Instead, he insisted, the NWC had as its purpose to reserve to the legislative, executive, and administrative arms of government the responsibility and authority to advance and protect the non-enumerated rights "where the likely violation of a human right stems from the operation of economic and social systems."[9]

Former Alberta premier Peter Lougheed, another of the Charter's key architects and one who was especially instrumental in the NWC's inclusion, defended the NWC on the basis that it preserved and gave continuing effect to Canada's tradition of parliamentary supremacy. While Lougheed did not countenance the pre-emptive invocation of section 33 – in fact, he later proposed a constitutional amendment prohibiting it as being "undemocratic" because such a practice would have what he assumed to be the *unintended* effect of precluding the judiciary from fulfilling its interpretive role in relation to the Charter's provisions – Lougheed was uncompromising in his position that the elected Parliament must be supreme over the appointed judiciary.[10]

Thomas Axworthy leads off this volume with an incisive account of the historic compromise reached in 1981 by Lougheed, Blakeney, and the other first ministers, save for Quebec's René Lévesque, which is largely represented by and embodied in the agreement to include the NWC in the Charter, thereby enabling Canada to patriate its Constitution from Westminster and to produce a con-stitutionally enshrined charter of rights and freedoms. But, as with most compromises over thorny questions of principle, purpose, and priority, the result is not always dispositive of meaning, inter-pretation, and effect.

There have been, as we know, numerous accounts of what, in the Charter's embryonic stages, may have been intended, expected, and also discouraged in the way of section 33's invocation and use. The contributors to this volume consider these along with the varying interpretations of the NWC's operative effects and with the theories of how the NWC functions in relation to other constitutional pro-visions, such as *inter alia*, the supremacy clause (section 52),[11] the fundamental freedoms provisions to which the NWC expressly applies (section 2),[12] the democracy clause to which it does not (section 3),[13] and, of course, the reasonable limits clause (section 1).[14] Kristopher Kinsinger provides a much-needed overview of the major threads in the arguments that have ensued among scholars and jurists alike and guides us through the essential literature on the topic in the forty years since the Charter's enactment.

While one might have expected that the NWC would be resorted to only responsively – that is, following a judicial declaration of constitutional invalidity – rather than pre-emptively,[15] nothing about the text of section 33 requires only responsive use. And so it would not be long before the one province that had not signed on to the patri-ation deal, Quebec, invoked the NWC not only pre-emptively – and, possibly, also retroactively – with general application to all Charter provisions referenced in section 33, but with reference to its entire statute book rather than to a specific piece of legislation.[16] Guillaume Rousseau and François Côté explain in this volume that this has given rise to a distinctive Quebec theory of the NWC – that is, to an approach to section 33 that is different in Quebec than elsewhere in the federation. Benoît Pelletier, who testified in support of Bill 21,

An Act Respecting the Laicity of the State,[17] defends Quebec's use as being a sort of manifestation of Quebec's wounded national pride asserting itself in the wake of its betrayal by the other premiers in what came to be known as the "night of the long knives,"[18] but also as evidence of Quebecers' actual love and embracing of the Charter. As section 33 is an integral – if controversial – provision of the Charter, its invocation as a means of asserting Quebec's own identity and cultural purpose within Canada serves, in Pelletier's understanding, as the mechanism that actually enhances the viability of Canadian federalism and advances the cause of national unity. Without the NWC, the argument goes, Quebec secession would be all the more probable.[19]

Whether the discreet use of section 33 in Quebec and, indeed, its use anywhere, squares with and even, possibly, enhances federalism, or whether it may actually produce the opposite effect, certainly remain matters of contention and feed into the question of whether, in light of the diversity of theories about and use of the NWC, we need some upgraded operating instructions for this extraordinary "tool" in the constitutional "toolbox" – as Premier Ford and his then-attorney general, Caroline Mulroney, once referred to the NWC.[20]

Changes to these operating instructions that have been proposed to date include ending pre-emptive invocation of the NWC,[21] ending omnibus and blanket invocation,[22] requiring a legislative supermajority for promulgation of an NWC invocation, requiring additional reconsideration and invocation following a general election,[23] requiring a public referendum to ratify or override the NWC invocation,[24] and restricting invocation to responses to decisions of the Supreme Court of Canada.[25]

Christopher Manfredi, who has previously proposed some of these changes, shares his reflections and proposals in this connection while defending the NWC as reflecting a political scientist's paradigmatic conception of judges and courts as essentially political actors and judicial policymakers and, therefore, as no more legitimate or authoritative arbiters of the balancing of competing rights and other political interests than are the legislatures. By the same token, Manfredi is especially troubled by the pre-emptive invocation of the NWC because it deprives society of the benefit of a judicial statement on the meaning of a constitutional right and, in that sense, runs contrary to the notion – explained at length by Dwight Newman[26] – of coordinate construction or interpretation, that is, the notion that both courts and legislators have a legitimate and important role to play in the matter of rights interpretation and analysis. The NWC, viewed in this framework, serves to remove from the judiciary the exclusive jurisdiction over declarations about how such balancing exercises ought to be resolved.

The matter of how section 33 fits into the whole Charter as an integral part rather than as some outlier provision, and the question of how both courts and legislatures are to go about their respective considerations of the Charter, are of particular interest to Mary Eberts, who brings to her deliberations a Supreme Court barrister's unique standpoint. She looks to the Charter itself for guidance and argues that there are cases in which courts can overrule and strike down laws in which the NWC has been invoked where a holistic analysis of the limitations on the Charter rights in issue – those rights referred to in section 33 (1) as well as on those not expressly covered by the NWC – commends a declaration or other remedy (under section 52 and, possibly, section 24 – the remedies clause[27]). Eberts examines the use and scope of the NWC within an interpretive framework that includes another critically important "notwithstanding" clause, namely, that in section 28 of the Charter – which guarantees that, notwithstanding anything in the Charter, the rights and freedoms referred to in it are guaranteed equally to male and female persons – and she concludes that, correctly interpreted, section 28 invalidates the discrimination against women in Quebec's Bill 21, in spite of Quebec's use of section 33.

We are left to consider whether legislatures ought to pass discrete rules governing the use of the NWC or whether those operating instructions should be given constitutional status by being inserted in the Charter itself. Or, if as some have argued,[28] the override is wholly inconsistent with what a liberal constitutional democracy requires in its basic law – particularly as we already have section 1 of the Charter, the "reasonable limits" clause, which lays out a regime for the justification of infringements that are neither inconsistent nor incompatible with what freedom and democracy require – might we not simply repeal the NWC altogether? Easier said than done, of course, especially after Charlottetown,[29] when the amending formula was, arguably, supplemented by a new convention, namely, the possible requirement of a national consultative referendum. It is also understood, especially in light of the arguments of Rousseau, Côté, and Pelletier, that repeal of the NWC would be a non-starter in any constitutional negotiations.

But against all such fantasizing, there exist the most serious and compelling arguments in support of section 33's contribution to a distinctively Canadian constitutional framework, one that Stephen Gardbaum referred to as the "Commonwealth Model,"[30] a sort of third way between "strong-form constitutionalism" (judicial supremacy) and "weak-form constitutionalism" (pure parliamentary supremacy). This model is one in which a certain healthy skepticism about the political legitimacy of judicial review is baked into the constitutional cake, and that commends not only the retention of the NWC but, indeed, its more, not less, frequent use.

The NWC is often thought of as exempting a federal, provincial, or territorial law from the application of and protections afforded by certain sections of the Charter, and as insulating an impugned law from Charter scrutiny.[31] But, as Robert Leckey and others[32] argue, this may be conceptually incorrect, as resorting to the remedies clause in the Charter is not necessarily precluded by invocation of the NWC – even if the ultimate remedy under section 52 of the Constitution Act[33] (the supremacy clause) would be fore-closed – and, further, that the court's authority and jurisdiction, indeed its responsibility, to declare Charter infringements not saved by section 1 are not ousted or extinguished by the invocation of the NWC.

Not surprisingly, this position has generated some controversy and, as Maxime St-Hilaire and Xavier Foccroulle Ménard argue herein, the invocation of the NWC effectively disposes of further judicial review. Once a law has been insulated by a statutory resort to its continued operation notwithstanding any of the Charter rights and freedoms referred to in section 33(1), there is, as they argue, "nothing further [for the court] to declare."

Elsewhere, Leckey has advanced the argument that a law that is found to limit or infringe a Charter right or freedom – that is, a law which is found to be inconsistent with a Charter provision – in respect of which the NWC has been invoked is, by virtue of that invocation, not unconstitutional because it has been rendered consistent with the Charter by resort to section 33.[34] Accordingly, a court would not strike down such a law as being of no force or effect. Grégoire Webber critically considers that analysis in this volume and argues that, while he and Leckey both agree that the NWC concerns itself with the continued operation of a law invoking the NWC and says nothing about any override or suspension of any rights or freedoms, a law which is inconsistent with a Charter provision is not thereby rendered consistent by virtue of the invocation. Instead, such a law is saved by virtue of an exception to the effect, set out in section 52, of the inconsistency. That exception is created by the NWC invocation. This seemingly esoteric distinction between Webber and Leckey turns out not to be merely semantic in nature but one of potential consequence for both the role and the substance of judicial review where the NWC is implicated.

A few short decades ago, Peter Hogg and Allison Bushell advanced the argument that there is a genuine "dialogue" of sorts that takes place between legislatures and courts in the context of constitutional challenges to laws, including where section 33 has been invoked.[35] Once a court pronounces on the constitutional validity of a law, the legislature may, in response, reconsider the law and modify it in some fashion, taking account of the court's understanding of where the line is drawn between consistency and inconsistency with the Constitution. Hogg and Bushell generated considerable debate and criticism, which itself prompted a reply and restatement from Hogg and Bushell, essentially defending their original conclusions.[36] This volume considers what sort of "dialogue" we may be left with when the NWC is invoked and what judicial review remains to be undertaken in such instances. There is broad, though not unanimous, consensus *inter alia* that the NWC should never, except possibly in cases of genuine emergency, be used pre-emptively, and further, that governments should be required to give a robust, transparent justification for invoking it and to be subject to a vigorous process of accountability and scrutiny by way of the legislative committee process and also by resort of affected parties to judicial review.

Ultimately, it becomes our collective responsibility as citizens to consider how the fallout from these inquiries squares with the sort of constitutional democracy we think we have – and the sort we wish to have. In a private exchange I had in the summer of 2021 with the late historian and human rights scholar Erna Paris, she bemoaned Quebec's Bill 96 (as it then was), along with the device that purports to insulate it from Charter scrutiny, as putting in doubt the question of whether Canada is, in fact, still a liberal democracy.[37] Jonathan Montpetit explores this very question in the specific context of Quebec history and politics. Tracing the tradition of liberal constitutionalism in the province beginning during the Quiet Revolution, he argues that by seeking to override not simply the Canadian

Charter but Quebec's Charter of Human Rights and Freedoms[38] as well, the CAQ government of François Legault is making a definitive break from the province's own tradition of liberal constitutionalism. Montpetit's chapter, which aligns with Paris's apprehension, goes to the heart of a central concern of this volume, to the very question of whether Canada's commonwealth model of constitutional democracy can admit of an override clause that even provisionally suspends the ordinary authority of fundamental rights provisions on the operation of laws expressly unanswerable to such authority, even provisionally.

There is, on the other hand, an impressive body of scholarship that highlights what it considers to be the all too common misconception that there is a rigid bifurcation of jurisdiction between the courts and the legislatures in which courts are uniquely endowed with the expertise and responsibility to not only adjudicate on rights and rights infringements but to define and explain the content of those rights, and that legislatures are uniquely charged with establishing policy and making laws. Instead, this critique contends both courts and legislative bodies have a role in constitutional interpretation. Dwight Newman, a leading proponent of this school, refers to the respective engagement of courts and legislatures in defining and interpreting rights and freedoms as one of "coordinate interpretation." As he frames it, the NWC "provides for democratic balancing between distinctly legal questions and issues that engage contested moral values."[39] And he seems to have the current majority of the Supreme Court on his side in this connection. Citing Newman in the recent City of Toronto case, the Chief Justice and Justice Brown state, "Where, therefore, a court invalidates legislation using s. 2(b) of the *Charter*, the legislature may give continued effect to *its* understanding of what the Constitution requires by invoking s. 33 and by meeting its stated conditions."[40]

Geoffrey Sigalet, like Manfredi, brings a political scientist's discipline and preoccupations to the conversation, defending the NWC as a decidedly political vehicle through which legislatures may act as a check on fallible and unelected judges. But more than merely advancing a conventional case for qualified parliamentary supremacy in cases which engage both the NWC and one or more of the rights and freedoms referred to in section 33(1), Sigalet explains that the NWC can operate as a means by which provinces might wish to signal a conception of rights and of fundamental freedoms and an understanding of ideal societal arrangements in Quebec civil society that are divergent from the predominant positions and attitudes in other parts of the country. In this sense, Quebec's invocation of the NWC to support Bill 21 is a vehicle through which Quebec expresses and, indeed, asserts its provincial identity. Sigalet's argument effectively moves the inquiry off the question of whether some uses of the NWC are offside by reason of the egregiousness of resulting rights limitations and onto broader questions about the political legitimacy and utility of a legislative override that renders unproductive or precludes judicial review altogether.

But we know, both from the text of the Charter and from forty years of experience, that the legislatures have not always waited for judicial determinations of unconstitutionality before resorting to the NWC. A practice in Quebec and, more recently, in Ontario,[41] is thus emerging in which the people, through their elected representatives, get the first, last, and possibly *only* crack at deciding which laws will operate. Lorraine Weinrib had argued, some thirty years ago, that section 33 "frees Canada from the crisis of judicial legitimacy that mars other rights protecting systems."[42] Today, as we consider the fallout from the seminal NWC decision of the Supreme Court of Canada in *Ford*, it is difficult not to adopt a somewhat less sanguine take on the NWC, especially in light of the complications and uncertainties produced by omnibus, retroactive, and pre-emptive resort to the clause.

Notwithstanding the guardrails of sunset clauses, limited and provisional application of the override, and the fact that we still do conduct periodic general elections, the idea that section 33 establishes a regime of "coordinate interpretation" is disconcerting news in some quarters, particularly among discrete and insular minorities and defenders of political pluralism who understand only too well the harm to minority interests that can sometimes be produced by majorities – or rather, by legislatures purporting to reflect the standards and aspirations of majorities – by making the so-called "will of the people" manifest in laws. This may appear to be something of an irony given that the earliest charters and declarations of rights and freedoms, at least in the West, were intended to guard against the arbitrary and abusive exercises of power by the few at the expense of the interests of the many. From Magna Carta Libertatum (the Great Charter of Freedoms)[43] to the Declaration of the Rights of Man and of the Citizen,[44] neither minority interests nor political pluralism were discrete concerns, although the principles extracted from the original texts have inspired the drafting of subsequent rights charters and grounded the advancement of claims for the protection of minority rights, including freedom of expression, conscience, and religion,[45] against the tyranny of unbridled majoritarianism.

In this volume, Caitlin Salvino discusses the particular vulnerability and precariousness of minority rights and freedoms as a function of NWC invocation. In particular, Salvino argues that while the drafters of the Charter may have intended the NWC to be used as a last resort, as Jean Chretien had stated in the House of Commons, and had embedded in section 33 structural safeguards of democratic accountability[46] as a bulwark against the deleterious effects on rights holders of abusive invocation, these safeguards do not adequately protect minority interests.

Marion Sandilands considers the effect of Quebec's Bill 21 and Bill 96[47] not only on minority rights but on human rights broadly, and makes the bold and remarkable claim that Quebec's use of both the NWC and section 52 of the (Quebec) Charter of Human Rights and Freedoms to insulate its declarations of Quebec nationhood in Bills 21 and 96 effectively oust the jurisdiction of both the Canadian and Quebec Charters, rendering them, at best, subordinate to laws in which the collective rights of the Quebec nation are promoted and, at worst, utterly without force. Sandilands argues that this has heralded a new legal order in Quebec, making it the only jurisdiction in Canada in which the human rights charters are not the supreme law(s) of the land. This, of course, aligns with Jonathan Montpetit's argument that Bills 21 and 96 herald the decline of liberal constitutionalism in Quebec.

Gregory Bordan also considers the impact of NWC in Quebec, with a particular focus on the court challenge to Bill 21. Concluding, as he does, that Bill 21 has a severely deleterious effect on minority rights in the province, including on the rights of religious and linguistic minorities, he advances a most original and serious argument for judicial review of NWC invocation by way of reference to section 1, while not arguing that NWC invocation is or can be subject to section 1 justification. Instead, Bordan argues that section 33 must be used within a constitutional framework that does not allow for the effective abrogation of the Charter's guaranteed rights and freedoms, while still giving significant room to legislatures to achieve a balance between those rights and freedoms and other societal interests. Section 1, Bordan argues, can be instructive in considering the limits that may apply to the power granted by section 33, particularly its two-step analysis.

Cara Zwibel and Jamie Cameron both advance arguments for an expansive reading of the right to vote under section 3 of the Charter, given that section 33 applies to the fundamental freedoms and legal and equality rights but not to democratic rights (sections 3–5). As the NWC can be used to override a number of rights and freedoms that are normally engaged in elections and in the lead-up to voting – such as freedom of expression and of the press, freedom of assembly and association, and freedom of conscience – the exclusion of democratic rights from the ambit of the NWC must, they argue, be interpreted as grounding "meaningful participation" in the electoral process. This means that courts could be asked to disallow and strike down uses of the NWC in instances in which invocation would have either the purpose or the effect of appreciably impacting our democratic structures. Zwibel argues further that this reading of section 3 also supports section 33 in effectively performing its democratic accountability function.

Cameron refers to democratic accountability as the bedrock principle of both sections 3 and 33. This is further reinforced by the fact that section 4 of the Charter provides for a maximum term of five years for any House of Commons or legislative assembly, except in times of real or apprehended war, which aligns with the five-year limitation on the effectiveness of an NWC invocation, as set out in section 33(3). Cameron argues that the legitimacy of section 33 and its theory of democratic accountability are contingent on an interpretation of section 3 that prohibits interference with the democratic process.

Tsvi Kahana examines the instances in which the NWC has been invoked and draws a different sort of line between those uses which pass muster under the Charter and those that should be disallowed. Kahana considers those invocations which are, on one basis or another, justifiable in a free and democratic society, and those that are not because they are effectively tyrannical in purpose or effect. He cites both Bill 21 in Quebec and Bill 307 ("Working Families"[48]) as instances of a tyrannical use of the NWC.

Sabreena Delhon brings an entirely different sort of critical appraisal of the NWC to the deliberations. As a democracy scholar and advocate, Delhon is concerned with the impact of the NWC invocation

on our civic culture and, in particular, on the political sensibilities of
some of our most vulnerable citizens, especially of those members of
discrete and insular minorities. She argues that the dialogic practice
engaged in by courts and legislatures, as envisaged by the framers of
the Charter and by constitutional scholars, would not favour or even
include consideration of the interests of many segments of the population who are or who feel disempowered in the current political and
constitutional environments. The background assumption undergirding the theory of robust judicial-legislative dialogue is that the political
sphere is open to all Canadians. But, Delhon argues, this assumption
does not match the social and economic realities of Canadian life. In
the result, the use of the NWC actually serves to erode trust and confidence in the political process and undermines hope and expectation
that political institutions will always act in the best interests of the
most vulnerable members of society, and also leaves these members
feeling alienated by and excluded from the justice system. In contrast
to the golden age of the Charter's early years, the Charter bloom is off
the rose in some segments of our population. This is consistent with
the democratic backsliding that characterizes our age, one in which
trust in government, in politicians, and in the authority of law itself
are at an all-time low. Against this backdrop, government invocation
of the NWC, even in the least controversial contexts, produces anxiety, insecurity, and trepidation in the hearts and minds of those least
empowered to participate, speak out, and advance their own causes
in the public square. Delhon argues that in order to remedy this sense
of alienation, institutions of democracy must work precipitously to
adapt and reflect our pluralistic, multiracial society and to solve problems of power by bringing motivation to make change into alignment
with authority to act.[49]

As the last four decades have shown, we cannot deny that the NWC
will be used in ways for ends and with consequences not necessarily anticipated or approved of by its original drafters. We are duty-
bound to return to first principles and to deliberate collectively on
one of the most important questions one might ask one's fellow citizens: what kind of constitutional democracy do we want? In the
context of our history of living with the override, the question might
be framed somewhat differently: what kind of constitutional democracy is consistent with a NWC, and what does a charter with such a
clause tell us about who we are as a country?

Commenting on the social benefit of laws, beyond their obvious function of either compelling or prohibiting conduct, former prime minister Pierre Elliott Trudeau wrote, "The purpose of the laws is to educate."[50] Perhaps this is partly what Leckey is getting at in ascribing to the courts the responsibility to declare rights infringements for the purpose of fostering an informed and enlightened civic engagement in those instances in which an impugned law is saved not by section 1 but rather by section 33.

In writing about section 33, Peter Russell wrote "that a democracy which puts its faith as much in its politically active citizenry as in its judges to be the guardians of liberty is stronger than one that would endeavour to vest ultimate responsibility for liberty and fundamental rights exclusively in its judiciary."[51] Russell was responding, in part, to John Whyte's critical essay on section 33, where he warned that "political authority will, at some point, be exercised oppressively; that is, it will be exercised to impose very serious burdens on groups of people when there is no rational justification for doing so."[52]

In this vein, one of our most esteemed of Canadian parliamentarians, Eugene Forsey, said of the NWC that it "is a dagger pointed at the heart of our fundamental freedoms, and it should be abolished ... Perhaps none of our legislatures will use the Notwithstanding Clause again. But it is there. And if this dagger is flung, the courts will be as powerless to protect our rights as they were before there was a Charter of Rights."[53]

So, whether one thinks of the NWC as a dagger or, in my Chekhovian imagination, a gun placed conspicuously on the set of Canada's constitutional drama, or whether we understand it as a check on an unaccountable judiciary and instrument of parliamentary supremacy and of democratic rights protection,[54] politicians, jurists, and citizens all have an opportunity and responsibility to reflect on what its invocation to date has meant for liberal constitutionalism and Canadian society and culture and on what, if any, changes to its use and text might be commended. It is hoped that the essays that follow will be read and considered with that civic responsibility in mind.

NOTES

1 Andrew P. Hutton, "Queen Signs Independence Proclamation," UPI
   Archives, 17 April 1982, https://www.upi.com/Archives/1982/04/17/
   Queen-signs-independence-proclamation/2782387867600/.
2 Canadian Charter of Rights and Freedoms, s. 33, Part 1 of the
   Constitution Act, 1982, being Schedule B to the Canada Act, 1982 (UK),
   1982 c. 11 [Charter], s. 52.

   33. (1) Parliament or the legislature of a province may expressly
   declare in an Act of Parliament or of the legislature, as the case may
   be, that the Act or a provision thereof shall operate notwithstanding a
   provision included in section 2 or sections 7 to 15 of this Charter.
   (2) An Act or a provision of an Act in respect of which a declaration
   made under this section is in effect shall have such operation as it
   would have but for the provision of this Charter referred to in the
   declaration.
   (3) A declaration made under section (1) shall cease to have effect
   five years after it comes into force or on such earlier date as may be
   specified in the declaration.
   (4) Parliament or the legislature of a province may re-enact a
   declaration made under section (1).
   (5) Section (3) applies in respect of a re-enactment made under
   section (4).

3 Canadian Charter of Rights and Freedoms.
4 Eric Adams and Erin Bower trace the history and evolution of the use of
   the NWC, putting in evidence the complexity, nuance, and changing
   attitudes to the NWC over time and tracing its origins not only to a set of
   compromises entered into by the Charter's negotiators and framers, but
   further back to a tradition of common law constitutionalism and rights
   protection. Eric M. Adams and Erin R.J. Bower, "Notwithstanding
   History: The Rights-Protecting Purposes of Section 33 of the Charter,"
   Review of Constitutional Studies 26, no. 2 (2022): 121, https://dx.doi.
   org/10.2139/ssrn.4185044.
5 "One must never place a loaded rifle on the stage if it isn't going to go off.
   It's wrong to make promises you don't mean to keep." Chekhov, letter to
   Aleksandr Semenovich Lazarev (pseudonym of A.S. Gruzinsky), 1
   November 1889, reported in Gurlyand, "Reminiscences of A.P. Chekhov,"
   Teatr I Iskusstvo, no. 28 (11 July 1904): 521; Leonid Sirota, "Chekhov's
   Gun: Dwight Newman's Defence of the Charter's Notwithstanding Clause

Is Unpersuasive," *Double Aspect* (blog), 10 May 2017, https://double
aspect.blog/2017/05/10/chekhovs-gun/.

6 Caitlin Salvino, "A Tool of Last Resort: A Comprehensive Account of the
   Notwithstanding Clause Political Uses 1982–2021," *Journal of
   Parliamentary and Political Law* 16, no. 1 (2022). In addition to the
   twenty-four instances of invocation documented by Salvino, there was one
   additional instance in November 2022 (first reading was given 31 October
   and Royal Assent on 3 November) in which the Ontario Government
   invoked, and then revoked, the NWC. This was in Bill 28, The Keeping
   Students in Class Act, 2022.

7 11 House of Commons Debates, 32nd Parl, 1st Sess (20 November 1981)
   at 13042–3 (Debates 20 November 1981).

8 13 Debates, 20 November 1981, Adams and Bower, "Notwithstanding
   History," 13042–3.

9 Allan Blakeney, "The Notwithstanding Clause, the Charter, and Canada's
   Patriated Constitution: What I Thought We Were Doing," *Constitutional
   Forum constitutionnel* 19, no. 1 (2010): 1-9, https://doi.org/10.21991/
   C9KD4W.

10 Peter Lougheed, "Why a Notwithstanding Clause?" *Points of View-
   Centre for Constitutional Studies* 6, no. 17 (1998).

11 Canadian Charter of Rights and Freedoms, s. 33, Part 1 of the
   Constitution Act, 1982, being Schedule B to the Canada Act, 1982 (UK),
   1982 c. 11 [Charter], s. 52.

12 Canadian Charter of Rights and Freedoms, s. 2 a–d.

13 Ibid., s. 3 (and 4 and 5).

14 Ibid., s. 1.

15 The overwhelming majority of contributors to this volume hold this view
   and, as reflected in the stated positions of two of the key negotiators at the
   table in November 1981, Prime Minister Chretien and Premier Lougheed
   (Salvino, "Tool of Last Resort," 11 House of Commons Debates, and
   Blakeney, "The Notwithstanding Clause"), the NWC was to be used to
   "correct absurd situations," "as a last resort" and in order that the
   legislature, and not the courts, "should have the last word." This, it seems
   logically, discloses an expectation that the NWC would be used only after
   a court had decided, thereby producing a potentially "absurd situation."

16 An Act Respecting the Constitution Act, 1982, CQLR, c-L-4.2, ss. 1, 2,
   5–7, which applied the NWC to Quebec's entire statute book, raising vex-
   ing questions about both the override's retroactive and pre-emptive use.

17 An Act Respecting the Laicity of the State, SQ 2019, c 12.

18 See Brian Bird's account in "Brian Bird: The Charter at Forty: The Legacy of Pierre Elliott Trudeau," *The Hub*, 4 March 2022, https://thehub.ca/2022-03-04/charter-at-forty-the-legacy-of-pierre-elliott-trudeau/.

19 Pelletier's submissions to the Commission were cited by Hugo Lavallée, "L'ex-ministre libéral Benoît Pelletier témoignera en faveur de la loi sur la laïcité," Radio Canada, 25 September 2020, https://ici.radio-canada.ca/nouvelle/1736368/ex-ministre-liberal-benoit-pelletier-temoignage-pour-faveur-loi-21-laicite. *"La justification la plus logique du recours à la disposition de dérogation consiste à dire que celle-ci est une composante nécessaire du fédéralisme, que cette clause permet de préserver la diversité d'opinions, de valeurs et d'aspirations politiques qui font la richesse de la fédération."*

20 Fatima Syed, "Mulroney's Reputation 'On the Line,' Say Critics, If She Won't Oppose Ford on Notwithstanding Clause," *National Observer*, 18 September 2018, https://www.nationalobserver.com/2018/09/18/news/mulroneys-reputation-line-say-critics-if-she-wont-oppose-ford-not-withstanding-clause. The cavalier phrase was used in the context of the Ontario government's introduction of the Better Local Government Act, 2018, S.O. 2018, c. 11 –Bill 5.

21 See Caitlin Salvino in this volume and Christopher P. Manfredi, *Judicial Power and the Charter: Canada and the Paradox of Liberal Constitutionalism*, 2nd ed. (London: Oxford University Press, 2001), 4, 193.

22 Peter H. Russell, "Standing Up for Notwithstanding," *Alberta Law Review* 29, no. 2 (1991): 293–309, https://doi.org/10.29173/alr1563.

23 Russell, note 18; Manfredi, note 17.

24 Scott Reid, "Penumbra for the People: Placing Judicial Supremacy under Popular Control," in *Rethinking the Constitution: Perspectives on Canadian Constitutional Reform, Interpretation and Theory*, ed. Anthony Peacock (Don Mills: Oxford University Press Canada, 1996), 203.

25 Tsvi Kahana, "The Notwithstanding Mechanism and Public Discussion: Lessons from the Ignored Practices of Section 33 of the Charter," *Canadian Public Administration* 44, no. 3 (September 2001): 255.

26 See Dwight Newman in this volume and "Canada's Notwithstanding Clause, Dialogue, and Constitutional Identities," in *Constitutional Dialogue: Rights, Democracy, Institutions*, ed. Geoffrey Sigalet, Grégoire Webber, and Rosalind Dixon (Cambridge: Cambridge University Press, 2019), 209.

27 Note 8, ss. 24 (1) and (2).

28 Deborah Coyne, *Canada's Faux Democracy: What Are We Going to Do about It?* (2021), https://deborahcoyne.ca/wp-content/uploads/Canadas-Faux-Democracy-What-are-we-going-to-do-about-it-by-Deborah-Coyne.pdf; Eugene Forsey, "Is There a Threat to Our Rights?" *Reader's Digest,* June 1989, 101–2.

29 Coyne, note 24.

30 Stephen Gardbaum, "The New Commonwealth Model of Constitutionalism," *The American Journal of Comparative Law* 49, no. 4 (Autumn 2001): 708–9; "Reassessing the New Commonwealth Model of Constitutionalism," *International Journal of Constitutional Law* 8, no. 2 (2001): 167, 168.

31 Coyne, note 24; The Government of Canada's own website states that invocation of section 33 "allows Parliament or the legislature of a province to derogate from sections of the Charter" and "effectively precludes judicial review of the legislation under the listed Charter sections," https://justice.gc.ca/eng/csj-sjc/rfc-dlc/ccrf-ccdl/check/art33.html.

32 Grégoire Webber, Eric Mendelsohn, and Robert Leckey, "The Faulty Received Wisdom around the Notwithstanding Clause," *Policy Options,* 10 May 2019, policyoptions.irpp.org/magazines/may-2019/faulty-wisdom-notwithstanding-clause; Robert Leckey and Eric Mendelsohn, "The Notwithstanding Clause: Legislatures, Courts, and the Electorate," *University of Toronto Law Journal* 72, no. 2 (2022): 189; See also Grégoire Webber, this volume, chapter 4.

33 Canadian Charter of Rights and Freedoms, section 52.

34 Leckey and Mendelson, note 29.

35 Peter Hogg and Allison Bushell, "The Charter Dialogue between Courts and Legislatures (Or Perhaps the Charter of Rights Isn't Such a Bad Thing After All)," *Osgoode Hall Law Journal* 35, no. 1 (Spring 1997); "Charter Dialogue Revisited: Or 'Much Ado About Metaphors,'" *Osgoode Hall Law Journal* 45, no. 1 (Spring 2007).

36 Christopher P. Manfredi and James B. Kelly, "Six Degrees of Dialogue: A Response to Hogg and Bushell," *Osgoode Hall Law Journal* 37, no. 3 (Fall 1999); Jamie Cameron, "Dialogue and Hierarchy in Charter Interpretation: A Comment on R. v. Mills," *Alberta Law Review* 38, no. 4 (2001): 1051.

37 Private exchange, 3 June 2021; See also Erna Paris, "After Decades of Playing Charter Chicken, Canada Is Now Home to What Is Effectively an Illiberal Democracy," *Globe and Mail,* 17 May 2021, https://www.theglobeandmail.com/opinionarticle-after-decades-of-playing-charter-chicken-canada-is-now-home-to-what-is/.

38 Charter of Human Rights and Freedoms, CQLR c C-12, s 52.

39 Newman, note 22.

40 *Toronto (City) v. Ontario (Attorney General)*, 2021 SCC 34, para 60.

41 Caitlin Salvino, "Tool of Last Resort."

42 Lorraine Weinrib, "Learning to Live With the Override," 35 *McGill Law Journal* 542, at 571.

43 Magna Carta, 1215.

44 France National Constituent Assembly, Declaration of the Rights of Man and of the Citizen Adopted by the National Assembly during Its Sessions on August 20, 21, 25, and 26, and Approved by the King (Paris: Mondharre & Jean, 1789).

45 France National Constituent Assembly, Declaration of the Rights of Man, Arts 10 and 11.

46 Section 33 (1): democratic accountability through the legislative process, and s. 33(3): democratic accountability through the electoral process.

47 Act Respecting Laicity of the State CQLR c L-0.3, see ss 33–34 ["Bill 21"]; An Act Respecting French, the Official and Common Language of Québec, SQ 2022, c 14 ["Bill 96"].

48 The Protecting Elections and Defending Democracy Act, 2021, S.O. 2021, c.31 – Bill 307.

49 Delhon draws on Hahrie Han's theory of the misalignment of motivation and authority in Han, "Problems of Power," *Stanford Social Innovation Review* 18, no. 1 (2019): A5–A6, https://doi.org/10.48558/3NWR-7085.

50 Pierre Trudeau, "A State Made to Measure," in *Approaches to Politics* (Toronto: Oxford University Press, 1970), 50.

51 Peter Russell, note 18.

52 J.D. Whyte, "On Not Standing for Notwithstanding," *Alberta Law Review* 28, no. 2 (1990): 347–57.

53 Forsey, note 24.

54 Adams and Bower, "Notwithstanding History."

PART ONE

Genesis and Context

An Historic Canadian Compromise: Forty Years after the Patriation of the Constitution, Should We Cheer a Little?

Thomas S. Axworthy

Compromise is odious to passionate natures because it seems a surrender; and to intellectual natures because it seems a confusion.

George Santayana[1]

It (the notwithstanding clause) was something you would rather not have, because you could guess as to who might use it. But my approach was that it may be a way to break the deadlock.

William Davis, Premier of Ontario[2]

More than forty years ago, in the first week of November 1981, the prime minister of Canada met the country's ten premiers in the Government Conference Centre – a former Ottawa railway station – to negotiate a constitutional settlement about three goals that had eluded Canadian leaders since 1927. These goals were: first, to end Canada's formal legal status as a colony of Great Britain; second, to achieve an amendment formula to change the Constitution to meet evolving conditions; and third, to enhance the rights of Canadians. Over four days – from Monday, 2 November to Thursday, 5 November 1981 – the leaders occasionally reached heights of eloquence as they defined their contending visions of Canada, sometimes stooping to invective and meanness more appropriate to street gang rumbles. I was an advisor to Pierre Trudeau during these negotiations and can report that right until the end, most participants despaired of ever achieving an agreement. But finally, and somewhat amazingly, during the evening of Wednesday, 4 November and the morning of Thursday, 5 November, the leaders cobbled together a series of compromises that allowed nine provinces (except for Quebec) and the government of Canada to unite in sending to Great Britain a resolution that finally ended Canada's quest for a new constitution.

Evaluating those compromises and assessing the results of the November 1981 constitutional bargain, now that more than a generation has passed, is the purpose of this chapter. In previous publications, I have written about the contending ideological frameworks that animated the participants ("Colliding Visions: The Debate over the Canadian Charter of Rights and Freedoms," 1985)[3] and the specifics behind the suggestion of a *non obstante* or notwithstanding clause that would restore parliamentary supremacy over much of the Charter of Rights and Freedoms ("Sword of Damocles or Paper Tiger: Canada's Continuing Debate over the Notwithstanding Clause," 2007).[4] As described below, my personal involvement in the constitution discussions will hopefully contribute in a small way to better understanding the context of the frantic negotiations of 2–5 November 1981. But, beyond personal impressions, I use the debate over the *non obstante* clause to examine the concept of compromise itself. What were the main compromises or trade-offs in the 1981 constitutional negotiations, why were they made, and how have they stood the test of time? Without the compromise over section 33, there would have been no constitutional settlement with the provinces; we would have had a national referendum on the federal package instead: would a referendum have led to a better result than the constitution we now have? Today, with polarization and partisanship expanding exponentially, compromise seems to be out of favour when compared to the delights of single-issue fervour. An examination of the compromises involved in patriating the Constitution and winning a Charter of Rights and Freedoms might remind us that compromise is at the heart of democratic politics.

THE ART OF COMPROMISE

The Merriam-Webster dictionary defines compromise as "a settlement of differences by arbitration, or consent reached by mutual concession." The two key words are *mutual* (i.e., you must deal with a party that has the power to influence the outcome) and *concession* (i.e., you must give in order to get). The art of effective compromise means bending without breaking – a trade-off between your longing or desired position and the possibilities of achieving it. You make a concession to get a desired result or to avoid a worse one if you assess that you are at risk of losing it all. Compromise is not the same as consensus, though it may lead to that result. When negotiators reach a consensus, they agree that a particular course of action is the best choice to make. But compromise is support for an inferior position according to your values or interests, which you felt compelled or were persuaded to make after assessing risks and possibilities. In the constitutional settlement of 1981, for example, two of the main actors had very different views. Jean Chretien not only defends the constitutional deal but extols it. In 2012, responding to criticism from Quebec nationalists, Chretien said Quebecers favoured ending Canada's status as a "legal colony" and "they use the Charter of Rights all the time in Quebec." "The courts," he said, "have gone further than expected" in expanding minority education rights – a boon for francophones outside Quebec and anglophones in Quebec. In his opinion, the use of the notwithstanding clause by provincial governments had so far been restrained, and it had the advantage of being a useful brake on potential judicial activism: "I'd rather have too many freedoms than not enough. But it is for the court to decide where there are limits because society evolves so rapidly. Yet, if the courts 'go too far,' Parliament will not accept it."[5] In his 2021 book *My Stories, My Times*, Mr Chretien continues to defend the constitutional compromises he was so instrumental in obtaining, but he does acknowledge "after 1982, whenever I met Pierre Elliott Trudeau, he rarely missed an opportunity to express his frustration at having been forced to accept Section 33, the so-called notwithstanding clause of the Charter, and always tendered me a gentle approach"[6]

Pierre Trudeau, in his retirement, certainly expressed doubts about key elements of the constitutional compromise: he ultimately accepted the compromises that Jean Chretien and William Davis urged upon him, but he never wavered from his opinion that the federal amendment proposal, which contained a Quebec veto on changes with a referendum provision to go to the people in a referendum if deadlock was intolerable, was superior to the Alberta proposal of seven provinces with 50 per cent of the population. He regretted that the Charter of Rights was not fully entrenched because governments could still diminish rights through the use of the notwithstanding clause, and had he gone to the country in a referendum to decide between the competing federal and provincial packages, Quebec would not have been left out of the final decision. He said in 1992, "I should have gone for an election or a referendum. Quebec wouldn't have been able to say it was left out because everyone would have been left out, and Canada would have gotten a better-amending formula and a better Charter."[7] Trudeau assumed in this statement, of course, that he would have won such a contest, though he would have had to win in every region, including the West. He might well have done so – the Charter was overwhelmingly popular with voters in every region – but it was a risk he was not willing to take in 1981. He mused, however, about the constitutional "what might have been" for the rest of his life.

Mr Chretien's defence of the 1981 compromise – in effect, federal acceptance of the Alberta amending formula in exchange for a Charter of Rights and Freedoms with a notwithstanding clause allowing parliamentary supremacy over judicial decisions in the areas of fundamental, legal, and equality rights – certainly reflects the mainstream tradition in extolling the necessity of compromise. Aristotle argued for the mean as the surest guide to live the good life. Thomas Hobbes argued in 1651 that because men are diverse in interest and not always harmonious in principle, they incline to war, so a way had to be found to adjudicate disputes without violence. His solution was a Leviathan or an all-powerful king. A generation on, however, the Glorious Revolution of 1688–89 dethroned a king and made Parliament the dominant political institution, so politics, legislatures, and parties became the way to reconcile interests. Compromise became the lubricant to make the system run. Edmund Burke argued that "all government – indeed, every human benefit and enjoyment, every virtue, and every prudent act – is founded on compromise and barter. We balance inconveniences; we give and take; we remit some rights that we may enjoy others."[8] After Burke and the development of the party system in the eighteenth century, the operative questions of politics became when to compromise and how far to go. So basic was compromise to the normal give and take of politics that John Stuart Mill, the great nineteenth-century philosopher but also the member of Parliament for the City of Westminster, wrote that, "One of the indispensable requisites in the practical conduct of politics, especially in the management of free institutions, is conciliation; a readiness to compromise."[9]

But Mr Trudeau's questions about the appropriateness of his readiness to compromise in 1981, given his political ideals, also find philosophical support. John Morley was a great British liberal voice in the nineteenth and early-twentieth centuries. He favoured Home Rule for Ireland, opposed the Boer War, and resigned from the British government in 1914 when Britain allied itself with Russia at the start of the First World War, given that the czar stood for everything that Morley opposed. Morley is also the author of *On Compromise*,[10] one of the best book-length examinations of this critical concept. Given his long involvement in politics and the high offices he held, Morley praised "the right kind of compromise" based on a "rigorous sense of what is real and practicable."[11] Yet he was troubled by the tendency "to lose some excellence of aim" in the rush to compromise. His book is about the relationship between principle and expediency. Principle, as he defines it, is the long-term interest, the product of thought and reflection. Expediency is the desire for immediate advantage. Compromise was a tool to achieve ends, but too often, the tool became an end in itself in the rush to have a deal. Burke said that no one would barter away "the jewel of his soul," but Morley was not so sure about this. In what he called the current "Age of Comfort," Morley worried that leaders were too quick to simply split the difference losing sight of the potential impact in the long term. He was opposed to "counting the narrow, immediate and personal expediency for everything" and believed that leaders had to have a "sense of intellectual responsibility,"[12] an admonition readily accepted by Pierre Trudeau in his approach to politics.

Compromise is overwhelmingly praised, but some compromises turn out to be the kind of disasters that Morley feared. In 1938, for example, British Prime Minister Neville Chamberlain negotiated the Munich Agreement with Adolph Hitler, which allowed German annexation of territories of Czechoslovakia despite past treaties guaranteeing Czechoslovakia military support. Chamberlain sacrificed morality to prevent war, but within a year, the Second World War came anyway, and ever since, the Munich Compromise has become a synonym for betrayal.

What criteria then can we apply to the contending views of Burke and Morley about compromise: Burke seeing it as necessary for the political system to function; Morley worried that principles are too easily sacrificed? John Stuart Mill created a set of enduring principles and ethics to apply to life generally (which greatly influenced

Morley), but as he also knew politics and served as a member of Parliament, he applied his standards to political compromise too. He always emphasized principle in his writings, but after getting involved in elected politics, he wrote, "I became practically conversant with the difficulties of moving bodies of men, the necessities of compromise, the art of sacrificing the non-essential to preserve the essential."[13] The art of compromise, then, is to sacrifice the non-essential for the essential – but what is essential? That is the question we will explore in assessing the three key compromises that defined the constitutional settlement of 1981.

THE AMENDING FORMULA

Compromise depends on what is real and practicable, John Morley advised. What was real and practicable in the 1981 negotiations was that Prime Minister Trudeau had begun negotiating a new constitution in 1968 with the provinces, and in 1981 he was still at it. "The Constitution was Trudeau's Magnificent Obsession," writes Christina McCall and Stephen Clarkson,[14] and by 1981 the endgame was underway. There is no need to go over the ins and outs of the long constitutional battle, but three salient points set the framework for the last-ditch bargaining sessions of November 1981. The first was that despite the Federalist victory in the 1980 Quebec referendum, the provinces reverted to their default position of opposing the federal goals of patriation and a charter of rights. After the failure of the September 1980 federal-provincial conference, Trudeau announced that the government of Canada would unilaterally go to Great Britain and ask the British Parliament to amend the Canadian Constitution one last time – with or without provincial support. The battle lines quickly formed: Ontario and New Brunswick supported the federal package, and the so-called "Gang of Eight" of eight provinces were opposed and resolved to fight the Trudeau initiatives in the courts and in lobbying the United Kingdom Parliament to say no. Rene Levesque and Peter Lougheed were the die-hard leaders of the Gang of Eight. Both believed if the Gang of Eight stayed united in opposition, they would succeed in persuading the British Parliament not to approve Trudeau's radical plan. In April 1981, to maintain the unity of the provinces opposed to the federal initiative, Quebec even signed on to the April 1981 Accord of the Gang of Eight, which promoted an Alberta proposed amendment formula of seven provinces and 50 per cent of the population, dropping in the process Quebec's traditional demand for a veto over constitutional change.

The second key point was that success in Great Britain for the federal package was not assured. Margaret Thatcher gave her word to Trudeau that she would support his initiative, but her parliamentary majority was a narrow one of only forty-four, and many Conservative MPs were not sympathetic to a package that had little provincial support and contained the innovation of a written entrenched Charter of Rights. There was a large Euro-skeptic faction in the Conservative caucus, and they opposed the European Court of Justice promoting the primacy of European Union law over Parliament's traditional authority. The debate in Canada over the Charter had many similarities with fears about written constitutions that so energized Conservative MPs in the United Kingdom. What would eventually be presented to the Parliament of the United Kingdom and what obstacles that package might face was a constant factor in the minds of all the negotiators in November 1981.

Third, the Supreme Court in Canada ruled in September 1981 that the federal package was legal in that the government of Canada could take to Great Britain a request that the British Parliament amend the Canadian Constitution without the consent of the provinces. But by a 6–3 majority, the court also ruled as a matter of constitutional convention a substantial degree of provincial consent was required (without defining what substantial meant). To maintain popular support for the federal package, Trudeau would have to try once again to negotiate with the provinces, which meant, in turn, that the unity of the Gang of Eight would have to be shattered. Some argued that given the court's ruling on legality, the Trudeau government should still attempt to go to London unilaterally. But I met Mr Trudeau at Harrington Lake soon after the court's ruling, and he understood the necessity of trying one more time to get the provinces aboard. We also discussed that if no agreement was achieved in November (the most likely outcome, we thought), Canadians would be asked in a referendum if they supported the Charter of Rights and the federal amending formula. One way or the other, we had to show the British Parliament that the federal package enjoyed substantial support.

The basic compromise of November 1981 was that the federal government accepted the Alberta amending formula in exchange for provincial acceptance of a Charter of Rights. And the tactic that broke up the Gang of Eight so that this swap could be consummated was Trudeau's initiative on Wednesday morning, 4 November, to suggest that a referendum might be the way to break the deadlock, a fallback position he had been contemplating at least since September 1981.

Pierre Trudeau believed that the source of legitimacy for any constitution was the people rather than Canada being a compact between the provinces. He presented to the House of Commons in June 1980, for example, a preamble to the Constitution (eventually dropped in the ensuing federal-provincial negotiations) that stated, "We, the people of Canada, proudly proclaim that we are and always shall be, with the help of God, a free and self-governing people ... We have chosen to live together in one sovereign country, a true federation, conceived as a constitutional monarchy and founded on democratic principles."[15] Therefore, it is not surprising that he included in the federal amending formula a referendum provision as a deadlock-breaking mechanism. He also briefed his allies William Davis of Ontario and Richard Hatfield of New Brunswick that at some point in the proceedings, he might suggest a national referendum with the requirement that the Charter of Rights and the federal amending formula (with the permanent referendum provision) be approved by a majority of electors in each of the regions of Atlantic Canada, Quebec, Ontario, and the West.

On the morning of Wednesday, 4 November, with the conference at a stalemate and near breaking up, Trudeau sprang his referendum idea, and Premier Levesque immediately agreed, believing perhaps that he would beat Trudeau in a second referendum and avenge the Parti Québécois' defeat on sovereignty association in May 1980. Trudeau immediately went to the media announcing a Quebec-Canada alliance to democratically break the impasse and then added mischievously, "And the cat is among the pigeons."[16]

The cat was among the pigeons in two backyards, both in the Gang of Eight and the provincial allies of Pierre Trudeau. The English-speaking premiers in the Gang of Eight were surprised at Levesque rising to Trudeau's challenge. The initial response was bravado, with Peter Lougheed saying, "We'll fight them, and we'll win."[17] But many premiers were not so sure that they could win a referendum opposing a charter of rights. This was due in part to one of the wisest decisions made by the Trudeau government in the entire constitutional saga. Cabinet had approved a draft Charter of Rights and Freedoms, but the government decided to open up the process by creating a Special Joint Committee on the Constitution and inviting MPs and the wider public to improve the Charter. The public response was tremendous: the committee met for fifty-six days, held 267 hours of hearings, and received more than 1,200 representations from individuals and groups,[18] and it soon became clear that Canadians wanted a charter of rights. But as Robert Sheppard and Michael Valpy write in *The National Deal*, "They wanted a much better one than was being offered."[19] Members of Parliament from all parties put forward 123 amendments to strengthen and improve the Charter, more than half of which were accepted by the government. Just as important, the committee hearings were televised, so for fifty-six days, Canadians saw an intense debate about rights, perhaps the greatest public education exercise that has ever engaged Canadians. Aboriginal rights, protection for the disabled, and strengthened guarantees for gender equality all emerged from this mass participation exercise in strengthening the Charter. A Bill of Rights may have been supported in the abstract by the public before the hearings of the Special Committee, but by the end of the process, the Charter had truly become a people's charter. The premiers found this out when they took out section 35 on aboriginal rights and applied the notwithstanding clause to section 28 on equality of persons in the final negotiations on 4 and 5 November. An enraged public soon forced them to retreat, and both provisions were restored.

So, the premiers were right to fear being on the wrong side of the debate in a national referendum on the Charter, as appeared likely after the Trudeau-Levesque referendum entente emerged at noon on 4 November. A scramble began Wednesday afternoon to find a compromise that would meet some federal objectives while hoping that Trudeau could be persuaded to meet provincial demands halfway. Saskatchewan took the lead in trying to craft this compromise. Saskatchewan had a critical supporter in this effort, and this was the government of Ontario. Premier Davis reluctantly supported the referendum provisions in the federal amending formula, but neither he nor Richard Hatfield wanted a winner-take-all national referendum on the Constitution. Davis thought a negotiated settlement was the best course and his delegation worked closely with Saskatchewan officials and ministers to bring this about. As described by Hugh Segal,

one of the premiers and closest advisors, Davis's view of the constitutional debate was "that there is considerable merit to both sides of
a question, and that the Canadian challenge is finding the instrument
that builds consensus around those points of merit."[20]

In the end, the Alberta amending formula, which treated the
provinces equally by dropping the federal provision of vetoes for
Quebec and Ontario and forever killed the concept of national
referendums being an entrenched part of the Constitution, was
reluctantly accepted by the federal government. This was the major
Gang of Eight demand (excluding Quebec, which simply wanted
the whole federal project derailed). Since 1982's proclamation
of the new Constitution, there have been eleven amendments to
the Constitution, most of them affecting only a single province.
There has been little national controversy over such amendments
until recently when in May 2021 Quebec introduced Bill 96 (with
the notwithstanding clause) to further French language primacy
by placing limits on enrollments in the English college system and
new requirements for medium-sized companies (with as few as
twenty-five workers) to work in French. To ensure this happens,
inspectors have been given almost unlimited powers of search and
seizure. Bill 96 also seeks to amend the Constitution under section 45 (requiring only the approval of the legislature concerned or
unilaterally) to affirm Quebec as a nation with French as its official language. Many argue that such an amendment would affect
Canada as a whole and should be considered under section 38 or
the general amendment formula of seven provinces making up 50
per cent of the population.[21] Bill 96 was passed on 24 May 2022,
with seventy-eight members of the National Assembly in favour
and twenty-nine opposed. There were large demonstrations by
the anglophone community against Bill 96 and the Legault government, and soon after the bill's passage, the English Montreal
School Board announced that it would be challenging the legislation in court since it enacted "a form of legal discrimination."
Since the Legault government has pre-emptively applied the notwithstanding clause to the entirety of Bill 96, some of the bill's
most striking provisions, such as expanded powers for the Quebec
language police, cannot be challenged under sections 7–15 of the
Charter, but the English Montreal School Board plans to challenge
using section 23 on minority language education rights which is
exempt from the scope of the notwithstanding clause.[22]

Bill 96 seeks to change the Constitution significantly through the use of the amendment procedure in section 45. Two significant proposed national amendments, however, have failed since 1982: the Meech Lake Accord failed to be approved by enough provinces in 1990 under the 7/50 provision within the three-year deadline of section 39 when the Manitoba and Newfoundland legislatures ran out of time to ratify, and the leaders who negotiated the Charlottetown proposals of 1992 decided to submit the package to voters in a national referendum though they were not legally bound to do so. The proposed amendment package was defeated when 54.3 per cent of Canadians said no, and only 45.7 per cent said yes. Canada has used the amendment formula negotiated in 1981 to change the Constitution but only in single provinces or the government of Canada by using sections 43 and 44: the famous 7/50 general amendment provisions of sections 38 and 39 – the heart of the Alberta amendment proposal – has yet to be successfully employed.

In the immediate aftermath of the 2–5 November negotiations, the federal government offered fiscal compensation to Quebec if education or cultural amendments passed, which the province opposed to try and lessen the sting of Quebec losing its traditional veto. And Prime Minister Chrétien later passed a bill requiring that the government of Canada first obtain the consent of Quebec, Ontario, and two provinces from both the western and Atlantic regions representing 50 per cent of the population of those two regions before proposing a constitutional amendment to Parliament. Though not entrenched in the Constitution, de facto, Quebec still has a veto.

Was the federal amendment proposal with its important referendum provisions essential, or has the country been able to make do with the Alberta amending formula? Canada's Constitution is hard to change under 7/50, but that is not necessarily a bad thing. The referendum provisions were central to Pierre Trudeau's concept of a country where people, not governments, would be the ultimate arbiters of constitutional change. But this centrality was not shared by allies like William Davis, and many in the federal cabinet were quite prepared to let referendums go too.

Referendums are a democratic way to settle constitutional disputes when governments cannot agree. The Mulroney government, for example, organized a national referendum on its Charlottetown proposals in 1992, and British Columbia and Alberta have passed laws requiring that any constitutional amendment first be submitted to a referendum before their legislatures can consider ratification. So, governments are free to turn to referendums if the situation demands it, and in our populist age we may see this device used more frequently. Still, by agreeing to drop his idea of formally entrenching a referendum provision into the Constitution in order to get provincial agreement on the larger constitutional package, especially the Charter, Mr Trudeau met Mills's criteria of keeping your eye on the essential prize.

MINORITY EDUCATION AND LANGUAGE RIGHTS

If accepting the provincially inspired amendment formulas was the major Gang of Eight demand, entrenching minority education and language rights was equally crucial to the federal government. Pierre Trudeau's vision of Canada was one where francophone and anglophone Canadians could live anywhere in the country and receive public services and educate their children in their own language. Provinces were reluctant to entrench minority language instruction where numbers warranted. When Roy Romanow, Roy McMurtry, and Jean Chretien met in a kitchen in the Government Conference Centre Wednesday afternoon to write a list of seven points that might constitute a deal, the provincial list had minority education rights only after a referendum (Chretien wrote on the paper "never").[23] The provinces eventually recognized that Pierre Trudeau would never sign a deal that did not entrench minority language rights; it was his ultimate bottom line. On Thursday morning, 5 November, eight English-speaking provinces agreed to entrench fully, and Manitoba signed the agreement but only with the caveat that the Manitoba Legislature would have to vote on section 23, which entrenched minority language and education rights. Following the Manitoba election of November 1981, which saw the Conservative government of Sterling Lyon defeated, the incoming NDP government of Howard Pawley informed the federal government that it supported the whole of the 5 November agreement.[24] Later, after further negotiations with Quebec, the federal government put into the Constitution the Canada Clause to protect the education rights of anglophones in Quebec. Making language and minority education provision an entrenched right is a major Canadian invention in the human rights field. Many countries grapple with how to protect language minorities from majoritarian democracy. The Canadian Charter of Rights and Freedoms shows them a way. As a Manitoban, I knew that the 1890 Manitoba Schools question had taken away minority rights from francophones and set Canada on a course of sectarian conflict. I felt especially proud that I was part of a government that had righted this historical wrong.

THE NOTWITHSTANDING CLAUSE

If the Alberta amending formula was the ultimate objective for the provinces and guaranteeing minority language and education rights was the same for the federal government, the last piece of the compromise puzzle was the acceptance by Pierre Trudeau of the notwithstanding or *non obstante* clause, which allowed legislatures to overturn judicial decisions protecting fundamental, legal, and equality rights. The critique of George Santayana about confusion in many compromises certainly applies to the *non obstante* clause: there is no logical reason why legislatures are prohibited from overturning democratic rights in the Canadian Constitution but are free to do so on fundamental rights like freedom of assembly. But logical or not, we do have a notwithstanding clause in our Constitution and like minority language and education rights, this is a unique feature of our Canadian rights framework, though I would argue a much less positive innovation than language protection.

I have written elsewhere a detailed study of the origins of the *non obstante* clause, so only a few points will be made in this chapter. The withstanding clause was a known entity already part of the provincial Bill of Rights, as in Alberta. Peter Lougheed had raised the idea at previous federal provincial conferences as a way to enshrine rights while maintaining legislative supremacy – a key objective for premiers like Sterling Lyon of Manitoba and Allan Blakeney of Saskatchewan. Paul Weiler of Harvard University had also achieved the dream of every academic of writing a timely article that influenced public policy by publishing a piece in 1980 in the Dalhousie Review[25] arguing that an override was a positive development since it would enable a rights dialogue between the judiciary and politicians (i.e., it was more than a deadlock-breaking compromise). Weiler's article found its way first to officials from British Columbia and then to other provincial delegations, and he was personally consulted by these delegations as well.

It was not, however, on Pierre Trudeau's agenda until very late in the game. On Tuesday night, 3 November 1981, Trudeau met his cabinet and said he might have to accept the Alberta amending formula in exchange for a fully entrenched Charter, but there was no hint that he might accept weakening the Charter itself. On Wednesday afternoon, 4 November, after Trudeau had broken up the Gang of Eight with his referendum proposal, the notwithstanding clause was one of the seven points on the Romanow-McMurtry list presented to Chretien as a possible way to get provincial buy-in for the idea of a Charter. Chretien told his colleagues, "You guys go and sell it to your premiers; I have a bigger job – I have to sell it to Trudeau."[26] But sell it he did. On the evening of 4 November, as provincial officials and premiers were meeting in Allan Blakeney's suite in the Chateau Laurier Hotel (no one called Quebec officials), ministers and officials were meeting at 24 Sussex to listen to Chretien explain that he had the makings of a deal – the Alberta amending formula in exchange for a Charter with minority language and education rights but with an override that would maintain legislative supremacy in key areas like equality rights. Then, a little after 10 p.m., Premier Davis called the prime minister and said he favoured the compromise Chretien was advocating, and that if Trudeau turned it down, Ontario would not support a unilateral package going to London. Trudeau gave Chretien a mandate to see how many provinces would come aboard. The next morning Chretien called the prime minister to say he had all of them except Quebec, and the deal was done.

During the years 1982–2021, according to the excellent research of Caitlin Salvino, there have been twenty-four pieces of provincial legislation that included the notwithstanding clause at the point of tabling in the legislature and sixteen cases where the laws have been promulgated and come into effect[27] (in some cases the intended laws were withdrawn or the law was not put into effect after passage, or the courts ruled on appeal on behalf of the government thereby negating the need for section 33). There was a flurry of initial usage in the 1980s, especially by Parti Québécois governments, which routinely used it on every piece of legislation. Still, Quebec was joined in these early years by Saskatchewan and the Yukon. Then there was a long hiatus with the use of section 33 until recently when Saskatchewan, New Brunswick, and Ontario joined with Quebec (always the most active user of the notwithstanding clause) in announcing the intended use of section 33. In 2017, Saskatchewan applied the notwithstanding clause to education legislation, and in 2019 New Brunswick introduced legislation applying the notwithstanding clause to a bill on vaccination policy. In 2019, Quebec used it to restrict the wearing of religious symbols in Bill 21, and in 2021 applied it to Bill 96 to further promote the use of French. Ontario threatened its use over municipal reorganization in 2018 and used it again in 2021 to enact legislation to allow restrictions on third-party political advertising. On 31 October 2022, Ontario introduced the Keeping Students in Class Act to avert a strike by education workers by imposing heavy fines if the workers used their right to strike and threatening to use section 33 to pre-empt legal challenges using the Charter. Using the notwithstanding clause pre-emptively in a contract dispute was a "travesty," according to federal Labour Minister Seamus O'Regan.[28] This is the third time in recent years that the Ford government has used or threatened to use section 33 – it seems to have become the go-to response of the Conservative government to possible Charter challenges.

But Quebec is still the most active province in invoking section 33. In 2021, according to Salvino, Quebec had six active acts with the notwithstanding clause, and Ontario had one. Quebec, by far, is the province that has most used the notwithstanding clause: with the promulgation of Bill 96 in May 2022, there have been sixteen pieces of Quebec legislation that invoked the notwithstanding clause and including the multiple renewals of several of those acts, Bill 96 would be the forty-first piece of legislation in the province to invoke the notwithstanding clause to remove the possibility of challenges to laws through the use of the Charter.

Supporters of the notwithstanding clause, like Peter Lougheed, knew the significance of taking away the rights of citizens, and he hoped that it would only be used on important matters after serious reflection. This standard has been slipping. When the Doug Ford government threatened to use the clause to ensure the reorganization of the Toronto City Council, the original supporters of the concept – Davis, Chretien, Romanow, and McMurtry – all criticized the Ontario government for using the clause on such a relatively minor matter.[29] In 2021, the Ford government actually used the notwithstanding clause to override a court decision on political financing, and in November 2022, it announced it would pre-emptively use the clause again, this time in a labour dispute with education workers. However, this casual or almost routine use of section 33 backfired. The proposed use of the clause in a contract dispute was condemned by Prime Minister Justin Trudeau, who said, "The suspension of people's rights is something you should only do in the most exceptional circumstances and I really hope that all politicians call out the overuse of the notwithstanding clause."[30] The CUPE union involved continued its strike, however, and unions across the province banded together to support CUPE and to protect their right to strike, even threatening a province-wide general strike. The Ford government then retreated and withdrew its draconian legislation in exchange for the CUPE union agreeing to take down their picket lines and return to the bargaining table. The Quebec government has been criticized, too, for using the clause in a pro-active manner to exclude the courts from even ruling on legislation like Bills 21 and 96, but it has ignored the criticism. These actions, however, are far from extraordinary: since 1982, the provinces have applied the notwithstanding clause nineteen times pre-emptively, many more times than in response to a court ruling.[31]

This is serious because you cannot have a political-judicial dialogue on rights, as proponents of the concept, like Paul Weiler, advocated, if governments exclude the courts from even having the opportunity to consider if the rights of citizens have been infringed. We are facing real dangers in the way current governments are using the power given to them in section 33.

The constitutional compromise of 1981 came together so quickly in the afternoon and evening of 4 November that there was very little time for reflection when the prime minister and premiers met at 9:30 a.m. on 5 November to seal the deal. Trudeau did raise the use of a sunset clause after five years so that governments that wanted to continue to overturn rights through the use of section 33 would have to start the legislative process over again. "I can live with that," said Lougheed, and, in the most famous use of the notwithstand-ing clause to restrict English on signs, Quebec, indeed, allowed its restrictions on signs to lapse after five years, though renewals of notwithstanding clauses in legislation are common.[32] There are ten pieces of Quebec legislation (often on pension administration) invoking the notwithstanding clause that have been renewed, some of them multiple times.

I wish the prime minister had similarly pressed Lougheed and the other premiers on lifting the application of section 33 to fundamental rights. In the debates over the Charter, the premiers had mostly been concerned about the implementation of equality and legal rights. Had we pressed on fundamental rights, Lougheed might have given in, though he later maintained it was a question of principle for him. As drafted in the Constitution, only a bare majority in a legislature is needed to pass legislation authorizing the use of the override. If Mr Trudeau had argued that there should be a supermajority of 60 per cent of the legislature, this would have maintained the principle of parliamentary supremacy so dear to premiers like Blakeney and Lyon, but in a practical sense it would have ensured that opposition parties would be involved (thereby making it unlikely to be used on trivial cases or forcing governments to search for other means to achieve their aims rather than using the override to take away rights). And the pre-emptive use of the override to prevent courts from even ruling on whether legislation is a violation of citizen rights is a real abuse of the original intent of the "framers" who advocated section 33 as a last resort after a court had ruled.

The federal government has never yet used the notwithstanding clause (Quebec, Yukon, Saskatchewan, Alberta, Ontario, and New Brunswick have invoked it). Prime Minister Paul Martin, indeed, once suggested that the national government should voluntarily remove its right to use section 33. The current federal government may not want to go as far as Martin advocated by eliminating its power to use section 33 entirely, but it should present a clause 33 reform package both to prevent potential future abuses and to set standards that the provinces might one day adopt. Peter Lougheed, one of the initiators of the notwithstanding clause compromise, thought hard about his creation, and in a 1991 lecture[33] suggested a reform package to prevent abuse, while still maintaining his core principle of legislative supremacy. Given the recent actions of some provinces, the Lougheed proposals are even more critical today than when he first raised them. The federal government should adopt the Lougheed plan and pass legislation outlining that if the federal parliament ever contemplated the use of section 33, it would:

- clearly outline the rationale for using the override so that citizens could evaluate the trade-offs;
- pledge that the override would never be used in a pre-emptive way and would only be applied after a court ruling;
- use of the override must be supported by 60 per cent of the members of Parliament.

CONCLUSION

Edmund Burke said that successful compromises involved giving up some rights so that we may enjoy others, and John Stuart Mill had similar advice in "sacrificing the non-essential to preserve the essential." How do the compromises involved in the settlement of 1981 stand up today? The Alberta amending formula has been used eleven times, mostly for single-province issues. The Charter broke new ground in entrenching minority education and language rights, and these innovations have stoked interest from around the world. After the premiers disgracefully took out Aboriginal rights from the November settlement, public opinion forced the premiers to retreat, and the courts have skillfully and boldly used section 35 on recognizing and affirming existing Aboriginal and treaty rights to begin the long road toward justice for our Indigenous peoples. Canada is no longer a legal colony of Great Britain. The Charter of Rights and Freedoms is used daily to enhance the rights of Canadians. The most contentious compromise was the acceptance of the notwithstanding clause, and there are genuine grounds for worry if governments get into the habit of diminishing rights and pre-empting judicial review. Quebec and Ontario are certainly doing their best currently to end the convention that section 33 should only be used in exceptional circumstances. But reforms can be made to make use of the clause a rare exception. It is up to Canadian citizens to begin to demand such reforms, and if they do, the political system will respond. This happened in Ontario in November 2022 when the Ford government had to retreat from its threatened use of section 33 in a contract dispute.

Pierre Trudeau was at the height of his powers in 1981, and he might have been able to win a national referendum on the Charter. In 1981, according to public surveys, 70–80 per cent of Canadians favoured an entrenched charter of rights. A survey released in June 1981, for example, found that 72 per cent of Canadians favoured an entrenched charter, with Atlantic Canadians the most favourable at 80 per cent, Quebec and Ontario respondents at 76 per cent, and the West at 65 per cent.[34] As the debate went on, the Charter became even more popular: a poll released by the Canada West Foundation in October 1981, for example, just before the November showdown with the premiers, showed 80 per cent of westerners favoured a bill or rights compared to 84 per cent of all Canadians.[35] The Charter, however, would have been only one part of the package that voters would have been asked to judge upon. In October 1981, a CROP survey asked how Canadians would vote in a constitutional referendum on the whole federal package, and 50 per cent of the sample would have voted yes, 33 per cent were opposed, and 18 per cent were undecided, a solid potential victory indeed. But to succeed, according to the criteria discussed at the November 1981 negotiations, the federal plan would have to win in every region. In Atlantic Canada, Quebec, and Ontario, support for the federal initiative was twenty points or more higher than the "no" side, but in the West 38 per cent of voters would support Trudeau, 44 per cent were opposed, and 18 per cent were undecided.[36] As one of the people who would have had a role in managing the federal referendum campaign, I can tell you that it would not have been a slam dunk.

Like Cyrano de Bergerac taking on one hundred enemies, Pierre Trudeau might have been able to defeat Peckford, Levesque, Blakeney, Lougheed, and the rest of the premiers in a national referendum on the Constitution. But the economy was in dreadful shape in 1981–82, and a referendum might have turned on regional or economic grievances rather than the Charter itself. The strategic imperative in elections is to frame the question uppermost in voters' minds when they make their choice: if the hypothetical question had been "Do you favour a Charter of Rights?" the constitutional referendum gamble would have succeeded. But if opponents had made a referendum instead turn on the question, "Do you approve of Pierre Trudeau's handling of the economy?" all bets would have been off. The advice of allies like Jean Chretien and William Davis, who both possessed great political intuition, was to take a pretty good – or at least a fair – deal, rather than risk it all in a national vote. It was prudent advice, and Mr Trudeau took it.

The results since 1982 have ratified Trudeau's choice of constitutional compromise over the risk of a winner-take-all referendum. He dropped what many regarded as the non-essential provision of the federal amendment formula with its referendum clause to compromise with the provinces by accepting their amendment formula. And, in truth, the Alberta-inspired amendment formula has functioned not too badly. In so doing, Trudeau won provincial acceptance of long-desired essential federal government objectives like patriation itself, minority language and education rights, and above all, an entrenched charter.

Prior to the birth of the Charter, Canada was not known as a human rights or judicial leader. In considering the actual performance of our Supreme Court on rights cases in the 1970s, Paul Weiler writes that it was not obviously apparent that "Canadian courts would do a clearly better job of defining our rights than would Canadian legislatures."[37] However, the Charter, even with the *non obstante* clause, initiated a major shift in authority to the judicial branch in the domain of human rights and our judges, under this surer legal footing, have been more activist in their defence of civil liberties.[38] Moreover, with the Charter, Canada broke new ground in linguistic and minority education rights and countries around the world became interested in the Canadian innovations. Canadian jurists and scholars are regularly invited abroad to speak to Canada's charter experience. At home, the adoption of the Charter has simply been transformative. The Charter of Rights and Freedoms was popular at its birth; it is even more popular now. An Environics study in April 2022 found that 88 per cent of Canadians believed the Charter of Rights to be a good thing, with only 4 per cent opposed. As Andrew Parkin, executive director of Environics, wrote about the study, "Whatever our differences, there is one part of the Constitution about which we almost unanimously agree ... if anything in this country unites us, it is support for the Charter."[39] The Charter has become an icon that defines us as a bilingual, multicultural society devoted to human rights, tolerance, and social justice. We are all Charter Canadians now, and this transformation is perhaps the biggest single achievement of the hard-pressed negotiators of 1981.

Soon after the constitutional settlement, reflecting the mood of the times with Quebec left out, disputes over the notwithstanding clause, and an unknown future for Indigenous rights, a review of the constitutional negotiations by several distinguished academics had the title, *And No One Cheered*.[40] That may or may not have been true then. In 2022, on the fortieth anniversary of the Charter and patriation, we should perhaps be a little more charitable and applaud the negotiators of the historic compromises of 1981 with at least a few hand claps.

NOTES

1 Introductory epigraph quoted in Alin Fumurescu, "No Compromise about Compromise" in *Compromise: A Political and Philosophical History* (Cambridge: Cambridge University Press, 2013), 25. Chapter 2 of Fumurescu's book greatly influenced the argument of this chapter.

2 Quoted in Ron Graham, *The Last Act: Pierre Trudeau, the Gang of Eight, and the Fight for Canada* (Toronto: Penguin Group, 2011), 159. Graham has written a dramatic account of the final week of negotiations. Robert Sheppard and Michael Valpy in *The National Deal* (Scarborough: Fleet Publishers, 1982) describe all the major events of the constitutional saga, 1980–82, and Peter Russell's *Constitutional Odyssey* (Toronto: University of Toronto Press, 2004) goes back to Confederation and places the patriation exercise within a broad historical context.

3 Thomas S. Axworthy, "Colliding Visions: The Debate over the Charter of Rights and Freedoms 1980–1981," in *Litigating the Values of a Nation*, eds. Joseph M. Weiler and Robin M. Elliot (Toronto: Carswell Co. Ltd, 1986).

4 Thomas S. Axworthy, "The Notwithstanding Clause: Sword of Damocles or Paper Tiger," *Policy Options*, 1 March 2007, https://policyoptions.irpp.org/magazines/equalization-and-the-federal-spending-power/the-notwithstanding-clause-sword-of-damocles-or-paper-tiger/.

5 Canadian Press, "Chretien: Patriation, Charter Benefited Quebec," *iPolitics*, 17 April 2012, https://www.ipolitics.ca/news/chretien-patriation-charter-benefited-quebec.

6 Jean Chretien, *My Stories, My Times Volume 2* (Toronto: Random House Canada, 2021), 202.

7 Quoted in Graham, *Last Act*, 259–60.

8 Edmund Burke, "Edmund Burke, On Conciliation with America," 1775, https://wisc.pb.unizin.org/ps601/chapter/edmund-burke-on-conciliation-with-america/.

9 Quoted in Rafael Cejudo, "J.S Mill and the Art of Compromise," *Human Affairs* 20, no. 4 (2010): 302.

10 John Morley, *On Compromise* (London: Macmillan, 1908). The book was first published in 1886.

11 Quoted in Fumurescu, "No Compromise about Compromise." This chapter has an extended discussion on Morley's thought.

12 Quoted in Bryan Dexter, "Morley and Compromise: The Future in Retrospect," *Foreign Affairs* 26, no. 2 (January 1948).

13 Quoted in Cejudo, "J.S. Mill," 302.

14 Stephen Clarkson and Christina McCall, *Trudeau and Our Times: Volume 1, The Magnificent Obsession* (Toronto: McClelland and Stewart Inc, 1990).

15 House of Commons Debates, 32nd Parliament, 1st Session: Volume 2, 10 June 1980.

16 Graham, *Last Act*, 94.

17 Shepard and Valpy, *National Deal*, 285.
18 Eddie Goldenberg, *The Way It Works* (Toronto: McClelland and Stewart Inc, 2006), 172.
19 Shepard and Valpy, *National Deal*, 135.
20 Nathan Nurgitz and Hugh Segal, *No Small Measure* (Ottawa: Deneau Publishers, 1983), 112.
21 Emmett Macfarlane, "Quebec's Attempt to Unilaterally Amend the Constitution Won't Fly," *Policy Options*, 14 May 2021, https://policy options.irpp.org/magazines/may-2021/quebecs-attempt-to-unilaterally-amend-the-canadian-constitution-wont-fly/.
22 Eric Andrew-Gee, "Opponents of Quebec's Bill 96 Prepare to Challenge Language Law in Court," *Globe and Mail*, 4 June 2022, https://www.theglobeandmail.com/canada/article-quebec-bill-96-french-language-law/.
23 Shepard and Valpy, *National Deal*, 289.
24 Sterling Lyon, premier of Manitoba, was one of the fiercest opponents of an entrenched Charter. He left the constitutional negotiations mid-way to return home to campaign in the provincial election he had called for 17 November 1981, leaving Attorney General Gerry Mercier to represent the province. Peter Lougheed called Lyon on the morning of 5 November to inform him of the impending deal and because of the inclusion of the notwithstanding clause, Lyon claimed to the Winnipeg Free Press on 6 November 1981 that "what we have ended up with today does represent a considerable watering down of the federal position." Gerry Mercier signed the 5 November agreement, but wrote beside his signature "subject to approval of Section 3(C) by the Legislative assembly of Manitoba." This was the part of the November 1981 agreement that entrenched section 23 on minority language and education rights. Howard Pawley's NDP, however, had opposed Lyon's constitutional position, especially on entrenchment of the Charter in a debate in the Manitoba legislature in May 1981 and Premier-elect Pawley called Prime Minister Trudeau soon after the November provincial election to say that Manitoba now supported fully the constitutional package. Special thanks are due to Michael Decter, former cabinet secretary of Manitoba, who clarified the sequence of events. The point is not a trivial one: James Matkin, a senior BC negotiator, wrote an essay in Weiler and Elliot, *Litigating the Values*, that the Manitoba caveat meant that "Manitoba did not sign without reservation and therefore, like, Quebec, did not commit unequivocally to support an entrenched Charter" (29). If the political spin after 5 November had been that two provinces – Manitoba and Quebec – were opposed or not fully on board with the deal, rather than the headlines that all the

English-speaking provinces were in favour and only Quebec had been left out, the public perception of ganging up on Quebec might have been greatly reduced.

25 Paul C. Weiler, "Of Judges and Rights: Should Canada Have a Constitutional Bill of Rights?" *Dalhousie Review* 60, no. 2 (1980).

26 Graham, *Last Act*, 194.

27 Caitlin Salvino, "A Tool of the 'Last Resort': A Comprehensive Account of the Notwithstanding Clause Political Use from 1982-2021," *Journal of Parliamentary and Political Law* 16, No. 1 (March 2022): 247–63. With Ontario's threat of the use of section 33 in a contract dispute with education workers in 2022, there have now been twenty-five times since 1982 that provinces or territories have threatened to use the clause.

28 "Trudeau Condemns Ontario Government," CBC News, 1 November 2022,https://www.cbc.ca/news/canada/toronto/early-session-debate-education-legislation-1.6636334.

29 "Creators of 'Notwithstanding Clause' Criticize Doug Ford for Using It," Durham Radio News, 15 September 2018, https://www.durham-radionews.com/archives/113539?fb_comment_id=2075145555881842_2075477565848641.

30 "Trudeau Condemns Ontario Government," CBC News. Trudeau said, "Using the notwithstanding clause to suspend workers' rights is wrong."

31 Salvino, "Tool of Last Resort." Alberta, Yukon, and New Brunswick have been the provinces which have joined Quebec in invoking the notwithstanding clause pre-emptively. Since Quebec has used section 33 more than any other provinces and usually pre-empts the courts from ruling on legislation, pre-emptive use far outweighs responding to court rulings which was the rationale used by the "framers" to justify use of the clause.

32 Salvino, "Tool of Last Resort." Quebec invoked the notwithstanding clause in the 1980s on different laws relating to the pension plan of teachers or retirement benefits of public employees and these have been renewed multiple times, the latest being in 2019. Salvino has useful tables that summarize when pieces of legislation using the notwithstanding clause have been enacted by the provinces (mostly Quebec), and if use of the clause has been renewed or not every five years. Her tables also show that the clause was used pre-emptively on these pieces of legislation too, so the courts have not had a chance to review such legislation in over forty years.

33 Peter Lougheed, "Why a Notwithstanding Clause?" *Points of View-Centre for Constitutional Studies* 6, no. 17 (1998).

34 "72% of Canadians favour an entrenched charter of rights." United Press Canada, "Canadian News Briefs," UPI Archives, 10 November 1981,

https://www.upi.com/Archives/1981/11/10/Canadian-News-Briefs/
8850374216400/.

35 "A Majority of Western Canadians Support a Bill of Rights," UPI
Archives, 21 October 1981, https://www.upi.com/Archives/1981/10/21/
A-majority-of-Western-Canadians-support-a-bill-of/9439372484800/.

36 Andrew Parkin, "Attitudes towards the Patriation of the Constitution and
the Charter of Rights, 1980–81," Environics Institute for Survey Research,
February 2022, https://www.environicsinstitute.org/docs/default-source/
default-document-library/patriation-1980s.pdf?sfvrsn=6af94cc_0.

37 Paul Weiler, "The Evolution of the Charter: A View from Outside,"
in *Litigating the Values of a Nation: The Canadian Charter of Rights and
Freedoms*, ed. Joseph M. Weiler and Robin M. Elliot (Toronto: Carswell,
1986), 55.

38 Ibid., 59.

39 Andrew Parkin, "Are Canadians Finally at Peace with their
Constitution?" *Globe and Mail*, 16 April 2022, https://www.theglobeand-
mail.com/opinion/article-are-canadians-finally-at-peace-with-their-
constitution/.

40 Keith Banting and Richard Simeon, eds, *And No One Cheered*
(Toronto: Methuen Publications, 1983).

2

The Evolving Debate over Section 33
of the Charter

Kristopher E.G. Kinsinger

The desirability and normative legitimacy of section 33 of the Canadian Charter of Rights and Freedoms has been a perennial debate within constitutional scholarship and commentary since the patriation of the Canadian Constitution in 1982.[1] Responses to this so-called "notwithstanding clause" and its prospective use have fallen along any number of points on a spectrum between vehement opposition and resigned acceptance to emphatic support and cautious optimism.[2] More recently, these debates have considered the operative effects of section 33's invocation, including how the clause functions in relation to other constitutional provisions. The purpose of this article is not to provide a complete survey of the voluminous scholarship on section 33 that has been published since 1982.[3] Rather, in the literature review that follows, I aim to provide a broadly representative summary of the assessments that have been offered of the notwithstanding clause over the course of the Charter's forty-year history.

I. THE NORMATIVE DEBATE

Early responses to section 33 were cautiously optimistic, if not outright supportive. Writing in 1984, Paul C. Weiler hailed the notwithstanding clause not merely as the product of a politically expedient calculus, but as "an intrinsically sound solution to the dilemma of rights and courts."[4] Under section 33, legislatures are prevented from routinely limiting fundamental rights and freedoms. "To make such a law prevail," Weiler explained, "the government would have to use a formula designed to draw the proposal to the attention of the opposition, the press and the general public."[5] In this regard, Weiler contended that the notwithstanding clause strikes a balance between legislative and judicial supremacy, one which "contemplates no serious danger of outright legislative oppression; certainly none sufficient to concede ultimate authority to Canadian judges and lawyers."[6]

Peter H. Russell similarly remarked that clauses such as section 33 offer a "process, more reasoned than court-packing and more accessible than constitutional amendment, through which the justice and wisdom of [judicial] decisions can be publicly discussed and possibly rejected."[7] This process is particularly apt, Russell explained, to the adjudication of contested freedoms such as expression, where courts are regularly called on to balance exercises of these fundamental guarantees against other competing interests. Far from relegating the judiciary to the margins of constitutional interpretation, he concludes, section 33 allows for meaningful judicial ventilation of rights without making such claims "ultimately adjudicable" to the point that "once the judiciary has spoken there must be closure on these issues."[8]

Conversely, the late Peter Hogg was more ambivalent regarding section 33's prospective use. In his landmark treatise on the Canadian Constitution, Hogg acknowledged that the clause "invites the question whether it is meaningful to speak about rights when the principal provisions of the Charter can be overcome by the enactment of an ordinary statute containing a notwithstanding declaration."[9] In practice, however, he predicted that the "signalling function" of the clause – by which governments alert critics that they "[believe] that [their] proposed legislation is inconsistent with the Charter" – would mitigate against abuse.[10] As such, Hogg held that, "It seems clear that [section 33] will be used infrequently and only when the legislating government is persuaded that there are powerful reasons of public policy to justify its use."[11] On this point, Hogg seemed willing to accept the legitimate role that section 33 could play in constitutional dialogue over rights adjudication: with the caveat that "there is widespread agreement that certain rights ought to take priority over the wish of the majority," through the process of judicial review, he stressed that "the definition of rights is often unclear," noting that "even clearly acknowledged rights must occasionally yield to other values."[12] The notwithstanding clause, from this perspective, offers a potential corrective for when judges reach "poorly informed [conclusions] about the costs and other consequences of their decision."[13]

Hogg expressed a similar view in a 1997 paper co-authored with Alison Bushell on "Charter dialogue," noting that the notwithstanding clause "allows the competent legislative body to re-enact [overturned laws] without interference from the courts," subject to a five-year sunset provision which "forces a periodic review of the use of section 33."[14] In this way, by allowing court decisions to be "reversed, modified, or avoided by the ordinary legislative process," section 33 (along with other limiting provisions such as section 1) helps to assuage concerns about the illegitimacy of judicial review.[15] This assessment, however, has not gone without criticism. In response to Hogg and Bushell's claim that provisions like section 33 facilitate constitutional dialogue, F.L. Morton maintained that, "This account fails to recognize the staying power of a new, judicially created status quo, especially when the issue cuts across the normal lines of partisan cleavage and divides a government caucus."[16] Politically speaking, Morton warned that "the effect of a Supreme Court Charter ruling declaring a policy unconstitutional is to transfer the considerable advantages of the policy status quo from one group of minority activists to the other."[17]

The "pessimistic view of section 33's place in the Charter's structural framework" was elsewhere given voice by Jamie Cameron.[18] As Cameron noted, the notwithstanding clause was hailed within the mythology of the Charter as a "uniquely Canadian" innovation protecting democratic integrity from the spectre of judicial activism, embodying a "middle ground" between constitutional and parliamentary supremacy.[19] Contrary to this narrative, Cameron insisted that section 33 "was never more than an exercise in wishful thinking."[20] To be sure, Cameron was not wholly unsympathetic to the claim that a provision like section 33 could theoretically help to promote institutional balance between courts and legislatures. In practice, however, she observed that legislators have been largely unwilling to invoke the notwithstanding clause "as a remedy for judicial activism."[21] Just as disuse of Parliament's power to disallow provincial legislation has delegitimized the provision to the point where its use now would likely ignite a constitutional crisis, reliance on section 33 to challenge judicial interpretations of the Charter has the potential to upset the (previously) established balance of Canadian constitutionalism.[22]

In this regard, Cameron suggested that the perceived illegitimacy of the notwithstanding clause is found in the paradox that "constitutional entitlements have a greater claim to legitimacy than ordinary legislation enacted under section 33" even while "the power to override constitutionally protected rights has no meaningful boundaries."[23] This is to say that the legitimacy of a constitutionally entrenched and judicially enforced bill of rights runs contrary to claims that the notwithstanding clause safeguards parliamentary supremacy.[24] The supposed middle ground that section 33 stakes out between competing supremacies lies uneasily within the landscape of Canadian constitutionalism. Cameron aptly remarked that the notwithstanding clause cannot be invoked "without violating principles of constitutionalism that predate the Charter and legitimize the judiciary's power to enforce its entitlements."[25] And yet, Canadian legal scholarship has typically held that legislative discretion to invoke the notwithstanding clause is (as far as the legal constitution is concerned) unfettered. In the absence of hard limits on its use, it is consequently difficult to reconcile section 33 with a constitutional project that seeks to circumscribe the state's authority over its citizens. As Cameron warned, "A source of authority cannot be legitimate unless it can be limited, and the problem is that section 33's power to override constitutionally protected rights is arbitrary."[26]

Concerns over section 33's precarious theoretical foundation have been more recently articulated by scholars who fear that the clause is at risk of being used to uphold restrictions on the rights of unpopular minority groups. In a 2019 article, Richard Mailey predicts that, "The rise of populist politics in Canada could eventually create a situational shift that would deeply undermine traditional justifications of the section 33 clause."[27] Like Morton before him, Mailey is unconvinced that section 33 promotes institutional dialogue between legislatures and courts. While, on its face, the notwithstanding clause "gives the legal power of final say on specific questions of constitutional interpretation to legislative institutions," Mailey notes that "the strength of the political convention that quickly developed against invocations of section 33" has resulted in judicial interpretations of the Charter almost always taking precedence over legislative priorities.[28] As such, the prospective benefit of section 33 "is not so much that it allows for an ongoing conversation or dialogue, but that it explicitly deals ... with the question of whose institutional will should prevail ... over how to interpret constitutional rights provisions."[29]

Institutional balance presumes the existence of a political culture in which reliance on the notwithstanding clause is truly seen
as exceptional.[30] Mailey warns, however, that this presumption
may not survive the germination of a "new populism" taking root
throughout the western world. New populists, he suggests, believe
that "their direct, almost mystical connection with the people ...
gives them the right and even the democratic obligation to take unilateral action on almost any issue, including by derogating openly
and persistently from constitutional rights commitments."[31] From
this perspective, section 33 may plausibly be read as preserving legislative supremacy while allowing for an "enhanced but still ultimately
minor role" for the judicial protection of rights.[32] Mailey contends,
however, that such an interpretation is contradictory: if the notwithstanding clause was meant to preserve legislative supremacy, then it
would follow that the Charter's framers "simultaneously intended
to bind and unbind ordinary legislative majorities to constitutional
law, to limit their sovereignty at the same time as preserving it."[33] It
remains to be seen, in Mailey's view, whether a principled reading of
section 33 can survive the sort of majoritarian supremacy which the
1982 act "rejects as a matter of basic principle."[34]

On this point, Brian Bird appositely notes that the persistent
"unease created by the existence and use of" section 33 points
toward the broader acceptance of "inescapably normative concepts
like freedom and equality."[35] As Bird contends, "The constitutional
commitment of a society to protect fundamental rights and freedoms
from unreasonable limitation by the state necessarily entails a commitment to a thicker version of the rule of law – to the rule of just
law – in that society."[36] While acknowledging that section 33 could
be justifiably used in a way that "serve[s] rather than subvert[s]
constitutionalism" – such as in response to courts which invalidate
legislation on the basis of "shaky constitutional reasoning" – Bird
warns that the risk of unjustifiable invocation is not one that can be
dismissed out of hand. "Where the notwithstanding clause is used
to oust or substantially imperil a Charter right or freedom without
justification," he concludes, "there is good reason ... to conclude
that such a use of the clause offends the rule of just law and is, for
that reason, illegitimate and even unlawful."[37]

Despite these concerns, some constitutional scholars maintain that
there is a constructive role for section 33 to play within Canada's constitutional order. Dwight Newman, for example, contends that the

clause "helps to establish a relatively unique mode of constitutionalism attentive to traditions of parliamentary democracy and respect
for distinctive identities within Canada."[38] That said, Newman also
suggests that the narrative of section 33 marking a "third way"
between judicial and legislative supremacy is too transnational and
too abstract, glossing over the ways in which the clause fits uniquely
within the architecture of the Canadian Constitution.[39] In particular, he rejects previous arguments by scholars such as Cameron
that invocations of the notwithstanding clause mark an internally
inconsistent "override" of agreed-upon Charter guarantees. The
"dominant purpose" of section 33 "is to permit a Canadian federal parliament or provincial legislative assembly to have the last
word on rights questions by making declarations to ensure the operation of particular statutory enactments"; any such declaration, he
emphasizes, "stems from the constitution itself, so it is not an override of the constitution but a constitutionally supported decision to
enact a statute regardless of view that judges might hold as to the
conformity of that statute with certain sections of the Charter."[40]

On this point, Newman submits that many jurists continue to
preclude a legitimate role for section 33 due to their entrenched
preference for judicial supremacy. Even the vision of legislative-
judicial dialogue promoted by scholars such as Hogg and Bushell
rests on the presumption that legislators will fulfill their role "within
the interpretive parameters as set by judges."[41] From this perspective, the era of "constitutional supremacy" supposedly ushered in
by the Charter all but excludes legislators from the task of constitutional guardianship and interpretation. In contrast to this vision,
Newman suggests that section 33 might be approached in a way that
facilitates "coordinate interpretation where both courts and legislative bodies have a role in constitutional interpretation."[42] While
conceding that section 33 ought not to be routinely invoked to the
point where legislators are "second-guessing judicial decisions on an
everyday basis," he maintains that the clause is more than a mere
"last resort" or "escape hatch," allowing for democratic balancing
between distinctly legal questions and issues that engage contested
moral values.[43] Far from removing legislative constraints on rights
issues, Newman concludes that section 33 "calls upon governments
to make deliberate, responsible choices" against the backdrop of
Canada's constitutionalist tradition, albeit in a manner that is itself
not justiciable "but ... is no less normatively binding for that fact."[44]

II. THE TECHNICAL DEBATE

Other recent debates over section 33 have (at least to some extent) sidestepped the preceding discussion over the constitutional desirability of such a provision, focusing instead on the technical legal effect of the clause's invocation.[45] In a 2019 essay, Grégoire Webber, Eric Mendelsohn, and Robert Leckey dispute (as Newman does) that section 33 allows legislatures to "override" rights and freedoms guaranteed by the Charter, as the received wisdom has long held.[46] The Supreme Court's decision in *Ford*, they contend, only commented on the formal requirements to invoke section 33, and was otherwise silent on how the clause shields the operation of impugned laws.[47] Neither the words "override" nor "judicial review" appear within the text of section 33, which instead protects "such operation as [a law] would have but for the provision of this Charter referred to in the declaration."[48] Normally, laws that are judicially found to be inconsistent with the Charter are rendered of "no force and effect" by virtue of section 52(1) of the 1982 Act.[49] Conversely, so long as it remains invoked, the notwithstanding clause merely removes the judiciary's ability to constitutionally invalidate legislation; section 33 thus neither exhausts the "judiciary's duty to say what the law is" nor "[ousts] the role of courts in ruling on Charter rights."[50]

From this, Webber, Mendelsohn, and Leckey suggest that the invocation of section 33 does not actually preclude judicial review to determine whether an impugned law would otherwise survive Charter scrutiny. Such a practice could yield certain advantages. Specifically, the authors contend that judicial review of legislation which invokes the notwithstanding clause could alert the electorate to laws that are substantively inconsistent with the Charter, allowing citizens (and in particular "minorities that might have little opportunity to make their voices heard by the democratic branches of government") to hold state actors to account.[51] Such was the case, they submit, in the Supreme Court's ruling in *Canada v Khadr*, in which a judicial declaration was made that the applicant's Charter rights had been infringed, but the court ultimately "left it to the government to right the wrong."[52]

Other scholars have adopted similar assessments of section 33. Shortly following the release of Weber, Mendelsohn, and Leckey's editorial, Leonid Sirota published an essay concurring with their interpretation.[53] While noting that section 33 "excludes the application of section 52(1)," he argues that there is nothing in the express wording of the clause to indicate that its invocation bars the application of section 24(1) of the Charter, which allows courts to award remedies "appropriate and just in the circumstances" to claimants whose guaranteed rights or freedoms have been "infringed or denied."[54] Sirota concedes that section 33's invocation changes the judicial "circumstances" surrounding an impugned law such that a declaration of invalidity would be inappropriate, but contends that "it would be wrong to make the leap from that incontrovertible truth to the much broader ... proposition that no judicial remedy is 'appropriate ... in the circumstances.'"[55] In such cases, a bare declaration of inconsistency (one that otherwise preserves a law's operation) stands to normatively vindicate a claimant's rights and "would seem to be a remedy that is (however minimally) just, and constitutionally appropriate in circumstances that include an operating 'notwithstanding clause.'"[56]

These novel interpretations of the notwithstanding clause have not gone without criticism. In response to the foregoing arguments, Maxime St-Hilaire and Xavier Foccroulle Ménard contend that a purposive interpretation of section 33 (one that accounts for the broader architecture of the Canadian Constitution) precludes the clause from being read in a strictly textualist manner.[57] Webber, Mendelsohn, and Leckey's focus on the inclusion of the word "operation" in section 33(2), they suggest, is flawed: "The exclusion of any substantive review (confirmed by the Supreme Court in *Ford*), the requirement of an express declaration of intent, and the temporary nature of the exception all support the argument that the function of section 33 is to allow legislators to exempt legislative provisions from any judicial debate on their respect for the constitutional rights from which they derogate."[58]

In support of this contention, St-Hilaire and Foccroulle Ménard cite Newman's argument that section 33 promotes "coordinate interpretation" of the Charter by constitutional actors, and in particular his conclusion that the clause was intended to ensure that "legislative bodies have the legal authority to substitute their view of a particular rights conflict or rights interpretation for the view at which courts have arrived."[59] The authors further dispute Webber, Mendelsohn, and Leckey's reading of the *Ford* decision, noting that the court's reasons carefully distinguished exceptions to rights from the limitation of rights within the context of section 1. They intuit from this that suspensions on the exercise of Charter guarantees pursuant to section 33 amount to constitutional exceptions, rather than limits, following which "courts simply have nothing to declare" with regard to the clause's legal effects.[60]

Following their co-authored 2019 editorial, Webber and Leckey/Mendelsohn respectively published further articles considering the technical effects of section 33's invocation. For his part, Webber focuses on the question of what the notwithstanding clause specifically makes exception to, identifying three potential answers: notwithstanding rights, notwithstanding judicial review, and notwithstanding remedy.[61] Disputing that section 33 constitutes an "override" of rights or otherwise "shield[s]" or "insulate[s]" laws from judicial review, Webber suggests that the use of the word "operation" in section 33(2) indicates that the primary purpose of the clause is to protect an invoking law's operability: "By invoking the notwithstanding clause, legislation is able to resist what would otherwise be the consequence of inconsistency with the rights and freedoms guaranteed in section 2 or sections 7 to 15 of the Charter, namely the loss of the legislation's operation ('force and effect') by reason of its invalidity."[62]

Under normal circumstances, Charter-infringing legislation is rendered inoperable by virtue of a judicial declaration of invalidity following a finding of inconsistency.[63] On this point, Webber considers Donna Greschner and Ken Norman's contention that section 33 should only be invoked following "a prior judicial determination that a law violates a Charter right or freedom," noting that, under this reading, "the clause cannot be invoked in legislation before such legislation has been subject to judicial review."[64] The notwithstanding clause, Webber ultimately concludes, does not prevent judicial review of a law's *prima facie* consistency with Charter guarantees; rather, section 33 simply prevents courts from rendering relief under section 52(1) of the 1982 Act by striking down the legislation in the event of inconsistency.[65]

Beyond this, Webber does not resolve the broader question of whether the court's role upon the invocation of section 33 "is fundamentally no different than the court's constitutional responsibilities in other Charter cases, such that the judicial role is undisturbed by any restrictions on immediate remedial consequences."[66] It is to this question that Leckey and Mendelsohn offer a more direct answer. Specifically, they suggest that Webber "misconstrues the

supremacy clause and misunderstands the significance of the overarching principle of constitutional supremacy in the Canadian legal
order."⁶⁷ Section 52(1) enshrines the principle that the Constitution
objects to the continued operation of an inconsistent law's operation; accordingly, Leckey and Mendelsohn dispute Webber's
three-step progression from inconsistency to invalidity to inoperability. The clause's function, they contend, is more straightforward:
"[Section 33] makes space within the Charter, and thus within the
Constitution of Canada, for laws that infringe rights by temporarily
ensuring their operation without regard to their impact on specific
rights and freedoms ... In this respect, the notwithstanding clause
functions similarly to [section] 1, signalling that the Charter, overall,
regards a law's impact on rights as permissible."⁶⁸

Despite their disagreement with Webber's thesis on this point,
Leckey and Mendelsohn argue that courts retain a critical constitutional role even when the notwithstanding clause is invoked.⁶⁹
Section 33(3) provides that declarations made under section 33(1)
"shall cease to have effect five years after it comes into force,"
thereby allowing for an electoral check on potential abuses of the
clause.⁷⁰ "For the electorate to play the constitution role assigned
to it by [section] 33(3)," Leckey and Mendelsohn thus conclude,
"it needs access to information about the impact of protected laws
on Charter rights," which may include "judicial conception[s] of
Charter rights" and declarations of "how they are impacted by protected laws."⁷¹

Not all scholars are convinced by the interpretations of section 33
respectively proposed by Webber and Leckey/Mendelsohn. Geoffrey
Sigalet, for example, notes that the wording of section 33(2) is "subjunctive," stating that laws invoking the clause "shall have such
operation as operation as [they] *would* have *but for*" certain guarantees in the Charter.⁷² This, Sigalet concludes, "implies a hypothetical
or counter-factual [state of affairs]" that "requires court to read the
law as having the same operation it would have in a world where the
Charter posed no threat to its consistency with the Constitution."⁷³
In Sigalet's view, laws that consequently invoke section 33 are incapable of being subjected to judicial review for *prima facie* consistency
with the Charter, precisely since the text of section 33(2) demands
that courts operate from a conceit that certain Charter entitlements
do not exist.⁷⁴

Other scholars seek to uncouple the preceding debates regarding section 33 (both normative and technical) from the assumptions that underpin "legal constitutionalist" accounts of the Charter. Such is the ambition of Stéphane Sérafin, Kerry Sun, and Xavier Foccroulle Ménard (SSM), who assess the clause from the perspective of the classical natural law tradition.[75] SSM set out an "alternative view of rights" that rejects the long-standing fear that section 33 could allow legislatures to circumvent constitutional entitlements. Specifically, SSM deny that the Charter is constitutive of the rights that it guarantees, arguing that the legal instrument of the Charter is posterior to the rights on which it confers constitutional effect. "On this alternative view," they explain, "the Charter is instead taken to simply specify or declare the existence of certain rights, to which it gives concrete effect as part of positive Canadian law."[76] More fundamentally, SSM dispute that the meaning of Charter rights lies within the sole purview of the judiciary. Positing that rights exist objectively (i.e., prior to positive legal enactment), SSM explain that rights need not "be consigned to the preserve of the judiciary if they are to qualify as rights properly speaking."[77] Concurring with Newman's view that section 33 allows for coordinate interpretation of the Charter, SSM thus conclude that the clause serves not only "as a recognition that the courts are not apt to undertake this task [of rights specification] in all circumstances," but also "as a prophylactic for the shortcomings of an overly judicialized rights discourse."[78]

CONCLUSION

The foregoing debates reveal the extent to which scholars continue to work through how section 33 fits within Canada's broader constitutional structure. Indeed, over the past decade, scholars have been forced to contend with the invocation of section 33 not merely as a hypothetical, but as a constitutional provision on which legislatures increasingly rely. Virtually all contributors to these debates rely on the concept of constitutional architecture (either explicitly or implicitly) in support of their respective interpretations of the notwithstanding clause. Yet many of these perspectives mask an ongoing preference to construe section 33 with primary reference to other sections contained within the 1982 Act.[79] The time is ripe for a more sophisticated understanding of how section 33 fits within the broader design of Canada's constitutional architecture, a call to which this volume's contributors have ably and readily responded.

NOTES

1 Canadian Charter of Rights and Freedoms [Charter], s 33, Part 1 of the Constitution Act, 1982, being Schedule B to the Canada Act 1982 (UK), 1982, c 11 [1982 Act].

2 See, for example, Howard Leeson, "Section 33, the Notwithstanding Clause: A Paper Tiger?" in *Judicial Power and Canadian Democracy*, ed. Paul Howe and Peter H. Russell (Montreal-Kingston: McGill-Queen's University Press, 2001), 297; Nicholas Stephanopoulos, "The Case for the Legislative Override," UCLA *Journal of International Law and Foreign Affairs* 10 (2005): 250; Janet L. Hiebert, "Parliamentary Bills of Rights: An Alternative Model?" *The Modern Law Review* 69, no. 1 (2006): 7–28; Yves Faguy, "Guidelines on the Use of the Notwithstanding Clause," CBA/ ABC *National*, 15 January 2020, https://www.nationalmagazine.ca/en-ca/ articles/cba-influence/resolutions/2020/guidelines-on-the-use-of-the- notwithstanding-claus; Ryan Alford, "Emergencies, Absolute Rights and the Legitimacy of the Notwithstanding Clause," *The Supreme Court Law Review* 101 (2021): 337.

3 Note that my focus in this section is primarily on legal scholarship, rather than debates which have taken place in the field of political science.

4 Paul C. Weiler, "Rights and Judges in a Democracy: A New Canadian Version," *University of Michigan Journal of Law Reform* 18, no. 1 (1984): 51–80.

5 Weiler, 81.

6 Ibid., 84.

7 Peter H. Russell, "Standing Up for Notwithstanding," *Alberta Law Review* 29, no. 2 (1991): 293–309.

8 Ibid.

9 Peter Hogg, *Constitutional Law of Canada*, student ed. (Toronto: Thomson Reuters, 2016), 39.

10 Ibid.

11 Ibid.

12 Ibid.

13 Ibid.

14 Peter W. Hogg and Allison A. Bushell, "The Charter Dialogue between Courts and Legislatures (Or Perhaps the Charter of Rights Isn't Such a

Bad Thing After All), *Osgoode Hall Law Journal* 35, no. 1
(Spring 1997): 83–4. That said, Hogg and Bushell also noted that,
"In practice, section 33 has become relatively unimportant, because of
the development of a political climate resistance to its use." It is unfortu-
nate that Hogg passed away without publicly commenting on the
expanded use of section 33. One cannot help but wonder whether laws
such as Bill 21 would have altered his assessment of the political
viability of the clause.

15 Hogg and Bushell, 80.

16 F.L. Morton, "Dialogue or Monologue?" in *Judicial Power and Canadian Democracy*, ed. Paul Howe and Peter H. Russell (Montreal-Kingston: McGill-Queen's University Press, 2001), 111–13.

17 Morton, 115.

18 Jamie Cameron, "The Charter's Legislative Override: Feat or Figment of the Constitutional Imagination?" in *Constitutionalism in the Charter Era*, ed. Grant Huscroft and Ian Brodie (Markham: LexisNexis, 2004), 139.

19 Ibid., 137, 139, 143.

20 Ibid., 140.

21 Ibid., 152.

22 On this point, I note that recent political developments have called into question many of the assumptions regarding section 33 that underpinned the scholarly literature during the 1990s and 2000s. As provincial govern-ments increasingly rely on the clause, several scholars have taken a less pessimistic view of section 33's prospective invocation. I consider several of these perspectives elsewhere in this article.

23 Cameron, 152.

24 Ibid., 154. On this point, it is worth noting that, despite assertions to the contrary, the term "parliamentary supremacy" does not accurately reflect the institutional balance of authority struck by the Canadian Constitution. As Guy Régimbald and Dwight Newman contend, "Due to the constitu-tional limits imposed on the principle, it would be in error to confuse the principle of Parliamentary sovereignty with that of Parliamentary supremacy. In the United Kingdom, where the courts do not have any powers of judicial review of Parliament and where this is no federal sys-tem, the terms 'sovereignty' and 'supremacy' can be used interchangeably. Rather, in Canada, the division of powers and the Charter makes it preferable to use the term 'Parliamentary sovereignty.'" See *The Law of the Canadian Constitution*, 2nd ed. (Toronto: LexisNexis, 2017), §3.64.

25 Cameron, "The Charter's Legislative Override," 157.

26 Ibid., 158.

27 Richard Mailey, "The Notwithstanding Clause and the New Populism," *Constitutional Forum constitutionnel* 28, no. 4 (2019): 9.

28 Ibid., 11.

29 Ibid.

30 Ibid.

31 Mailey.

32 Ibid., 12.

33 Ibid., 13.

34 Ibid., 13–14.

35 Brian Bird, "The Notwithstanding Clause and the Rule of Law," in *Supreme Court Law Review*, 2nd Series, Volume 101 (LexisNexis Canada, 2021), 299–301.

36 Ibid., 302.

37 Ibid., 303. See also Evan Fox-Decent, "Is the Rule of Law Really Indifferent to Human Rights?" *Law and Philosophy* 27, no. 6 (November 2008): 533–7.

38 Dwight Newman, "Canada's Notwithstanding Clause, Dialogue, and Constitutional Identities," Paper delivered at Oxford University, 7 June 2017, 4, https://dx.doi.org/10.2139/ssrn.3019781.

39 Ibid. Indeed, Newman notes that, contrary to received mythology, section 33 "was not a spur-of-the-moment invention" during the final stages of patriation, but had been under discussion as early as 1979, and bears striking similarities to the saving provision which had been included in the quasi-constitutional Canadian Bill of Rights, SC 1960, c 44 [Bill of Rights].

40 Newman, "Canada's Notwithstanding Clause," 9.

41 Ibid., 10.

42 Ibid.

43 Ibid., 11–12.

44 Ibid., 12–13.

45 In one sense, it is impossible to divorce the debate over the legal effect of section 33 from the discourse regarding the clause's normative legitimacy. Competing views as to how section 33 operates are reinforced by normative assumptions about the institutional balance that ought to be struck between legislatures and courts.

46 Grégoire Webber, Eric Mendelsohn, and Robert Leckey, "The Faulty Received Wisdom around the Notwithstanding Clause," *Policy Options*, 10 May 2019, policyoptions.irpp.org/magazines/may-2019/faulty-wisdom-notwithstanding-clause.

47 Weber, Mendelsohn, and Leckey, citing *Ford v Quebec (Attorney General)* [1988] 2 SCR 712.
48 Weber, Mendelsohn, and Leckey, citing Canadian Charter of Rights and Freedoms, s 33(2).
49 1982 Act, Canadian Charter of Rights and Freedoms, s 52(1).
50 Weber, Mendelsohn, and Leckey, "Faulty Received Wisdom," citing *Ford v Quebec (Attorney General)*, [1988] 2 SCR 712.
51 Weber, Mendelsohn, and Leckey.
52 Weber, Mendelsohn, and Leckey, citing *Canada (Prime Minister) v Khadr*, 2010 SCC 3.
53 Leonid Sirota, "Concurring Opinion," *Double Aspect* (blog), 23 May 2019, https://doubleaspect.blog/2019/05/23/concurring-opinion/.
54 Sirota, citing Canadian Charter of Rights and Freedoms, ss 24(1), 52(1).
55 Ibid.
56 Ibid.
57 Maxime St-Hilaire and Xaiver Foccroulle Ménard, "Nothing to Declare: A Response to Grégoire Webber, Eric Mendelsohn, Robert Leckey, and Léonid Sirota on the Effects of the Notwithstanding Clause," *Constitutional Forum* 29, no. 1 (2020): 38–9.
58 Ibid., 40.
59 St-Hilaire and Foccroulle Ménard, citing Newman, "Canada's Notwithstanding Clause," 13.
60 St-Hilaire and Foccroulle Ménard, 40–1. The authors thus also conclude that Webber, Mendelsohn, and Leckey's reliance on the *Khadr* decision is misguided, insofar as the applicant's rights in that particular case "had not been derogated from by means of valid applicable statutory provisions" (41). In response to this argument, Leckey and Mendelsohn contend in a subsequent article (considered below) that "if activating the notwithstanding clause made rights inapplicable to a protected law – a formulation absent from the constitutional text – it would be redundant to specify that the law shall have its operation despite those rights" (as section 33 does) since "that consequence would arise automatically." "The Notwithstanding Clause: Legislatures, Courts and the Electorate," *University of Toronto Law Journal* 72, no. 2 (2022): 8–9, https://papers.ssrn.com/sol3/papers.cfm?abstract_id=3841568.
61 Grégoire Webber, "Notwithstanding Rights, Review, or Remedy? On the Notwithstanding Clause on the Operation of Legislation," *University of Toronto Law Journal* 71 (2021): 1–2, https://ssrn.com/abstract=3935891.
62 Ibid., 13–14.

63 Ibid., 11–12, 14. Webber acknowledges the rebuttal of whether, based on a holistic interpretation of the Charter, "It [is] ... better to read the notwithstanding clause's reference to the operation of legislation as also securing the legislation's validity and consistency." In reply, he concedes that, "The progression from consistency to validity to operability is indeed analytically sequenced, such that one may usually infer that operable legislation is valid and is valid because it is consistent with the constitution," but argues that "such inference may be disrupted either by constitutional doctrines like paramountcy (whereby operable provincial legislation is not, by reason of being inoperable, *also* invalid and inconsistent with the constitution) or by a constitution provision like the notwithstanding clause, which disrupts the analytical sequence at the third step." See 15–16.

64 Webber, 16, citing Donna Greschner and Ken Norman, "The Courts and Section 33," *Queen's Law Journal* 12, no. 2 (1987): 155–88.

65 Webber, 17.

66 Ibid., 26.

67 Leckey and Mendelsohn, "Legislatures, Courts, and the Electorate"; Webber, "Notwithstanding Rights," 6.

68 Leckey and Mendelsohn, "Legislatures, Courts, and the Electorate," 10.

69 Ibid., 10, 16.

70 Canadian Charter of Rights and Freedoms, s 33(3).

71 Leckey and Mendelsohn, "Legislatures, Courts, and the Electorate"; Webber, "Notwithstanding Rights," 16–17.

72 Geoffrey T. Sigalet, "The Truck and the Brakes: Understanding the Charter's Limitations and Notwithstanding Clauses Symmetrically," *Supreme Court Law Review* 105 (2022): 192–222, citing Canadian Charter of Rights and Freedoms, s 33(2) [emphasis added]. See also Geoffrey T. Sigalet, "Legislated Rights as Trumps: Why the Notwithstanding Clause Overrides Judicial Review," *Osgoode Hall Law Journal* 61, no. 1 (forthcoming).

73 Sigalet.

74 Sigalet, 223. It strikes me that an important distinction might be made here between whether this conceit requires courts to act as if impacted Charter entitlements *no longer exist* or *as if they never existed in the first place*. The former interpretation could support an argument that section 33 facilitates derogation not just from specific Charter guarantees, but also potentially from their underlying subject matter; conversely, the latter reading would indicate that, to the extent that a guarantee's subject matter

pre-dates the Charter, courts may still undertake judicial review from the vantage point of pre-1982 constitutional provisions and entitlements.

75 Stéphane Sérafin, Kerry Sun, and Xavier Foccroulle Ménard, "Notwithstanding Judicial Specification: The Notwithstanding Clause within a Juridical Order," *Supreme Court Law Review* 110 (2023). See also Kerry Sun, Stéphane Sérafin, and Xavier Foccroulle Ménard, "Notwithstanding the Courts? Directing the Canadian Charter toward the Common Good," *Ius & Iustitium* (blog), 1 July 2021, https://iusetiustitium.com/notwithstanding-the-courts-directing-the-canadian-charter-toward-the-common-good/.

76 Sérafin, Sun, and Ménard, "Notwithstanding Judicial Specification," 137.

77 Ibid.

78 Ibid.

79 On this point, that Leckey and Mendelsohn support their interpretation of section 33 with reference to pre-1982 principles and doctrines such as parliamentary sovereignty, federalism, the separation of powers, and judicial discretion. Leckey and Mendelsohn, "Legislatures, Courts, and the Electorate," 20–30.

PART TWO

Fundamentals

While this volume goes to some lengths to expose the notwith-standing clause (NWC) to critical scrutiny and, indeed, to questions about substantive shortcomings and even about its very legitimacy as a most consequential provision in the constitution of a liberal democracy, it begins not with the premise that it is flawed, illegitimate, or otherwise problematic, but with a robust statement of its role, purpose, and operation.

Dwight Newman explains how the NWC serves to facilitate ongoing coordinate approaches to rights protection and fulfillment, to maintain the particularly significant value of democratic participation as a structuring feature of our constitutional order, and to offer a mechanism for the protection of diverse identities within Canada.

Gregoire Webber then deconstructs and explains the structure and operational intricacies of the NWC. At issue is whether its limiting effect on constitutionally prescribed rights and freedoms is to undermine the supremacy clause in section 52 of the Constitution Act, 1982, which renders "of no force or effect ... any law that is inconsistent with the provisions of the Constitution," or whether "it signals an exception ... to the legal effect of the supremacy clause, providing a temporal exception to the denial of legislation's operation by reason of its inconsistency with targeted rights and freedoms." Webber concludes that it is the latter. In his exposé of the NWC in relation both to the constitutionally enumerated rights and freedoms specified in the invoking legislation, and to the supremacy clause which stipulates the general effect of those laws which are found to be inconsistent with the provisions of the Constitution, Webber shifts the analytical paradigm from one focused on rights infringement, suspension, and "override," to one trained on the operation of the law in support of which the NWC has been invoked. While Webber's essay could just as well have been included in the next section of the volume, "Judicial Review," its analysis of the basic structure and operation of the NWC in relation to other relevant provisions of the Constitution commend it to the reader's consideration of the "Fundamentals."

3

Key Foundations for the Notwithstanding Clause in Institutional Capacities, Democratic Participatory Values, and Dimensions of Canadian Identities

Dwight Newman

The presence and the use of the notwithstanding clause mark a distinctive feature of Canadian constitutionalism. The notwithstanding clause has underlying justifications in the differing institutional capacities of different branches of government, in democratic participatory values, and in dimensions of Canadian identity.[1] In this contribution, I discuss aspects of these justifications and draw out their significance for the appropriateness of using the notwithstanding clause and for the broader implications of the notwithstanding clause as part of Canadian constitutionalism. Counter to so much academic commentary trying to find different ways to undermine or to limit the notwithstanding clause,[2] my approach not only recognizes it as a legally accessible mechanism within the Canadian Constitution but identifies underlying justifications for its presence and use that mark its coherence with broader values and norms.

Before turning to these points in full, several preliminary points are important by way of background. First, this approach engages with a natural reading of the central features of the key parts of the text of the notwithstanding clause:

(1) Parliament or the legislature of a province may expressly declare in an Act of Parliament or of the legislature, as the case may be, that the Act or a provision thereof shall operate

notwithstanding a provision included in section 2 or sections 7
to 15 of this Charter.
(2) An Act or a provision of an Act in respect of which a declaration made under this section is in effect shall have such operation
as it would have but for the provision of this Charter referred to
in the declaration.[3]

The use of the notwithstanding clause is a decision for another
branch of government: the legislative branch. By an express *non
obstante* declaration, its legislation can be effective despite what
would otherwise have been concluded by the judiciary concerning
the implications of sections 2 and 7 to 15 of the Charter. Aside from
the time limit in section 33(3), and the democratic accountability of
legislative bodies, the sole textual restriction on the use of the clause
is the requirement of an express declaration. Upon that express
declaration, legislation that might otherwise have been considered
invalid by the judiciary instead remains effective. It cannot be said
to be "valid," for that terminology would be inconsistent with the
time limit, so it is said to operate, using a terminology appropriate
to any *non obstante* clause guaranteeing the enforceability of one
provision over another.

Second, taking this approach does not involve any denial of the
motivated historical roots of the notwithstanding clause. As highlighted well by Tom Axworthy's contribution within this collection,[4]
the ultimate presence of the notwithstanding clause within the
Canadian Charter of Rights and Freedoms depended upon a process of historic compromise that made it possible to patriate the
Canadian Constitution. However, the fact that constitutions come
from historical compromises is not a reason to read them in compromised ways. Nor it is a reason to think differently about particular
clauses of constitutions that were specifically involved in the negotiated compromises necessary to constitutional development. That the
notwithstanding clause was, as the Supreme Court of Canada puts
it, "an undeniable aspect of the constitutional bargain,"[5] does not
diminish its significance. If anyone took such a position, it would
pose risks for all other parts of the Constitution, each of which was
in some measure part of the necessary compromises of real-life political action and constitution-making.

For example, early case law about the minority language rights
clauses of the Charter honed in on their history and treated their

guarantees as more attenuated because they were connected to compromises within the negotiation process.[6] Later case law has rightfully seen a move away from any suggestion that this history should lead to reading those clauses in more limited ways.[7] Anyone who would argue that the notwithstanding clause should be hemmed in by new restraints because of its historical path as part of a constitutional compromise – or who would treat it as a source of embarrassment on account of this history – would be adopting an argument normatively structured in a way that would undermine language rights guarantees and, indeed, other human rights guarantees within the Charter.[8] The historical process must drive, rather, investigation into the nature of the notwithstanding clause as part of a uniquely Canadian Constitution and a clause that speaks to dimensions of Canada differently than the constitution of some other country would. That is the approach to history that this chapter ultimately employs.

Third, there is a danger of inaccuracy if academics read the Canadian Constitution as if it adopted American-style strong-form judicial review mixed with some additions like additional protection of minority rights and then use those features to purport to interpret and thus to delimit the genuinely unique provision of the notwithstanding clause. As developed in the work of Stephen Gardbaum, the presence of the notwithstanding clause in the constitutional text places Canada within a different spectrum of commonwealth models of constitutionalism that are not oriented to American-style strong-form judicial review.[9] Obviously, Canada made many constitutional choices different than those contained within the American text, such as in the deliberate different drafting of rights guarantees like those in section 15 or in section 7, even if the Supreme Court of Canada was ready in some contexts to depart rapidly from the effort at a different Canadian model.[10] The inclusion of the notwithstanding clause similarly marks out a very different model, and it will not do to attempt to develop limits on the notwithstanding clause based on an understanding of what the rest of the Constitution would mean for this unique clause in the absence of this clause. Rather, there must be an effort to understand what the underlying meaning of this different model, within which the notwithstanding clause functions, in relation to institutional capacities of branches of government, democratic participatory values, and dimensions of Canadian identity.

This chapter is oriented ultimately around those considerations, addressed respectively in parts II, II, and IV of the chapter. The notwithstanding clause is part of a distinct constitutional structure rather than a clause to be read away as if it were a strange add-on to an otherwise existing constitution. Before turning in parts III, IV, and V to how the notwithstanding clause functions in relation to the institutional capacities of branches of government, democratic participatory values, and dimensions of Canadian identity, part I clears the path by showing how important recent scholarly comments supporting limits on the notwithstanding clause inadvertently fall into the problem of reading the notwithstanding as an add-on even as they claim to be seeking to avoid that error.

I. TRANSCENDING INCOMPLETE HOLISTIC INTERPRETATIONS

By way of general constitutional methodology, it is important to see the notwithstanding clause as part of Canada's Constitution and to let it live as part of the Constitution rather than taking the view that there should be special restrictions put upon it based on the rest of the Constitution or views about what the rest of the Constitution would have meant without the notwithstanding clause. This approach fundamentally follows from the idea of holistic interpretation, from reading the Constitution as a whole rather than as a set of random legal propositions written down alongside each other. Only holistic interpretation fully befits a constitution, for the nature of a constitution in setting out the fundamental arrangements of the state and limits upon state action must function as a unity if it is to be anything worthy of the name.

Some past phases of scholarship on the notwithstanding clause treated it as something not belonging in the Constitution that needed to be interpreted anyway and that might thus be interpreted in light of values present in the rest of the Constitution without its presence. While a new wave of scholarship on the notwithstanding clause has seen scholars indicating that they respect the need to consider the notwithstanding clause in an integrated way as part of constitutional interpretation, I would respectfully suggest that they ultimately stop short of doing so, even if inadvertently, and thus cannot be taken as offering appropriate interpretations of the clause. Two key examples stand out.

First, it is worth referencing the important recent scholarly contribution of Robert Leckey and Eric Mendelsohn in their 2022 article on the notwithstanding clause.[11] In it, they have rightfully taken an approach that seeks to read section 33 as part of the Canadian Constitution, not seeing it as something outside the Constitution but as what they implicitly admit is an "important constitutional feature."[12] They say that they want to offer "an account of how subsections 33(1), 33(2), and 33(3) interact and fit into the Constitution of Canada."[13]

The specific approach to section 33 in this article seems to mark something of a new tack for Leckey and Mendelsohn. They had previously written with Grégoire Webber and relied upon his methodologies in their argument when it fit with their desired result.[14] However, Webber's approach unfortunately depends too much upon what I would respectfully consider a somewhat idiosyncratic reading of text pronounced forth as definitively resolving a complex legal debate. Webber says that past analyses have not focused enough attention on the words "operate" and "operation" in section 33 and that attention to these words will lead to a different understanding of the notwithstanding clause.[15] The argument fixates on these words, tracing through distinctions from Aquinas to Australia, while continuing to be subject to critiques even on that very narrow textual reading in ways highlighted by Geoff Sigalet.[16]

Leckey and Mendelsohn now want to surmount the textually isolated tendencies of Webber's pronouncements on the meaning of specific words in the constitutional text with their laudable aspiration toward a more holistic reading that understands section 33 as part of the Charter. However, their application of the idea of holistic constitutional interpretation is ultimately limited. Their argument ultimately uses other constitutional features to read new limits onto the notwithstanding clause, rather than discussing what it means to see the notwithstanding clause as among Canada's key constitutional features and thus as itself a constitutional feature that might appropriately lead to a different reading of these other features. Thus, they draw upon federalism, the role of the courts, and other elements as found elsewhere in the Constitution so as to interpret and ultimately limit aspects of section 33.[17] They do this rather than letting those concepts be understood in light of the presence of section 33. In other words, they end up in adumbrated readings of the notwithstanding clause shaped by an implicit assumption that other constitutional features take priority over it, thus failing to offer a genuinely holistic reading of the Constitution. The notwithstanding clause should not simply be hemmed in by the rest of the Constitution but should be understood as helping to shape the rest of the Constitution as well. Leckey and Mendelsohn do not examine what the notwithstanding clause might imply for how to understand the other values they reference, and achieving a holistic reading requires further examination of what the notwithstanding clause itself means and what it could thus mean for how to understand other aspects of the Canadian Constitution.

In saying as much, I do not wish to minimize the sophistication of their discussion. First, it would appear that they perceive it as potentially appropriate to adjust the read of other constitutional values in light of the notwithstanding clause, such as in a brief suggestion that the presence of the notwithstanding clause has something to say about how to understand parliamentary sovereignty within the Canadian constitutional order.[18] However, the actual resulting constraints on judges are minimal and amount to disapproval of judicial statements directly commenting on how citizens should vote in elections, which would be independently supported on any account of separation of powers without any reference to the notwithstanding clause.[19] Second, they do not simply impose limits on it, but engage in reasoning on why they think the notwithstanding clause should be shaped by other constitutional values grounded in the constitutional text. Part of how they argue that the notwithstanding clause should be read as subject to democratic values stems from their reading of the text itself, notably section 33(3)'s implicit inclusion of a democratic check on parliamentary and legislative uses of section 33 in so far as it aligns the sunset period on a use of the clause with the maximum time length of a parliament or legislative assembly.[20] However, their approach ultimately attaches itself to a few words of text without fully engaging with how the presence of the notwithstanding clause actually reshapes the Charter's whole statement on rights more generally. Perhaps most illustrative of this phenomenon is their argument that there may be section 24 remedies granted even where the notwithstanding clause is in place.[21] Since a use of the notwithstanding clause has inherently declared legislation to operate despite judicial interpretations of Charter rights, to say that section 24 may nonetheless operate against the legislation is to attempt to render section 33 nugatory and meaningless, surely not an approach in keeping with holistic constitutional interpretation in the context of a constitution with section 33 part of it.

Second, it is worth at least briefly referencing the extensively researched historical examination of the notwithstanding clause recently published by Eric Adams and Erin Bower.[22] They rightly highlight the reality that a "deeper constitutional history suggests that the notwithstanding clause is not best characterized as the last-minute invention of desperate politicians intent on brokering a deal," but stems from a long tradition of constitutionalism.[23] Aside from any quibbles with the history, on which they have in any event done a great service in drawing together a number of sources, what is striking about their article is that they end up interpreting the notwithstanding clause as within the long traditions of balancing in Canadian Charter jurisprudence and then conclude that nothing precludes judicial review of legislation protected with the notwithstanding clause, with them alleging that such judicial review preserves the spirit of balancing.[24] I summarize matters thus at some risk of oversimplification, but the normative part of their article is very short after a longer history, and this account does arguably get at its core. That core allows too much weight to a very generalized idea of "balancing" much like that in Charter case law, thus dodging the central point that the notwithstanding clause might naturally be understood as putting certain issues outside the scope of Charter jurisprudence, at least for the period of time in which legislative bodies took up a role in offering a determinative interpretation. While they similarly quest after holistic interpretation, a holistic interpretation needs to consider how the notwithstanding clause pursues central purposes within Canadian constitutionalism, to which I now turn.

II. INSTITUTIONAL ROLES IN THE CANADIAN CONTEXT

Even while marking a historical break in some ways, the Canadian Charter of Rights and Freedoms displayed fundamental continuities with historical constitutional traditions in others. Many provisions of the Charter displayed significant continuities with the Canadian Bill of Rights, including in the transposition of significant parts of the text.[25] The Bill of Rights, in turn, built upon longer-standing ideals within Canadian parliamentary tradition.[26] In certain general terms, the Charter thus maintained fundamental connections with Canadian parliamentary tradition.

The very structure of the way in which the Charter guaranteed the rights and freedoms recognized within it fits with this description, with the notwithstanding clause being a key part of this structure. The Canadian Charter does not set out judicially protected rights in unlimited ways but has section 1 simultaneously expressing both the guarantee of rights and the possibilities for limits of rights and section 33 differently locating the power to make determinations on the ultimate implications of significant parts of the Charter. The very structure of the Charter manifests a braiding of judicial rights review with ongoing institutional roles for parliaments and legislatures in a coordinate interpretation of rights.[27]

The notwithstanding clause was not some random last-minute addition by a mad drafter. It followed upon previous bills of rights in the Canadian context containing similar clauses.[28] The possibility of including a notwithstanding clause was present throughout various phases of the constitutional discussions of the 1960s and 1970s and thus an "available" idea.[29] Such a clause was urged by premiers who have subsequently described the profound underlying thinking behind such a clause, notably Alberta Premier Peter Lougheed and Saskatchewan Premier Allan Blakeney.[30] At an early phase of the last period of negotiations, Quebec actually introduced a potential draft version of the Charter that contained a version of the notwithstanding clause. The discussion of the era also saw an important theoretical contribution by the renowned Harvard-based Canadian labour law scholar Paul Weiler, who offered justifications for such a clause in institutional considerations about rights protection.[31] The idea was very much present through a significant period, and it marked a way of braiding judicial rights review and the parliamentary system, something in keeping with the significant theoretical contribution of Stephen Gardbaum in recognizing the diversity of possible models of rights protection and the way in which commonwealth states have adopted a different model than the United States did. Within such models, there is an ongoing role for parliaments and legislatures in interpreting rights.

The innovation present in the notwithstanding clause spoke in some ways beyond traditional concerns of constitutionalism and embedded many different prospects. In his account of reasons for the notwithstanding clause, Blakeney wrote of how the Charter included a narrow set of civil and political rights but did not and could not include all moral rights – rights that could justifiably be asserted against governments but that were not best protected through courts.[32] Among the moral rights in this category, he considered many social and economic rights to be best protected through democratic processes, through social solidarity, and through social and political activism. Those rights are not in the Charter, and those who would argue against governments ever using the notwithstanding clause would deny the ability of governments to defend moral rights not in the Charter text against overreaching judicial interpretations of the textually included rights. Figures like Blakeney foresaw the potential risks of the Charter becoming a straitjacket on policymakers and fought for a provision that secured the possibility of ongoing democratic work through the parliamentary process on challenging political issues.

In recent years, some scholars have come close to saying that Gardbaum's account of commonwealth models of rights review is outdated essentially because Gardbaum's account is no longer brand new and because a new wave of scholarship has included some articles once again arguing for limitation of the notwithstanding clause.[33] However, an account of how the Canadian Charter is located within a broader spectrum of commonwealth models does not become untrue simply because it is no longer a brand new observation. Emerging arguments for new limits on the notwithstanding clause must be assessed against constitutional text, context, and purposes,[34] and all of those considerations continue to support the notwithstanding clause as a key part of the Canadian approach to the respective roles of courts and legislative mechanisms in the interpretation and application of rights. Parliaments and legislatures have an ongoing and important role in the interpretation of rights, including through the power under section 33 to substitute their interpretation of rights for that of judges shaped within a certain elite context with potentially different perspectives on some of the moral choices involved within rights interpretation.

There is an important challenge to this approach that involves questioning the reality of the account, suggesting that it provides an idealized picture of parliaments that does not match their actual record on discussing potential uses of section 33.[35] Particularly noteworthy in this regard is the important paper of Léonid Sirota, with Sirota engaging in the actual empirical exercise of reading the legislative debates preceding various adoptions of the not-withstanding clause.[36] He finds that this debate is significantly less rich and robust than one might wish, and he concludes that this empirical reality raises questions about a normative justification for the use of the clause in the coordinate role of parliamentary and legislative interpretations of rights within commonwealth constitutional models.

While that reading certainly demonstrates reasons to be concerned about our democratic institutions, taking it to give reasons against the use of section 33 would both adopt an argument that proves too much and adopt an argument further weakening our institutions. First, the argument proves too much. A reading of parliamentary debates on various topics might find various discussions insufficiently erudite to satisfy some academics and insufficiently detailed to engage with all of the policy issues involved in various pieces of legislation. The nature of democratic representation is such that even non-lawyers are allowed to speak in parliaments and in democratic debates – sometimes imprecisely, sometimes without as much education as others, and sometimes even crudely. As highlighted in some of Aileen Kavanagh's work, there are dangers of courts or legal figures analyzing the quality of legislative debates demanding legalistic discussions in ways that may not emerge in the context of a nonetheless functioning democratic argument.[37] Moreover, that legislative debate is not always as rich as one could hope does not mean that it cannot be, and there is also empirical work showing rich discussions of rights issues within parliamentary processes, albeit in complex ways.[38]

Second, to remove power is to remove responsibility. The more matters that move from legislative control to judicial control, the less responsibility legislators bear. Arguments for taking away roles from parliaments and legislatures on the basis one wishes there were better debates lead toward removing more responsibility and thus are likely to further worsen democratic processes. Treating parliamentarians like infants risks making them such.

Commonwealth models of constitutionalism have taken a variety of forms not involving strong-form judicial rights review but involving more nuanced roles for bills of rights or similar instruments integrated with the parliamentary tradition. Logically, those who rush to assume that the notwithstanding clause undermines the idea of liberal democracy should also stand ready to condemn countries like the United Kingdom, Australia, and New Zealand as rogue states outside the bounds of liberal democracy. They also presumably are asserting that only strong-form rights-based review like that in the United States can work to achieve liberal democracy, embracing the American model of human rights protection as preferable to that from the rogue states of the commonwealth. Such consequences of many critiques of the notwithstanding clause must give us pause. Parliamentary interpretation of rights has had an important role in many respects within the British parliamentary tradition, the longest-standing form of liberal democracy to survive over the centuries. In a world in which liberal democracies have prevailed in only a very limited space and time, we should not rush to dispose of one of its most successful models. Canada's notwithstanding clause creatively bridges that model in certain ways with elements of American-style rights review, thus seeking to learn from different traditions in constructive ways. Its innovative bridging of institutional capacities is one of its important justifications.

III. THE NOTWITHSTANDING CLAUSE AND DEMOCRATIC PARTICIPATORY VALUES

In maintaining the place of the parliamentary tradition in engaging with rights, the notwithstanding clause implicitly preserves what Jeremy Waldron has called the "right of rights," that of democratic participation.[39] Democratic participation is central to the vision of the notwithstanding clause, as is evident in the very structure of its location within the Charter. What the Charter leaves outside the scope of the notwithstanding clause includes minority language rights (themselves significant to various other issues but also to participation) as well as sections 3 through 6 of the Charter. The democratic and mobility rights contained in sections 3 through 6 protect rights of voice and rights of exit.[40] This location speaks to the relationship of the notwithstanding clause to other considerations. The notwithstanding clause is there in large part to support democratic participation.

On a democratic participation understanding of why ongoing parliamentary engagement with rights is significant, if rights affect too much policymaking and rights are within the purview only of courts, one places ever more policy in the hands of courts. The self-proclaimed guardians of rights become our guardians in more concerning ways. The notwithstanding clause, by contrast, maintains a much more complex scheme that sees both courts and parliaments engaging in interpretation of rights, with democratic electors serving as an ultimate check on the system and thus maintaining a democratic legitimacy and democratic responsibility on the entire system.

There are important critiques to be made of a Waldron-based approach to democratic participation as a justification for the notwithstanding clause. First, one can ask questions about whether democratic participation is an overriding value in quite the way presumed in calling it the "right of rights."[41] Second, some have argued that the preservation of democratic participation may entail other policies, some of which might even involve limitations on the notwithstanding clause.[42] Third, one can ask questions about how to maintain an institutional location through which an individual whose rights are violated can seek a response to that violation, with the implicit point attached to this that legislatures do not analyze rights of individuals but enact general policies and that there must then remain a venue for such claims in rights-oriented courts if rights are to continue to mean something.[43]

I have never adhered to Waldron's full approach to the notwithstanding clause, in which he would actually seek to amend the notwithstanding clause so as to be yet more powerful. I would see it as problematic were legislators to become the sole interpreters of rights, as would occur if they were to routinely use the notwithstanding clause. I seek only to refer to the very significant place of democratic participation in any constitutional order meant to be consensually imposed and meant to respond to the local knowledge of citizens with very different identities than those of elite judges. Thus, I would accept the critique that democratic participation may not be the sole overriding value, even while suggesting that liberal legalism has moved so far from democratic participation that the value of democratic participation must be significantly reasserted. I would also accept that uses of the notwithstanding clause that threaten democratic participation raise serious concern, even while not considering it to follow that the solution is to reinsert judicial supervision of the people. Rather, there must be real efforts at rebuilding civil society and recovering long-standing institutions of responsible government and redeveloping educational systems for strong citizenship. Following a path of putting more and more power into the hands of judges is simply not a substitute for re-empowering people.

The text of section 33 permits restrictions on the fundamental freedoms of section 2. While any such restrictions are of profound concern to me – as has been the general ignorance and lack of use of many parts of section 2, thus generating a set of "forgotten freedoms"[44] – respect for the constitutional text makes it necessary to seek to understand the way in which restrictions on section 2 freedoms that would appear to support democratic participation are nonetheless permitted by a clause oriented to the value of democratic participation. Even these freedoms raise some complex interpretive issues, some challenges of how to understand them well in the face of new challenges, and there may be instances in which parliaments and legislatures must take the solemn step of inserting their different interpretations even on these fundamental freedoms.[45] In doing so, they speak generally, but so do appellate courts. The individual facing the overbearing power of the state must have the opportunity to challenge that exercise of power. But the possibility of democratic uses of the notwithstanding clause on challenging issues do not negate that. The shape of the courts and various practical barriers on access to them have much more effect on individuals' opportunities to challenge exercises of state power. Those worrying about the notwithstanding clause could better put their efforts into those issues, particularly since the next section will let us see that many actual uses of the notwithstanding clause are very different than presumed by its detractors.

IV. THE NOTWITHSTANDING CLAUSE AND DIVERSE IDENTITIES IN CANADA

The notwithstanding clause also responds to the diverse identities of Canada in some rich ways. Three examples stand out, involving the direct protection of minority identities, the protection of diverse provincial identities, and the potential for federal uses of the clause in support of Indigenous peoples.

Turning first to the direct protection of minority identities, here the quantitative record on the clause matters. Depending on how one counts Quebec's omnibus use of the clause that inserted it into each statute, one could say that there have been hundreds of uses of the notwithstanding clause, thus establishing a robust record of use of the clause, notably in indicating some of the ongoing differences of Quebec within the federation as the primary francophone heartland within an English-dominated North America.

If one does not count uses of the clause in that way, it is nonetheless notable that a significant proportion of the uses of the clause have been often under-noticed and relatively uncontroversial uses of the clause by provinces in defence of minority identity interests against actual or potential risks to those rights from the courts. In Saskatchewan, the legislature adopted a bill to avoid sudden shifts in students in rural schools potentially caused by a problematic lower court decision that imperiled constitutionally guaranteed Catholic denominational schooling.[46] While a later appellate decision avoided the need to bring the legislation into force,[47] the Saskatchewan legislative use acted to protect minority religious rights from an overbearing court that actively imperiled them. In Yukon's early use of the notwithstanding clause, it acted to protect Indigenous representation in certain governance contexts from potential risks from then-unknown interpretations of Charter equality rights.[48] And a number of pieces of Quebec legislation using the notwithstanding clause have similarly involved various remedial uses, including protections of minority and Indigenous communities, similarly in the face of potential litigation risks otherwise potentially posed. Though many continue to wander about as if they did not know of them, these uses were detailed in Tsvi Kahana's important doctoral thesis on the notwithstanding clause in 2000, in which Kahana identified a number of under-noticed uses of the notwithstanding clause in Quebec legislation.[49] While the omnibus use and the use on behalf of Quebec's language legislation are better known, others were less controversial and evidence the point. One concerned an age-based distinction in legislation on agricultural operations that was used temporarily. Four involved safeguarding pension eligibility rules against potential equality rights challenges and had been re-enacted more than once (in the context of section 33's five-year time limit). Six involved protecting minority rights in relation to denominational schooling or Indigenous educational opportunities against possible constitutional challenges.[50] There are various situations in which courts have been the threat to minority rights, and legislatures using the notwithstanding clause have been protectors of minorities.

In describing matters this way, I do not of course want to brush away the hard cases. There are instances in which parliaments or legislatures have used the notwithstanding clause that have been more controversial and, indeed, in which many located outside those provinces have been less able to see the justification for the use of the clause. At the same time, it is precisely in such cases that there must also be serious attention to why some of our fellow citizens might see there being justifications for the uses of the clause. To reach out seeking to understand our fellow citizens ought to be a principal aim of not only political leadership but scholarly leadership as well. There is no doubt that there are hard cases, but they must be considered in detail and they must be understood as standing alongside a record of the notwithstanding clause often being used to protect minorities against courts.

It is not possible to engage fully here with what is no doubt the most controversial use of the notwithstanding clause, that contained in Quebec's Bill 21 of 2019, what has now become the Act Respecting the Laicity of the State.[51] I cannot make a full defence of it, for it adopts a vision of state secularism at odds with that held by almost everyone from Canada's anglophone provinces. However, if one considers the Quebec legislation imposing limits on the wearing of religious symbols within Quebec's public service alongside various restrictions on religious symbols in different European countries, many upheld within the European human rights system, it may be that this highly controversial use of the notwithstanding clause is actually an example of a provincial legislature setting forth a different interpretation of the implications of particular rights and freedoms within a range of possible interpretations of human rights norms. The legislation warrants ongoing attention, and even skepticism, but it simply does not offer a knockdown argument against the notwithstanding clause in the way sometimes suggested.

The dialogue among the premiers during the constitutional drafting process saw references to the notwithstanding clause permitting different provincial choices on some issues. That idea sits more easily with the Charter than some might first think. It is worth noting that Canada does not even have the same Charter across the country. The province of New Brunswick has a different Charter text than does the rest of the country, as it made use of the section 43 bilateral amending formula to add section 16.1 to the Charter, uniquely applicable to New Brunswick's different circumstances on linguistic communities. Where some changes can be effected through amending formulae, others can be achieved through the notwithstanding clause, which can be used in ways that enable the preservation of diverse provincial identities. Quebec obviously has a distinctive tradition in this regard, and there is an important Quebec scholarship of the notwithstanding clause that many anglophone legal scholars tended not to read, likely out of a combination of limitations on language capacities and some simple disinclinations. Scholars like Guillaume Rousseau and François Côté have been important figures in forcing that scholarship to the attention of Canada's anglophone legal academic community.[52] A key underlying message is that in a diverse Canada, various parts of the federation must be able to act so as to preserve their distinct identities. That message resonates with many western Canadian voices as well, and it is thus unsurprising that the greatest enthusiasm for the notwithstanding clause in the historical negotiations was from Alberta, Saskatchewan, and Quebec, albeit with other provinces also ready to be supportive. The clause allows provinces to depart from centralized judicial interpretations on some matters and, more generally, to preserve provincial distinctiveness within the federation.

While it is provincial governments that have used the notwithstanding clause in response to threats to diverse identities posed by centralized political power, and the need for such uses would appear less commonly to arise at the federal level, there is an unexplored context in which there is real potential for federal uses of the clause to be supportive of the diverse identities within Canada. Here, I refer to the context of Indigenous peoples in situations where section 25 of the Charter does not offer sufficient protection to distinctive Indigenous identities. Section 25, which purports to shield Aboriginal and treaty rights from adverse effects from the Charter has, of course, been notoriously underdeveloped, with courts often shying away from developing any content to it.[53] That may change if the Supreme Court of Canada does develop the section 25 test – something that may occur in the context of its engagement with the *Dickson v. Vuntut Gwitchin First Nation* case.[54] However, whether section 25 remains undeveloped or undergoes some development, there would be potential in some contexts to use section 33 as an additional mechanism of shielding Indigenous peoples from having their societies reshaped by interpretations of the Charter by courts that end up being insufficiently attentive to Indigenous worldviews and perspectives.

In just what contexts these issues are most significant is of course a complex matter. However, to take just one example on which an important Indigenous legal scholar has published, David Milward has identified a number of ways in which judicial interpretations of the Charter are particularly restrictive of traditional Indigenous criminal justice practices.[55] Some of his particular proposals, such as his desire to see a revival of corporal punishment even for adults, might be controversial – with this particular proposal being in potential tension not only with international human rights law, but also with the Truth and Reconciliation Commission's insistence that corporal punishment even of children must be banned in response to past colonial wrongs and, implicitly, its lack of accord with Indigenous practices.[56] But his broader points would raise issues with how some dimensions of how elite judges interpret the Charter may be a particular misfit with Indigenous communities.

While the Charter text does not directly permit Indigenous governments to access the notwithstanding clause if section 25 is an inadequate shield, one could envision a potential federal use of the clause within federal legislative jurisdiction to support Indigenous peoples in different ways. One approach could be more in response to specific requests for a use of the clause put by particular Indigenous communities to the federal government. However, the seeming ongoing supervision by the federal government involved in this approach would arguably make it unwelcome and inappropriate. An alternative might be a larger statutory framework within which Indigenous lawmakers could derive federal delegated powers to use the notwithstanding clause, thus empowering Indigenous peoples to make selective choices about contexts in which they would depart from judicial impositions of particular interpretations of the Charter on them. Whether particular Indigenous communities identify with the Charter or not, such a framework could be of use, whether to permit selective prioritization of threatened Indigenous practices after careful consideration of competing interpretations of the Charter or to assure necessary recognition of a legal ability to block imposition of consequences from an instrument with which an Indigenous community does not identify. In either case, the federal government supporting making section 33 available would be another way in which the structure of section 33 enables protection of diverse communities within Canada.

CONCLUSION

Canada's notwithstanding clause is a distinctive constitutional mechanism. Some rush to denounce it as some sort of aberration or as some sort of dangerous loaded gun. However, many of the critiques of it, or calls for restrictions on it, misland. A full evaluation of the notwithstanding clause must understand it to have profound justifications as well. These include facilitating ongoing coordinate approaches to rights protection and fulfillment, maintaining the particularly significant value of democratic participation as a structuring feature of our constitutional order, and offering a mechanism for the protection of diverse identities within Canada.

Saying that the clause has these justifications does not answer all questions about it. Saying that it is an important feature of Canadian constitutionalism will not solve every potential problem to which it admittedly might give rise. Constitutions are not magical, and they cannot be the sum of our hopes and dreams. Constitutions structure a civic space in which we must discuss and debate, in which we must carry on deep-rooted traditions of profound value, and in which we must engage in ongoing learning and prudent innovation. The challenges of citizenship will never be met by surrender to a judicial guardianship. Citizenship asks more of all of us and invites us to engage with the other, something fostered through the sort of discussion and debate in collections like that in which I am honoured to be able to publish these reflections. May this collection inspire us to yet more debate and yet more thinking.

NOTES

1   This chapter builds upon and extends from my past argument in Dwight Newman, "Canada's Notwithstanding Clause, Dialogue, and Constitutional Identities," in *Constitutional Dialogue: Rights, Democracy, Institutions*, ed. Geoffrey Sigalet, Grégoire Webber, and Rosalind Dixon (New York: Cambridge University Press, 2019), 209. See also Dwight Newman, "Allen Blakeney and the Dignity of Democratic Debate on Rights," in *Back to Blakeney: Reviving the Democratic State*, ed. David McGrane et al. (Regina: University of Regina Press, 2019). In these writings, I have defended an approach to the clause that does not read additional limits into it and that sees it as recognizing the parliamentary and legislative role in interpreting rights. For what appears to be a recent

approval of that view by the majority of the Supreme Court of Canada, see *City of Toronto v. Attorney General of Ontario*, 2021 SCC 34 at para. 60 (majority stating that "s. 33 preserves a limited right of legislative override. Where, therefore, a court invalidates legislation using s. 2(b) of the Charter, the legislature may give continued effect to *its* understanding of what the Constitution requires by invoking s. 33 and by meeting its stated conditions").

2 Earlier phases saw some arguments for the outright abolition of the clause. See, for example, John Whyte, "On Not Standing for Notwithstanding," *Alberta Law Review* 28, no. 2 (1990): 347. Others argued for significant limits on the clause going beyond those accepted by the Supreme Court of Canada, whether based on a purported acceptance of the clause so long as it was subject to very significant restraints or based on assumptions that the clause is fundamentally problematic. See, for example: Lorraine Eisenstat Weinrib, "Learning to Live with the Override," *McGill Law Review* 35 (1990): 541; Donna Greschner and Ken Norman, "The Courts and Section 33," *Queen's Law Review* 12 (1987): 155. There were, of course, also important academic defenders of the clause. See, for example: Peter H. Russell, "Standing Up for Notwithstanding," *Alberta Law Review* 29 (1991): 293; Christopher P. Manfredi, *Judicial Power and the Charter* (Oxford: Oxford University Press, 1993).

3 Constitution Act, 1982.

4 See chapter 1. See also Thomas S. Axworthy, "Colliding Visions: The Debate Over the Canadian Charter of Rights and Freedoms, 1980–81," *The Journal of Commonwealth & Comparative Politics* 24, no. 3 (1986): 239.

5 *City of Toronto v. Attorney General of Ontario*, 2021 SCC 34 at para. 60.

6 See *MacDonald v. City of Montreal* [1986] 1 SCR 460; *Société des Acadiens du Nouveau-Brunswick v. Association of Parents for Fairness in Education* [1986] 1 SCR 549; *Bilodeau v Manitoba* [1986] 1 SCR 449.

7 See generally the discussion of this shift in *R v Beaulac* [1999] 1 SCR 768. See also Leslie Green, "Are Language Rights Fundamental?" *Osgoode Hall Law Journal* 25 (1987): 639–46 (noting that "the historical pedigree of some provision does not repudiate its justifications") and passim.

8 As noted by Justice Bastarache for the court in a discussion of the language rights context, "Though constitutional language rights result from a political compromise, this is not a characteristic that uniquely applies to such rights." A. Riddell, "À la recherche du temps perdu: la Cour suprême et l'interprétation des droits linguistiques constitutionnels dans les années

80," *Les Cahiers de droit* 29, no. 3 (1988), 829–46. Riddell underlines that a political compromise also led to the adoption of ss. 7 and 15 of the Charter and argues, at page 848, that there is no basis in the constitutional history of Canada for holding that any such political compromises require a restrictive interpretation of constitutional guarantees. I agree that the existence of a political compromise is without consequence with regard to the scope of language rights, para. 24. The same principle would imply that any political compromise associated with the notwithstanding clause must be without consequence for it.

9 See: Stephen Gardbaum, "The New Commonwealth Model of Constitutionalism," *The American Journal of Comparative Law* 49, no. 4 (2001): 707; Stephen Gardbaum, *The New Commonwealth Model of Constitutionalism: Theory and Practice* (Cambridge: Cambridge University Press, 2013).

10 *Re: B.C. Motor Vehicle Act* [1985] 2 SCR 486.

11 Robert Leckey and Eric Mendelsohn, "The Notwithstanding Clause: Legislatures, Courts, and the Electorate," *University of Toronto Law Journal* 72, no. 2 (2022): 189.

12 Leckey and Mendelsohn, 189–90, arguing for reading section 33, "in the light of other important constitutional features."

13 Ibid., 191.

14 Grégoire Webber, Eric Mendelsohn, and Robert Leckey, "The Faulty Received Wisdom around the Notwithstanding Clause," *Policy Options*, 10 May 2019, policyoptions.irpp.org/magazines/may-2019/faulty-wisdom-notwithstanding-clause. For an important response, see Maxime St-Hilaire and Xaiver Foccroulle Ménard, "Nothing to Declare: A Response to Grégoire Webber, Eric Mendelsohn, Robert Leckey, and Léonid Sirota on the Effects of the Notwithstanding Clause," *Constitutional Forum* 29, no. 1 (2020): 38–9.

15 See, for example, Grégoire Webber, "Notwithstanding Rights, Review, or Remedy? On the Notwithstanding Clause on the Operation of Legislation," *University of Toronto Law Journal* 71 (2021): 1–2, https://ssrn.com/abstract=3935891.

16 In chapter 7, Geoffrey Sigalet makes compelling arguments against Webber's reading of the text. See also Geoffrey T. Sigalet, "Legislated Rights as Trumps: Why the Notwithstanding Clause Overrides Judicial Review," *Osgoode Hall Law Journal* 61, no. 1 (forthcoming).

17 Leckey and Mendelsohn, "The Notwithstanding Clause."

18 Ibid., 203–5.

19 Ibid., 205.

20 Ibid., 198–200.

21 Ibid., 209.

22 Eric M. Adams and Erin R.J. Bower, "Notwithstanding History: The Rights-Protecting Purposes of Section 33 of the Charter," *Review of Constitutional Studies* 26, no. 2 (2022): 121, https://dx.doi.org/10.2139/ssrn.4185044.

23 Ibid.

24 Ibid.

25 See, for example: Dwight Newman and Lorelle Binnion, "The Exclusion of Property Rights from the Charter: Correcting the Historical Record," *Alberta Law Review* 52 (2015): 543 (discussing the move of many provisions from the Bill of Rights, with property rights being an exception); Dwight Newman, "God in the Constitution: The Supremacy of God Clause in the Preamble to the Canadian Charter of Rights and Freedoms," *Supreme Court Law Review* 105 (2022): 39 (discussing how the Bill of Rights affected many clauses of the Charter).

26 See various discussions in Brian Bird and Derek Ross, eds., *Forgotten Foundations of the Canadian Constitution* (Toronto: LexisNexis, 2022).

27 On coordinate interpretation generally, see Dennis Baker, *Not Quite Supreme: The Courts and Coordinate Constitutional Interpretation* (Montreal: McGill-Queen's University Press, 2010). On the notwithstanding clause as facilitating a sort of "court curbing," see also the interesting discussion in Andrea Lawlor and Erin Crandall, "The Canadian Charter's Notwithstanding Clause as an Institutionalized Mechanism of Court Curbing," *American Review of Canadian Studies* 53, no. 1 (2023).

28 See Canadian Bill of Rights, S.C. 1960, c. 44, s. 2; Alberta Bill of Rights, R.S.A. 1980, c. A-16, s. 2; Saskatchewan Human Rights Code, S.S. 1979, c. S-24.1, s. 44; [Quebec] Charter of Human Rights and Freedoms, R.S.Q., c. C-12, s. 52.

29 See Barry Strayer, "The Evolution of the Charter," in *Patriation and Its Consequences: Constitution Making in Canada*, eds. Lois Harder and Steve Patten (Vancouver: University of British Columbia Press, 2015), 90.

30 See: Peter Lougheed, "Why a Notwithstanding Clause?" *Points of View-Centre for Constitutional Studies* 6, no. 17 (1998); Allan Blakeney, "The Notwithstanding Clause, the Charter, and Canada's Patriated Constitution: What I Thought We Were Doing," *Constitutional Forum constitutionnel* 19, no. 1 (2010): 1–9, https://doi.org/10.21991/C9KD4W.

31 Paul C. Weiler, "Of Judges and Rights: Should Canada Have a Constitutional Bill of Rights?" *Dalhousie Review* 60, no. 2 (1980).

32 See discussion in Newman, "Canada's Notwithstanding Clause," 216–17.

33 Such a suggestion was made in her conference presentation by Jamie Cameron. See also her revised form in chapter 17.

34 These elements have been identified as primary on constitutional interpretation in a number of Supreme Court of Canada cases. See, for example, *R. v. Comeau*, 2018 SCC 15 [2018] 1 S.C.R. 342 at para. 52.

35 I appreciate Peter Biro and Nathalie des Rosiers initially pushing me on this point, on which I was fortunate to learn further from the paper of Léonid Sirota.

36 Léonid Sirota, "Do Legislators Debate Rights When They Make Laws Notwithstanding the Charter?" Legacies of Patriation Conference, University of Alberta Centre for Constitutional Studies, Edmonton, April 2022 (not yet published).

37 See discussion of the legalistic pressures in Aileen Kavanagh, "Proportionality and Parliamentary Debates: Exploring Some Forbidden Territory," *Oxford Journal of Legal Studies* 34, no. 3 (2014): 443.

38 See, for example, Meg Russell and Daniel Gover, *Legislation at Westminster: Parliamentary Actors and Influence in the Making of British Law* (Oxford: Oxford University Press, 2019).

39 Jeremy Waldron, *Law and Disagreement* (Oxford: Oxford University Press, 1999), 254.

40 The concepts of voice and exit here are those of Albert O. Hirschman, *Exit, Voice, and Loyalty: Responses to Decline in Firms, Organizations, and States* (Cambridge: Harvard University Press, 1990), which I have previously applied in other political theory contexts in Dwight Newman, *Community and Collective Rights: A Theoretical Framework for Rights Held by Groups* (Oxford: Hart Publishing, 2013). On mobility rights, section 6, of course, protects rights other than exit rights, including many rights oriented to economic participation, but one could understand part of what it protects as to include exit rights.

41 Michael Pal has made this point in not-yet-published work: Michael Pal, "Democracy and the Notwithstanding Clause," The Public Law Conference, University College Dublin, Dublin, July 2022.

42 Pal. This idea is also present in a different way in Jamie Cameron's chapter: see chapter 17.

43 Here I have been influenced by not-yet-published work by George Letsas: George Letsas, "In Praise of Human Rights Courts," IVR World Congress 2022, Bucharest, July 2022.

44 See generally Dwight Newman, Derek B.M. Ross, and Brian Bird, eds, *The Forgotten Fundamental Freedoms of the Charter* (Toronto: LexisNexis, 2020).

45 Ontario's November 2022 use of the clause in strike-breaking legislation (Keeping Students in Class Act, 2022, S.O. 2022, c. 19) was obviously controversial, and abandoned days later. But it was arguably foreseeable in the context of judicial decisions establishing the right to strike that were in contrast with prior decisions of the very same judicial body, combined with the aspiration for finality always present in back-to-work legislation. The key judicial decision also contained significant technical errors, such as citing to incorrect versions of constitutions and overridden cases: Dwight Newman, "A Court Gone Astray on the Right to Strike," *National Post*, 26 February 2015.

46 School Choice Protection Act, S.S. 2018, c. 39.

47 See *Good Spirit School Division No. 204 v Christ the Teacher Roman Catholic Separate School Division No. 212*, 2017 SKQB 109, rev'd by *Saskatchewan v Good Spirit School Division No. 204*, 2020 SKCA 34, leave to appeal to Supreme Court of Canada denied 25 February 2021. Those who say Saskatchewan should have waited for an appellate decision would have caused four years of uncertainty, even were a stay to be in place, such that parents and children might have commenced making different choices about schools in ways detrimental to minority religious educational institutions. The use of the notwithstanding clause brought rapid clarity in a way that no judicial mechanism could have without much faster court processes.

48 Land Planning and Development Act, S.Y. 1982, s. 39.

49 Tsvi Kahana, *The Partnership Model of the Canadian Notwithstanding Mechanism: Failure and Hope* (SJD Thesis, University of Toronto, 2000), Appendix 2, 293.

50 Ibid.

51 Act Respecting the Laicity of the State, R.S.Q., c. L-0.3.

52 See: Guillaume Rousseau and François Côté, "A Distinctive Quebec Theory and Practice of the Notwithstanding Clause: When Collective Interests Outweigh Individual Rights," *Revue générale de droit* 47 (2017): 237; François Côté, "From Ford v. Québec to the Act Respecting the Laicity of the State: À Distinctive Quebec Theory and Practice of the Notwithstanding Clause," *The Supreme Court Law Review* 94 (2020): 463.

53 See, for example, *R. v. Kapp*, 2008 SCC 41, in which all but one justice avoided dealing with the opportunity squarely raised by the case to develop a framework for section 25 of the Charter.

54 The Supreme Court of Canada granted leave in early 2022 from *Dickson v. Vuntut Gwitchin First Nation*, 2021 YKCA 5, a case which directly engages these issues once again.

55 David Milward, *Aboriginal Justice and the Charter: Realizing a Culturally Sensitive Interpretation of Legal Rights* (Vancouver: University of British Columbia Press, 2013).

56 Call to action number 6 of the TRC's final report calls for the removal of section 43 of the Criminal Code, thus calling for the removal of any defence to spanking a child.

4

The Notwithstanding Clause, the Operation of Legislation, and Judicial Review

Grégoire Webber

I. AN INCOMPLETELY THEORIZED AGREEMENT

Every reader of the notwithstanding clause first confronts the words that empower Parliament or the legislature of a province to "expressly declare" in legislation that an "Act or a provision ... shall operate notwithstanding" the Charter's guarantees of fundamental freedoms, legal rights, and equality rights.[1] For many readers, these words empower a legislature to legislate notwithstanding rights and the reference to the "operation" of an act or one of its provisions is passed over in silence. Yet for the reader who proceeds in reading the notwithstanding clause beyond its opening words, the question of the "operation" of legislation cannot long be ignored, for the clause next tells us that, for any act or provision "in respect of which a declaration" has been made, that act or provision "shall have such operation as it would have but for the provision of this Charter referred to in the declaration."[2] The combination of the imperative "shall have" with the conditional "would have" makes for a complex reference to the operation of legislation. And yet, this complex reference is decisive for understanding what the notwithstanding clause achieves – its legal effect. So what could it mean?

That was a question that Robert Leckey and I explored in a discussion in April 2019. He had been in correspondence with Eric Mendelsohn about the legal meaning of the clause and, together, we set out to contribute to the public debate on the clause that was animated by Bill 21, An Act Respecting the Laicity of the State.[3] The Government of Quebec had introduced Bill 21 before the National

Assembly in March 2019 and the provisions of the bill included an
"express declaration" on the operation of the proposed legislation.
Much of the debate on the notwithstanding clause proceeded on
certain assumptions about what the clause empowers a legislature
to do, assumptions about the legal effect on rights and on judicial
review of an express declaration under the notwithstanding clause.
In short order, Leckey, Mendelsohn, and I published in May 2019 an
essay in *Policy Options* exposing what we called "the faulty received
wisdom around the notwithstanding clause."[4]

That wisdom provides that the notwithstanding clause is an
"override provision"[5] that empowers the legislature to legislate
notwithstanding rights, to "override" them,[6] to "derogate" from
them,[7] or to "suspend" them,[8] with the result that no court challenge may lie in judicial review against legislation for violating such
rights and freedoms. We argued that there is no support in the text
of the notwithstanding clause for such received wisdom: neither the
word "override" nor many of its close cousins appear in the clause
and there is no reference to "judicial review" or other language
that would affirm that legislation invoking the clause shall not be
questioned or reviewed in any court. Rather, the focus of both the
express declaration and the legal effect of such a declaration is firmly
on the operation of legislation. Noting that the French version of the
clause employs the term "*effet*" where the English version employs
"operation," we recalled that these same two terms are found in the
Constitution's supremacy clause, which denies to legislation that is
inconsistent with the supreme law of Canada its "force or effect"
or, to employ the French nomenclature, renders "*inopérantes*" the
provisions of any inconsistent legislation.[9] The relationship between
the notwithstanding clause and the Constitution's supremacy clause
is, we said, "the key to understanding" what the legislature achieves
by making an express declaration.[10] We argued that the legal effect
of the notwithstanding clause is to secure the operation of legislation
and that, in so doing, the clause leaves legislation open to challenge
in court, such that "a court may determine whether the law violates
Charter rights" and "may declare that the law violates rights."[11] We
highlighted how judicial review could serve an educational function
in highlighting for voters whether legislation violates rights, could
provide a forum for minorities to make their voices heard, and could
inform legislation's political standing on whether to repeal or, in
time, to renew an express declaration.

Before agreeing upon a final version of our essay, Leckey, Mendelsohn, and I explored some possible differences on what more was open to a court after finding that a law was inconsistent with rights targeted in an express declaration. We resolved to say less rather than more on this question with a view to minimizing our joint argument's complexity and controversy. Our focus was to draw the reader's attention to the operation of legislation and, in so doing, to highlight how the clause was not best read as authorizing the override of rights or as eliminating the possibility of judicial review. Our goal was to revisit the received wisdom.

In so doing, we settled on one of three versions of an "incompletely theorized agreement."[12] Perhaps the best-known version of such agreements is agreement on a particular outcome, as when judges on an appellate court "agree on the result and on relatively narrow or low-level explanations for it," all without agreeing or needing to agree on "fundamental principle."[13] Another version is agreement on "a general principle" that leaves "incompletely specified" what the principle "entails in particular cases."[14] A bill of rights is often a paradigmatic illustration of such agreement, whereby there is ready assent to declarations like "freedom of expression," in part because the resolution of disputes surrounding hate speech, commercial and election advertising, and more is left for "a later day."[15]

Leckey, Mendelsohn, and I had settled on a third version of an incompletely theorized agreement, being an agreement on a "mid-level principle," all without agreeing on "the more general theory that accounts for it."[16] As we pursued the further development of our argument, we confronted the need to "complete" that more general theory. In so doing, we discovered some differences on (a) whether legislation found by a court to be in violation of a right could be said to be invalid despite containing an express declaration (I thought yes), and (b) whether our argumentative strategy should be narrowly legal-technical or more purposive (I thought the former could secure broader agreement among skeptics of our conclusion). We resolved to outline two ways in which one could complete the theoretical foundations of our *Policy Options* position, agreeing it to be in the service of our shared position to outline more than one way in which that position could be supported.

One way was published in the Fall 2021 issue of the *University of Toronto Law Journal*, in which I argued that the notwithstanding clause left it open to a court to find legislation (a) inconsistent with targeted rights and freedoms, (b) unconstitutional as a result, but (c) not of "no force or effect" so long as the express declaration invoking the clause secured the legislation's operation.[17] A second way was published in the Spring 2022 issue of the *University of Toronto Law Journal,* in which Leckey and Mendelsohn argued the notwithstanding clause (a) left it open to a court to find legislation invoking the clause inconsistent with targeted rights and freedoms, but (b) that legislation was not for that reason inconsistent with the Constitution, with the consequence that (c) the operation of legislation is secured by the clause.[18] The differences between our positions are not great and our argumentative strategies are, in my view, wholly complementary. Save for a difference of opinion on whether the notwithstanding clause secures the validity of legislation that is inconsistent with rights and freedoms targeted in an express declaration (to which I return below), my legal-technical arguments and Leckey and Mendelsohn's arguments appealing to constitutional purpose and principle are, in my view, mutually supporting.

In this chapter, I return to the "more general theory" that informs my argument on the notwithstanding clause (section II) before reviewing the alternative general theory presented by Leckey and Mendelsohn (section III). I then attempt some answers to challenges offered by my co-authors and others to the interpretation of the clause that I outline (section IV) and conclude with some reflections on the judicial virtues (section V).

II. INCONSISTENT, INVALID, BUT OPERABLE

The legal effect of the notwithstanding clause comes into play only after a judicial finding of inconsistency between legislation and a Charter right or freedom, a finding that is possible because the rights and freedoms targeted in an express declaration are not overridden and judicial review is not blocked. That is the idea I defended in "Notwithstanding Rights, Review, or Remedy?" in which I noted that the key expressions in the notwithstanding clause – "shall operate" and "shall have such operation as it would have" (in the French version: "*a effet*" and "*a l'effet qu'elle aurait*") – have escaped interrogation in much of the literature, and this despite the fact that these expressions are the engine of the notwithstanding clause: they and only they settle the legal effect of an express declaration by the legislature.

But what is the "operation" of legislation? The Colonial Laws Validity Act, 1865 – a dated, now spent Act of the Imperial Parliament – offers some instruction. By appealing to a hierarchy of legally inferior and superior laws, the act provided that colonial laws, such as those of Canada, are "void or *inoperative* on the ground of repugnancy to the law of England."[19] The operation of the legally inferior colonial legislation was here related to its validity, which was denied (rendered "void") by reason of a conflict ("repugnancy") with the legally superior English law. The superiority of the law of England over the law of Canada was terminated by the Statute of Westminster, 1931, albeit subject to the continuing superiority of the British North America Acts, 1867 to 1930.[20] As is well known to students of our Constitution, the division of legislative powers under what we now call the Constitution Act, 1867 have rendered a great many Canadian statutes void and inoperable, with courts ruling federal or provincial statutes to have exceeded the jurisdiction awarded to the enacting legislature by the Imperial Parliament in the British North America Act, 1867.

Our interest in the Colonial Laws Validity Act, 1865 is not historical, however. It is rather in how the act helps articulate how the *operation* of inferior law is related to its *validity*, which is to be denied by reason of a *"repugnancy"* (inconsistency) with legally superior law. The 1865 Act helps to express an order, a sequence from (a) the consistency of inferior to superior law to (b) the validity of inferior law to (c) the operation of inferior law. That same sequence can be stated in the reverse and as a series of conditions as follows: inferior law is operative *if* it is valid and it is valid *if* it is consistent with legally superior law.

The Supreme Court of Canada has affirmed that the supremacy clause in the Constitution Act, 1982 continues the "constitutional jurisprudence, developed under the Colonial Laws Validity Act, 1865,"[21] namely the jurisprudence of denying the operation of legislation held to be repugnant to constitutionally superior law. This conclusion was not immediately straightforward for the court, at least insofar as the supremacy clause does not employ the same key words of "repugnancy," "void," and "inoperative" as are found in the 1865 Act. Instead of "repugnancy," the supremacy clause employs the term "inconsistent" (in the French version: *"incompatibles"*) and instead of "inoperative," the supremacy clause denies legislation's "force or effect" (in the French version, the provisions of inconsistent legislation are said to be "*inopérantes*") on grounds of such inconsistency. As for the idea of "void" from the 1865 Act, there is no equivalent in the supremacy clause at all.

Yet, despite these differences, the Supreme Court affirmed that the "words 'of no force or effect'" in the supremacy clause "mean that a law thus inconsistent with the Constitution has no force or effect *because it is invalid.*"[22] The sequence from inconsistency to invalidity to inoperability from the 1865 Act was carried forward into the Constitution's supremacy clause: a law is of "no force or effect" ("inoperative") by reason of being "invalid" ("void") on account of its "inconsistency" with ("repugnancy to") the Constitution. The Supreme Court could have strengthened its reasoning by noting that, although the English version of the supremacy clause employs the expression "no force or effect" to replace what the 1865 Act had captured by the term "inoperative," the French version of the clause makes no such substitution: it provides that laws that are inconsistent ("*incompatibles*") with the Constitution are "*inopérantes*" ("inoperable"). It follows that the English version of the supremacy clause could have provided, without any loss of meaning, that "any law that is inconsistent with the provisions of the Constitution is, to the extent of the inconsistency, *inoperable.*"

With these constitutional fundamentals in place, it is possible to demonstrate why understanding the relationship between the Constitution's supremacy clause and the Charter's notwithstanding clause is indeed the key to understanding the legal effect of the notwithstanding clause. Given that the "operation" of legislation is dependent on legislation's "validity," and given that such "validity" is dependent on legislation's "consistency" with the Constitution, the all-important affirmation in the notwithstanding clause that legislation "*shall have such operation as it would have but for* the provision of this Charter referred to in the declaration" comes into view.[23] The legal effect of the clause is to secure legislation's operation (to award it "such operation as it would have"), even if legislation is inconsistent with rights and freedoms targeted in an express declaration ("but for the provision of this Charter referred to in the declaration" that would otherwise deny legislation its operation). What would analytically follow as a matter course from legislation's inconsistency with the Charter's provisions – i.e., the legislation's loss of operation – does not follow because the notwithstanding clause empowers the legislature to secure for its legislation "such operation as it would have but for" the targeted rights and freedoms. Absent the notwithstanding clause, those rights and freedoms would deny legislation's operation because legislation that is inconsistent with constitutional rights is of no force or effect.

In the analytical sequence from inconsistency to invalidity to inoperability, it is significant that the notwithstanding clause settles only the question of legislation's operation. The notwithstanding clause makes no mention of legislation's consistency with targeted rights and freedoms and it makes no mention of legislation's validity. With this general theory in place, the incompletely theorized agreement of our *Policy Options* essay can be returned to. The notwithstanding clause leaves open for resolution the question of legislation's consistency, such that a court may adjudicate the consistency of legislation with targeted rights and freedoms and, if it concludes that legislation is inconsistent with those rights and freedoms, a court may declare such inconsistency. With such a declaration, it follows as a matter of course that the legislation is invalid. The progression from the first (consistency) to the second (validity) of the analytical steps is not a matter of discretion, but rather inheres in the very relationship between superior and inferior law. As recently reaffirmed by the Supreme Court, "The supremacy clause refers to the hierarchy of laws in the constitutional order," and "courts are called upon to resolve conflicts between the Constitution and ordinary statutes."[24] The resolution of such conflicts is always to be in favour of the hierarchically superior law.

The progression from the second (invalidity) to the third (inoperability) of the analytical steps is also not a matter of discretion. As judicially affirmed, "The courts are commanded under [the supremacy clause] of the Constitution Act, 1982 to declare ... inoperative" legislation that is inconsistent with the Constitution.[25] Yet, the command of the supremacy clause is here interrupted by the notwithstanding clause, which provides that legislation "shall have such operation as it would have but for the provision of this Charter referred to in the declaration." The interruption to the command of the supremacy clause is a contingent one, however: it lasts only so long as the express declaration is in force. Once that declaration expires or is revoked, the progression from the invalidity to the inoperability of legislation takes hold and legislation ceases to be of force and effect all without the need for a new judicial declaration.

III. INCONSISTENT, BUT VALID AND OPERABLE

For Leckey and Mendelsohn, the notwithstanding clause secures the operation of legislation by denying that legislation is invalid with the Constitution even if it is inconsistent with the rights and freedoms targeted in an express declaration. They explain that, "For the purposes of the supremacy clause, a court assesses a law's consistency with the entire Constitution" and "not with a provision of the Charter, standing alone."[26] Their explanation continues by affirming that the legal effect of the notwithstanding clause "prevents a protected law's breach of Charter rights from amounting to 'inconsistency' with the Constitution of Canada for purposes of the supremacy clause."[27] Given that there is no inconsistency between a law invoking the notwithstanding clause and the Constitution, the operation of legislation is secured. Their argument draws an analogy to the Charter's limitation clause,[28] reasoning that just as "a law that limits a Charter guarantee in a way that is justifiable under [the limitation clause] is not 'inconsistent' with the Charter in the sense of the supremacy clause,"[29] so too does the notwithstanding clause "forestall a conclusion that a law is inconsistent with the Constitution of Canada under the supremacy clause."[30]

I have some reservations about this alternative reading of the notwithstanding clause. One reservation is with respect to the claim that the supremacy clause evaluates the consistency of legislation with the "entire Constitution" as opposed to with any one of the Constitution's provisions. To be sure, the French version of the supremacy clause affirms that "La Constitution du Canada ... *rend inopérantes les dispositions incompatibles de toute autre règle de droit*," but the English version affirms, with greater specificity, that "any law that is inconsistent with *the provisions of the Constitution* is, to the extent of the inconsistency, of no force or effect."[31] The provisions of the Charter are provisions of the Constitution and I remain uncertain why an inconsistency with those provisions would fail to engage the supremacy clause.

To draw attention to this distinction between the whole Constitution and the provisions of the Constitution is not to deny that the whole of the Constitution is relevant to evaluating the consistency of legislation with any one of the Constitution's provisions. As Leckey and Mendelsohn carefully review, there are a full range of constitutional provisions and principles that inform one's interpretation of *each one of* the Constitution's provisions and their purposive reading of the notwithstanding clause is, in my view, wholly convincing.[32] Each provision is to be read in light of the others and of the Constitution entire, and no "part of the Constitution" is to be "abrogated or diminished by another part."[33] But it remains that, for Leckey and Mendelsohn, there can be an inconsistency with a provision of the Constitution that does not amount to an inconsistency with the Constitution itself and therein lies my hesitation. I am minded to think that the better interpretative approach is to say that consistency with the entire Constitution implies consistency with every one of its provisions.

Perhaps Leckey and Mendelsohn's strongest argument is their analogy to the Charter's limitations clause. On their understanding, "a rights-limiting law that is 'saved'" by the Charter's limitations clause is inconsistent with a provision of the Constitution but "avoids inconsistency with the Constitution."[34] The Supreme Court's frequent recourse to terms like "infringe,"[35] "*prima facie* infringe,"[36] "derogate,"[37] "breach,"[38] "contravene,"[39] "abridge,"[40] and "impair"[41] to describe legislation's limitation of a right lends support to Leckey and Mendelsohn's understanding, as does the sometime reference to the limitation clause as a "saving provision."[42] These key words may be read to suggest that an inconsistency between legislation and one provision of the Constitution (a Charter provision guaranteeing a right or freedom) is rescued by a different provision of the Constitution (the Charter's limitation clause), such that an inconsistency with one provision of the Constitution does not amount to an inconsistency with the entire Constitution.

Despite the strength of this analogy, I am minded to resist the reading offered by Leckey and Mendelsohn by appeal to a legal postulate or axiom almost too plain to state. It is that no law, not least the supreme law, is to be read as authorizing the violation of its very provisions. The Charter's limitation clause, after all, affirms that the rights and freedoms of the Charter are "subject ... to" – not *opposed to* or *inconsistent with* – reasonable limits. But we can set aside questions about the best reading of the limitation clause, for our focus is on the notwithstanding clause and the wording of that clause does not, on my reading, support a claim that the clause "forestall[s] a conclusion that a law is inconsistent with the Constitution of Canada."[43] I take Leckey and Mendelsohn to reason that since legislation's operation is secured by the notwithstanding clause, then so too must legislation's consistency with the Constitution be secured by the clause. I return to this challenge in the next section. For now, I highlight that my concern with this view is that it may weaken the case for judicial review. If it is taken as settled by the notwithstanding clause that there is no inconsistency between legislation and the Constitution, a court would not be asked to rule on whether legislation conforms to the supreme law of Canada. The task of determining whether "a law is inconsistent with the Constitution" is, as recently recalled by the Supreme Court, "an ordinary judicial task of determining a question of law,"[44] and I am minded to think that a court is provided with a firmer basis for the exercise of jurisdiction if it is recognized that the notwithstanding clause secures only legislation's "operation" and leaves it to a court to determine whether legislation is consistent with the Constitution.

IV. TWO REPLIES TO CHALLENGES

Since Leckey, Mendelsohn, and I first set out our criticism of the received wisdom on the notwithstanding clause, we have benefited from the careful engagement of many colleagues.[45] In my 2021 article, I attempted to reply to four early challenges to the conclusion that we sought to defend: (1) on whether the rights and freedoms targeted by an express declaration are suspended or inapplicable; (2) on mootness; (3) on the Supreme Court's holding in *Ford v Quebec* that "there is no warrant for importing" into the notwithstanding clause "grounds for substantive review";[46] and (4) on the significance of interpretive aids surrounding the notwithstanding clause.[47] I here attempt replies to two new challenges.[48] Now as then, I hope to stay true to Socrates's instruction that to be defeated in argument is a benefit to be welcomed, not a burden to be avoided, for one is relieved of error.[49] That is one reason among many to be charitable rather than combative in one's scholarly disposition.

One new challenge is raised by Leckey and Mendelsohn, who argue that it "is a conceptual error to characterize as 'invalid' or 'inconsistent' with the Constitution a law expressly allowed by it to operate."[50] They correctly affirm that "the supremacy clause enshrines the principle that, as between the Constitution and any law repugnant to it, the Constitution prevails and the other law yields" and that a law that is "inconsistent with the Constitution within the sense of the supremacy clause means that the Constitution objects to the law's continued operation."[51] My argument relies on the truth of these propositions in attempting to make sense of the significance of the key word "operation" in the notwithstanding clause. There is, on my view, "no judicial discretion to intervene between a finding of inconsistency and the conclusion that inconsistent legislation is invalid" and, in turn, there is "also no judicial discretion to intervene between a finding of invalidity and the conclusion that invalid legislation is of no force or effect."[52] But, in the case of the notwithstanding clause, the intervention that breaks the analytical sequence from invalidity to inoperability "is not judicial, but constitutional": by the very terms of the notwithstanding clause, legislation's invalidity does not deny legislation's operability *because* the legislation "shall have such operation as it would have but for" the targeted rights and freedoms.[53] In so doing, the notwithstanding clause "signals an exception to – not a contradiction with – the legal effect of the supremacy clause, providing a temporal exception to the denial of legislation's operation by reason of its inconsistency with targeted rights and freedoms."[54] In the end, little turns on the distinction between the reading favoured by Leckey and Mendelsohn and my own, save that one advantage of my reading is that a judicial finding of inconsistency between legislation and targeted rights and freedoms entails the legislation's invalidity, which in turn entails the legislation's inoperability as soon as the express declaration under the notwithstanding clause expires.

A second new challenge is articulated by Geoffrey Sigalet in his contribution to this volume.[55] Sigalet reads the reference in the notwithstanding clause to how any act or provision in respect of which an express declaration has been made "shall have such operation as it would have but for the provision of this Charter referred to in the declaration" in the subjunctive mood. According to this mood, we are instructed to award legislation "such operation as it would have" in a counterfactual world in which the rights and freedoms targeted in an expression declaration did not exist. Even if we grant the correctness of Sigalet's reading for evaluating the operation of legislation, I do not think it leads to the conclusion he reaches, which is to deny judicial review on the basis that we are to assume a world in which the targeted rights and freedoms do not exist. After all, on his argument, the counterfactual world in which rights and freedoms do not exist holds for the purposes of legislation's *operation*: that is the focus of the notwithstanding clause and of the subjunctive mood he identifies. That counterfactual world does not extend to legislation's consistency with rights or freedoms or to legislation's invalidity for violating those rights and freedoms. The notwithstanding clause focuses only on legislation's operation, leaving legislation's consistency with rights and freedoms a matter open to judicial determination.

V. ON THE JUDICIAL VIRTUES

In the months intervening between my joint May 2020 *Policy Options* essay with Leckey and Mendelsohn and our respective Fall 2021 and Spring 2022 journal articles, the Quebec Superior Court ruled in April 2021 on the constitutional challenge to the enacted Bill 21.[56] A version of our *Policy Options* argument was put before the Superior Court by counsel seeking a declaration that various provisions of the law were inconsistent with targeted rights and freedoms.[57] The court affirmed that it had the judicial discretion to make a declaration, reasoning that the wording of the notwithstanding clause "[*n']exclurait pas une demande de jugement déclaratoire.*"[58] Yet, for reasons of judicial economy and a concern that a declaration of inconsistency would amount to ruling on the merits of the legislature's recourse to the notwithstanding clause, the court declined the invitation.[59]

The court exercised what, in the conclusion of my Fall 2021 article, I referred to as the "passive virtues."[60] I there outlined some considerations that a court could explore in evaluating whether to exercise the jurisdiction awarded to it on our reading of the notwithstanding clause. Absent from the considerations that I there explored is one that has emerged since Leckey, Mendelsohn, and I first sought to contribute to debates on the notwithstanding clause: the increased use of the clause by two provincial legislatures, seemingly with the aim of exempting its legislation from judicial challenge and scrutiny.[61] In such circumstances, where recourse to the clause is not exceptional and where political justification for invoking it is not forthcoming, the judicial virtues may well recommend that a court resist the attempted escape from challenge and scrutiny. After all, determining whether legislation is inconsistent with the Constitution calls on "an ordinary judicial task that involves resolving a question of law."[62] In resolving that question, a court will provide an all-important forum for those whose voices were left unheard and unheeded in the legislative process.

NOTES

1 Canadian Charter of Rights and Freedoms, s 33(1), Part I of the Constitution Act, 1982, being Schedule B to the Canada Act 1982 (UK), 1982, c 11 [Charter]. Subsection (1) provides:

(1) Parliament or the legislature of a province may expressly declare in an Act of Parliament or of the legislature, as the case may be, that the Act or a provision thereof shall operate notwithstanding a provision included in section 2 or sections 7 to 15 of this Charter.

(1) Le Parlement ou la législature d'une province peut adopter une loi où il est expressément déclaré que celle-ci ou une de ses dispositions a effet indépendamment d'une disposition donnée de l'article 2 ou des articles 7 à 15 de la présente charte.

2 Canadian Charter of Rights and Freedoms, s 33(2). Subsection (2) provides:

(2) An Act or a provision of an Act in respect of which a declaration made under this section is in effect shall have such operation as it would have but for the provision of this Charter referred to in the declaration.

(2) La loi ou la disposition qui fait l'objet d'une déclaration conforme au présent article et en vigueur a l'effet qu'elle aurait sauf la disposition en cause de la charte.

3 1st Sess, 42nd Leg, Quebec, 2019 (assented to 16 June 2019), S.Q. 2019, c. 12.

4 Grégoire Webber, Eric Mendelsohn, and Robert Leckey, "The Faulty Received Wisdom around the Notwithstanding Clause," *Policy Options*, 10 May 2019, policyoptions.irpp.org/magazines/may-2019/faulty-wisdom-notwithstanding-clause.

5 *Ford v Quebec* [1988] 2 SCR 712 at paras 1 et subs. The court's expression referred to the express declaration in the Act Respecting the Constitution Act, 1982, S.Q. 1982, c. 21.

6 See, for example, Peter W. Hogg, "Override of Rights" in *Constitutional Law of Canada*, Student Edition (Toronto: Thomson Reuters, 2018).

7 See, for example, Jeremy Webber, *The Constitution of Canada: A Contextual Analysis* (Oxford: Hart Publishing, 2015), 189.

8 See, for example, Pierre Elliott Trudeau, *Memoirs* (Toronto: McLelland & Stewart, 1993), 322.

9 Constitution Act, 1982, s 52(1). Subsection 52(1) provides:

(1) The Constitution of Canada is the supreme law of Canada, and any law that is inconsistent with the provisions of the Constitution is, to the extent of the inconsistency, of no force or effect.

(1) La Constitution du Canada est la loi suprême du Canada; elle rend inopérantes les dispositions incompatibles de toute autre règle de droit.

10 Webber, Mendelsohn, and Leckey, "Faulty Received Wisdom."

11 Ibid.

12 Cass R. Sunstein, "Incompletely Theorized Agreements," *Harvard Law Review* 108 (1995): 1733–9.

13 Ibid., 1735–6.

14 Ibid., 1739.

15 I explore this feature of bills of rights in Grégoire Webber, *The Negotiable Constitution: On the Limitation of Rights* (Cambridge: Cambridge University Press, 2009), 1–12, 160–73.

16 Sunstein, "Incompletely Theorized Agreements," 1739.

17 Grégoire Webber, "Notwithstanding Rights, Review, or Remedy? On the Notwithstanding Clause on the Operation of Legislation," *University of Toronto Law Journal* 71 (2021): 1–2, https://ssrn.com/abstract=3935891.

18 Robert Leckey and Eric Mendelsohn, "The Notwithstanding Clause: Legislatures, Courts, and the Electorate," *University of Toronto Law Journal* 72, no. 2 (2022). See further Robert Leckey in this volume.

19 Colonial Laws Validity Act, 1865, 28 & 29 Vict. c. 63 (UK), s. 3 (emphasis added), to be read with s. 2. See *Manitoba Language Rights Reference* [1985] 1 SCR 721 at 746.

20 Statute of Westminster, 1931, 22 Geo. V, c. 4 (U.K.), ss. 2, 7.

21 *Manitoba Language Rights Reference*, 746. See also *Operation Dismantle v The Queen* [1985] 1 SCR 441 at para 86.

22 *Manitoba Language Rights Reference*, 746 (emphasis added). See further *R v Sullivan*, 2022 SCC 19 at para 48.

23 Canadian Charter of Rights and Freedoms, s 33(2) (emphasis added).

24 *R v Sullivan*, para. 48.

25 *Mossop v Canada* [1993] 1 SCR 554 at 582.

26 Leckey and Mendelsohn, "The Notwithstanding Clause," 193.

27 Ibid., 196.

28 Canadian Charter of Rights and Freedoms, s 1.

29 Leckey and Mendelsohn, "The Notwithstanding Clause," 193.

30 Ibid., 196.

31 Constitution Act, 1982, s 52(1) (emphasis added). The French version may be less friendly to Leckey and Mendelsohn than first appears, as the reference to "*toute autre règle* de droit" may be best read to imply that the Constitution is itself a series of "règles de droit" and that it is these and not the Constitution entire that render inoperable any inconsistent legislative provisions.

32 The greatest share of their article is devoted to showing how it is in keeping with a range of constitutional provisions and principles to subject

legislation invoking the notwithstanding clause to judicial review. Leckey and Mendelsohn, "The Notwithstanding Clause," 196–214.

33 *New Brunswick Broadcasting Co v Nova Scotia (Speaker of the House of Assembly)* [1993] 1 SCR 319 at 373.

34 Leckey and Mendelsohn, "The Notwithstanding Clause," 196.

35 See *RJR-MacDonald v Canada* [1995] 3 SCR 199 at para 129.

36 See *Canadian Foundation for Children, Youth and the Law v Canada* [2004] 1 SCR 76 at para 73.

37 See *M v H* [1999] 2 SCR 3 at para 333.

38 See *Gosselin v Quebec* [2002] 4 SCR 429 at para 140.

39 See *Edmonton Journal v Alberta* [1989] 2 SCR 1326 at 1342.

40 See *R v Edwards Books and Art* [1986] 2 SCR 713 at 768.

41 See *Vriend v Alberta* [1998] 1 SCR 493 at para 108.

42 See *R v Morgentaler* [1988] 1 SCR 30, 73; *RJR-MacDonald*, para 127; *Thomson Newspapers v Canada* [1998] 1 SCR 877 at para 79.

43 Leckey and Mendelsohn "The Notwithstanding Clause," 196.

44 *R v Sullivan*, paras 43 and 45.

45 Though many colleagues have offered welcome challenges, some have supported our conclusion by drawing on other sources. See Eric M. Adams and Erin R.J. Bower, "Notwithstanding History: The Rights-Protecting Purposes of Section 33 of the Charter," *Review of Constitutional Studies* 26, no. 2 (2022): 121, https://dx.doi.org/10.2139/ssrn.4185044.

46 *Ford v Quebec*, 740.

47 Webber, "Notwithstanding Rights," 533–7. The first challenge was set out in Maxime St-Hilaire and Xaiver Foccroulle Ménard, "Nothing to Declare: A Response to Grégoire Webber, Eric Mendelsohn, Robert Leckey, and Léonid Sirota on the Effects of the Notwithstanding Clause," *Constitutional Forum* 29, no. 1 (2020): 38–9. See also Maxime St-Hilaire, Xavier Foccroulle Ménard, and Antoine Dutrisac in this volume.

48 I leave to one side the challenges drawing on the classical legal tradition articulated in Stéphane Sérafin, Kerry Sun, and Xavier Foccroulle Ménard, "Notwithstanding Judicial Specification: The Notwithstanding Clause within a Juridical Order," *The Supreme Court Law Review* 110 (2d) (2023): 135. Although I have explored the history of ideas relating to our modern understanding of rights by exploring the Latin *ius*, the inspiration for my understanding of rights is not the classical tradition but instead the moral specificationist literature in moral rights theory and Hohfeld's analytical scheme of rights. See: John Oberdiek, "Specifying Rights Out of Necessity," *Oxford Journal of Legal Studies* 28 (2008): 127; W.N. Hohfeld, *Fundamental Legal Conceptions as Applied in Judicial*

Reasoning (New Haven: Yale University Press, 1919). In exploring the Latin *ius*, my scholarly disposition was akin to John Gardner's reference to "an intellectual squirrel," "scouring assiduously for truths across many supposedly rival positions and traditions." *Law as a Leap of Faith* (Oxford: Oxford University Press, 2012), vi.

49 Plato, "Gorgias," in *Plato: Complete Works*, ed. J.M. Cooper (Indianapolis and Cambridge: Hackett Publishing, 1997), 457c-458b.

50 Leckey and Mendelsohn, "The Notwithstanding Clause," 193.

51 Ibid.

52 Webber, "Notwithstanding Rights," 528.

53 Ibid.

54 Ibid., 525.

55 Geoffrey Sigalet, in this volume. See further Geoffrey T. Sigalet, "Legislated Rights as Trumps: Why the Notwithstanding Clause Overrides Judicial Review," *Osgoode Hall Law Journal* 61, no. 1 (2023).

56 *Hak c Québec (Procureur général)* 2021 QCCS 1466.

57 Ibid., paras 785–800.

58 Ibid., para 798.

59 Ibid., paras 799, 798.

60 Webber, "Notwithstanding Rights," 537–8, with reference to Alexander M. Bickel, "The Passive Virtues," *Harvard Law Review* 75 (1961): 40.

61 See: Protecting Elections and Defending Democracy Act, 2021, S.O. 2021, c. 31, s. 53.1(1) (Ontario); An Act respecting French, the official and common language of Québec, S.Q. 2022, c. 14, ss. 121, 217 (Quebec); and Keeping Students in Class Act, 2022, S.O. 2022, c. 19, s. 13(1) (Ontario, since repealed).

62 *R v Sullivan*, 49.

PART THREE

Judicial Review

It may seem an odd exercise of editorial discretion to begin a section on judicial review with a consideration of the role and choices of the legislatures in enacting laws and determining the scope, application, and timing of notwithstanding clause (NWC) invocation rather than with an exploration of the role of the courts in responding to Charter challenges, or to requests for judicial intervention or interpretation. And yet, we must understand those legislative roles and exercises of discretion in order to take the full measure of judicial review which is, inescapably, reactive to lawmaking. Robert Leckey thus explores the ways legislative choices may significantly affect the degree to which the voting public will know or suspect how a protected law affects Charter rights and how these choices resonate differently with theoretical justifications for the NWC. He discusses broad versus targeted invocations of the NWC, pre-emptive and responsive invocation and the significance, for public accountability and democratic discourse, of judicial review, even where invocation has already decided the matter of constitutionality.

In their response to Leckey on the matter of what, if any role, the courts might play once the NWC has been invoked, Maxime St-Hilaire, Xavier Foccroulle Ménard, and Antoine Dutrisac, relying on the *Ford* case in the Supreme Court, reaffirm and elaborate upon their argument that invocation of the NWC effectively forecloses the option of judicial review, not merely from the standpoint of constitutional architecture, but as a matter of textual logic and integrity.

Geoffrey Sigalet largely concurs with St-Hilaire et al., but takes the arguments against the availability of judicial review to another plane, arguing that the courts are not merely legally – i.e., jurisdictionally – prevented from entertaining Charter challenges in respect of which the formalities of section 33 as to applicable Charter sections have been met, but they are morally bound to not intervene where the nwc has been properly invoked. The normative argument against judicial review is predicated on the idea that the nwc was designed to establish a second system of checks and balances, the first being judicial consideration of questions about the constitutionality of laws. Here, the nwc gives the legislative branch the prerogative to consider the soundness of affected judicial pronouncements and, if invoked pre-emptively, to obviate the need for or option of judicial intervention altogether. In this respect, Sigalet characterizes the judicial role – or an aspect of it – as inescapably political and even strategic in nature, and views the NWC as a constitutional vehicle through which society may defer to legitimate political institutions – the legislatures – to decide certain fundamentally political questions.

Christopher Manfredi, like Sigalet, argues that courts and judges are inherently political and strategic actors and that they are frequently engaging in policy making when they purport merely to be adjudicating as neutral interpreters of the relevant legislative and constitutional text. But beyond considering the political nature of judging, Manfredi reiterates and expands upon his long-standing argument that, as recognized and mandated by the NWC, legislatures have a role, and the corresponding capacity, at least as important as that of the courts in upholding and defending the Constitution and, more precisely, in interpreting what it intends and means, especially as to the content and definition of the rights and freedoms enumerated therein. Manfredi characterizes the regime introduced with the advent of the Charter and, within it, the NWC, as one not of either judicial or legislative supremacy, but as one of "constitutional supremacy," in which it is the Constitution itself that both informs and sits above all other actors and institutions. Ultimately, he sees the NWC's justification and purpose as residing in its role in remedying the "critical paradox of liberal constitutionalism. ... If judicial review evolves such that political power in its judicial form is limited only by a constitution whose meaning courts alone define, then judicial power is no longer itself constrained by constitutional limits."

5

Legislative Choices in Using Section 33 and Judicial Scrutiny

Robert Leckey

Section 33 of the Canadian Charter of Rights and Freedoms, known as the notwithstanding clause, allows a legislature to declare that a law shall "have such operation as it would have" but for one or more provisions of the Canadian Charter referred to in the declaration.[1] Such a protected law is thereby shielded from judicial strike-down for unjustifiably limiting a Charter guarantee. A legislature may shield a law from one or more of a subset of Charter provisions: the "fundamental freedoms" (section 2), the "legal rights" (sections 7–14), and the "equality rights" (section 15).[2] Although debates on the mechanism have arguably neglected this point, each use of the notwithstanding clause involves consequential choices. One choice relates to what is protected. For example, a legislature may activate section 33 to shield one provision or more, or an entire statute. A second relates to the identity and number of Charter provisions from which protection is granted. A legislature may shield its law from one or more guarantees – or from all those amenable to section 33. A third choice relates to timing and the relationship to litigation: namely, whether the legislature shields a law pre-emptively or does so after the government loses a Charter challenge in court. This chapter addresses two broad implications of such legislative choices.

First, these choices may significantly affect the degree to which the voting public will know how a protected law affects Charter rights. For instance, activation of section 33 to protect a law from one Charter guarantee may communicate with relative precision the legislative drafters' anticipation of how the law would affect rights bearers. By contrast, a broader activation that shields the law from sections 2 and 7 to 15 may do so much less.

Second, uses of section 33, characterized by these legislative choices, resonate differently with theoretical justifications for the notwithstanding clause. The examples that underlie scholarly debates about section 33 – expressly or tacitly – are thus more important than is sometimes acknowledged. Specifically, it is worth being alert to which scenario or scenarios the interlocutors take as likely or paradigmatic. Consider the view (to which we return below) of the notwithstanding clause as a safety valve that lets the government disagree with the judiciary on rights. A targeted and restrained use of section 33 after a judgment declares that a law limits a Charter right unjustifiably is much more consistent with this view than is a broad invocation.

The analysis here unfolds against a dataset that, while small, shows broader invocations to have recently outnumbered targeted ones. Sensitivity to the varieties of uses of the notwithstanding clause merits a place in political and legal debates, especially as the device enjoys "something of a renaissance,"[3] with early, if inconclusive, evidence of "the beginning of a new era in which the use of s. 33 is normalized."[4]

This chapter's argument about how various uses of section 33 affect transparency and political actors' accountability to the electorate for their choices builds on earlier contributions.[5] Flatteringly, those contributions have inspired engagement by distinguished colleagues. Indeed, the engagement is such that chapters in this volume cast themselves as a "retrospective,"[6] or a consolidation of "all of the arguments, objections and precise responses presented to date."[7] While I refer to some of this work along the way, my present aim is to shed new light on the implications of legislative design choices when using section 33.

In the essay I co-authored with Mendelsohn, we argue that while the notwithstanding clause may give the legislature the "last word" on whether a protected law can produce legal effects, it does not do so on the law's impact on rights and its justification. Nor does it make those questions legally meaningless or silence the judiciary. We argue that, in appropriate cases, on application by a plaintiff with standing, a court may scrutinize a law protected by section 33 in the light of arguments and evidence. The court may declare whether the law limits Charter rights and, if so, whether such limits are demonstrably justifiable in a free and democratic society, in the terms of section 1.[8] Such a declaration, following a traditional Charter analysis, would not stop the law's operation. But it could enhance the electorate's ability to play its constitutional role informedly. The connection to the present chapter is that "the potential value of a judicial assessment of a protected law's impact on Charter rights depends on the context,"[9] including the legislative choices in activating the notwithstanding clause.

I. SCRUTINY OF PROTECTED LAWS

Nothing in the notwithstanding clause precludes the judiciary from reviewing a law protected by section 33. Subsection 33(2), which Mendelsohn and I call the mechanism's "effects clause," states that a law shall have the operation it would have but for Charter rights. Its focus is ensuring that a protected law produces its effects, not on precluding the courts from studying such a law.[10] While we welcome a healthy debate about how best to interpret subsection 33(2), some seem to minimize the interpretive choices we see as unavoidable, contending instead that the text unequivocally precludes judicial review.[11] We argue that by playing its established constitutional role of analyzing whether a law limits Charter rights and, if so, whether such limits are justifiable in the terms of section 1, a court can inform the public about the legal effects of the legislature's political choice to use section 33. Moreover, in appropriate cases, a court should exercise its discretion by doing so. Such a declaration would aid an applicant in expeditiously seeking a declaration of invalidity when a law's protection by section 33 lapses. We emphasize the court's potential role in informing the public; the idea is not that the legislature needs the court's guidance. In any event, the government can always seek the judiciary's view through a reference.

The path we envisage – an application, a trial, judicial analysis, and ultimately a declaration regarding a protected law – fits with established procedure and judicial practice. An applicant seeking such a declaration would need to follow ordinary procedure. In line with the approach to declaratory relief, a court asked to examine a protected law would inquire whether a plaintiff or plaintiffs with a genuine interest in the dispute were bringing evidence of the law's effects on their rights. This assessment by the court would address the warnings against ruling on Charter cases "in a factual vacuum."[12] The governmental respondent would have an interest in opposing the declaration, given the potential political consequences of a detailed analysis of a protected law's impact on Charter rights. Although

the government might decline to participate, courts have tools for
responding where a governmental party does so. They might rely
on evidence submitted by a nongovernmental party defending the
protected law, or by interveners. If necessary, courts can appoint an
amicus curiae. The court would retain its usual ability to discipline
unfounded claims by awards for costs. Courts could use their familiar tools for screening out cases that would entail an imprudent use
of judicial resources, such as one that would be hypothetical or theoretical, not real, or political, not legal.[13] A protected law's impact
on Charter rights is a real legal matter since Charter rights remain in
effect while section 33 operates.[14]

I noted above that the effects clause says nothing to preclude judicial review of a protected law. Cognizant of the multiple inputs to
constitutional interpretation, our article incorporates other elements
into our reading of section 33(2) as leaving open space for courts
to scrutinize protected laws. Our endeavour is one of interpreting
section 33 by the techniques and sources of constitutional
interpretation, integrating the notwithstanding clause into the
Charter and the constitution of Canada. It does not depend on section 33's status as the result of political compromise.[15]

A salient fact is that the notwithstanding clause reserves a role for
the voting public, acting through the democratic process. The sunset
clause in subsection 33(3) – by which a declaration under subsection 33(1) "shall cease to have effect five years after it comes into
force" or at an earlier specified date – "force[s] reconsideration by
the Parliament or Legislature of each exercise of the power at five-
year intervals (intervals in which elections will have been held)."[16]
While legislators and legislatures are answerable to their electorates
as a general matter, subsection 33(3) underlines that their legitimacy
in matters concerning the notwithstanding clause derives from democratic support.[17] Their decisions to activate section 33 or to renew
its protections are subject to approval via the democratic process.
Through this process, the public may express judgments about legislative decisions to use the notwithstanding clause and political
actors' commitments to renew such use or let it lapse.

Unwritten principles, which may influence interpretation of the
constitutional text,[18] bolster the case for discerning in section 33 a
conception of democratic responsibility by which the voting public is
called to consider legislative trade-offs about rights. One is the principle of democracy, recognized by the Supreme Court of Canada as

"an essential interpretive consideration."[19] By the Supreme Court's conception, this principle acknowledges that a "democratic system of government is committed to considering ... dissenting voices"[20] and that it would be "a grave mistake to equate the legitimacy [of democratic institutions] with the 'sovereign will' or majority rule alone."[21] A second fundamental principle, the protection of minorities, inclines against reading section 33 as opening a black box into which Charter rights and minorities vanish.[22] Other principles and constitutional elements, including parliamentary sovereignty, federalism, and the constitutional role of the superior courts, help in integrating section 33 into the Constitution and delineating the courts' potential role in scrutinizing a protected law.[23]

For the electorate to play the constitutional role assigned to it by subsection 33(3), it needs access to information about how protected laws affect Charter rights. Judicial scrutiny of a protected law might mitigate two impediments to knowledge brought into view by the Supreme Court's appeal in *Ford v Quebec (Attorney General)*[24] and related scholarship. One is the difficulty, even impossibility, of knowing the impact that laws will have on Charter rights and rights holders, pre-enactment or post-enactment, before or absent legal proceedings in which concrete claims are asserted and adjudicated based on arguments and evidence.[25] The second flows from the Supreme Court's adoption, in *Ford*, of a formal – rather than substantive – approach to the conditions for activating section 33. *Ford* accepted that a legislature may protect a law by using the notwithstanding clause pre-emptively, prior to any Charter challenge. Furthermore, a legislature need not specify which Charter right or rights the protected law is predicted to affect. This formal or minimalist approach to activation of the notwithstanding clause makes it more important to construe the effects clause as permitting publicity about a protected law's concrete impact on rights.[26] As Eric Adams and Erin Bower put it, "The mechanics of the sunset provision only make sense if courts retain a role in assessing and identifying, but not remedying, legislation that unjustifiably infringes one of the select Charter rights covered by section 33."[27]

Our proposition aligns with the notion that it does not make sense for section 33 to allow a legislature indefinitely "to subordinate potential rights claims of which it is unaware or uncertain."[28] A similar intuition that it would be wrong for section 33 to have effects in an informational vacuum about the effects on Charter rights underpins suggestions about when a legislature may activate the mechanism legitimately. It has been proposed that legislatures should resort to section 33 only after a judicial determination that the law unjustifiably limits rights.[29] The difference is that those authors saw the need for information about a law's impact on Charter rights pre-enactment, whereas our approach opens an avenue for producing such "crucial information"[30] post-enactment.

II. CHARACTERIZING USES OF THE NOTWITHSTANDING CLAUSE

In our article, Mendelsohn and I address the widespread supposition that, by using section 33, "A legislature concedes that it violates Charter rights (or disagrees with the Supreme Court's interpretation thereof)."[31] To do so, we adduced the example of Quebec's controversial laicity law, Bill 21.[32] This part elaborates on my reflections that our example arose from different legislative choices than may the examples foremost in the minds of those who share that supposition. After spelling out these choices, with examples, successive parts will connect them to the varying value of a judicial declaration and the implications for scholarly debates.

Having decided to activate the notwithstanding clause, legislative drafters and elected lawmakers make choices respecting at least four matters. One concerns the extent of the legislation to have its operation despite Charter rights. In an article that provided empirical data about uses of section 33 up to 2001, Tsvi Kahana addressed this feature as "What is deviating?"[33] In a "targeted" or "surgical"[34] approach, a legislature may shield just one provision of a statute. An example comes from Saskatchewan. A first-instance decision had held that providing governmental funding to a Roman Catholic school for the benefit of students not of that faith unjustifiably limited the state's duty of religious neutrality, under paragraph 2(a) of the Canadian Charter, and the equality rights in subsection 15(1).[35] For the court, such funding fell outside the constitutional protection of denominational schools.[36] That decision was eventually reversed on appeal.[37] In the meantime, however, the legislature had amended the Education Act, 1995.[38] It added a subsection 2.2(1): "Pursuant to subsection 33(1) of the Canadian Charter of Rights and Freedoms, section 2.1" – which provides for the payment of provincial grants to boards of education without regard to the religious affiliation of pupils or their parents or guardians – "is declared to operate notwithstanding sections 2 and 15 of the Canadian Charter of Rights and Freedoms."[39]

In a less targeted fashion, legislative drafters may shield multiple provisions of a statute. Following the Supreme Court of Canada's decision in *Ford*, the National Assembly of Quebec modified the Charter of the French Language,[40] declaring that section 58 of the latter and the first paragraph of its section 68 would operate notwithstanding paragraph 2(b) of the Canadian Charter.[41] A legislature may also shield an entire statute from one or more provisions of the Charter. A statute enjoys the protection of the notwithstanding clause in the cases of Quebec's Bill 21,[42] regarding secularism and religious symbols; its Bill 96,[43] which amended the Charter of the French Language and numerous other laws; and Ontario's electoral reform of 2021.[44] Among other things, the latter reform doubled donation limits, extended the per-vote subsidy for political parties, and adjusted limits on third-party advertising. New Brunswick's Bill 11, which would have made proof of vaccination mandatory for children attending school, initially included a clause 4 that would have activated the notwithstanding clause in respect of the whole statute.[45] Most dramatically, a legislature may shield its statute book from one or more provisions of the Canadian Charter. The National Assembly of Quebec did so in 1982, activating section 33 in respect of all provincial legislation. This move was an "act of political protest against the fact that the Charter was entrenched without the Government of Quebec's consent."[46] The Supreme Court of Canada upheld the validity of this omnibus recourse to section 33 in *Ford*.

Another choice concerns the number and identity of the Charter provisions despite which the law will have its effect. Kahana refers here to "section of Canadian Charter deviated from,"[47] though "sections" in the plural would be preferable. For her part, Caitlin Salvino contrasts "broad" and "targeted" invocations of the notwithstanding clause.[48] At one end of a spectrum, a comparatively restrained approach might provide that an enactment shall operate notwithstanding one or more of the Charter's sections 2 and 7 to 15. The National Assembly has shielded part of its Charter of the French Language from the provision guaranteeing freedom of expression, paragraph 2(b).[49] As mentioned, Saskatchewan's School Choice Protection Act activates the notwithstanding clause to assure protection from only sections 2 and 15 of the Canadian Charter.

Ontario's short-lived legislation to prevent a strike by employees of school boards was declared to operate notwithstanding sections 2, 7, and 15.[50] At the other extreme, a legislature might declare that a protected law shall operate notwithstanding all of sections 2 and 7 to 15, a "blanket"[51] or "wall to wall" invocation.[52] Quebec's Bill 21 and Bill 96 and Ontario's electoral law triggered protection from the fullest set of Charter provisions possible.[53]

A third choice concerns timing and the relationship to Charter litigation. A legislature may activate the notwithstanding clause after an adverse decision, at first instance, on appeal, or from the Supreme Court of Canada. The Saskatchewan legislature's education law responded to a loss at trial. Its victory on appeal rendered nugatory the activation of section 33. A legislature may also activate the notwithstanding clause upstream of any litigation. Think here of Quebec's Bill 21, its Bill 96, and Ontario's electoral reform.

A fourth choice concerns elected lawmakers' speech about recourse to the notwithstanding clause. Choices here may be formal or substantive. Substantively, lawmakers may admit that they are legislating with a view to limiting a Charter right unjustifiably. They might recognize that they are legislating in furtherance of an interpretation of rights different from that of the judiciary. They may also deny that they are infringing rights. Formally, lawmakers may speak in the legislative assembly or outside it, as in press conferences or on social media. After legal experts informed the public that the use of the notwithstanding clause proposed in Bill 96 would negate the right to be free from unreasonable searches and seizures, the government of Quebec paid for newspaper ads denying that the Office québécois de la langue française had engaged, or ever would engage, in searches or seizures.[54] Lawmakers may also express a view in the activating legislation. Quebec's Bill 21 – which Mendelsohn and I cited to answer the supposition that using section 33 necessarily concedes a violation of rights – is an arresting example. It contains what is, in essence, a legislative denial that the law violates rights. Specifically, Bill 21 activates section 33 to ensure the operation of measures that appear to infringe Charter guarantees such as freedom of religion, freedom of expression, and the right to equality. But it affirms that its animating principle of the "laicity of the State [sic]" is "based" on principles including "the equality of all citizens" and "freedom of conscience and freedom of religion."[55] Geoffrey Sigalet has suggested that "legislatures, intent on using section 33 to signal majoritarian opposition to judicial decisions[,] could relish courts issuing ineffective declarations of Charter inconsistency if this helps signal their opposition to rights views that are unpopular in their province."[56] This intriguing possibility is evidently not the case with Quebec's Bill 21, given the governmental and legislative denial of infringing rights.[57]

III. VARYING VALUE OF DECLARATIONS

In our article, Mendelsohn and I recognize that the potential value of a judicial assessment of a protected law's impact on Charter rights depends on the context. We suggest that, in deciding whether to exercise its discretion to scrutinize a protected law, a court might ask itself questions including the following: Would a declaration meaningfully inform the public on the legal matter of a law's impact on Charter rights? Did the legislative process consider and recognize these effects? Exercise of the traditional judicial function of declaring where a law unjustifiably limits Charter rights may inform the public more meaningfully in some scenarios than in others. I look back now to the choices identified in the preceding section. The concern here is how such choices collectively shape the degree to which a legislature's activation of section 33 is sufficiently transparent for the electorate to judge it. Judicial scrutiny and an eventual declaration will have a much greater informational value where the effects of activating the notwithstanding clause are opaque to the electorate.

Where the legislature invokes section 33 to protect one provision from one Charter guarantee, it may send the public a relatively clear message about what it is doing. In other scenarios, it may be harder for the public to evaluate the legislature's choice informedly and the judiciary may consequently have more to contribute. Where the activation covers one statute or more, or a statute book, it may be difficult for the public to know the impacts on rights bearers of the recourse to the notwithstanding clause. Similarly, where the legislature seeks protection for a law from all of sections 2 and 7 to 15, it does not disclose precisely the constitutional problems flagged by the governmental lawyers. In such cases, the legislative drafters have not "specified" the right or rights most severely affected.[58] Those who take it for granted that a legislature concedes a rights violation by using section 33 may be thinking of a restrained use, such as one that shelters a law from one Charter guarantee. It seems implausible to read a blanket invocation of section 33 in respect of sections 2 and 7 to 15 as conceding violations of each guarantee in question.

As for timing and relationship with litigation, where the legislature activated the notwithstanding clause after litigation, and no "significant change in the circumstances or evidence" has arisen,[59] the electorate will know the protected law's impact. It is conceivable that after a substantial time or if there is a "significant change," the judgment from the litigation may be less probative about the rights violations in issue. Pre-emptive activation of the notwithstanding clause may make it harder for the public to know how a law, in operation, affects rights bearers.[60] So may legislative speech that denies a violation of Charter rights. In such instances, a judicial declaration respecting a protected law's impact on Charter rights may meaningfully inform the electorate.

Two caveats are in order about the present discussion's focus on how legislative choices in activating section 33 affect the public's knowledge about the impact on Charter rights. One is that it leaves for another day questions about the respect that the legislative branch may owe to fundamental rights and, perhaps as a matter of interinstitutional comity, to the judiciary and its constitutional role. In the litigation relating to Bill 21, the trial judge expressed concern that the blanket activation of the notwithstanding clauses in the Canadian Charter and the Quebec Charter constituted a "flippant and unconsidered" use of legislative prerogatives,[61] signalling "a certain banalization and indifference."[62] These remarks bespeak tacit premises that may merit unpacking.

The other caveat is that the opacity of a protected law's impact on Charter rights is not directly correlated to its severity. In this way, a "wall to wall" use of the notwithstanding clause – which does little to signal its expected effects on rights – might engender less suffering than a targeted, restrained, and thus more "specified" use (to return to Weinrib's term). Think of a provision authorizing torture allowed to operate notwithstanding solely section 12's "right not to be subject to any cruel and unusual punishment." In other words, the present analysis may be more helpful in discerning the extent to which the courts have an informational role to play than the degree of moral culpability attaching to lawmakers' choices.[63] This part has shown that the epistemic value of a judicial declaration depends substantially on several legislative choices. This chapter turns next to the scholarly implications.

IV. LATENT SCHOLARLY PREMISES

Legislative choices resulting in a targeted or restrained use of the notwithstanding clause align better than broader or less restrained uses with some accounts of what the notwithstanding clause allows legislatures to do. While a robust literature discusses justifications for the notwithstanding clause with an eye to the aspirations of those involved in negotiating it, here I foreground Dwight New-man's recent chapter as a fruitful example,[64] complemented by reference to Sigalet's scholarship. Newman recounts how Allan Blakeney, premier of Saskatchewan, conceived of the notwithstanding clause as allowing the legislature to act in furtherance of moral rights going beyond the legal rights in the Charter.[65] As for Alberta's Peter Lougheed, he wrote of the notwithstanding clause as "permit[ting] a certain responsiveness to interpretations of rights with which there is ultimate democratic disagreement."[66]

Both conceptions – allowing the protection of rights outside the Charter and enabling legislative disagreement with judicial interpretations of rights – presuppose a legislature that is committed, in general, to fundamental rights. From an historical perspective, the notwithstanding clause in the Canadian Charter, as those in earlier rights instruments, aimed "to enhance deliberate deliberation about rights and their limits, demanding a legislative process that took rights seriously, imposed limits explicitly, and engaged with judicial reasoning with the dignity of reasonable disagreement."[67] Both conceptions suggest that legislative drafters will identify a conflict or potential conflict between an intended legislative policy and a Charter right (or a judicial interpretation of one). For example, a legislature might "us[e] section 33 to express disagreement about the scope and content of rights,"[68] or it might "enact statutory specifications of rights that operate notwithstanding their disagreement with those preferred by courts,"[69] with "'notwithstanding' declarations as potential constructions of rights."[70]

In contrast, these conceptions, and the associated aspirations for legislative collaboration in respecting fundamental rights, say little or nothing about the blanket invocation of section 33 to shield an entire regime (or a statute book) from the largest possible group of Charter rights. Such a use of the mechanism is not a form of active engagement in the rights project. It is not a message about where, by the elected lawmakers' assessment, the courts got it wrong, or about how better to specify rights and reasonable limits defining their contours in given circumstances. Rather, it is an opting-out or withdrawal from engaging with rights, a signal that the legislature is pursuing its aim in opposition to the set of fundamental rights and freedoms. For example, the "sweeping, pre-emptive use of the not-withstanding clause" by Quebec in Bill 96 "signals that the defence of the French language isn't a social aim that is compatible with fundamental rights," but is, rather, "antagonistic to them."[71]

Taking different uses of section 33 – the upshot of varying choices identified in part II – as paradigmatic or emblematic may steer scholars to different concerns about the mechanism. The targeted and restrained use of the notwithstanding clause in the Saskatchewan schools case may strike scholars favourable to the notwithstanding clause as especially attractive. Newman, presumably writing before the recent evidence of political actors' "greater willingness"[72] to deploy section 33 broadly, draws again on ideas associated with Lougheed. He reads the use of section 33 following the Saskatchewan schools judgment as "reflect[ing] a statement that a different inter-pretation of rights ought to apply than that instantiated by a judicial decision."[73] As Sigalet puts it, the notwithstanding clause "allows Saskatchewan's statute to construct the scope of how the duty of state neutrality, drawn from the Charter right to freedom of reli-gion, relates to constitutional protections for historically vulnerable religious institutions."[74] Newman adds that the case "belies sugges-tions that uses of the notwithstanding clause will be by majorities out to oppress minorities."[75] Rather, "It is actually a case that sees the government protecting the integrity of the (minority) Catholic school system from threats by the courts and the rights of individual parents and children to exercise choice in schooling based on com-plex matters of faith."[76]

Now, one example may "belie" the proposition that section 33 will only be used to oppress minorities. It is hard to see, however, how it displaces the worry that it will often be so used, a worry intensified by Quebec's uses of the device in Bill 21 and Bill 96. Recognizing that Newman and Sigalet take the Saskatchewan case as significant helped me to recognize my positionality. Like many who care about religious minorities and "complex matters of faith,"[77] I have focused on Quebec's Bill 21.[78] I do so as I wrestle with what the notwith-standing clause makes possible in a federation that is ostensibly committed to fundamental rights and the protection of minorities, and with what it may ask of judges.[79] In defence of Mendelsohn's and my article, our contention that courts can scrutinize a protected law and declare its impact on rights, and sometimes should do so, is not a one-size-fits-all approach. Our argument builds in flexibility for the range of choices discussed in part II. It remains the case, though, that Bill 21 may have coloured the argument in ways of which we were less than wholly aware. Looking to past scholarship, one might seek to discern what kinds of use of section 33 the authors took as paradigmatic. For the future, interlocutors in the debates might undertake self-reflection and disclose their starting points.

This chapter calls for greater attention to the variety of ways that a legislature may activate the notwithstanding clause in the Canadian Charter of Rights and Freedoms. Some uses may telegraph to the electorate the legislature's trade-offs about Charter rights or its points of disagreement with judicial interpretations of those guarantees. Other uses may not. In such cases, the potential role for the courts is most significant.

Turning to constitutional and political theory, it is worth asking whether discussions bear on ideal legislatures or real ones. In a way that may be counterintuitive for some theorists, it seems important to grapple with empirical questions when discussing section 33. Some justifications for the mechanism are more compelling in the light of some varieties of use than of others. In a context that has witnessed an uptick in recourse to section 33, this chapter invites attention to questions of scope and timing. Beyond that, other empirical questions deserve attention. Which kinds of uses of the notwithstanding clause are more frequent? Which most harm those minorities who are unlikely to exercise influence through the majoritarian channels of the parliamentary process? How often does a legislature use section 33 to practice rights protection or engage in rights discourse, as opposed to showing disdain for fundamental rights and the role of the independent courts as a check on majoritarian power? If we are to have lucid debates about the notwithstanding clause, it may be helpful to adduce evidence about how it is used and to disclose the varieties we have foremost in mind.

NOTES

For comments, I am grateful to Patrick Baud, Anne Campbell, Félix-Antoine Lestage, Eric Mendelsohn, and Laurent Ruffo-Caracchini, as well as to participants at The Notwithstanding Clause at 40: Canadian Constitutional Democracy at a Crossroads, Massey College (11 and 12 April 2022), and an external reviewer.

1 Part I of the Constitution Act, 1982, section 33, being Schedule B to the Canada Act 1982 (UK), 1982, c 11 [Canadian Charter or Charter].
2 Constitution Act, section 33(1).
3 Peter W. Hogg and Wade K. Wright, *Constitutional Law of Canada*, 5th ed., vol. 2 (Toronto: Thomson Reuters, 2007) (loose-leaf updated 7/2023, release 1), 39–6.
4 Ibid., 39–9.
5 Grégoire Webber, Eric Mendelsohn, and Robert Leckey, "The Faulty Received Wisdom around the Notwithstanding Clause," *Policy Options*, 10 May 2019, policyoptions.irpp.org/magazines/may-2019/faulty-wisdom-notwithstanding-clause; Robert Leckey, "Advocacy Notwithstanding the Notwithstanding Clause," *Constitutional Forum constitutionnel* 28, no. 4 (2019); Robert Leckey and Eric Mendelsohn, "The Notwithstanding Clause: Legislatures, Courts, and the Electorate," *University of Toronto Law Journal* 72, no. 2 (2022): 189–215.
6 Grégoire Webber, this volume, chapter 4.
7 Maxime St-Hilaire, Xavier Foccroulle Ménard, and Antoine Dutrisac, this volume, chapter 6.
8 *R v Oakes* [1986] 1 SCR 103, 26 DLR (4th) 200.
9 Leckey and Mendelsohn, "Notwithstanding Clause," 213.
10 Grégoire Webber, "Notwithstanding Rights, Review, or Remedy? On the Notwithstanding Clause on the Operation of Legislation," *University of Toronto Law Journal* 71 (2021): 510–38, 518 ("absence of a privative or ouster clause or other mention of judicial review from the wording of the notwithstanding clause"); Grégoire Webber, this volume, chapter 4 ("there is no reference to 'judicial review' or other language that would affirm that legislation invoking the clause shall not be questioned or reviewed in any court"); Eric M. Adams and Erin R.J. Bower, "Notwithstanding History: The Rights-Protecting Purposes of Section 33 of the Charter," *Review of Constitutional Studies* 26, no. 2 (2022): 121–44, 142 ("nothing in the text of the notwithstanding clause or its context or purposes suggests that it precludes judicial engagement with the question of whether a

particular Charter right has been infringed and justifiably limited or not" when the legislature resorts to section 33).

11   Maxime St-Hilaire, Xavier Foccroulle Ménard, and Antoine Dutrisac, this volume, chapter 6, and Geoffrey Sigalet, this volume, chapter 7, argue in different ways that section 33 makes judicial review impossible while it protects legislation. Sigalet argues that section 33(2) "prohibits judicial review." See also: Geoffrey T. Sigalet, "The Truck and the Brakes: Understanding the Charter's Limitations and Notwithstanding Clauses Symmetrically," *Supreme Court Law Review* 105 (2022): 194–218; Geoffrey T. Sigalet, "Legislated Rights as Trumps: Why the Notwithstanding Clause Overrides Judicial Review," *Osgoode Hall Law Journal* 61, no. 1 (forthcoming); even that it does so "directly" (Sigalet, "Legislated Rights as Trumps."). Whether or not section 33(2) is best understood as telling courts not to examine protected laws, it is a stretch to say that it "prohibits" their doing so ("to forbid (an action, event, commodity, etc.) by a command, statute, law, or other authority; to inter-dict" (*Oxford English Dictionary*, online, *sv* "prohibit")), let alone that it does so "directly." Sigalet's subtle argument about the subjunctive mood or conditional tense of section 33(2) involves attention to alternative wording that the drafters might have used. Yet he does not consider how easily the drafters could have drawn on the familiar language of privative clauses had their chief aim been barring access to a reviewing court.

12   *MacKay v Manitoba* [1989] 2 SCR 357 at 361, 61 DLR (4th) 385.

13   While courts routinely exercise discretion in such screening, interpreting section 33 as allowing courts to decide to examine a protected law may reduce the certainty associated with some conceptions of the rule of law. See, for example, Antonin Scalia, "The Rule of Law as a Law of Rules," *University of Chicago Law Review* 56, no. 4 (1989): 1175–88.

14   St-Hilaire and his co-authors disagree with this proposition, favouring a view with which Mendelsohn and I engaged ("Notwithstanding Clause," 194–5).

15   See Dwight Newman, this volume, chapter 3.

16   Hogg and Wright, *Constitutional Law of Canada*, 39–10; See also: Guy Régimbald and Dwight Newman, *The Law of the Canadian Constitution*, 2nd ed. (Markham, ON: LexisNexis, 2017), 608, para 21.13; Jamie Cameron, this volume, chapter 17. For the innovative suggestion that associating the five-year limit for each use of section 33 with the maximum interval between elections is "unconvincing," see St-Hilaire, Foccroulle Ménard, and Dutrisac, this volume, chapter 6.

17 During the conference, Jamie Cameron spoke of democratic accountability
    as the "bedrock" of the legitimacy of the notwithstanding clause. See her
    contribution in this volume, chapter 17.

18 *Reference re Secession of Quebec* [1998] 2 SCR 217 at para 52, 161 DLR
    (4th) 385 [*Secession Reference*]; *Toronto (City) v Ontario (Attorney
    General)*, 2021 SCC 34 at para 55, Wagner CJ and Brown J.

19 *Secession Reference*, para 62.

20 Ibid., para 68.

21 Ibid., para 67.

22 See further the contributions by Caitlin Salvino, this volume, chapter 18.

23 Leckey and Mendelsohn, "Notwithstanding Clause," 203–9.

24 [1988] 2 SCR 712, 54 DLR (4th) 577 [*Ford*].

25 *Ford*, 741 (The legislature "may not be in a position to judge with any
    degree of certainty" which Charter provisions might be successfully   .
    invoked against legislation).

26 There are varying readings of *Ford*. Webber, Mendelsohn, and I read it as
    addressing the conditions a legislature must meet to activate the notwith-
    standing clause (Webber, "Notwithstanding Rights," 536; Leckey and
    Mendelsohn, "Notwithstanding Clause," 191 n10), leaving it open for a
    court to examine a protected law's impact on rights (see similarly Adams
    and Bower, "Notwithstanding History," 141). I know no basis for think-
    ing that the justices hearing *Ford* considered this possibility, distinct from
    "substantive review of the legislative policy in exercising the override
    authority in a particular case" (*Ford*, 740), let alone that they rejected it.
    But St-Hilaire, Foccroulle Ménard, and Dutrisac, in this volume, chapter
    6, read *Ford* otherwise. They suggest diplomatically that any "honest
    reading" of the appeal yields the conclusion that section 33 makes rights
    inapplicable to the protected legislation, preventing any judicial declara-
    tion that a protected law infringes rights.

27 Adams and Bower, "Notwithstanding History," 142.

28 Lorraine Eisenstat Weinrib, "Learning to Live with the Override," *McGill
    Law Journal* 35, no. 3 (1990): 541–71, 556 (criticizing *Ford* for not
    requiring the legislature to specify the impact on rights in the legislation
    activating the notwithstanding clause).

29 For the view of section 33 as a safety valve on the part of a premier who
    negotiated the Charter, see Dwight Newman, "Canada's Notwithstanding
    Clause, Dialogue, and Constitutional Identities," in *Constitutional Dialogue:
    Rights, Democracy, Institutions*, eds. Geoffrey Sigalet, Gregoire Webber, and
    Rosalind Dixon (Cambridge: Cambridge University Press, 2019), 209–18,
    discussing Peter Lougheed, "Why a Notwithstanding Clause?" *Points of*

View-Centre for Constitutional Studies 6, no. 17 (1998), publishing the
Marv Leitch QC Lecture, delivered at the University of Calgary, 20
November 1991. For scholarly presentation of the proposition that a legisla-
ture should not use section 33 upstream of litigation, see, for example,
Donna Greschner and Ken Norman, "The Courts and Section 33," *Queen's
Law Journal* 12, no. 2 (1987): 155–98, 187–97. For argument that a legisla-
ture should not use section 33 until the Supreme Court of Canada has ruled
on the law, allowing "courts [to] deliberate through judicial decisions and
legislatures [to] decide whether to accept the courts' conclusions," see Tsvi
Kahana, "Understanding the Notwithstanding Mechanism," *University of
Toronto Law Journal* 52, no. 2 (2002): 221–74, 225.

30 Adams and Bower, "Notwithstanding History," 142.
31 Leckey and Mendelsohn, "Notwithstanding Clause," 213.
32 Bill 21, An Act Respecting the Laicity of the State, SQ 2019, c 12 [Bill 21].
33 Kahana, "Understanding the Notwithstanding Mechanism," 260–5; For
    an updating of Kahana's survey of uses of the notwithstanding clause, see
    Caitlin Salvino, "A Tool of Last Resort: A Comprehensive Account of the
    Notwithstanding Clause Political Uses 1982–2021," *Journal of
    Parliamentary and Political Law* 16, no. 1 (2022): 11–58.
34 Sigalet, "Legislated Rights as Trumps."
35 *Good Spirit School Division No 204 v Christ the Teacher Roman Catholic
    Separate School Division No 212*, 2017 SKQB 109, [2017] 9 WWR 673.
36 Constitution Act, 1867 (UK), 30 & 31 Vict, c 3, s 93, reprinted in RSC
    1985, App II, No 5; The Saskatchewan Act, 1905, 4–5 Edw VII, c 42
    (Can), ss 3, 17(1), reprinted in RSC 1985, App II, No 21.
37 *Saskatchewan v Good Spirit School Division No 204*, 2020 SKCA 34, 445
    DLR (4th) 179.
38 SS 1995, c E-0.2.
39 The School Choice Protection Act, SS 2018, c 39, s 3.
40 CQLR c C-11.
41 An Act to Amend the Charter of the French Language, SQ 1988, c 54, s
    10.
42 Bill 21, An Act Respecting the Laicity of the State, section 34.
43 Bill 96, An Act Respecting French, the Official and Common Language of
    Québec, SQ 2022, c 14, s 217. The activation of the notwithstanding
    clause, in that provision, refers to "this Act and the amendments it makes,
    other than those made by sections 1 to 122," but ss 1–122 are shielded
    from the Canadian Charter by section 121's insertion into the Charter of
    the French Language of a new section 214 that activates the notwithstand-
    ing clause for that instrument.

44 Bill 307, Protecting Elections and Defending Democracy Act, 2021, SO
     2021, c 31, s 4, amending the Election Finances Act, RSO 1990, c E7.
     For a challenge based on section 3 of the Canadian Charter, see *Working
     Families Coalition (Canada) Inc v Ontario*, 2023 ONCA 139, leave to
     appeal granted, SCC File No 40725 (9 November 2023).

45 Bill 11, An Act Respecting Proof of Immunization, 59th Leg, 3rd Sess
     (defeated on third reading, 18 June 2020). The invocation of the notwith-
     standing clause was removed by the Standing Committee on Economic
     Policy, on 16 June 2020. Canadian Press, "New Brunswick committee
     drops notwithstanding clause from vaccination bill," CTV News
     (17 June 2020), https://atlantic.ctvnews.ca/new-brunswick-committee-drops-
     notwithstanding-clause-from-vaccination-bill-1.4987933.

46 Tsvi Kahana, "The Notwithstanding Mechanism and Public Discussion:
     Lessons from the Ignored Practices of Section 33 of the Charter,"
     Canadian Public Administration 44, no. 3 (September 2001): 255–91, 281
     n1; See further Henri Brun, Guy Tremblay, and Eugénie Brouillet, *Droit
     constitutionnel*, 6th ed. (Cowansville, QC: Yvon Blais, 2014), 969, para
     XII–2.17; See also Benoît Pelletier, this volume, chapter 9.

47 Kahana, "Understanding the Notwithstanding Mechanism," 260–5.

48 Salvino, "A Tool of Last Resort," 17.

49 An Act to Amend the Charter of the French Language, SQ 1988, c 54, s
     10.

50 Bill 28, Keeping Students in Class Act, 2022, SO 2022, c 19, s 13(1),
     repealed by Bill 35, Keeping Students in Class Repeal Act, 2022, SO 2022,
     c 20.

51 See, for example, Weinrib, "Learning to Live," 599.

52 See, for example, Pierre Trudel, "L'abus de dérogation," *Le Devoir,* 28
     September 2021, https://www.ledevoir.com/opinion/chroniques/635823/
     chronique-l-abus-de-derogation [author's translation of *"mur à mur"*].

53 While it falls outside this volume's focus on section 33 of the Canadian
     Charter, legislation can simultaneously trigger a notwithstanding mechan-
     ism in a quasi-constitutional rights instrument, such as the Canadian Bill
     of Rights, SC 1960, c 44, Quebec's Charter of Human Rights and
     Freedoms, CQLR c C-12 [Quebec Charter], or the human-rights code of
     another province. Enactment by the National Assembly of legislation that
     operates notwithstanding the Quebec Charter is unrelated to concerns
     about the patriation process in the early 1980s and the consequent
     (il)legitimacy of the Canadian Charter. For discussion of the idea of
     "autonomizing" the Quebec Charter by allowing it to operate while acti-
     vating section 33 of the Canadian Charter, see Louis-Philippe Lampron,

"La Loi sur la laïcité de l'État et les conditions de la fondation juridique d'un modèle interculturel au Québec," *Canadian Journal of Law and Society* 36, no. 2 (2021): 323–37, 330.

54 Steve Rukavina, "Legal Experts Fact-Check Quebec Ad Campaign That Aims to Correct 'Falsehoods' on Controversial Language Law," CBC News, 3 June 2022, https://www.cbc.ca/news/canada/montreal/legal-experts-fact-check-quebec-ad-campaign-that-aims-to-correct-falsehoods-on-controversial-language-law-1.6474927.

55 Bill 21, An Act Respecting the Laicity of the State, section 2.

56 In this volume.

57 Sigalet, given his laudable attention to political morality and democratic will, might be interested by polling data on Bill 21 from August 2022. The survey produced by the Association for Canadian Studies, in collaboration with SurveyMonkey and polling house Léger, reported that 64.5 per cent of Quebecers surveyed believed that it would be important for the Supreme Court of Canada to give its opinion as to whether Bill 21 is discriminatory; only 46.7 per cent of those surveyed would continue to support the law if the courts "confirmed" that it violated the charters of rights and freedoms. Association d'études canadiennes, *La Loi 21 : Discours, perceptions & impacts, Sondage* AEC *mai-juin 2022*, https://acs-metropolis.ca/wp-content/uploads/2022/08/Rapport_Sondage-Loi-21_AEC_Leger-12.pdf; see also Émilie Nicolas, "Les mythes et réalités de la loi 21," *Le Devoir*, 11 August 2022, https://www.ledevoir.com/opinion/chroniques/743721/les-mythes-et-realites-de-la-loi-21.

58 Weinrib, "Learning to Live," 556.

59 *Canada (Attorney General) v Bedford*, 2013 SCC 72, [2013] 3 SCR 1101 at para 44.

60 It may also frustrate the role of the courts as interpreters of Charter rights, even if – by a conception of coordinate construction – they are not the sole interpreters. See Dennis Baker, *Not Quite Supreme: The Courts and Coordinate Constitutional Interpretation* (Montreal: McGill-Queen's University Press, 2010. See also Christopher Manfredi, this volume, chapter 8. For the view that a pre-emptive use – upstream of a law's application to facts by a court – reflects the civilian tradition's preference for abstract norms, see Guillaume Rousseau and François Côté, this volume, chapter 10.

61 *Hak c Procureur général du Québec*, 2021 QCCS 1466 at para 770 (appeal to QCCA under reserve) [author's translation]. Blanchard J emphasized that, "Remarkably and relevantly, Bill 21 was the first legislation to derogate simultaneously from sections 1 to 38 of the Quebec Charter and

section 2 and 7 to 15 of the Canadian Charter" (para 768 [author's translation]).

62 *Hak c Procureur général du Québec*, para 768 [author's translation].

63 Or, to draw on Tsvi Kahana's contribution in this volume, the degree of "tyranny" shown by the legislature.

64 Newman's understanding by which section 33 was "not an incoherent compromise" ("Canada's Notwithstanding Clause," 214) contrasts with readings of section 33 as less principled. See, for example, Janet L. Hiebert, "The Notwithstanding Clause: Why Non-use Does Not Necessarily Equate with Abiding by Judicial Norms" in *The Oxford Handbook of the Canadian Constitution*, eds. Peter Oliver, Patrick Macklem, and Nathalie Des Rosiers (New York: Oxford University Press, 2017), 695 ("not the product of any grand normative theory about constitutional design").

65 Newman, "Canada's Notwithstanding Clause," 216.

66 Ibid., 218; See also Adams and Bower, "Notwithstanding History," 138–9.

67 Adams and Bower, 142. See also 139.

68 Sigalet, "The Truck," 209. See also: Adams and Bower, "Notwithstanding History," 222 ("a legitimate way for legislatures to express disagreements about rights"); Sigalet, "Legislated Rights as Trumps" ("capacity to trump judicial mistakes concerning the just meaning of rights as they relate to different persons and states of affairs"; "use the notwithstanding clause to correct abuses of judicial review that threaten to undemocratically replace reasonable legislative constructions of rights").

69 Sigalet, "The Truck," 211. See also 221 ("use notwithstanding declarations in ways that deliberately seek to protect rights by specifying their boundaries").

70 Sigalet, "The Truck," 222; Sigalet, "Legislated Rights as Trumps" ("ability to enact legislative interpretations of rights using the notwithstanding clause"); Sigalet, this volume, chapter 7 (legislatures having "the power and responsibility to construct the meaning of Charter rights").

71 Robert Leckey, "Bill 96: An Attack on Justice and Fundamental Rights," *Policy Options*, 20 May 2022, https://policyoptions.irpp.org/magazines/may-2022/bill-96-fundamental-rights/.

72 Hogg and Wright, *Constitutional Law of Canada*, 39–15.

73 Newman, "Canada's Notwithstanding Clause," 228–9. Mark Mancini and Geoffrey Sigalet write that the Saskatchewan legislature's "use of the notwithstanding clause shows how it can be employed in a way that constructs and protects reasonable understandings of Charter rights." "What

Constitutes the Legitimate Use of the Notwithstanding Clause?" *Policy Options*, 20 January 2020, https://policyoptions.irpp.org/magazines/january-2020/what-constitutes-the-legitimate-use-of-the-notwithstanding-clause/).

74 Sigalet, "Legislated Rights as Trumps." See also Newman, "Canada's Notwithstanding Clause" (legislatures jointly responsible with courts "to establish the valid scope of the right to religiously neutral state action as it relates to the right of historically protected denominations to public funds").

75 Newman, "Canada's Notwithstanding Clause," 229.

76 Ibid.

77 Ibid. See, for example: Rebecca Jones, Nathaniel Reilly, and Colleen Sheppard, "Contesting Discrimination in Quebec's Bill 21: Constitutional Limits on Opting out of Human Rights," *Directions* (2019); Frédéric Mégret, "Lost in Translation? Bill 21, Human Rights and the Margin of Appreciation," *McGill Law Journal* 66, no. 1 (2020): 213–52; Frédéric Mégret, "Ban on Religious Symbols in the Public Service: Quebec's Bill 21 in a Global Pluralist Perspective," *Global Constitutionalism* 11, no. 2 (2022): 217–48.

78 See the introduction to Grégoire Webber, this volume, chapter 4.

79 For our proposal that "the superior courts' role as the guardians of the Constitution and their duty to consider rights claims in appropriate cases may require them to exit their comfort zone," see Leckey and Mendelsohn, "Notwithstanding Clause," 211.

6

Judicial Declarations Notwithstanding the Use of the Notwithstanding Clause? A Response to a (Non-)Rejoinder

Maxime St-Hilaire, Xavier Foccroulle Ménard, and Antoine Dutrisac

Section 33 of the Canadian Charter of Rights and Freedom is trending again.[1] Since 2018, provincial legislatures across Canada have invoked its use five times, and at least twice successfully: Quebec's An Act Respecting the Laicity of the State[2] passed and was brought into force in 2019 and, in 2021, the same occurred with Ontario's Protecting Elections and Defending Democracy Act, 2021.[3] More recently, section 33 has been invoked by the legislature in Quebec in enacting An Act Respecting French, the Official and Common Language of Quebec.[4] In parallel to these legislative activities, a new creative doctrinal approach to section 33 has developed, seeking to disrupt the historically shared understanding and conceptualization of the so-called "notwithstanding clause." The takeaway of such an approach is that the use of section 33 in legislation does not prevent courts from declaring an inconsistency between the legislation and Charter rights and freedoms. Two of us first reviewed, discussed, and analyzed these developments at their beginnings in our 2020 article "Nothing to Declare,"[5] in which we dismissed these novel arguments as valid alternatives to the reasons given by the Supreme Court of Canada in the *Ford* decision in 1988.[6] The shared position always has been that section 33 suspends the application of the provisions guaranteeing the rights and freedoms in the first place so that there is no inconsistency with rights and freedoms to declare.

Since then, those advancing these novel arguments on section 33 doubled down on their creativity and further developed their doctrinal approach. Some of our initial objections were addressed, and some were left unanswered. More worrying, they now provide irreconcilable arguments substantiated by opposing methodologies.[7] This schism reveals a great difficulty flowing from the fact that *Ford* was correctly decided and that the notwithstanding clause takes out any possibility of judicial review between given legislative provisions and the targeted Charter provisions – courts indeed must act as if these were simply not found in the Charter. To do justice to the seriousness of this debate and to the main interlocutors involved, it is crucial to clearly review, discuss, and analyze once more all of the arguments, objections, and precise responses presented to date, carefully tracking the chronological unfolding of the debate at hand. We will demonstrate how none of the novel arguments advanced are ultimately convincing and why the Supreme Court of Canada should maintain its interpretation of section 33 as set out in *Ford*.

1. THE RISING DEBATE ON THE NOTWITHSTANDING CLAUSE

1.1 An Initial Challenge to the Orthodox Interpretation

A new challenge to the orthodox interpretation of the effects of the notwithstanding clause was first brought forth by professors Grégoire Webber and Robert Leckey as well as lawyer Eric Mendelsohn in their 2019 blog entry, "The faulty received wisdom around the notwithstanding clause."[8] In turn, Leonid Sirota jumped into the fray in support of this position in a blog post titled "Concurring Opinion."[9] Leckey then developed his own position further in his short paper, "Advocacy Notwithstanding the Notwithstanding Clause."[10] The initial challenge is important because it is the source of what will develop into a serious debate on the effects of the notwithstanding clause. As the debate unfolds, we will note departures in the current positions of the main participants from the initial challenge presented. From here then, we are in a better position to track the various discussions, arguments, and responses received to date so as to not obscure a sound conclusion on how to interpret the notwithstanding clause.

Five distinct arguments were made by the authors: (1) a textualist interpretation of the term "operation" in section 33(2) of the Charter; (2) a jurisprudential argument based on *Ford*; (3) a jurisprudential argument based on *Khadr*;[11] (4) a comparative law argument based on declarations of incompatibility in the United Kingdom, New Zealand, and Australia; and finally (5) a law of remedies argument pertaining to the applicability of section 24 of the Charter.

The first argument, albeit textualist in nature, is literalist as it purely relies on the wording of section 33(2) of the Charter, which states that an act in respect of which a declaration under section 33(1) is made "shall have such operation as it would have but for the provision of this Charter referred to in the declaration."[12] "Operation" here is to be read along with section 52 of the Constitution Act, 1982, which states that a provision inconsistent with the Charter has "no force or effect," or according to the French version: *"rend inopérantes les dispositions incompatibles."* They claim this indicates that the effect of the notwithstanding clause is to shield only the operation of legislation, "even if that legislation violates a right or freedom guaranteed in the Charter," so that courts still hold the power to examine the inconsistency of legislation subject to a declaration under section 33 and therefore "declare that the law violates rights."[13] They support this narrow, literalist interpretation by highlighting the absence of the words "override" or "judicial review" in the text of section 33.

The second argument supporting their interpretation of section 33 is a particular reading of the Supreme Court of Canada's ruling in *Ford*. While they recognize *Ford* is the fullest discussion of section 33 found in our case law to date, they affirm that it did not address the *effects* of deploying the notwithstanding provision.[14] In *Ford*, they claim that the court was not asked about the "significance of shielding a law's operation,"[15] and did not rule on it. While not fully fleshed out at this stage of the debate, their reliance on the incompleteness of the court's examination of section 33 in *Ford* looms large in all of their arguments, allowing them to frame their novel interpretation as part of the yet uncharted territory of the "operation" of section 33, and not as a revised reading of long-established case law.

The third argument is based on a particular reading of the *Khadr* decision. The Supreme Court of Canada concluded in *Khadr* that the appropriate remedy for the infringement on the section 7 rights of the respondent Omar Ahmed Khadr was a declaratory one, leaving it to the government to "decide how best to respond to this

judgement."[16] This use of a declaratory relief by the court in *Khadr*
is presented as an example of the court's "duty to say what the law
is"[17] because the Supreme Court of Canada pronounces itself on the
inconsistency of a governmental decision with the Charter, despite
not providing specific remedies. In their analogy with section 33, the
"shield" of the notwithstanding declaration is akin to the restraint
shown by the court when exercising constitutional remedial powers
to intervene in matters of foreign affairs.[18] In both cases, a limitation
on remedies is seen as giving ample room to the court to declare the
violation of rights. Read in this light, the *Khadr* decision represents
an irreducible power of the court to declare inconsistency.

The fourth argument is comparative as it relies on the human rights
regime of the United Kingdom, New Zealand, and Australia, which
all share the possibility for judges to declare legislation incompatible
with rights without "affecting the operation of the legislation."[19]
From the legal regimes of these members of the commonwealth,[20]
the authors conclude that a narrow interpretation of section 33 is
fully consistent with the respect for parliamentary supremacy since
the aforementioned jurisdictions share this principle with Canada.

This fifth argument was brought forth by Sirota[21] and was taken up
and expanded by Leckey.[22] Sirota highlights that the Charter general
remedy clause at section 24 is not subject to section 33. It follows, he
argues, that plaintiffs would not be barred from obtaining a judicial
declaration of inconsistency with rights that are validly targeted by
a section 33 declaration as remedy, since judges "must still strive to
issue a 'just' remedy within the constraints of section 33."[23] In his
paper, Leckey builds upon this argument and claims that a section
24(1) remedy could go as far as to award damages. It is significant
for him that there are instances where state action is deemed valid
and yet may nevertheless give rise to civil liability.[24] Leckey argues
that the same logic applies to section 33.

1.2 Rebuttal of the Initial Challenge: There is Nothing to Declare

Each of these initial arguments has been answered by two of us.[25]
We shall reiterate.

The response to the first argument is anchored in the long-standing
principle of a purpose-based – "purposive" or even "teleological" –
interpretation of the Charter,[26] and in the correlative genuine concern

for the meaning of the text to be informed by context, as opposed to a literalist approach. In assessing the purpose of a provision, the overall scheme and architecture of the provision itself and of the Constitution as a whole cannot be ignored.[27] The literalist reading of section 33(2), as presented by Webber, Leckey, and Mendelsohn, cannot on its own reveal the purpose of the notwithstanding clause when the overall scheme of the provision and of the Charter confirms a different reading. As we put it in "Nothing to Declare," "The exclusion of any substantive review (confirmed by the Supreme Court of Canada in *Ford*), the requirement of an express declaration of intent, and the temporary nature of the exception all support the argument that the function of section 33 is to allow legislators to exempt legislative provisions from any judicial debate on their respect for the constitutional rights from which they derogate."[28] This interpretation is supplemented by taking into account the vast "extrinsic evidence" of the framers intent, as examined by Dwight Newman, revealing that section 33 was intended as a way for Parliament and provincial legislatures to temporarily suspend judicial review.[29] What seems to us an unbiased and well-balanced use of the recognized interpretational tools for constitutional texts confirms that section 33 should be construed as barring any judicial review between the legislation invoking it and the Charter provisions to which it is excepting from.

The jurisprudential argument based on *Ford* is answered by making clear *why* the court did not contemplate making a declaration about the inconsistency of section 58 of the Charter of the French Language and 2b of the Charter. The court explicitly refused to answer the inconsistency question because of the valid declaration of exception to sections 2 and 7 to 15 of the Charter.[30] The insistence of the judges to distinguish between exception to rights and limitation under section 1, the acceptance by the court of an "omnibus clause" that would bar all legislation from the same provincial parliament from review under 2 and 7 to 15 of the Charter, the refusal to consider any substantial condition to the exercise of section 33, all indicates that the "significance" of section 33 was fully taken into account in *Ford* – it was clearly seen as temporarily "overriding" or "suspending the application" of the Charter provision targeted by a valid declaration under section 33. The court did consider the effect of section 33, and ruled that it did not have the power to substantively review the provisions of the Charter of the French Language under Charter rights that were validly suspended.

The third argument of Webber, Leckey, and Mendelsohn relying on *Khadr* misses the mark. While courts can, within their jurisdiction, declare violations of rights instead of granting the remedy sought, nothing demonstrates or even suggests that limitations on remedies can be analogous to the notwithstanding clause. In *Khadr*, the section 7 provisions of the Charter had not been subject to a derogation, and nothing in their reasoning helps bridge the conceptual gap between hypothetical infringements on derogated provisions and the declaratory powers of the courts in cases where remedies are limited. To put it simply, had section 7 provisions been validly derogated from in *Khadr*, the court could not and, in all likelihood, would not have granted a declaratory relief.

Our understanding here is consistent with the historical reluctance of the Anglo-American legal tradition toward judicial declarations, which were inspired by civilist systems.[31] The long-established principle of "no right without a remedy" (*ubi jus ibi remedium*)[32] has the corollary of "no remedy without rights," which highlights how foreign to the common law a declaration of incompatibility with rights that are temporarily inapplicable is. That is why the court in *Ewert*[33] cited "jurisdiction" and the necessity for the dispute before the courts to be "real and not theoretical" as criteria to consider a judicial declaration, otherwise a "narrow remedy." Our position is that courts have no jurisdiction to make declarations based on provisions (be they constitutional, statutory, or regulatory) which have validly been made temporarily inapplicable.

The comparative argument also fails due to the particulars of the constitutional regimes and the hierarchical differences between the legal instruments being compared. Although all legal instruments involved contain rights-bearing provisions, it is a misleading analogy to compare human rights regimes governed by the principle of parliamentary sovereignty with our supra-legislative constitutional protection of human rights in the Charter. Both the British Human Rights Act, 1998[34] and the New Zealand Bill of Rights Act, 1990 (NZBRA)[35] are statutes enacted by Parliament. These have no formal constitutional status. As for the targeted provisions themselves, only section 4 of the British statute allows for the courts to make a "declaration of incompatibility" which "does not affect the validity, continuing operation or enforcement of the provision in respect of which it is given."[36] The NZBRA only provides that the courts may not declare any legislative act "impliedly repealed or revoked, or to be in any way invalid or ineffective."[37] Under these ordinary statutory regimes, such declaratory power of courts ensure that "applicable" rights do not remain without any judicial remedy. This is different from the Charter regime in Canada, where remedy is always available for violations of guaranteed rights and freedoms.

The British Human Rights Act and NZBRA provisions deal with conflicting ordinary laws of the same hierarchical level, enabling the courts, despite the inherent validity and operation of the subsequent law, to declare an inconsistency. Conversely, section 33 suspends the application of certain constitutional provisions entirely; indeed, section 33 temporarily strips the supra-legislative instrument of its default invalidating power that stems from any inconsistency between ordinary legislation and the Constitution precisely because there can be no inconsistency with an inapplicable provision. A "horizontal" conflict of laws, such as one in the United Kingdom or New Zealand, can be resolved in a number of ways since inconsistency between statutes enacted by the same body does not make either invalid. Although the common law and interpretation statutes supply rules for resolving conflicts, legislatures can expressly depart from them by providing that a legislation prevail over any other legislation with which they conflict, as is the case with the Human Rights Act, 1998. The best comparison is that of the paramountcy doctrine: the legislation over which another has prevailed continues to exist, albeit deprived of legal effect. When a legislation conflicts with Charter provisions, there is a "vertical" conflict instead, in which case it is not a possibility but a duty of the court placed in front of such constitutional inconsistency to recognize the inferior provisions as invalid, per section 52 of the Charter.[38] The same default invalidating force of a supra-legislative instrument is not present in the British Human Rights Act nor in the NZBRA, meaning that, again contrary to the Charter, the declaratory power each contains is a poor example of how an inconsistent, thus invalid, norm can nevertheless be operable in a "rigid" constitutional framework like Webber, Leckey, and Mendelsohn suggest.

On the fifth argument, the fact that section 24 is not subject to section 33 does not support the claim that courts may grant a declaration or another remedy despite the valid use of section 33.[39] There is no need to include section 24 among the provisions that can be suspended because, as the heading above sections 32–33 indicates, section 33 relates to the "application of the Charter," and section 24, as per its heading, relates to its "enforcement." That section 33 allows the temporary exception of legislation to the application of certain Charter provisions, which are themselves substantive, means that there is no enforcement possible. We cannot expect from the constituent authority to make every logical implication explicit. The reasoning goes as follows: since there is no application of the right-bearing provision as if the provision was not included in the Charter at all, there can be no judicial application of the guaranteed right(s), and therefore there is no "declaration" or other judicial remedy possible. We invited readers to a thought experiment on 24(2):[40] Within this view, would the courts have the power to exclude evidence obtained in "violation" of Charter rights-provisions from which statutory provisions are validly excepted? The answer should, of course, remain a resounding no.

The responses given in "Nothing to Declare" were meant to address the formulations of the initial challenge directly, and in this they might not have been stated in their purest form. Some of the aforementioned responses are fundamental, while some are just incidental implications. For the sake of clarity, we shall summarize. The overall architecture of the Charter, coupled with a genuine concern for the meaning of the text to be informed by context and the extrinsic evidence of the framers' intent, all suggest that the purpose of section 33 is to temporarily suspend the application of the provisions that are validly derogated from and remove them from judicial debate – where the validity of the declaration of derogation itself is only a matter of form, as was decided in *Ford*. Accordingly, no remedy whatsoever can be enforced following section 24, and no judicial declaration of inconsistency can be made. This is in line with the long tradition of the common law regarding remedies' relation to rights and with the established case law. An honest reading of *Ford* reveals that the Supreme Court of Canada's jurisprudence supports this interpretation. The decision not to substantially review the consistency of the Charter of the French Language with the Charter is derived from the court's constitutional interpretation of the effects and substance of section 33. Foreign examples from human rights in regimes where parliamentary sovereignty does not know any rigid constitutional limits cannot be imported into the Canadian context because these are not found in a supra-legislative instrument that carves out an exception to rights-provisions in any way.

2. THE CURRENT DEBATE ON THE NOTWITHSTANDING CLAUSE

We now turn to a second series of articles that developed further this novel interpretation of the notwithstanding clause and partially answered some of our objections. Since the initial challenge in 2019, however, the main participants now provide irreconcilable and, at times, openly conflicting arguments substantiated by opposing methodologies. In one camp, Webber led the way with his article "Notwithstanding Rights, Review or Remedy?"[41] in which he clarified and fully developed his literalist approach focusing on the word "operation" found at section 33(2). In the other camp, Leckey and Mendelsohn opted for a broader discussion on "how courts *should* decide when to scrutinize protected laws" in their more recent article, "The Notwithstanding Clause: Legislature, Courts, and the Electorate,"[42] drawing on the "unwritten" principles of the Constitution. These two different approaches presently include conceptual breaking points and inconsistencies with the initial challenge, which we consider symptoms of the untenable nature of their initial position. In what follows, we will review their current view against what they brought forward in their initial challenge and identify all changes and developments.

2.1 The Term "Operation" at Section 33(2)

In "Notwithstanding Remedy," Webber suggests three possible answers to the following question: To what does the notwithstanding clause of the Charter make exception? Orthodox answers are that section 33 allows legislatures to suspend the supra-legislative rights and freedoms as guaranteed by the Charter provisions in sections 2 and 7 to 15, or that it protects the enacted legislation from judicial review in relation to these questions or both.[43] Webber contends instead that the notwithstanding clause makes exception to the remedy that would normally flow from a finding of inconsistency between the legislation provisions and the Charter rights

and freedoms – which remedy is the striking down of the legislation provisions under section 52 of the Charter, also known as the
supremacy clause.

This alternative answer is admittedly novel and dissident. Webber
himself says that while there is no consensus on the purpose of
section 33, we do have an uncritical broad-yet-shallow consensus
on its effects.[44] In fact, he claims, section 33(2) has not been thor-
oughly interpreted.[45] He does not explicitly explain exactly what
this consensus is about either. Is section 33 an exception to rights
or to judicial review? Further, he writes that, "The answers 'notwithstanding rights' and 'notwithstanding review' together more or
less exhaust what is said about the legal effect of the clause when
it is invoked by the legislature.[46] Indeed, so settled are these two
answers that they are sometimes appealed to interchangeably, the
one being the consequence of the other."[47] The range of views on
the effects of the notwithstanding clause appears to be too broad
even to call it a consensus.[48]

Webber supports his unorthodox stance by insisting on the fact that
words like "override" and "derogation" (in French, "dérogation"),
which would lend support to the orthodox views, are "not found in
the wording of the clause itself."[49] The text of section 33, in fact, uses
the word "operate," which relates to the remedy of rendering legislation inconsistent with the Charter of "no force and effect" found
at section 52, effectively striking down such legislation. Indeed, the
word "operate" in section 33(2) is key in indicating that the legal
effect of the clause is focused on "legislation and its operation and
not [on] rights or review."[50] Webber invokes the Supreme Court of
Canada's analytical sequence of the supremacy clause in *Manitoba
Language Rights Reference*, which starts with the inconsistency of
the legislation with the Charter provisions, to the invalidity of such
inconsistent legislation, and to its inoperability.[51] On the analytical
sequence leading to the striking down, or "inoperability" as coined,
courts must first determine inconsistency, then invalidity, and then
inoperability – where he claims that any step of the sequence may be
separated from the others. The term operation is "a term of art"[52]
that specifically refers to the latter step of the analytical sequence,
meaning that the notwithstanding clause only targets the stage of
"inoperability," leaving the possibility for the courts to declare any
inconsistency with provisions that are validly derogated from. In

other words, with the use of "operate," section 33(2) refers to the latter part of the sequence and protects statutes invoking it from being inoperable. As a consequence, the use of the word "operate" and its related notion of "operation" at section 33(2) means, for Webber, that the effects of the notwithstanding clause are to make exception to the striking-down remedy of section 52 upon a finding of inconsistency with Charter rights and freedoms.

This conclusion raises eyebrows. The correct reading of the word "operate" here is that the statutory provisions shall operate temporarily without the application of specific Charter provisions. That is, section 33 renders the targeted Charter provisions inapplicable to a given legislation, which means that the same Charter provisions cannot be applied to them by any court whatsoever. In other words, the statute provisions will have the effect they would have "but for the provision of this Charter referred to in the declaration," and one of the effects is that these statute provisions will not be subject to any judicial remedy based on an inapplicable Charter provision.

What strikes immediately to the careful reader is the use of the term "provision" when referring to the part of the Charter from which a legislation may derogate upon a legislature declaring so. Nowhere in the text of the notwithstanding clause can the notions of "rights" or "freedoms" can be found. To make his argument, Webber suggests that the focus of section 33(2) "is on legislation and its operation," but he omits to mention "provision," which arguably is, in fact, the most important term. Citing section 33 is necessary:

33 (1) Parliament or the legislature of a province may expressly declare in an Act of Parliament or of the legislature, as the case may be, that the Act or a provision thereof shall operate notwithstanding a provision included in section 2 or sections 7 to 15 of this Charter.
(2) An Act or a provision of an Act in respect of which a declaration made under this section is in effect shall have such operation as it would have but for the provision of this Charter referred to in the declaration.[53]

To emphasize the word "provision" just as much as Webber emphasizes "operation" poses a problem for his suggestion that the effect of the notwithstanding clause is to "secure the operation of legislation despite such legislation's inconsistency with targeted rights and freedoms and despite the legislation's invalidity that follows from such inconsistency."[54] Under Webber's interpretation, it is the violation of targeted Charter rights and freedoms by the protected legislation that begins the reasoning sequence with inconsistency, moving to invalidity, and ending with inoperability. The problem here is that no violation of rights or freedoms is conceptually possible to start the sequence in the first place because the legislation invoking section 33 is derogating from the application of the provisions that guarantee these very rights and freedoms. If the provisions crystallizing the rights or freedoms in the supra-legislative instrument are targeted by section 33 and thus become not applicable, the protected legislation cannot be inconsistent in any way with the rights and freedoms guaranteed by these inapplicable provisions, nor can the protected legislation be found to be invalid. The operability question simply never arises.

As we said, instead of replying to the teleological argument, Webber comes up with a few more textual ones. Indeed, even Leckey and Mendelsohn are of the opinion that Webber "focused on the meaning of s 33(2) in isolation"[55] and that his theory "is not parsimonious."[56] Webber believes, "It is of note that the notwithstanding clause makes no reference to judicial review and is not formulated as a privative or ouster clause."[57] In doing so, Webber eludes the claim that section 33 is all about enabling legislators to temporarily take away certain specific constitutional issues or questions – that is, whether *or not* certain statutory *provisions* infringe upon certain rights, as these are protected by specific Charter provisions. The relation between a provision and the corresponding right is understood best by looking at section 1 and section 52, which respectively state that the Charter guarantees rights and freedom "set out in it," and that any law "inconsistent with the provisions" is of no force and effect. Read along with section 33, it appears that the notwithstanding clause denies the very entrenchment of rights by virtue of a Charter provision. In a way that confuses inconsistency with the supreme law (or the Constitution) with inconsistency with "rights," Webber takes for granted that when statutory provisions do not infringe Charter rights, or when they do so in a manner that is justified under section 1, then, "The notwithstanding clause serves no immediate purpose."[58] This is no argument in the context of the current debate, where it is argued that it surely serves a purpose to allow legislators to temporarily take away from courts the *question* of the consistency of given statutory provisions with identified rights-bearing provisions of the Charter.

Webber incorrectly claims that section 33 is about cases of Charter rights "infringements," and from there, he adds that the constituent authority had three choices of effect for a declaration under section 33(1) to enact at section 33(2): providing for the protected statutory provisions' *consistency* with the Charter provisions referred to in the declaration; providing for these statutory provisions' *validity* notwithstanding their infringing the rights protected by the Charter provisions referred to in the declaration; or providing (only) for these protected statutory provisions' *operation* or *effect.*[59] It is, according to him, this third choice the constituent authority made in 1982. Therefore, the argument goes, nothing prevents courts basing themselves on Charter provisions referred to in a valid and applicable declaration made under section 33(1) from declaring statutory provisions inconsistent with the Constitution and consequently invalid. We have to say again that this argument is unconvincing. In reality, the choice made in 1982 is different altogether because the effects of section 33 are to make targeted Charter provisions temporarily inapplicable to specific statutory provisions so that the question is taken away from courts entirely. Indeed, to make specific Charter provisions inapplicable means that there cannot be any inconsistency in the first place. In cases where operability is different from validity, in division of powers cases, for instance, or when two valid laws by a same legislator conflict – which is not the case as far as section 52 CA 1982 is concerned[60] – the logic is the following: in order to be applicable, a provision must first be valid, and in order for it to be operative, it must be both valid and applicable. Yet, a provision which is inapplicable cannot be operative, and a provision that is invalid cannot be applicable and, therefore, cannot be operative either. The very idea that courts will give effect to a provision that they could hold either inapplicable or invalid is alien to our law.[61] It is conceptually impossible to isolate the latter step of the analytical sequence from the first two that must precede and are necessary to it: inconsistency must happen first for invalidity to even arise, and only then can courts look into inoperability.[62] To interpret section 33 as authorizing courts to declare inconsistency with the supreme law while simultaneously preserving its "operation" is aberrant to our constitutional order.

The purpose of section 33 is to allow legislators to temporarily make certain Charter provisions inapplicable, by courts, to specific statutory provisions. Again, section 33 regards the application of the Charter, not the remedies through which courts may enforce it. In our legal system, superior courts have for now no jurisdiction to apply, be it in a "mere declaration," inapplicable Charter rights provisions, to make "declarations of inconsistency" with the very rights guaranteed. Since these provisions are not applicable and not applying, there cannot be any rights violation – there cannot be an inconsistency with Charter rights to begin with. Courts have no authority to grant a remedy where there is no right. Therefore, there is no point explicitly denying judicial review based on non-applicable provisions; moreover in our law, privative clauses only protect decisions from review, not provisions, and there cannot be any decision about inapplicable constitutional provisions to protect.

Toward the end of "Notwithstanding Remedy," Webber does address the fact that section 33 is placed under a heading titled "Application of Charter" and, more precisely, the fact that section 33(1) is placed under a marginal note titled, "Exception where express declaration" and, in French, "*Dérogation par declaration expresse.*" On this, he writes: "Such appeals to the heading title and marginal notes all beg the question. While one may readily agree that it is of some significance that the heading refers to the 'application' of the Charter and the marginal note refers to an exception' or '*dérogation*,' such references do not, without more, settle what about the Charter's application is qualified and what is made exception to or derogated from."[63] And yet, there is, in fact, a lot more. The heading under which section 33 is placed is supported by everything we have discussed thus far, and further, the fact that there is another heading, titled "Enforcement," under which section 24 is placed. If section 33 had been intended to have the purpose and effect Webber wants to give it, it would have been placed along section 24 under the "Enforcement" part.

Even if we ignore its headings altogether, the Charter has a structure – constitutive but not exhaustive of its "architecture" – and in this structure, the purpose is to allow for a limited exception to the application of the Charter. Just before section 33, section 32(1) of the Charter reads: "32(1) This Charter applies: (a) to the Parliament and government of Canada in respect of all matters within the authority of Parliament including all matters relating to the Yukon

Territory and Northwest Territories; and (b) to the legislature and government of each province in respect of all matters within the authority of the legislature of each province."

Following this general applicability provision, section 32(2) makes a temporary exception to its applicability: "32(2) Notwithstanding subsection (1), section 15 shall not have effect until three years after this section comes into force."

It is of interest to note that the French version of section 32(2) and section 33(2) both use the term "*a effet*," and both dispositions use the term "notwithstanding" to refer to excluded Charter provisions. There can be no debate around the legal effect of section 32(2): There is no judicial remedy available under section 15 until three years because it is not yet applicable. As we saw, our interlocutors defend a radically different meaning of section 33, despite the similar term used and the fact that the notwithstanding clause follows immediately after section 32 and is the only remaining section of the "Application" header.[64] This is why, even without referring to any purpose or extrinsic evidence, the meaning of section 33(2), when read coherently with the Charter as a whole and its immediate context, is to temporarily suspend the applicability of Charter provisions.

This interpretation is supported by, among other things, the fact that what precedes the notwithstanding clause matches the extrinsic evidence, the fact that there is a current consensus on its effects, from which Webber's interpretation is dissenting, and the fact that the Supreme Court of Canada confirmed this purpose in *Ford*.

Leckey and Mendelsohn conceded that our defence of the orthodox position, that is, the inapplicability of certain Charter provisions to (also) specified legislative provisions when section 33 is invoked, "fits more comfortably within the constitutional framework than does Webber's."[65] Yet they found it unpersuasive. For them, "If activating the notwithstanding clause made rights inapplicable to a protected law," it would be "redundant" to specify that the protected statutory provisions shall have their operation despite the derogation from Charter provisions. On the extrinsic evidence, Leckey and Mendelsohn notably "heed the Supreme of Canada's signal of the limited interpretive value of statements by those involved in constitutional drafting."[66] This is, for a large part, why they accompany their interpretation of section 33 with "non-technical" strongly normative political "interpretive" arguments, in a Dworkinian sense.[67] We address these novel arguments in section 2.4 below.

Leckey and Mendelsohn avoid focusing too heavily on the word "operate" and make a slightly different argument, which they claim is a simpler explanation: the use of the notwithstanding clause prevents "a protected law ... from being inconsistent with the Constitution of Canada in the sense of the supremacy clause. The effects clause thereby precludes remedies to cure inconsistency with the Constitution, such as striking down."[68] They find no need to discuss the Blackstonian analytical sequence from inconsistency, to invalidity, to inoperability implied at section 52 because it leads to a conceptual error, which they suggest Webber is guilty of: "That a law is inconsistent with the Constitution within the sense of the supremacy clause means that the Constitution objects to the law's continued operation, in whole or in part. It is a conceptual error to characterize as 'invalid' or 'inconsistent' with the Constitution a law expressly allowed by it to operate."[69] This echoes our position regarding an invalid but operable legislation as an aberration.[70] Nevertheless, for them, the necessary effects of section 33 strictly relate to section 52 and only prevent the specific remedy of striking down any legislation "inconsistent" with the Charter.[71] The argument of Leckey and Mendelsohn, therefore, leads to the same practical result: courts may declare mere incompatibility notwithstanding the notwithstanding clause since such may be grounded in section 24.[72]

This view, however, does not solve the greater conceptual problem with judicial declarations of inconsistency of a protected legislation with the Charter provisions from which it excepts application. We have already explained that for a remedy to be granted under the Charter, there must be a violation of right or freedom. Section 24(1) specifically reads: "Anyone whose rights or freedoms, as guaranteed by this Charter, have been infringed or denied may apply to a court of competent jurisdiction to obtain such remedy as the court considers appropriate and just in the circumstances." Here, no infringement with rights and freedom as guaranteed by the Charter at sections 2 and 7 to 15 can materialize because section 33 suspends the application of the targeted provisions guaranteeing these rights and freedoms. These are the real necessary effects of the notwithstanding clause. We find comfort in the conceptual justificatory gap between Webber on one side and Leckey and Mendelsohn on the other with regards to the notwithstanding clause because it ultimately reveals unstable views that are not as solidly grounded in the constitutional text as is the orthodox position that we have always defended. The correct understanding of section 33 is the most simple and broad: the use of section 33 Charter-rights violation renders *questions* temporarily non-justiciable, for it temporarily makes certain Charter provisions guaranteeing these rights outright inapplicable by courts to specific legislative provisions.

Leckey and Mendelsohn make the unlikely claim that, "The notwithstanding clause functions similarly to s. 1, signalling that the Charter, overall, regards a law's impact on rights as permissible."[73] This just ignores the possibility that section 33 is about temporarily de-judicializing some specific and limited Charter *issues* relating to actual and identified legislative provisions. Leckey and Mendelsohn's additional argument that "if activating the notwithstanding clause made rights inapplicable to a protected law," it would be "redundant" to specify that the protected statutory provisions shall have their operation despite the derogated-from Charter provisions, does not work either. Infusing in legislature and Parliament a power to make a declaration and specifying the effects of said declaration in a separate paragraph of a section is coherent: there is no redundancy between what a provision was intended to do and how it does it. It is only in being unwilling to contemplate that to have "such operation as it would have but for the provision of this Charter referred to in the declaration" at section 33(2) amounts to an immunity from substantive judicial review that one can conclude to a redundancy. In other words, the redundancy argument is question-begging and does not hold.

Even on its "technical-legal" merits, the textualist argument is not a logical reading of the Constitution as a whole. There are simply too many hoops to jump through to make it work, which leads to counterintuitive results, like affirming the similar function of section 1 and section 33, having constitutionally invalid but operable norms, a meaning of "operable" that differs from section 52 and section 33, headers that do not mean anything and rights enforced by a Charter even when the provisions guaranteeing them are absent, to name a few.

2.2 The Jurisprudential Argument Based on Ford

Webber addresses the *Ford* objection directly, recalling that in *Ford* the Supreme Court of Canada ruled that section 33 "lays down requirements of form only, and [that] there is no warrant for importing into it grounds for substantive review of the legislative policy in exercising the overriding authority in a particular case," but claiming that is a challenge that "misses its mark."[74] Why? First, because there would be a distinction to be made between substantive review of the sort implied by mere "declarations of inconsistency" and substantive review of "the legislative policy in exercising the overriding authority in a particular case."[75] Second, because, in *Ford*, the Supreme Court of Canada would have been asked to rule on only some readings of the notwithstanding clause, but not the one Webber advances, namely because the court did not analyze section 33(2).

Leckey and Mendelsohn write that "for present purposes," they "accept as authoritative the construal of s. 33(1) in *Ford*," but that "in light of ... subsequent developments and the Supreme Court of Canada's willingness for its Charter jurisprudence to evolve ... s. 33(1) is ripe for judicial reconsideration."[76] At the same time, they maintain that "the effects clause has never been construed authoritatively,"[77] for "the Court's major appeal on the notwithstanding clause, *Ford v. Quebec (Attorney General)* ... addressed the conditions in s. 33(1) that Parliament of Canada or a provincial legislature must meet to engage that mechanism's protection."[78] They add that only in *obiter dicta* in *Ontario (Attorney General) v G*[79] and *Gosselin v Quebec*[80] has the Supreme Court of Canada ever "spoken ... of a protected law as exempted from the application of Charter rights."[81]

They also acknowledge the rejection by the Supreme Court of Canada in *Ford* of the argument that, "The nature of the guaranteed right or freedom must be sufficiently drawn to the attention of the members of the legislature and of the public so that the relative seriousness of what is proposed may be perceived and reacted to through the democratic process."[82] But they opine that the rejection of this argument only applies to the dismissal of the claim that the legislator invoking section 33 must specify a law's impact on rights in its declaration. "Significantly," they write, "the Court's recognition of the informal or epistemic limits on the legislature when it activates s. 33 does not entail that, in the five-years intervals during which the effects clause precludes a remedy to cure a law's inconsistency with rights [precludes the striking down of the law], nobody should know that impact [through a judicial opinion]."[83] Straight from there, they go as far as to write that, "*Ford* thus militates against reading the effects clause [section 33(2)] as categorically barring access to the independent institution that can expertly specify a law's impact on Charter rights."[84]

It is one thing to argue against a Supreme Court of Canada's interpretation of a constitutional provision and another to misconstrue a constitutional question as "not settled" when it is. By diminishing the clarity of the court's ruling on the effect of section 33 in *Ford*, our interlocutors aim to make way for their original and unorthodox reading, but this notion that there was a silence on the effect of section 33 in *Ford* should be quickly dispelled. First, the question as set out in *Ford* was the infringement of sections 58 and 69 of the Charter of French Language on the freedom of expression guaranteed by section 2(b) of the Charter.[85] The court ruled on the consistency of said provisions with the Constitution; they had no choice but to rule on the effect of section 33. To answer to the Charter of French Language constitutional consistency, the court had to first consider the applicability of section 2(b): "The application of the Canadian Charter of Rights and Freedoms turns initially on whether there is a valid and applicable override provision."[86] A few paragraphs later, the court unequivocally affirms that in order to examine if there is inconsistency between 2(b) of the Canadian Charter and sections 58 and 69 of the Charter of French Language provisions, the notwithstanding declaration under section 33 must be invalid.[87] Again, the following question is stated at par. 21: "Is section 58 or s. 69 of the Charter of the French Language protected from the application of s. 2(b) of the Canadian Charter of Rights and Freedoms by a valid and applicable override provision enacted in conformity with s. 33 of the Canadian Charter?"[88] That question is answered by the following: "Therefore, s. 52 of An Act to amend the Charter of the French Language is a valid and subsisting exercise of the override authority conferred by s. 33 of the Canadian Charter of Rights and Freedoms that protects s. 58 of the Charter of the French Language from the application of s. 2(b) of the Canadian Charter."[89] We think it is obvious that *Ford* stated that the legal effect of section 33 is to suspend the application of the relevant Charter provisions, making it impossible to declare inconsistency. Not only was it stated, but it was necessary to rule on the constitutional questions at issue. Courts are not free to do indirectly what they cannot do directly, that is, reviewing the use of the notwithstanding clause on substantive grounds, even if the result is a mere declaration of inconsistency.[90]

Another reason not to interpret *Ford* restrictively is the fact that the court decided to rule on certain questions of applicable law at the time of the judgment instead of at the date of facts,[91] invoking the need to "settle" all questions concerning the validity of enacting the override declaration under section 33 to set precedent and guide future cases.[92] This marks an intention to make the decision a principled authoritative precedent (*arrêt de principe*) aimed at clearing up any confusion regarding the exercise of section 33. A novel doctrinal approach that sets its target on a constitutional interpretation that is uncontroversial cannot have the benefit of claiming the court's "silence" when the court's reasons do not address the specific theories it proposes years later. Granted, the court did not give a full explanation on *why* the suspension of the relevant Charter provisions was the effect of section 33, perhaps because it is self-evident from the scheme of the Constitution. But one thing is certain: *Ford* is a principled decision that ruled decisively on the effect of section 33 because the court openly affirmed its intention to settle all questions for other pending and future cases.

2.3 Unanswered Arguments

THE JURISPRUDENTIAL ARGUMENT BASED ON *KHADR*
Webber does not mention the *Khadr* case in his article. In "Nothing to Declare," two of us wrote about "suspended rights" instead of the more precise notion of "inapplicable provisions," inviting Webber to oppose that section 33 does not suspend rights, but only the operation or effect, of targeted statutory provisions. As we have developed here, we now insist on the fact that section 33 renders inapplicable said *provisions*. This makes it clear that the analogy between section 33 and remedial deference to the executive branch of the government is inadequate. There is no disagreement on the correct interpretation of *Khadr*, and the position expressed in "Nothing to Declare" was that there is no irreducible judicial power to declare violation of rights when non-applicable provisions are the legal source of these rights, which we think is not controversial. Ultimately, the relevance of *Khadr* depends on a prior conclusion as to the effects of section 33, which leads us back to the first argument discussed. It is likely that Webber agrees that there can be no judicial declaration of "inconsistency" or "incompatibility" with the Charter over a non-violation of Charter rights.

In their response, Leckey and Mendelsohn develop their argument about the irreducible power of the court to declare inconsistency, now anchoring it in the constitutional role of superior courts.[93] Although *Khadr* is not at the forefront, the basis of the argument remains unchanged: the court has made stand-alone declarations of rights when other remedies were not available, a sign of their constitutional duty as "guardians of the constitution."[94] The jurisprudential focus of the authors now switches to *Gosselin*,[95] which is viewed as significant because "it makes plain that, in appropriate cases, courts have a duty to adjudicate rights claims despite lacking the power to strike down rights-infringing laws." The authors continue to affirm that the court declining to hear such cases would amount to a "shirking of judicial responsibility."[96] The parallel drawn between a declaration of rights when faced with remedy limitations and a declaration about rights that are excepted from by section 33 is surprising considering the earlier recognition, in their section titled "Necessary effects," that the legal effect of section 33 is to prevent a protected law from amounting to inconsistency as it relates to the supremacy clause.[97]

The notion of "rights claims" in *Gosselin* echoes what the Supreme Court of Canada says in *Manitoba Metis Federation*, being that sometimes a declaratory remedy is the only way to give effect to a duty or a right.[98] The claim still needs to be founded on an applicable right and be otherwise valid. In *Manitoba Metis Federation*, the only way to give effect to the "honour of the Crown" was to issue a declaratory remedy, but that remedy is only available because the claim is not defeated by either a statute of limitations or the doctrine of laches.[99] Inapplicable provisions simply cannot make up a valid claim that can be the object of a remedy, even if it is only declaratory; in that sense, they are in the same category as claims barred by statute of limitations or founded on repealed statute.

THE COMPARATIVE LAW ARGUMENT

In his essay, Webber includes a completed part V titled "Commonwealth comparisons," which does not address our response provided on comparative law to the initial challenge. However, he did concede that, "Without doubt, Canada's Charter is unlike the other Commonwealth bills of rights in any number of respects: it is of constitutional, not statutory rank; judicial review for compliance with Charter rights and freedoms is grounded in the Constitution's supremacy clause, not in a statutory rights instrument; and the role of courts under the Charter is best described as one of strong-form review, unlike the weak-form review that animates the judicial role in United Kingdom, Australia, and New Zealand."[100] Actually, Webber goes as far as to warn his reader that, "By reviewing these Commonwealth comparisons, no attempt is made to support the reading of the notwithstanding clause set out above – that reading stands or falls on its legal-technical merits."[101] As we'll see below, Webber tried to maintain his misleading comparative argument while trying to immunize it from criticism by presenting it as philosophical, theoretical, or otherwise not "technically" legal. This is ultimately untenable: one cannot benefit from the "indirect" support for such interpretation of section 33, but not the responsibility of what such interpretation entails.

As for Leckey and Mendelsohn, they offer no greater support to the comparative law argument, as they simply overlook this argument altogether.

THE REMEDY ARGUMENT BASED ON SECTION 24
In his new essay with Mendelsohn, Leckey did not address the objections provided to his initial position, nor did he try to defend the implications of his theory for the interpretation of section 24(2) as we enjoined him. It is safe at this stage to consider this argument moot.

2.4 A Novel Argument:
The "Unwritten" Principles and Section 33(3)

The "sunset" clause at section 33(3) stipulates that a declaration under section 33(1) ceases to have effect after five years and must then be re-enacted every five years under sections 33(4) and 33(5) to continue having effect. Leckey and Mendelsohn argue that since the renewable five year time limit coincides with the maximum time between general legislative elections set by section 4 of the Charter, courts have the responsibility, and therefore the power, at the demand of a party which has standing, to advise the electorate on whether protected legislative provisions infringe rights which are protected by the Charter provisions they derogate from.[102] This argument is mainly founded on the existence of "unwritten" principles of the Constitution as set out in *Reference re Secession of Quebec*,[103] which should guide our interpretation of section 33. Although the principles of "democracy" and "protection of minorities" serve as the backbone of their argument, Leckey and Mendelsohn also explain how their argument coheres with other principles like federalism, parliamentary sovereignty, and separation of powers.[104]

Leckey and Mendelsohn seek to make their argument "interpretive," in contrast with the "legal-technical" exercise aimed at "identifying what the law is," merging the law as it is with the law as it should be, notably through invoking the unwritten constitutional principles of "democracy" and the "protection of minorities." The authors describe the interpretative content of the "democracy" principle as encompassing a consideration for "dissenting voices," which, together with the "protection of minorities" itself, they think should guide our interpretation of section 33 as preserving a space for judges to tell the population about potential infringements on targeted provisions of the Charter. We will not challenge the Dworkinian idea that legal interpretation requires one to make a "principled, context-specific"[105] choice between competing constitutional interpretations by opposing to it an impossibly pure legal positivism. We note, however, that "interpretivism" and the use of "principles" can easily multiply the subjective interpretations, many so remote from the intent of the legislative act that they cease to be the result of a serious and rigorous legal exercise and become an exercise of political activism.[106] Here, Leckey and Mendelsohn fail to strike the right equilibrium by using selective and underdeveloped meanings of both principles, "democracy" and "protection of minorities,"[107] to advance a counterintuitive reading of sections 33(2) and 33(3), which depart from the meaning of these legislative provisions. Pace Leckey and Mendelsohn, it is insufficient to simply mention these unwritten constitutional principles to conclude as to their meaning and implications. Any use of either "democracy" or "protection of minorities" in constitutional interpretation is helpful only insofar as it is grounded in a thorough study of their meaning and implications, including how they have been theorized and discussed in case law and doctrine.

Even though a same legislature may always abrogate a declaration enacted under section 33 of the Charter, we agree with Peter W. Hogg that section 33(3) "force reconsideration by the Parliament or Legislature of each exercise of the power at five-years intervals."[108] However, Leckey and Mendelsohn are taking shortcuts when they write: "Critically, five years is the maximum term of legislative bodies. Implicit in s. 33, then, is a link to general elections."[109] While general elections are held in Canada in a span of five years, many things can happen between intervals: minority governments, repealed statute, repealed declaration under section 33, and so on. In truth, the statement rests on the faulty assumption that the use of section 33 in legislation is deemed sufficiently important in itself to the electorate to constitute an election issue and will remain an active issue in the next election. The "implicit" link between the sunset clause period and the general elections process is tenuous and unconvincing. Furthermore, the asynchronicity of the judicial process with the political election cycle, as well as the inherent delays and contingency of any examination by courts, should make us doubtful of meaningfully drawing any link between electoral timing and constitutional provisions.

Even so, the principle of democracy has already been considered at the time of enactment and is reflected by the determinations in sections 33(3) and 33(4) themselves. The claim is that democracy is committed to considering dissenting voices. Thus, the voice of the judiciary is welcomed as a counterweight to majority rule.[110] There is no further investigation as to the democratic process, the making of the legislature, the nature of legislation, and the role of the judiciary in a democracy.[111] What Leckey and Mendelsohn are suggesting are additional conclusions that are not supported by the very policy considerations embodied in the text of the notwithstanding clause. The scheme of the Constitution requires giving effect to democracy as it is currently found in section 33, and to resist the judicial branch taking power that it was specifically deprived of, in the name of preserving democracy, from the very branch that is supposed to enact legislation representative of democratic will, the legislature.

Recall that Leckey and Mendelsohn emphasized to "heed the Supreme Court of Canada's signal of the limited interpretive value of statements by those involved in constitutional drafting."[112] So far, so good. We should stress, however, that "limited" does not mean "inexistent": in many past cases, the court made extensive use of extrinsic evidence, even in Charter cases.[113] There is also a notable difference between the mere "statements of those involved in constitutional drafting," and the analysis of the political compromise that was struck when the Constitution was enacted by the constituent as a corporate body, especially on an element as vital to the federative order as the notwithstanding clause. In the case of linguistic rights, the court expressed the importance for constitutional interpretation to recognize "historically important compromise"[114] – some interpretations undermine that compromise and should be discarded.[115] The court also reminds us that this compromise as the purpose of a section of the Constitution should not be defeated by a literalist reading of any of its parts: "The Confederation compromise in relation to education is found in the whole of s. 93, not in its individual parts ... But they are insulated from Charter ... as part of the Confederation compromise."[116] One could argue that language rights at section 93 of the Constitution Act of 1867 makes up a different kind of compromise than that one struck during repatriation. Indeed, it is common for scholars to speak of the Charter as a moral coming-of-age, whereas the Constitution Act of 1867 tends to be categorized as a mere political deal. Such distinction based on personal observations, however, remains unfounded, especially in the case of section 33. In truth, the Supreme Court of Canada in *Toronto (City) v. Ontario (Attorney General)* assesses the constitutional role of unwritten principles with great care for the "constitutional bargain" that is section 33.[117] As detailed by Thomas Axworthy in chapter 1, the notwithstanding clause is the *sine qua non* condition for the acceptance by the provinces of the Charter as superior legal instrument.[118] We maintain that it should be interpreted as such, taking into account the political context of its inception. The approach taken by Leckey and Mendelsohn artificially redefines a delicate compromise between provinces and Parliament, disregarding the constituent's choice at the time of patriation and enactment of the Charter in 1982.[119]

The compromise on the notwithstanding clause is clear, and the orthodox position, as well as the *Ford* decision, indicate that it always has been. As Newman demonstrates, the most reliable reflections to understand the historical purpose and meaning of the notwithstanding clause are that of prairie premiers Allan Blakeney of Saskatchewan and Peter Lougheed of Alberta because they were its primary champions and drafters.[120] Historical evidence suggests that Blakeney and Lougheed gained provincial support for section 33 as a means to contest judicial review.[121] While both premiers supported patriation without the Charter in 1981, they each came, along with Sterling Lyon of Manitoba, to support the Charter as part of patriation, provided that the notwithstanding clause be included as it was first brought forth by Lougheed in 1979 at the meeting of

First Ministers.[122] It is Lougheed, in particular, who convinced Lyon to accept the Charter with the notwithstanding clause despite the premier of Manitoba being the most opposed to it.[123] All premiers, with the exception of Quebec, got around to accepting the five-year expiration to the section 33 protection and limits on its application to democracy, mobility, and language rights.[124] We should also note that Blakeney and Lougheed ardently resisted the attempt by Bill Davis of Ontario to remove section 2 fundamental freedoms from the scope of application of the notwithstanding clause.[125]

This is why in *Vriend v. Alberta*, the Supreme Court of Canada characterized section 33 as an "override provision" and the ultimate "parliamentary safeguard."[126] In *Vriend*, the court wrote: "Moreover, s. 33, the notwithstanding clause, establishes that the final word in our constitutional structure is, in fact, left to the legislature and not the courts."[127] This argument from constitutional structure can be linked to the court's statements in *City of Toronto* about the role of unwritten principles regarding the constitutional structure of the Charter: "And that structure, recorded in the Constitution's text (as we discuss below), is interpreted with the aid of unwritten constitutional principles ... Structures are not comprised of unattached externalities; they are embodiments of their constituent, conjoined parts. The structure of our Constitution is identified by way of its actual provisions, recorded in its text."[128] Here, the interpretation of unwritten principles by Leckey and Mendelsohn runs contrary to the text structure when they are supposed to supplement it.

Fundamentally, Leckey and Mendelsohn mistakenly consider the court's opinion on legislation and constitutional rights as universally beneficial, even when not legally warranted. They write: "For the electorate to play the constitutional role assigned to it by s. 33(3), however, it needs access to information about the impact of protected laws on Charter rights. Moreover, information about the judicial conception of Charter rights and the courts' assessment of how they are impacted by protected laws can be relevant inputs."[129] We commend that our interlocutors refer to the "judicial conception of Charter rights" for this evidences that they recognize the possibility of other conceptions of these rights. Their undefended and unexamined statement is nevertheless highly contested and vulnerable to the opposite outcome. As it happens, one of the main arguments for the legitimate use of section 33 is precisely that some determinations of rights and freedoms are outside the purview of the judiciary.[130]

Leckey and Mendelsohn's position evades this debate and simply assumes that there can be no legitimate balancing of rights outside the scope of the judiciary and that the impact of a judicial declaration can only be salutary to all.[131] Therefore, they never contemplate nor respond to the claim that section 33 is, in fact, about allowing legislators to formally, temporarily, and limitedly discard this judicial conception of Charter rights. Instead, Leckey and Mendelsohn simply take for granted, under an allusive and underdeveloped "rich conception of democracy," not only that judicial insight is always relevant but that a legal constituent may not legitimately make the choice to allow legislators to temporarily de-judicialize some specific constitutional rights issues.

It is a false belief that every modern and democratic liberal state ought to have judicial review of laws following a rigid supra-legislative inventory of fundamental rights – which, to name one example, the United Kingdom ignores. It is a choice of the constituent. In 1982, ours made his choice: he accompanied our supra-legislative instrument with the temporary faculty for the legislator to suspend the judicial review of certain specific rights by rendering the targeted Charter rights-provision inapplicable to a protected legislation under section 33, in a temporary manner and under conditions of form as set out in the *Ford* decision. There are constitutionalists who are incapable of admitting that, in a rule-of-law liberal state, some questions pertaining to rights and freedoms could be de-judicialized. According to them, the opinion of the court is always welcomed. Such excess feeds the new craze, both academic and profane, of criticizing judicial review as giving rise to a "government of judges." As a consequence, we respond to Leckey's call on the "responsibility" of jurists[132] by saying that responsible jurists, starting with judges, will rather be found among those who will not answer it.

CONCLUSION

To conclude, none of the arguments as part of the initial challenge hold. Any textualist interpretation of the term "operation" in section 33(2) of the Charter must be consistent with the overall scheme and architecture of the provision itself and of the Constitution, with decided precedent – in this case, the *Ford* decision – and the massive available extrinsic evidence of its purpose. The jurisprudential argument based on *Ford* is founded on a selective reading of

Ford, which does address the effects of the notwithstanding clause and concludes that the courts may only review if the clause itself was validly used under proper conditions of form. The jurisprudential argument based on *Khadr* is not an apt analogy as there was no derogation involved. The comparative law argument does not address the specific case at hand of section 33 suspending the application of certain constitutional provisions, thus temporarily stripping the supra-legislative instrument of its default invalidating power that stems from any inconsistency between ordinary legislation and the Constitution. The law of remedies argument cannot work because section 33 is about the application of Charter provisions and is of a completely different nature than the remedies clauses found at section 24.

In addition, none of the creative arguments for section 33's new meaning and new legal effects defended by Webber or Leckey and Mendelsohn are persuasive, each failing in their own terms. The argument defended by Webber fails because he focuses on the word "operation" while overlooking that what is maintained is the full operation of protected legislation notwithstanding other Charter provisions and, therefore, notwithstanding courts. As set out in *Ford*, the effect of section 33 is to outright suspend the application of targeted Charter provisions to the protected legislation. It is conceptually impossible for a protected legislation to be judicially recognized as inconsistent with Charter rights if the very provisions guaranteeing these rights are inapplicable. There cannot be judicial review of inapplicable provisions. There is, therefore, nothing to declare. The argument of Leckey and Mendelsohn fails because their position leads to the same result as Webber, and there is nothing to declare. Their argument fails even further in that the unwritten principles argument in favour of judicial declarations of violations with Charter guarantees are founded on the value of democracy embedded in the text of section 33 as a whole, when it was, in fact, to guard democracy itself that section 33 was included as an exception mechanism to the application of targeted Charter provisions. The text reflects and embodies the democratic value of allowing the democratically elected legislatures to derogate from non-elected judicial interpretations of Charter rights and freedoms in their relationship with identified legislative provisions, leaving the courts with nothing to declare.

Everything we have discussed indicates that the orthodox position which we have continuously defended must prevail. The scheme of the Constitution of Canada, the text of all its provisions, the *Ford* decision, the extrinsic evidence, the contextual account of comparative foreign law, and every single other element worth considering to interpret section 33 lead to the conclusion that the notwithstanding clause suspends targeted rights-guaranteeing provisions of the Charter, rendering them inapplicable to protected legislation. Under these circumstances, for the times section 33 is temporarily invoked, there cannot be any judicial review of the protected legislation in relation to these inapplicable provisions, and as a consequence, there cannot be any remedy for a non-existent Charter rights violation, be it a "mere" declaration of "inconsistency."

NOTES

1 Part I of the Constitution Act, 1982, being Schedule B to the Canada Act, 1982 (UK), 1982, c 11 [Charter].
2 CQLR c L-0.3 [Bill 21].
3 Protecting Elections and Defending Democracy Act, 2021, S.O. 2021, c. 31, s. 53.1(1).
4 Bill 96, An Act Respecting French, the Official and Common Language of Québec, 2nd Sess, 42nd Leg, Quebec, 2022 (assented to 1 June 2022), SQ 2022, c 14 [Bill 96].
5 Maxime St-Hilaire and Xavier Foccroulle Ménard, "Nothing to Declare: A Response to Grégoire Webber, Eric Mendelsohn, Robert Leckey, and Léonid Sirota on the Effects of the Notwithstanding Clause," *Constitutional Forum* 29, no. 1 (2020): 38–9 ["Nothing to Declare"].
6 *Ford v Quebec (AG)*, [1988] 2 SCR 712, 54 DLR (4th) 577 [*Ford*].
7 See Grégoire Webber, this volume, chapter 4.
8 Grégoire Webber, Eric Mendelsohn, and Robert Leckey, "The Faulty Received Wisdom around the Notwithstanding Clause," *Policy Options*, 10 May 2019, policyoptions.irpp.org/magazines/may-2019/faulty-wisdom-notwithstanding-clause ["The Faulty Received Wisdom around the Notwithstanding Clause"].
9 Leonid Sirota, "Concurring Opinion," *Double Aspect* (blog), 23 May 2019, https://doubleaspect.blog/2019/05/23/concurring-opinion/ ["Concurring Opinion"].
10 Robert Leckey, "Advocacy Notwithstanding the Notwithstanding Clause," *Constitutional Forum constitutionnel* 28, no. 4 (2019).
11 *Canada (Prime Minister) v Khadr*, 2010 SCC 3 [*Khadr*].
12 Charter, s. 33(2).

13 Webber, Mendelsohn, and Leckey, "Faulty Received Wisdom."
14 Ibid.
15 Ibid.
16 *Khadr*, para 39.
17 Webber, Mendelsohn, and Leckey, "Faulty Received Wisdom."
18 *Khadr*, para 39.
19 Webber, Mendelsohn, and Leckey, "Faulty Received Wisdom."
20 We note that all these jurisdictions are of the common law tradition, and no jurisdictions of the civilist tradition were mentioned.
21 Sirota, "Concurring Opinion."
22 Leckey, "Advocacy Notwithstanding."
23 Sirota, "Concurring Opinion."
24 Leckey, "Advocacy Notwithstanding."
25 St-Hilaire and Foccroulle Ménard, "Nothing to Declare." Note that we do not claim that the Supreme Court of Canada is conducting such purposive approach correctly in all cases, but merely that this is the methodology established to interpret Charter provisions.
26 St-Hilaire and Foccroulle Ménard, 39.
27 See *Hunter et al. v Southam Inc.* [1984] 2 SCR 145, 11 DLR (4th) 641.
28 St-Hilaire and Foccroulle Ménard, "Nothing to Declare," 40.
29 Dwight Newman, "Canada's Notwithstanding Clause, Dialogue, and Constitutional Identities," in *Constitutional Dialogue: Rights, Democracy, Institutions*, eds. Geoffrey Sigalet, Gregoire Webber, and Rosalind Dixon (Cambridge: Cambridge University Press, 2019), 209.
30 *Ford*, para 33.
31 St-Hilaire and Foccroulle Ménard, "Nothing to Declare," 44.
32 Jonathan Law and Elizabeth A. Martin, *A Dictionary of Law*, 7th ed. (Oxford: Oxford University Press, 2014); *Ashby v White* (1703) 14 St Tr 695, 92 ER 126. The right precedes and constitutes the remedy. See John Gardner, *From Personal Life to Private Law* (Oxford: Oxford University Press, 2018), 204: "The law says ubi ius, ibi remedium. That is a norm, a doctrine, a principle of particular legal systems or legal traditions. It says that when there is a right recognized by the law, a legal right, there ought to be a legal remedy for its breach. It is not a conceptual truth, and nor is it advanced as one. It does not say that nothing is a legal right until there is a legal remedy for its breach. In fact, it contradicts that proposition. If nothing is a legal right until there is a legal remedy, then the fact that something is a legal right could not be a reason to furnish a legal remedy."
33 *Ewert v Canada*, 2018 SCC 30, at para 81 [*Ewert*]. ·
34 Human Rights Act 1998 (c. 42) [British Human Rights Act].

35 New Zealand Bill of Rights Act 1990, No 109 [NZBRA].

36 British Human Rights Act, section 4.

37 NZBRA, section 4.

38 See also the statement of the Court in *Tranchemontagne v. Ontario (Director, Disability Support Program)*, 2006 SCC 14 at para 35: "A provision declared invalid pursuant to s. 52 of the Constitution Act, 1982 was never validly enacted to begin with. It never existed as valid law because the legislature enacting it never had the authority to pass it. But when a provision is inapplicable pursuant to s. 47 of the Code, there is no statement being made as to its validity. The legislature had the power to enact the conflicting provision; it just so happens that the legislature also enacted another law that takes precedence." For a more detailed explanation, see Maxime St-Hilaire and Patrick F. Baud, "Legal Roadblocks to a Quebec Constitution," in *A Written Constitution for Quebec*, eds. Richard Albert and Leonid Sirota (McGill-Queen's University Press, 2023), 62–5.

39 St-Hilaire and Foccroulle Ménard, "Nothing to Declare," 46.

40 Ibid.

41 Grégoire Webber, "Notwithstanding Rights, Review, or Remedy? On the Notwithstanding Clause on the Operation of Legislation," *University of Toronto Law Journal* 71 (2021): 1–2, https://ssrn.com/abstract=3935891 ["Notwithstanding Remedy"].

42 Robert Leckey and Eric Mendelsohn, "The Notwithstanding Clause: Legislatures, Courts, and the Electorate," *University of Toronto Law Journal* 72, no. 2 (2022): 189 ["Notwithstanding Clause"].

43 Leckey and Mendelsohn, 515–18. We must clarify that these answers only pertain to the legal effects of the notwithstanding clause as informed by its purpose, and not to its purpose per se and overall legitimacy. In offering a robust defence of section 33 as protection against judicial review, Geoff Sigalet confuses the debate on effects with the debate on purpose. See "The Trucks and the Brakes: Understanding the Charter's Limitations and Notwithstanding Clauses Symmetrically," *The Supreme Court Law Review* 105 (2022): 189–216. Webber, Leckey, Mendelsohn, St-Hilaire, and Foccroulle Ménard discuss the effects of the notwithstanding clause (see notes 39, 40, and 5), whereas Newman, Hiebert, Sérafin, Sun, and Foccroulle Ménard discuss the purpose and legitimacy of the notwithstanding clause (see notes 29, 121, and 133).

44 Leckey and Mendelsohn, "Notwithstanding Clause," 515.

45 Ibid., 519.

46 Ibid., 518.

47 Ibid.

48 In his recent article, Sigalet responds to Webber, Leckey, and Mendelsohn by making the case that the effects of the notwithstanding clause are to preclude the protected legislation from judicial review, which means that courts are not allowed to declare the inconsistency between a protected legislation and the target Charter provisions. See Sigalet, "Trucks and Brakes." We agree with Sigalet that the notwithstanding clause prohibits judicial review of the protected legislation and that courts have nothing to declare.

49 Leckey and Mendelsohn, "Notwithstanding Clause," 516.

50 Ibid., 518.

51 Ibid., 520. See *Manitoba Language Rights Reference* [1985] 1 SCR 721 at 746, 19 DLR (4th) 1.

52 Leckey and Mendelsohn, "Notwithstanding Clause," 519.

53 Charter, section 33.

54 Leckey and Mendelsohn, "Notwithstanding Clause," 527.

55 Ibid., 191.

56 Ibid., 193.

57 Webber, "Notwithstanding Rights," 518.

58 Ibid., 524.

59 Ibid.

60 *Manitoba Language Rights Reference* [1985] 1 SCR 721, 19 DLR (4th) 1.

61 That is, outside the specific case of temporary suspensions of declarations of invalidity.

62 This is consistent with the common law tradition as explained by Blackstone. See *Canada (AG) v Hislop*, 2007 SCC 10 at para 84, citing Blackstone, *Commentaries on the Laws of England*, vol. 1 (Oxford: Clarendon Press, 1765), 69–70.

63 Webber, "Notwithstanding Rights," 536.

64 Headings "were systematically and deliberately included as an integral part of the Charter" and must be taken into consideration by courts "when engaged in the process of discerning the meaning and application of the provisions of the Charter." In constitutional interpretation, the importance of headings is tied to, among other things, the homogeneity of the underlying provisions. See *Law Society of Upper Canada v. Skapinker* [1984] 1 SCR 357, at para 22. "At a minimum the heading must be examined and some attempt made to discern the intent of the makers of the document from the language of the heading." See para 23.

65 Leckey and Mendelsohn, "Notwithstanding Clause," 194.

66 Ibid., 197.

67 Ibid., 191. Any reference to Dworkin here flows from our characterization in trying to appreciate the argument in its best light, as our understanding is that Leckey is not a Dworkinian scholar, but a postmodern legal scholar.
68 Leckey and Mendelsohn, "Notwithstanding Clause," 190.
69 Ibid., 193.
70 Leckey, "Advocacy Notwithstanding the Notwithstanding Clause."
71 We leave aside the debate on whether section 52 is a remedial provision (Roach; *Ontario (Attorney General) v. G*, 2020 SCC 38) or a substantive provision (Strayer; Marcotte; *Nova Scotia (Workers' Compensation Board) v. Martin* [2003] 2 S.C.R. 504, 2003 SCC 54).
72 Leckey and Mendelsohn, "Notwithstanding Clause," 209.
73 See how *Ford* stressed the distinction between section 1 and section 33 of the Charter.
74 Webber, "Notwithstanding Rights," 536.
75 Ibid., 535–6.
76 Leckey and Mendelsohn, "Notwithstanding Clause," 202, footnote 64.
77 Ibid., 191.
78 Ibid., 191 footnote 10.
79 *Ontario (Attorney General) v G*, 2020 SCC 38, at para 137.
80 *Gosselin v. Quebec (Attorney General)*, 2002 SCC 84, at para 15.
81 Leckey and Mendelsohn, "Notwithstanding Clause," 194.
82 *Ford*, 738.
83 Leckey and Mendelsohn, "Notwithstanding Clause," 202.
84 Ibid.
85 *Ford*, 721.
86 Ibid.
87 Ibid., 732.
88 Ibid., 742.
89 Ibid.
90 *Hak c. Procureur général du Québec*, 2021 QCCS 1466 at para 798.
91 These questions pertain to the omnibus character and the retrospective aspect of the enactment contained in an Act Respecting the Constitution Act, 1982. See *Ford*, 742–3.
92 *Ford*.
93 Ibid., 206.
94 Ibid., 207.
95 *Gosselin v Quebec* (Attorney General), 2002 SCC 84, [2002] 4 SCR 429 [*Gosselin*].
96 Leckey and Mendelsohn, "Notwithstanding Clause," 207.
97 Ibid., 196.

98 *Manitoba Metis Federation Inc. v Canada (Attorney General)*, 2013 SCC 14 [2013] 1 SCR 623.

99 *Manitoba Metis Federation Inc. v Canada (Attorney General)*, paras 143–4.

100 Webber, "Notwithstanding Rights," 528.

101 Ibid., 529.

102 For a reiteration of this idea, see Leckey, this volume, chapter 5.

103 *Reference re Secession of Quebec*, 1998 CanLII 793 (SCC) [1998] 2 SCR 217. [*Secession Reference*].

104 Leckey and Mendelsohn, "Notwithstanding Clause," 203 and ss.

105 Ibid., 191.

106 See *Toronto (City) v. Ontario (Attorney General)*, 2021 SCC 34.

107 For instance, absent from the discussion on the "protection of minorities" is that Quebec's use of the notwithstanding clause is itself an expression of the will of a minority nationally and in North America, as was aptly observed by the Supreme Court itself in the *Secession Reference* when discussing the principle of federalism, *Toronto (City) v. Ontario (Attorney General)*, para 59. On this subject, see: Guillaume Rousseau and François Côté, "A Distinctive Quebec Theory and Practice of the Notwithstanding Clause: When Collective Interests Outweigh Individual Rights," *Revue générale de droit* 47, no. 2 (2017): 343; André Binette, "Le pouvoir dérogatoire de l'article 33 de la Charte canadienne des droits et libertés et la structure de la Constitution du Canada," *Revue du Barreau,* Special Issue (2003): 107.

108 Peter Hogg, *Constitutional Law in Canada*, vol. 2 (Toronto: Thomson Reuters, 2018), 39–5.

109 Leckey and Mendelsohn, "Notwithstanding Clause," 198.

110 Ibid., 200.

111 For the complete discussion on "democracy" and "dissenting voices" in *Secession Reference*, paras 63–9.

112 Leckey and Mendelsohn, "Notwithstanding Clause," 197.

113 Pierre-André Côté, *Interprétation des lois*, 4th ed. (Montreal: Thémis, 2009), 502–3.

114 *Reference re Bill 30, An Act to Amend the Education Act (Ont.)*, [1987] 1 SCR 1148, para 29.

115 Ibid., para 57.

116 Ibid., para 64.

117 *Toronto (city) v. Ontario (Attorney General)*, 2021 SCC 34, para 60.

118 See Axworthy, this volume, chapter 1.

119 This creates confusion in new scholarship. See notably Eric M. Adams and Erin R.J. Bower, "Notwithstanding History: The Rights-Protecting

Purposes of Section 33 of the Charter," *Review of Constitutional Studies* 26, no. 2 (2022): 121, https://dx.doi.org/10.2139/ssrn.4185044. The authors cite the correct and relevant sources, identify the right historical protagonists and arguments, and confirm the rights-protecting purposes of the notwithstanding clause by the legislatures. Nothing in their historical review suggests a role for courts; quite the contrary, everything supports the idea that the notwithstanding clause limits the role of the courts to grant greater place to the legislatures. Near the end, at page 141, the authors adopt the erroneous idea that "courts retain an important role to play in assessing and adjudicating Charter rights infringements, notwithstanding the successful invocation of the notwithstanding provision," despite that there cannot be any infringement with inapplicable Charter rights which are excepted from by the legislation invoking such notwithstanding provision. We contend that the historical review of Adams and Bower at pages 121–39 confirms the orthodox position we have always defended and aligns with the *Ford* decision.

120 Newman, "Canada's Notwithstanding Clause," 224.
121 Janet L. Hiebert, "Compromise and the Notwithstanding Clause: Why the Dominant Narrative Distorts Our Understanding," in *Contested Constitutionalism: Reflections on the Canadian Charter of Rights and Freedoms*, ed. James B. Kelly and Christopher P. Manfredi (Vancouver: UBC Press, 2010), 115–16.
122 See Barry Strayer, "The Evolution of the Charter," in *Patriation and its Consequences*, eds. L. Harder and S. Patten (Vancouver: University of British Columbia Press, 2015), 72–90.
123 See Howard A. Leeson, *The Patriation Minutes* (Edmonton: Centre for Constitutional Studies, University of Alberta), 29, 31, 42, and 64.
124 Ibid., 70.
125 Ibid., 66, 69.
126 *Vriend v. Alberta* [1998] 1 SCR 493, para 178.
127 *Vriend v. Alberta* [1998] 1 SCR 493.
128 *Toronto (city) v. Ontario (Attorney General)*, 2021 SCC 34, at para 53. In this passage, the court also reiterates the priority of a purposive interpretation: "This is why our colleague can offer no example of legislation that would undermine the structure of the Constitution that cannot be addressed as we propose, which is via purposive textual interpretation."
129 Leckey and Mendelsohn, "Notwithstanding Clause," 201.
130 See: Stéphane Sérafin, Kerry Sun, and Xavier Foccroulle Ménard, "Notwithstanding Judicial Specification: The Notwithstanding Clause within a Juridical Order," in *Supreme Court Law Review*, 2nd series, vol.

110, ed. Maxime St-Hilaire, Ryan Alford, and Kristopher Kinsinger (LexisNexis, 2023); Newman, "Canada's Notwithstanding Clause"; Hiebert, "Compromise." But see also Maxime St-Hilaire, "Les Leçons de Jordan, III : à quelles conditions est-il légitime de déroger aux droits constitutionnels fondamentaux?" *Constitutional Forum constitutionnel* 26, no. 3 (2017).

131   We should note that we do not take a position in this text on the debate of the legitimate use of the notwithstanding clause as is developed by Newman, Hiebert, Sérafin, Sun, and Foccroulle Ménard. See notes 29, 121, and 133. We are simply highlighting that the "interpretive" argument of Leckey and Mendelsohn needs to engage with the relevant scholarship on such debate if it uses the principle of "democracy" to conclude on the effects of the notwithstanding clause.

132   Leckey, "Advocacy Notwithstanding."

7

Notwithstanding Judicial Review: Legal and Political Reasons Why Courts Cannot Review Laws Invoking Section 33

Geoffrey Sigalet

Should Canadian courts review laws invoking the infamous "not-withstanding clause" of the Charter of Rights and Freedoms? In this article I will argue that the answer to the question of whether courts "ought" to review such laws is: no. They should not because they legally cannot do so and, even if they could, they should not for reasons of political morality.

Courts should not review laws invoking section 33 because the legal effect of the notwithstanding clause prohibits this. Section 33(1) ensures that questions about the consistency of laws invoking the not-withstanding clause with selected Charter provisions are moot. Even more importantly, the mood of section 33(2) of the notwithstanding clause requires courts to treat certain Charter provisions *as though* they don't apply to laws making use of it. This prevents courts from substantively reviewing laws that make use of the notwithstanding clause, while leaving questions about the consistency of such laws up to the political branches (and the citizens who elect them).

Politically, the notwithstanding clause serves as a kind of legislative veto point for checking the judiciary's veto power over legislation related to Charter rights. It allows legislatures to review judicial decision-making without directly undermining judicial independence. The politicization of Charter issues by laws invoking the notwithstanding clause means that even if courts could legally review the substance of these enactments, doing so threatens to politically undermine more constructive forms of legislative review.

It turns out that the normative case against the judicial review of laws invoking section 33 may be aligned with the strategic incentives of courts. Strategic modelling of judicial decision-making shows us that just as the disuse of the notwithstanding clause can remove constraints on judicial policy-making, increased usage of the clause can institutionally constrain judicial power. Increased provincial uses of section 33 have likely shattered whatever older norm once existed against using the clause to challenge judicial decision-making. Reviewing laws that use the notwithstanding clause to curb judicial power, and holding them operational notwithstanding their inconsistency with rights, could *embolden* court curbing where legislative policy preferences are closer to public opinion than judicial preferences. Here I used the term "ineffectual judicial review" to refer to judicial decisions that review laws invoking section 33 and declare them to be violations of Charter rights that nonetheless "operate" under the protection of section 33(2). The obvious federalism angle to this is that ineffectual judicial review risks appearing more nakedly political, thereby providing an opening for provincial legislatures to tie judicial preferences to the political preferences of the federal politicians who appoint them. In other words, the cost of courts directly but ineffectually challenging laws meant to curb judicial power could be to encourage provincial legislatures to use the notwithstanding clause as a means of signalling to provincial audiences that they are resisting centralist intrusions on their jurisdiction, rather than as an instrument of constructive rights dialogue about specific rights issues.

I. JUDICIAL REVIEW NOTWITHSTANDING SECTION 33?

Ever since the Supreme Court of Canada's landmark case of *Ford v. Quebec*, the received wisdom concerning section 33 of the Charter has been that it prohibits judicial review.[1] The first parts of section 33 of the Charter read:

(1) Parliament or the legislature of a province may expressly declare in an Act of Parliament or of the legislature, as the case may be, that the Act or a provision thereof shall operate notwithstanding a provision included in section 2 or sections 7 to 15 of this Charter.

(2) An Act or a provision of an Act in respect of which a declaration made under this section is in effect shall have such operation as it would have but for the provision of this Charter referred to in the declaration.[2]

In *Ford*, the Supreme Court held that the clause "lays down requirements of form only, and there is no warrant for importing into it grounds for substantive review of legislative policy."[3] In other words, the courts are prohibited from reviewing statutes that declare that they operate "notwithstanding" certain provisions of the Charter, at least until these declarations expire without renewal after five years.

This "received wisdom" has been questioned in the past by somewhat wild and unpersuasive arguments,[4] but more recently it has become subject to a new debate that takes seriously the wording of section 33(2)'s statement that a law invoking the notwithstanding clause "shall have such operation as it would but for the provision of this Charter referred to in the declaration."

In 2019 Quebec enacted the *Loi sur la laïcité de l'État*,[5] also known as *Loi 21*, which invoked the notwithstanding clause to protect prohibitions on some public servants wearing religious symbols from being struck down for violating Charter rights – particularly the section 2(a) right to religious freedom. In the wake of *Loi 21*, Grégoire Webber, Eric Mendelsohn, and Robert Leckey argued that the text of section 33(2) authorised the judicial power to declare laws to be inconsistent with Charter rights in cases where legislatures invoke section 33.[6] As evidenced by their chapters in this volume, Webber, Mendelsohn, and Leckey eventually disagreed about the textual case for the judicial power to review laws invoking the notwithstanding clause.

Webber developed the view that because section 33(2) protects the "operation" of laws, it does not protect their constitutional consistency and validity, and as a result it thereby only prohibits courts from holding such laws inoperative.[7] This view leaves open the possibility that courts might review laws invoking section 33 and make declarations that they are unconstitutional violations of certain Charter rights that nevertheless operate as an exception to the supremacy of the Constitution per section 52 of the Constitution Act, 1982. Leckey and Mendelsohn developed the alternative view that section 33(2) protects the constitutional validity of laws even if they violate Charter rights.[8] Note that Webber takes his view to explain how section 33(2) justifies the legality of the judicial review of laws invoking section 33, while suggesting that it may be prudent for courts to exercise what Alexander Bickel called the "passive virtues" in refusing to exercise such a politically charged type of adjudication.[9] Leckey and Mendelsohn openly advocate for courts to take on the heroic task of alerting the public to violations of rights by offering declarations that statutes like *Loi* 21 violate rights. I should note that both of these lines of argument show a great deal of ingenuity and attention to detail, and it's hard not to admire that.

Litigators have picked up on these clever academic arguments, although they have thankfully so far failed to persuade courts. For example, in *Hak v Quebec* respondents challenged Quebec's use of the notwithstanding clause in *Loi* 21.[10] The Quebec Superior Court held that *Loi* 21's use of the notwithstanding clause is "judicially unassailable" (*juridiquement inattaquable*) and that courts should refuse to offer formal declarations about whether Charter rights are violated.[11] But the court left open questions about why arguments for the review of laws invoking section 33 are misguided, and such questions will surely interest appellate courts reviewing the trial court decision.

II. THE LEGAL CASE AGAINST JUDICIAL REVIEW

There are both legal and political reasons for rejecting the substantive judicial review of laws invoking the notwithstanding clause. This section will review two important legal arguments prohibiting such review.[12] Legally, laws invoking the clause cannot be substantively reviewed because questions about the rights consistency of laws invoking it are moot, and because the mood of section 33(2) means that laws must be treated *as if* certain sections of the Charter don't apply to them.

The first legal argument against the review of section 33 is that the meaning of "notwithstanding" ensures that laws are constitutionally paramount over the Charter provisions they select.[13] Canadian courts understand statutory notwithstanding clauses as the legislature's instruction to interpret part of the law as a "paramount provision" when seeking to avoid conflicts between provisions in order "to produce coherent, internally consistent legislation."[14] The same should go for the constitutional meaning of statutes that invoke section 33 "notwithstanding" certain Charter provisions.

That means that laws invoking section 33 are not necessarily inconsistent with the provisions of the Charter they select, but they have constitutional priority in case there are conflicts. This means that laws invoking section 33 do not "suspend" or "override" the enumerated rights and freedoms they apply to, as argued in early scholarship by Maxime St-Hilaire and Xavier F. Ménard.[15] Indeed, it is telling that the notwithstanding clause does not even apply notwithstanding "rights and freedoms," but rather against "a provision included in section 2 or in sections 7 to 15 of this Charter."[16] Read on its own, without looking to section 33(2), laws invoking section 33(1) gain priority over any *provisions* of the Charter they properly select *in the case of conflicts*, but do not express conflicts with the rights and freedoms enumerated in these provisions.[17] As such, questions about the consistency of these laws with the Charter are moot and not fit for judicial review. Another thing to note about this argument is that it means that laws invoking section 33 can express reasonable views about rights.

The second legal argument is more subtle: the mood of section 33(2) requires courts to treat laws invoking the notwithstanding clause *as though* selected Charter provisions do not apply to them, even though it remains open to legislators and citizens to assess the consistency of such laws with constitutional rights and freedoms. This is the case for the mood of both the English and French texts of section 33.

The mood of section 33(2) is in the subjunctive in the English text: the text says that laws "shall have such operation as they would but for the provision of the Charter referred to." In English, the indicative mood signals actual states-of-affairs, stuff that really exists or is happening.[18] The subjunctive mood signals counter-factual or hypothetical states-of-affairs.[19] Imagine ordering a meal from a waiter in a restaurant. An example of an indicative order is: "I'll have the rainbow trout without any sauce." The waiter is directed to bring one thing (rainbow trout) without another thing (sauce). A subjunctive order is a stranger thing, because it will involve asking someone to do something as though a counter-factual or hypothetical state-of-affairs obtained.

An example of a subjunctive order is: "I'll eat whatever is *vegetarian*, but for my sake consider *fish* a *vegetable*." The waiter is instructed to bring a set of things (vegetables), including one type of thing that lies outside of that set (fish), by pretending that outlying thing belongs naturally to the ordered set (trout qua veggie). If the waiter brought the customer a rainbow trout with the pronouncement "here is your non-vegetarian meal, madame," he would be disobedient. If the waiter set down a plate of rainbow trout in front of the customer while saying "here is your *vegetarian* meal, madame," he would be more obedient for his drole emphasis.

The subjunctive language of section 33(2) asks the reader to think that laws invoking section 33 "shall have the operation they would have but for the Charter provisions" in the sense that the laws operate *as they would if the Charter provisions did not exist*. These statutes constitutionally operate as though the Charter provisions don't exist. As long as we're pretending that the Charter provisions don't exist in relation to these laws, the laws cannot be reviewed for consistency with these Charter provisions.

The subtlety here is that, of course, the Charter provisions *do exist*, even though we are told to treat them *as if* they don't in relation to laws invoking section 33. Laws invoking section 33 don't temporarily amend or suspend the Constitution; rather, section 33 alters the constitutional status of statutes that invoke it. The notwithstanding clause alters the status of statutes by constitutionally requiring laws invoking it to be treated as though the Charter provisions they select do not exist as grounds for questioning their operation. Because Charter provisions do exist, it remains open to the political branches and wider citizenry to question their consistency with laws invoking section 33. This means that the text of section 33(2) is at odds with both Webber and Leckey and Mendelsohn's lines of argument.

If section 33(2) were written in the indicative, it wouldn't use the word "would" and it could be read as protecting *only* the operation of the laws, not their constitutional consistency and validity. This is Webber's reading, which is mistaken because the clause seems to be written in the subjunctive. However, attention to the mood of the clause suggests that *either* the English clause is subjunctive, and thereby protects the constitutionality of legislative judgments about rights by prohibiting substantive judicial review, or else it is indicative, and could accordingly be read as legally opening the door for courts to declare statutes invoking it invalid and *unconstitutional*, but not inoperable, because the notwithstanding clause protects only the "operation" of laws.[20] These readings act as an interpretive pincer to exclude Leckey and Mendelsohn's argument that section 33(2) protects the constitutionality of laws without barring courts from reviewing and declaring their inconsistency with selected Charter rights. If laws invoking the notwithstanding clause operate as though selected Charter provisions do not exist to be applied to them, then courts may not assess their constitutional consistency with rights enumerated in those provisions. If laws invoking the notwithstanding clause only have their operation guaranteed by section 33(2), then they may be reviewable for unconstitutionally violating enumerated rights.

In this volume, Webber attempts to save his view by noting that even if the mood of section 33(2) is subjunctive, "the counter-factual world in which rights and freedoms do not exist holds for the purposes of legislation's *operation*."[21] But this fails to appreciate the meaning of the counter-factual. The counter-factual world in which laws operate as though certain rights and freedoms do not exist is one where the law could not be challenged as invalid for violating such rights. Why? Because the path to questioning a law's operation starts with questioning its constitutional validity (although in rare cases valid laws can also be inoperable), and so the world where the law operates as though certain rights and freedoms do not exist is one where the law operates free from the primary type of question used to impugn its operation: questions about its validity. Webber's reading of section 33(2) does not fit with the subjunctive mood because the counter-factual world where laws operate as they would but for certain rights is not a world where *invalid* laws operate as though rights don't exist. That would implausibly read the clause as at least half-indicative, saying the Charter provisions exist and apply to laws invoking the notwithstanding clause but do not exist and apply to the operation of those laws. The true counter-factual world is one where laws are valid and operable because they operate as though certain rights do not exist as grounds for questioning their operation, which also means that such rights do not exist as grounds for questioning their validity as part of the chain of reasoning about questioning their operation. The truth is that Webber is reading section 33(2) as an indicative exception to the rule that operational laws are valid, but no such indicative exception exists in the text of section 33(2) because it is subjunctive. Indeed, there is no authorization for invalid but operative laws anywhere in the text of the Constitution. The idea of invalid but operational laws is repugnant to our constitutional tradition; it has only been deployed by the Supreme Court in order to avoid even more repugnant outcomes (i.e., invalidating all of Manitoba's statutes), and this casts doubt on Webber's reading *even if* section 33(2) was written in the indicative mood.

What about the French text? The French text of section 33(2) requires courts to treat laws properly invoking the notwithstanding clause as having the *"l'effet"* (operation) *"qu'elle aurait"* (that they would have), *"sauf la disposition en cause de la chartre"* (but for the Charter provision in question). The mood of the French rendering of the clause in the *le conditionnel passé* shares the English subjunctive's counter-factual sense of laws operating as though the Charter provisions in question don't apply to them. In this way, the mood of section 33(2) prohibits judicial review in both of Canada's official languages.

But it would be wrong to think that nothing has been gained from these legal arguments for the judicial review of laws that make use of the notwithstanding clause. In truth, the legal arguments for courts reviewing laws invoking section 33 are not only cleverly mistaken, but also useful for sharpening our understanding of the technical way in which the notwithstanding clause overrides judicial review, as opposed to rights or remedies.

III. THE POLITICAL CASE AGAINST JUDICIAL REVIEW

The political case for not subjecting laws invoking section 33 to judicial review is clear and twofold: judicial review of the clause could illegitimately check the legitimate use of a clause that was intended to serve as a check on abuses of judicial review; courts reviewing laws that invoke the clause could *embolden* the very kinds of court curbing that critics of section 33 fear.

As Dwight Newman as adeptly shown, the notwithstanding clause was crafted to ensure that legislatures have a say in contesting judicial interpretations of rights.[22] This can have democratic benefits given how moralized much judicial reasoning about rights is, and particularly reasoning about "reasonable limits" on rights under the *Oakes* test. The notwithstanding clause is a political check on the possibility that unelected courts will undemocratically abuse the power of judicial review under the Charter. I think we can all think of cases where this power has been abused, even if we disagree about which ones. For example, I have argued that Saskatchewan's use of section 33 to protect funding for non-Catholic students at constitutionally protected and provincially funded Catholic schools *protects* the right to religious freedom in that province.[23] The trial court striking down such funding for non-Catholics at Catholic schools arguably made public funding for Catholic schools *less religiously neutral* and conflicted with Canada's tradition of religious freedom.[24] It turned out that the province won its appeal of the trial decision, but its use of section 33 protected its understanding of religious freedom in the face of uncertainty and a potential loss in the appeal.

Having the courts review these invocations would be like trying to ineffectually check the ability of legislatures to check judicial power. Consider if the litigants in the Saskatchewan school funding case were able to challenge the law invoking section 33 even as the province appealed the trial courts' invalidation of the earlier law. The appellate courts would then be questioning the substantive decision of the trial court while a new trial arose questioning whether Saskatchewan's new law violated rights notwithstanding section 33. This would not only be wasteful but openly disparaging to the legislature's constitutional power to enact laws in disagreement with the judiciary – even while it appeals substantively identical laws struck down at the trial level. Not only will such declarations be moot, they will also be potentially duplicative and confusing.

And in cases where legislatures pre-emptively use section 33 to forestall anticipated judicial disagreement, the judicial review of such laws will risk appearing as a naked attempt to short-circuit the idea that legislatures have the power and responsibility to construct the meaning of Charter rights. Subsection 33(3) limits the extent to which a legislature can prohibit substantive judicial review without a renewed electoral mandate (which must be sought every five years), and courts reviewing laws before then would be complicit in speaking out their constitutional turn. If we want legislatures to develop a standard for using section 33 to engage in substantive disagreements in constructive dialogues with courts about rights, having courts question the legislative ability to have a say about rights that differs from the judiciary seems like it could further discourage this.[25]

Proponents of the judicial review of laws invoking section 33 have not adequately considered that legislatures, especially provincial legislatures, intent on using section 33 to signal majoritarian opposition to judicial decisions could *relish* courts issuing ineffective declarations of Charter inconsistency if this helps signal their opposition to rights views that are unpopular in their province.

In order to appreciate this, it is necessary to review the strategic environment in which judicial review takes place. Judges are not apolitical angels sent from Laurentian heaven. They are lawyers appointed to the bench through a partisan political process that has implicated courts in Canadian politics since confederation. Canadian judges clearly wield political power in accordance with their political attitudes.[26] However, as political actors, judges exercise power under specific institutional and strategic constraints.[27]

Judges in constitutional systems with independent courts seek to strategically maximize their interests with internal consideration for disagreement between the preferences of judges on apex courts and how future courts might reverse their decisions,[28] Judicial behaviour is also strategically conditioned by external considerations such as "court-curbing" threats to judicial independence (e.g., political restructuring of the judiciary; jurisdiction stripping; limits on judicial budgets and salaries; the override of, or refusal to implement, judicial decisions).[29] Christopher Manfredi has drawn on the strategic model of judicial behaviour to argue that as the threat of legislative resistance to judicial review under the Charter has diminished, judicial review has become more aggressively remedial and activist.[30] Manfredi argues that section 33 counts as a kind of court-curbing instrument and that the declining use of the notwithstanding clause explains the different levels of remedial judicial activism in cases such as *R. v. Morgentaler (2)* and *Vriend v. Alberta*.[31]

In *Morgentaler (2)*, the Supreme Court faced the possible use of section 33 by a Conservative majority in the House of Commons to override any judicial decision invalidating federal restrictions on abortion. And only 23 per cent of the Canadian public at that time favoured unrestricted access to abortion.[32] The court actually produced four separate reasons that narrowing held that state processes violate the right to security of the person so far as they restrict and delay access to abortion procedures in ways that increase risks to the health of the mother.[33]

This narrow holding left room (and continues to leave room) for a parliamentary response restricting abortion access, but the Mulroney government's attempt to legislate new abortion restrictions was ultimately frustrated by a tie vote (43–43) in the Senate.[34] In Manfredi's view, the prospect of a legislative override of the court's decision incentivized the justices to nullify the Criminal Code's abortion restrictions on narrower grounds to encourage a legislative response that maintained some restrictions on abortion without overriding the judicial policy preferences.[35]

The inability of Parliament to respond to *Morgentaler (2)*, combined with the negative association of section 33 with Québécois nationalism in the wake of *Ford v. Quebec*, may have encouraged the court to become more activist in its remedies for Charter violations. In *Vriend*, the court unanimously "read in" protections against discrimination based on sexual orientation into Alberta's human rights statute in order to make the law compliant with section 15 equality rights, despite Alberta deliberately omitting such protections from the law.[36] One variable helping to explain this aggressive exercise of judicial review is that a majority of Canadians supported extending protections against discrimination based on sexual orientation.[37] But perhaps even more importantly, the notwithstanding clause had become politically unpopular, to the extent that Alberta premier Ralph Klein was forced to backtrack on plans to use section 33 to protect against judicial interference in another policy area.[38]

Rather than presenting Alberta with the possibility of a policy response to redress the rights question on its own terms, the court presented "the province with a dichotomous choice between accepting the court's human rights policy preferences or invoking the notwithstanding clause."[39] The decline of the notwithstanding clause as a probable means by which legislatures could contest judicial policy preferences incentivized the court to maximize its preferences by using the remedy of "reading in" to directly impose its policy preference on Alberta. One important variable explaining the difference between the narrower and more deferential judicial decision in *Morgentaler* and the more aggressive decision in *Vriend* was that the probable use of the notwithstanding clause declined during this period.

What does this strategic background tell us about the political effects of allowing courts to review laws invoking section 33? It can tell us something about what we might expect, and what courts might expect, in a shifting strategic environment. The strategic environment that surrounded the court in *Vriend* has certainly changed. To be sure, the federal use of the notwithstanding clause remains improbable (although federal Conservative politicians have recently discussed it as a policy option), but at the provincial level the clause has become much more of an acceptable policy tool. Starting in 2018, the notwithstanding clause has been used by provincial legislatures on six occasions, with three of the bills invoking section 33 enacted into law and one on its way.[40] And unlike in the period between *Morgentaler* and *Vriend*, the clause has been invoked by multiple provinces outside of Quebec's *Loi 21*, with recent uses by Ontario,[41] New Brunswick,[42] and Saskatchewan.[43] This shows a significantly increased probability in provincial uses of section 33 when compared with the four invocations of section 33 (three of which were enacted in Quebec, one invoked but then retracted by Alberta's Klein government in 1998)[44] in the ten years between *Morgentaler* in 1988 and *Vriend* in 1998.

It remains to be seen whether this shift will continue, but it seems possible that the judicial review of laws invoking the notwithstanding clause could accelerate the trend. A key factor in this process is federalism. One obvious variable helping to explain the disparity between provincial uses of section 33 and federal disuse is that the federal government has control over appointments to appellate courts, including the Supreme Court of Canada. This allows the federal government to influence the policy preferences of appellate judges over the long haul, and thereby offers the federal government a kind of "soft" court-curbing device that isn't available to the provinces.[45] Without the ability to politically influence the direction of Charter jurisprudence, the notwithstanding clause becomes an attractive tool for resisting the judicial imposition of centralizing views on rights questions at odds with the views of citizens in certain provinces.

In other words, section 33 is sometimes used by provincial legislatures to resist views on rights that are more popular in other parts of the country, and with federally appointed legal elites, than in their province. Courts could *encourage* such uses of section 33 if they review these laws and promote the provincial legislature's resistance to the federalist/elite view. In such cases where majority views in one province are significantly at odds with views on rights imposed by federal courts, feeble "declarations" that laws invoking section 33 violate Charter rights could serve as free advertising for provincial parties seeking to position themselves as champions of provincial autonomy and difference. Of course, it is possible that judicial declarations could concern legislatures insofar as their renewal is in political jeopardy, as such declarations could be taken to invalidate statutes with expired invocations of section 33. Even so, it seems unlikely that the (debatable) "gain" of an ineffectual declaration that a law infringes rights will outweigh the risk of playing into the hands of legislators seeking to advertise their opposition to centralizing rights politics. This not only helps explain why courts may be politically hesitant to get involved in the judicial review of laws invoking section 33, apart from the strong legal case against doing so, but also why their own strategic interests may lie in avoiding this.

CONCLUSION

As a court-curbing mechanism, the notwithstanding clause is a democratically admirable Canadian innovation because it curbs judicial power without directly threatening judicial independence. Although it can certainly be abused, just like the power of judicial review itself, it is also subject to specific constitutional limitations that enable legislatures to contest judicial forays into policymaking without threatening judicial independence. When a legislature abuses section 33 to override the determinate meaning of Charter rights, the remedy is at the next election's ballot box, but the offending statute itself restricts judicial power without directly interfering with judiciary. In contrast with other court-curbing measures (such as highly polarized appointments processes, court packing, jurisdiction stripping, etc.), the notwithstanding clause does not directly interfere with the judicial decision-making process, nor with the composition of the judiciary. This just adds to the sound legal and political reasons for approving of this mechanism, and these reasons counsel courts to avoid tampering with the very part of the Constitution that intentionally limits their power. The results of such tampering might not be as salutary as some might expect.

NOTES

1 Grégoire Webber, "Notwithstanding Rights, Review, or Remedy? On the Notwithstanding Clause on the Operation of Legislation," *University of Toronto Law Journal* 71 (2021): 1–2, https://ssrn.com/abstract=3935891.

2 Canadian Charter of Rights and Freedoms, s 33(1), Part I of the Constitution Act, 1982, being Schedule B to the Canada Act 1982 (UK), 1982, c 11 [Charter].

3 *Ford v Quebec (AG)*, [1988] 2 SCR 712 at para 33 [*Ford*].

4   For example, Brian Slattery, "Legislation," *The Canadian Bar Review* 61, no. 1 (1983): 391.

5   Act Respecting the Laicity of the State, CQLR c L-0.3 [*Loi 21*].

6   See Grégoire Webber, Eric Mendelsohn, and Robert Leckey, "The Faulty Wisdom around the Notwithstanding Clause," *Policy Options Politiques*, 10 May 2019, policyoptions.irpp.org/magazines/may-2019/faulty-wisdom-notwithstanding-clause/.

7   Webber, "Notwithstanding Rights."

8   See Robert Leckey and Eric Mendelsohn, "The Notwithstanding Clause: Legislatures, Courts, and the Electorate," *University of Toronto Law Journal* 72, no. 2 (2022): 189.

9   Webber, "Notwithstanding Rights."

10 See *Hak c Québec (PG)*, 2021 QCCS 1466 [*Hak*].

11 *Hak*, para 4. The court also held that the section 28's equal guarantee of all rights to both sexes is an interpretive clause that cannot be used to trump section 33 (paras 869, 874, 875).

12 I elaborate on these arguments at greater length in "Legislated Rights as Trumps: Why the Notwithstanding Clause Overrides Judicial Review," *Osgoode Hall Law Journal* 61, no. 1 (forthcoming).

13 See Ruth Sullivan, *Statutory Interpretation* (Toronto: Irwin Law, 2007), 305.

14 Sullivan, *Statutory Interpretation*.

15 See Maxime St-Hilaire and Xaiver Foccroulle Ménard, "Nothing to Declare: A Response to Grégoire Webber, Eric Mendelsohn, Robert Leckey, and Léonid Sirota on the Effects of the Notwithstanding Clause," *Constitutional Forum* 29, no. 1 (2020): 38–9. I should note that Ménard has recently joined two other co-authors to revise his view of section 33 as a means of specifying rights in relation to the common good. This view is very much compatible with the reading of the text offered in this article. See Kerry Sun, Stéphane Séraphin, and Xavier F. Ménard, "Notwithstanding the Courts? Directing the Canadian Charter toward the Common Good," *IusetIustitium* (blog), 1 July 2021, iusetiustitium.com/notwithstanding-the-courts-directing-the-canadian-charter-toward-the-common-good/.

16 Canadian Charter of Rights and Freedoms, s 33(1).

17 Asher Honickman, "Deconstructing Section 28," *Advocates for the Rule of Law*, 29 June 2019, www.ruleoflaw.ca/deconstructing-section-28/.

18 See Bas Aertes, *Oxford Modern English Grammar* (Oxford: Oxford University Press, 2011), 275–314.

19 See Aertes, *Oxford Modern English Grammar*.

20 Webber, "Notwithstanding Rights."

21 Grégoire Webber, this volume, chapter 4.
22 Dwight Newman, this volume, chapter 3; Dwight Newman, "Canada's Notwithstanding Clause, Dialogue, and Constitutional Identities," in *Constitutional Dialogue: Rights, Democracy, Institutions*, ed. Geoffrey Sigalet, Grégoire Webber, and Rosalind Dixon (Cambridge: Cambridge University Press, 2019), 209–24.
23 See Mark Mancini and Geoffrey Sigalet, "What Constitutes the Legitimate Use of the Notwithstanding Clause?" *Policy Options Politiques*, 20 January 2020, policyoptions.irpp.org/magazines/january-2020/what-constitutes-the-legitimate-use-of-the-notwithstanding-clause/.
24 *Good Spirit School Division No 204 v Christ the Teacher Roman Catholic Separate School Division No 212*, 2017 SKQB 109 at paras 451–5.
25 For a "constructive" theory of rights dialogue see Geoffrey Sigalet, "Dialogue and Domination," in *Constitutional Dialogue: Rights, Democracy, Institutions*, ed. Geoffrey Sigalet, Grégoire Webber, and Rosalind Dixon (Cambridge: Cambridge University Press, 2019), 85–126.
26 C.L. Ostberg and Matthew E. Wetstein, *Attitudinal Decision Making in the Supreme Court of Canada* (Vancouver: UBC Press, 2007).
27 Lee Epstein and Jack Knight, *The Choices Justices Make* (Washington, DC: Congressional Quarterly Press, 1998).
28 Epstein and Knight, *Choices Justices Make*, xiii.
29 Alyx Mark and Michael A. Zilis, "Restraining the Court: Assessing Accounts of Congressional Attempts to Limit Supreme Court Authority," *Legislative Studies Quarterly* 43, no. 1 (2018), 141–3.
30 Christopher Manfredi, "Strategic Behaviour and the Charter," in *The Myth of the Sacred*, ed. Patrick James, Donald E. Ableson, and Michael Lusztig (Kingston-Montreal: McGill-Queen's University Press, 2002), 156.
31 Manfredi, "Strategic Behaviour."
32 Ibid., 160.
33 *R. v. Morgentaler* [1988] 1 S.C.R. 30.
34 F.L. Morton and Rainer Knopff, *The Charter Revolution and the Court Party* (Peterborough: Broadview Press, 2000), 162–3.
35 Manfredi "Strategic Behaviour," 165.
36 *Vriend v. Alberta* [1998] 1 S.C.R. 493.
37 Manfredi, "Strategic Behaviour," 163.
38 Ibid.
39 Ibid., 164.
40 Quebec's Bill 96 is, in the opinion of the author, quite likely to pass with an effective invocation of section 33. See Bill 96: An Act Respecting

French, the Official and Common Language of Quebec (1st Sess., 42nd Leg., Quebec, 2022).

41 Efficient Local Government Act, 2018 (1st Sess., 42nd Leg., Ontario, 2018); An Act to Amend the Election Finances Act, 2021 R.S.O. 1990, c. E.7, s. 53.1; Keeping Students in Class Act, 2022, S.O. 2022 c.19 s. 13.

42 An Act Respecting Proof of Vaccination (3rd Sess., 59th Leg., New Brunswick, 2019).

43 The School Choice Protection Act, 2018 S.S. 2018, c. 39, s. 3.

44 Rousseau and Cote, this volume, chapter 10.

45 F.L. Morton "The Effect of the Canadian Charter of Rights on Canadian Federalism," *Publius* 25, no. 3 (1995), 181.

8

Courts, Legislatures, and the Politics of Judicial Decision-Making (or Perhaps the Notwithstanding Clause Isn't Such a Bad Thing after All)

Christopher Manfredi

The opportunity to participate in this volume of reflective essays on the notwithstanding clause at forty is a welcome one as it provides an occasion to return to themes that have been central to my intellectual life and academic career.[1] The title of my essay is, of course, a playful reference to the title of the article by Peter Hogg and Allison Bushell that launched the era of "dialogue theory" in Canada.[2] As set out by them, dialogue theory recognized the notwithstanding clause as an important architectural element of the Charter that moderates judicial supremacy by giving legislatures a power to modify or reverse rights-based judicial decisions. Unfortunately, Hogg and Bushell's recognition of the notwithstanding clause's legitimacy as an indispensable element of dialogue theory came at a moment when the clause was on the verge of falling into desuetude if that had not yet already occurred. Indeed, within five years of the original dialogue article, the Supreme Court arguably dismissed it as a viable understanding of the relationship between courts and legislatures in *Sauvé v. Canada* (2002).[3]

The recent, and somewhat unexpected, resurgence of the notwithstanding clause in legislation enacted by Saskatchewan, Ontario, and Quebec has sparked new interest in its theoretical grounding and practical implications, as well as further criticism of its very place in a constitutionally entrenched rights protecting document. As reflected in work by other scholars represented in this volume, there is, on the one hand, renewed interest in the clause as the basis for an approach to constitutional interpretation grounded in coordinate construction and, on the other hand, discussions of how courts themselves can limit its impact by careful reading of the clause's text.[4] More provocatively, in March 2022 Sarah Burningham offered an argument in favour of invoking the notwithstanding clause if the Supreme Court were to strike down section 33.1 of the Criminal Code, which negated the extreme intoxication defence established by the court in *R. v. Daviault* (1994).[5] With the courts having done just that in *R. v. Sullivan* (2022),[6] Burningham's argument may get a real-world test.

These recent developments around both the politics and scholarship of the notwithstanding clause provide an auspicious context in which to reflect on its forty-year history. My essay proceeds in three steps. It begins by setting out my disciplinary biases as a political scientist in a field generally dominated by legal scholars. This section describes courts as strategic political actors and considers how the notwithstanding clause affects their strategic relationship to legislatures. It then moves to consider my original defence of the notwithstanding clause, its textual deficiencies, and my proposals to address those deficiencies. Finally, I offer my thoughts on its recent use and the debates around those uses. Readers will recognize many of the arguments advanced in this essay from earlier publications, but that is fitting in a forty-year retrospective on a poorly understood component of the 1982 constitutional agreement.

THE POLITICAL SCIENCE OF JUDICIAL DECISION-MAKING

Since C. Herman Pritchett's classic study of the Roosevelt Court in the United States, political scientists have recognized that judicial decision-making, particularly in final courts of appeal, is driven by factors other rather than legal considerations.[7] There are several reasons for this aspect of decision-making in these courts.[8] First, cases reach them precisely because the applicable legal rules are ambiguous, and legal ambiguity enhances the importance of individual judicial attitudes and policy goals. Second, institutional characteristics such as discretionary jurisdiction and the absence of higher court review elevate policy over law. In short, the fundamental premise of the political analysis of law and courts is that justices are goal-oriented actors who seek to embed their policy preferences in legal rules.[9]

In addition to the role that policy plays in final appellate court decision-making, political scientists have also recognized that judges, like other political actors, face institutional constraints that force them to act strategically in pursuing their policy objectives, despite provisions designed to insulate them from ordinary political pressures.[10] These constraints – which force justices to consider other actors' preferences, the choices they expect others to make, and the context in which they operate[11] – produce strategic behaviour on two distinct levels. First, justices are constrained individually by rules that govern their interactions with colleagues. Most obviously, the successful transformation of individual policy preferences into law on multi-member appellate courts requires coalition building to produce majority support for decisions. Second, justices are constrained collectively by rules that govern the relationship between courts and other political institutions. They must be cognizant of the capacity of other institutions either to negate specific policy decisions or to challenge the legitimacy of the court itself. The achievement of short-term policy objectives depends to a significant degree on a court's institutional power and prestige,[12] and both inaction and over-extension can undermine the institutional legitimacy of courts within the political process. These institutional constraints generate a wide range of strategic behaviour, including internal bargaining, prospective thinking, agenda manipulation, and strategic opinion writing.[13]

One conclusion to which the political science of judicial decision-making leads is that Supreme Court policymaking is more than simply a by-product of the court's ordinary adjudicative function. As institutions involved in the creation of public policy, courts "exercise power on the basis of their judgment that their actions will produce socially desirable results."[14] Judicial policymaking is a two-step process in which textual interpretation is used to establish jurisdiction over a social problem, while the precise solution to that problem flows from a judgment, based on legally non-authoritative sources, about what constitutes the most socially beneficial decision.[15] Courts thus transform policy goals into legal doctrine in order to establish their authority over particular social problems and to legitimate the implementation of a particular solution.[16] The Supreme Court of Canada's judgments in cases like *Vriend* (1998) and *M. v. H.* (1999) are good illustrations of this dynamic.[17] In both cases the court saw a policy vacuum, used its interpretation of equality rights under section 15 of the Charter to assert jurisdiction over the problem, and specified a new policy to fill the perceived gap.

One of the important issues raised by judicial policymaking concerns the process by which judges identify "socially desirable results." According to one view, judges should, and do, take their cues from "widely held principle[s] of social morality."[18] While this standard makes judicial determination of social desirability seemingly less arbitrary, it is problematic for at least two reasons. First, it does not address the question, "Widely held by whom?" This is particularly problematic in the context of federalism, which grants areas of policy autonomy to subnational political units precisely to allow for the implementation of divergent social moralities. Second, the emphasis on *"widely held* social morality" (emphasis added) is inconsistent with perhaps the most important rationale for rights-based judicial review, which is to provide counter-majoritarian protection for minority rights. Yet, if judicial policymaking exists merely to implement what is already a "widely held" belief, then one could argue that it is unnecessary except as an acceleration mechanism.

In many respects, the court exercises its policymaking functions during the application of the *Oakes* test under the reasonable limits clause of section 1 of the Charter. As readers of this volume will know, the *Oakes* test contains two elements. First, a government seeking to defend a limit on rights must show that its legislative objective relates "to concerns that are *pressing and substantial* in a free and democratic society" (emphasis added). Second, the limit itself must be proportionate to the legislative objective, which courts determine according to a three-pronged test. To pass the first prong, the limit must be rationally connected to the legislative objective. Next, the government must show that, by impairing the relevant right or freedom as little as possible, the limit in question represents the least restrictive means of achieving the objective. Finally, it must be clear that the collective benefits of the limit outweigh its costs to the individual.

Although the *Oakes* test provides the basic framework for section 1 analysis, the court has held that this framework's application should vary according to both the type and intended beneficiaries of a public policy. In 1989, the court drew an explicit distinction between policies where legislatures are mediating the claims of competing groups and

those where government "is best characterized as the singular antag-
onist of an individual."[19] For policies of the first type, Chief Justice
Brian Dickson suggested, the court should be circumspect in assessing
legislative objectives and means. By contrast, the second type of policy frees the court to exercise its review function more aggressively.
However, the court has been inconsistent in following the implications
of its apparently general rule of judicial deference in socio-economic
policy cases.[20] For example, in RJR *Macdonald v. A.-G. Canada*
(1995), where a majority nullified restrictions on tobacco advertising, the court stated that "to carry judicial deference to the point of
accepting Parliament's view simply on the basis that the problem is
serious and the solution difficult, would be to diminish the role of
the courts in the constitutional process and to weaken the structure
of rights upon which our constitution and our nation is founded."[21]
In sum, the court has demonstrated an unwillingness to follow even
self-imposed limits on its judicial review function, and its control over
the interpretation and application of section 1 allows it to expand and
contract those limits to suit its immediate policy objectives.

How does the notwithstanding clause affect the strategic relationship between courts and legislatures? Its inclusion in the Charter
initially made it more difficult for the court to assert final authority
over the articulation and enforcement of constitutional rights because
it provided a clear institutional mechanism for legislatures to resist
assertions of judicial power. The clause generated uncertainty about
the locus of constitutional supremacy, which encouraged strategic
moderation of judicial review to avoid a political confrontation that
might undermine the court's long-term institutional status.

Nowhere is this perhaps more evident than in the Supreme Court's
January 1988 abortion decision.[22] The political context of the decision meant that there was at least the possibility that the Progressive
Conservative government of the day could find public support to
override a judicial declaration of a constitutional right to abortion.
This possibility presented the court with a strategic dilemma. On
the one hand, maintaining its Charter-based institutional authority to participate in controversial policy debates meant that the
court could not simply avoid the abortion issue, as it had in 1976.
On the other hand, faced with uncertainty about whether judicial
nullification of the federal abortion policy would trigger a legislative override, the justices confronted the possibility that the court
might "lose" its first direct confrontation with Parliament over a

highly visible policy issue. In the long-term, this outcome could have seriously undermined any future claims the court might make to constitutional supremacy. Chief Justice Dickson's solution to the dilemma was to nullify the existing law while maximizing the set of alternatives to legislative override. He did this by discovering administrative flaws in the operation of the abortion law while making it quite clear that it was "neither necessary nor wise" to "explore the broadest implications" of liberty in analyzing the abortion provisions.[23] One plausible explanation for this cautious approach was the viability of section 33.

As I discuss in the next section, the notwithstanding clause's legitimacy suffered a significant setback later in 1988 because of Quebec's use of it in the context of responding to the court's judgment in *Ford v. Quebec* (1988).[24] A decade later, the Alberta government learned a very hard lesson about the politics of section 33. On 10 March, Alberta introduced a bill to compensate victims of provincial eugenic sterilization laws that were in effect from 1929 to 1972. One element of the bill was a provision to prohibit victims from suing for additional compensation, and the government proposed to shield that provision from judicial review through the notwithstanding clause. In purely legal terms, there was nothing particularly unusual about this provision. For example, provincial workers' compensation and no-fault automobile insurance regimes also prohibit individual lawsuits as a quid pro quo for a simplified system of guaranteed compensation. On an emotional level, however, wielding the notwithstanding clause against this vulnerable group smacked of mean-spiritedness. As a result, one day after introducing the bill, the provincial attorney general withdrew it under intense political pressure. Alberta's premier Ralph Klein explained the decision to withdraw the bill in the following terms: "It became abundantly clear that to individuals in this country the Charter of Rights and Freedoms is paramount and the use of any tool ... to undermine [it] is something that should be used only in very, very rare circumstances."[25] Not surprisingly, one month later, the Alberta government summarily dismissed the idea of invoking the notwithstanding clause after the court's decision in *Vriend* (the very case in which the court recognized "dialogue theory") that its human rights act must be read as providing protection on the basis of sexual orientation.

The debate over same-sex marriage appeared for a time to revive interest in section 33. In fact, in March 2000 a private member's bill – the Marriage Amendment Act – was passed in Alberta that defined marriage exclusively as an opposite-sex union and contained a notwithstanding clause to protect that definition from Charter review. Although undoubtedly unconstitutional on federalism grounds, the bill indicated the possibility that a social innovation as fundamental as changing the legal definition of marriage might provoke sufficient political resistance to revitalize the legislative override. Ironically, it was precisely this possibility that may have made the notwithstanding clause even more difficult to invoke.

On 16 September 2003, the federal opposition introduced a motion in Parliament "to reaffirm that marriage is and should remain the union of one man and one woman to the exclusion of all others, and that Parliament take all necessary steps within the jurisdiction of the Parliament of Canada to preserve this definition of marriage in Canada." The motion presented members of the governing Liberal Party with a dilemma: most of them had supported an almost identical motion in 1999, but the government's new policy was that the definition of marriage should be changed to include same-sex unions. The prime minister suggested that those members could vote differently in 2003 in good conscience because a vote for the motion would be a vote against the Charter of Rights and Freedoms. Why? Because "all necessary steps" might include invoking the notwithstanding clause, and to invoke the notwithstanding clause would undermine the Charter. The prime minister's gambit worked: by the narrowest of margins (the speaker casting the tie-breaking vote against it), the House of Commons rejected an amendment to remove the reference to "all necessary steps," leading to the rejection of the main motion by a vote of 137–132. The successful transformation of a motion about the definition of marriage into a de facto referendum on the notwithstanding clause affirmed perceptions of a growing constitutional convention that it should never be invoked by any legislative body.[26]

To summarize, inclusion of a legislative override provision in the Charter generated uncertainty about the institutional locus of constitutional supremacy. For a Supreme Court vested with newly expanded powers of judicial review, this uncertainty created conditions for the strategic use of those powers to avoid a political confrontation that might undermine its long-term institutional status. However, the unfolding of events from late 1988 into the early 2000s gradually shifted the balance of power toward the courts.

Changing institutional constraints affected the nature of strategic judicial behaviour,[27] and as the likely use of section 33 declined, the assertion of judicial power increased.

THE NOTWITHSTANDING CLAUSE AND LIBERAL CONSTITUTIONALISM: A DEFENCE AND REFORM PROPOSALS

In December 1988, four months after I began my academic career at McGill University, the Supreme Court struck down important provisions of Quebec's Bill 101. Quebec responded with Bill 178, which it immunized from judicial review by invoking the notwithstanding clause. The reaction was swift and negative, with a consensus emerging that the clause was at best inconsistent with the idea of constitutionally entrenched rights, and at worst a constitutional abomination. Most famously, Prime Minister Brian Mulroney called it "that major fatal flaw of 1981, which reduces your individual rights and mine." The notwithstanding clause, Mulroney continued, "holds rights hostage" and renders the entire Constitution suspect. Any constitution, he concluded, "that does not protect the inalienable and imprescriptible individual rights of individual Canadians is not worth the paper it is written on."[28]

With the hubris of youth, I decided to write a book that argued that section 33 was, in fact, a *positive* contribution to liberal constitutionalism in Canada. I argued that opposition to the notwithstanding clause was the product of an historical accident and three conceptual errors. The historical accident was that Canadians experienced a use of section 33 they found objectionable before the Supreme Court rendered a politically unpopular Charter decision. The first conceptual error involved a misunderstanding of the constitutional role of legislatures and courts in liberal constitutional theory. There is nothing in that theory that assigns the task of constitutional interpretation exclusively to courts; legislatures also have a legitimate and important role to play as posited by the theory of coordinate construction.[29] The second conceptual error stemmed from a basic misunderstanding of the legislative process as being characterized by the haphazard adoption of measures motivated by majority tyranny. To be sure, legislatures can act both irrationally and arbitrarily, and judicial review provides an important check on these pathologies of legislative behaviour. Nevertheless, judicial supremacy may be a cure worse than the disease since courts suffer from their own institutional pathologies when it comes to evaluating complex policy choices. The final conceptual error was a basic misunderstanding of the nature of Charter adjudication. Although Charter cases raise fundamental questions about rights or moral principles, the dispute in most cases is about whether the legislature has chosen the least restrictive means of achieving an important policy objective. Yet, even if Charter cases did involve serious disputes about fundamental moral principles on a regular basis, there would be no reason to leave the resolution of those disputes in the exclusive hands of Supreme Court justices.

The legitimacy of the notwithstanding clause must lie, therefore, in its contribution to *constitutional* supremacy (rather than preservation of legislative supremacy) by recognizing the equal responsibility and authority of legislatures to interpret the Charter. I suggested, therefore, that "section 33 can have a positive impact by encouraging a more politically vital discourse on the meaning of rights and their relationship to competing constitutional visions than what emanates from the judicial monologue that results from a regime of judicial supremacy."[30] Although I claim no direct influence for it, this idea became expressed as the core proposition of "dialogue theory," which means that I was very much in favour of dialogue theory before I was against it!

Although I argued that the notwithstanding clause is consistent with liberal constitutionalism, this did not mean that it was perfect in its original form. The clause suffered from three deficiencies: (1) it presented itself as an opportunity for legislatures to *override rights* themselves; (2) it could be used *pre-emptively*; and (3) it had very weak *political accountability* mechanisms. All three deficiencies were evident in Bill 178. Although Bill 178 followed a Supreme Court decision, it was in fact a pre-emptive use of the clause because Bill 178 did not re-enact the identical provisions nullified by the court in *Ford*. It would have been preferable for Quebec to allow Bill 178's provisions – which, after all, simply followed principles articulated in the court's reasonable limits analysis – to be tested in litigation. However, for obvious political reasons, Quebec decided to assert legislative authority over language policy by pre-emptive use of the notwithstanding clause.

To address these deficiencies, I proposed three changes to the text of the notwithstanding clause.[31] First, I proposed the following

change to section 33(1) of the Charter: "May expressly declare …
that the Act or a provision thereof shall operate notwithstanding *a*
final judicial decision that the Act or a provision thereof abrogates
or unreasonably limits a provision." The purpose of this change
was two-fold: to make it clear that the legislature was overriding
a judicial interpretation of a right rather than the right itself, and
to prevent pre-emptive use of the notwithstanding clause. Second, I
proposed that the text be amended to require a three-fifths majority
to enact the clause, a proposal designed to ensure that there was
widespread political consensus that the judicial interpretation of
a right being overridden was indeed flawed. Finally, I proposed to
augment the five-year sunset clause already embedded in section 33
with the proviso that "notwithstanding declarations" also cease to
have effect with the dissolution of the parliament or legislature that
made the declaration. This would strengthen the political accountability mechanism by ensuring that the declaration and its potential
re-enactment would become an electoral issue.

I presented these textual amendments as one strategy for making the notwithstanding clause even more compatible with liberal
constitutional theory. The core principle of that theory is the subordi-
nation of all political power, including judicial power, to procedural
and substantive constitutional rules. While it is true that no constitution can long survive if its meaning "is frozen in time to the moment
of adoption," liberal constitutionalism does not establish a judicial
monopoly over the process of adapting constitutions to changing
social circumstances. In addition to formal amendment, legislatures
and executives must play a role in the continuous process of adap-
tation. In Canada, the procedural rules of the Constitution have
been kept flexible with relatively little judicial assistance through
the evolution of constitutional conventions.[32] Moreover, the original
formulation of the living tree doctrine allowed Canadian governments to pursue innovative policy choices consistent with novel
interpretations of constitutional language. Contrary to the assertion
of many critics of the notwithstanding clause, who would prefer a
judicial monopoly over constitutional interpretation, such a monopoly can produce more rigidity than flexibility.

Not surprisingly, these reform proposals attracted little attention
and gained no traction. Instead, as I sketched out in the previous
section of this essay, the notwithstanding clause became a less
and less viable option for legislatures dissatisfied with judicial

interpretations of rights. My youthful hubris gradually gave way to early-middle-aged cynicism, and I became increasingly pessimistic that the notwithstanding clause would, in fact, encourage "a more politically vital discourse on the meaning of rights and their relationship to competing constitutional visions."

This cynicism manifested itself in two ways. One was a series of articles, beginning in 1999, critical of dialogue theory as it had emerged from Hogg and Bushell.[33] In addition to criticizing conceptual and operational aspects of the Hogg-Bushell work, I considered it overly simplistic, ahistorical, and apolitical to ground a theory of dialogic constitutionalism in the mere existence of the notwithstanding clause. Although legislatures certainly *could* reverse judicial decisions by override, the advocates of strong judicial power – if not of supremacy – had altered the political context to put the presumptive advantage in debates about rights squarely in the hands of the Supreme Court. The second manifestation was a second edition of *Judicial Power and the Charter* aimed at updating its review of the court's impact on public policy and understanding how legislatures had lost most, if not all, of their authority to define rights, as opposed to simply re-evaluating "the balance struck by the courts between constitutional rights and other interests."[34]

THE NOTWITHSTANDING CLAUSE AT FORTY: NEW LIFE OR CONTINUED DECLINE?

Three decades after Bill 178 turned the notwithstanding clause into something of a third rail of Canadian constitutional politics, three provinces invoked it in very high-profile ways over a period of five years. In 2017, Saskatchewan invoked the clause in legislation responding to a Court of Queen's Bench ruling that it was unconstitutional to fund non-Catholic students to attend Catholic separate schools. Quebec invoked the clause in two controversial pieces of legislation in 2019 and 2022: An Act Respecting the Laicity of the State (2019) and An Act Respecting French, the Official and Common Language of Quebec (2022). Finally, Ontario included the clause in An Act to Amend the Election Finances Act (2021) and An Act to Resolve Labour Disputes Involving School Board Employees Represented by the Canadian Union of Public Employees (2022, known as Bill 28). The two Quebec uses of the clause and the 2022 Ontario use (Bill 28) were clearly pre-emptive, while the 2021

Ontario and the Saskatchewan uses might be described as "partially pre-emptive," since they were enacted in lieu of appealing the judicial decisions to which they were a response.

Although these uses of the notwithstanding clause generated some scholarly support for its revival,[35] it is fair to say that they largely remobilized critics who thought the clause had become irrelevant to Charter discourse. In particular, the persistence of pre-emptive uses produced interesting work by Leckey, Webber, and Mendelsohn.[36] At the core of this work is the assertion that there is a judicial remedy to pre-emptive uses of the notwithstanding clause. This line of argument asserts that, although section 33 of the Charter precludes the operation of a law, it does not foreclose judicial review of the statute. To be more precise, although the notwithstanding clause renders unavailable invalidation of a statute as a remedy under section 51 of the Constitution Act, it leaves open the possibility of judicial declarations of unconstitutionality under section 24(1) of the Charter.

This argument is an intriguing one, and it certainly avoids the necessity of amending the text of section 33 as I recommended in 1993. Its principal defect, however, is that it perpetuates the idea of judicial supremacy in defining both the substance of constitutional rights and the reasonable limits that may attach to them. In this sense, it entrenches the perception that legislatures are overriding rights when they invoke the notwithstanding clause, as opposed to disagreeing with a judicial interpretation of rights. Moreover, although it provides judicial recourse against pre-emptive notwithstanding clauses, it does not prevent them.

Ironically, the recent saga of Ontario's Bill 28 supports the notion that the appropriate – and effective – recourse to illegitimate uses of the notwithstanding clause is political. To be very clear: although nothing in the text of the notwithstanding clause prevented its pre-emptive use in Bill 28, such a use is not justified under my theory of the clause's inherent consistency with constitutional supremacy (even to "override" a right the court had only inserted into the Charter in 2015 by reversing its earlier precedent from 1987).[37] Not surprisingly, the political opposition was swift and effective: within only a few days of Royal Assent, the Ontario government backed away from its decision, and formally repealed Bill 28 eleven days after it received Royal Assent (Bill 35). In many ways, the Bill 28 saga resembles Alberta's experience in March 1998, discussed earlier in this chapter.

Nevertheless, the recent Quebec and Ontario uses of the notwithstanding clause, and to a lesser extent the Saskatchewan use, have mostly served to perpetuate the conceptual errors underlying opposition to the clause on which I focused in 1993. However, as Sarah Burningham suggested in March 2022, the court's decision in *R. v. Sullivan* (2022) could have generated sufficiently negative public opinion to correct Bill 178's historical accident of an objectionable use of the notwithstanding clause occurring prior to a politically unpopular Charter decision. At issue in *Sullivan* was the constitutionality of the ironically numbered section 33.1 of the Criminal Code, which nullified the defence of extreme intoxication the court established in *R. v. Daviault* (1994). Given that section 33.1 of the Criminal Code directly repudiated the *Daviault* holding – Kent Roach has described it as an "in your face" legislative response[38] – the court's options were limited had it wanted to uphold its constitutionality. For example, because section 33.1 simply negated the right articulated in *Daviault*, the court could not easily have determined that it was a reasonable limit on that right. The court could have taken refuge in the three dissenting votes in *Daviault* to take the very radical path of declaring that the case was wrongly decided, thereby rendering section 33.1 redundant. Instead, it reached the unanimous judgment that section 33.1 was unconstitutional.

Subsequently, the only option available to the federal government, had it wished to negate the defence of extreme intoxication, was to invoke the notwithstanding clause, and Burningham made a strong case in favour of it doing so. However, the court's own strategic calculation that there was little risk of this occurring appears to have been confirmed, at least at the time of writing this chapter. Indeed, the generally negative media and scholarly reactions to the recent provincial uses of the clause – especially in Ontario and Quebec – probably reduced that risk further. Rather than providing a new foundation for the notwithstanding clause's legitimacy, those uses have probably accelerated its decline.

CONCLUSION

Defending the notwithstanding clause has been an uphill battle from the beginning. In particular, the political circumstances that produced it inhibited the public development of a coherent theoretical justification for the clause. The most extensive public discussion of this provision occurred on 20 November 1981, when then Justice Minister Jean Chrétien introduced the constitutional resolution containing the Charter into the House of Commons. Even then, Chrétien's remarks on section 33 covered only eleven paragraphs and were aimed primarily at assuring the House that it did not "emasculate" the Charter. The only theoretical point that Chrétien stressed in these remarks was that section 33 would be an infrequently used "safety valve" which would ensure "that legislatures rather than judges have the final say on important matters of public policy." Section 33, Chrétien argued, would allow legislatures "to correct absurd situations without going through the difficulty of obtaining constitutional amendments."[39] Paradoxically, Chrétien's defence of the notwithstanding clause rested on a tension between judicial supremacy and legislative supremacy, with the clause ultimately deciding this tension in favour of legislative supremacy in critical instances.

The paradox is that the constitutional regime established in 1982 was neither a continuation of the existing regime of legislative supremacy nor a new regime of judicial supremacy: it was a regime of *constitutional* supremacy. Indeed, there is no doubt that section 52(1) of the Constitution Act, 1982 and section 24(1) of the Charter explicitly establish a political regime of constitutional supremacy in which limits on political power are enforced through constitutional judicial review of statutes, regulations, and official conduct. Nor was the notwithstanding clause intended to inhibit the expansion of judicial power under the Charter: constitutionally entrenched bills of rights inevitably enhance the power of final courts of appeal. Although it is useful and important to debate the normative implications of this shift in power, its legitimacy or illegitimacy is somewhat beside the point. Greater and more active use of judicial power under the Charter is simply a fact. At its core, judicial activism is the willingness of courts to reverse or otherwise alter the policy decisions of legislatures and executives. A court that never did this would be entirely deferential; a court that always did it would be completely activist. In the real world, of course, no court's behaviour reflects either of these extremes. In practice, this means that *every* court is at least somewhat activist. Although reasonable people may disagree whether a court has been *too* activist or exercised its activism outside the parameters of its constitutional authority, it is possible to compare levels of activism across different courts or on the same court at different periods of time.

The justification for the notwithstanding clause lies not in its preservation of legislative supremacy or potential suppression of judicial activism, but in its role in remedying a critical paradox of liberal constitutionalism. The paradox lies in this: if judicial review evolves such that political power in its judicial form is limited only by a constitution whose meaning courts alone define, then judicial power is no longer itself constrained by constitutional limits. The notwithstanding clause recognizes that courts can make mistakes when defining and applying rights, and it provides a more elegant, expeditious, and politically accountable mechanism for legislatures to respond to those occasions. Ultimately, a constitution's meaning must belong to the people who must live under it. The notwithstanding clause makes that possible.

NOTES

1 This essay reflects my personal views as a judicial politics scholar and professor of political science and should not be associated with my position as a senior academic administrator at McGill University, nor should it be considered as representing the position of McGill University.

2 Peter Hogg and Allison Bushell, "The Charter Dialogue Between Courts and Legislatures (Or Perhaps the Charter of Rights Isn't Such a Bad Thing After All," *Osgoode Hall Law Journal* 35, no. 1 (1997): 75–124.

3 *Sauvé v. Canada* [2002] 3 SCR 519. See Christopher P. Manfredi, "The Day the Dialogue Died: A Comment on Sauvé v. Canada," *Osgoode Hall Law Journal* 45, no. 1 (2007): 105–23. Readers should know that I served as an expert witness for the government of Canada in this litigation.

4 For coordinate construction, see the papers by Newman and Sigalet. For judicial mitigation of the clause, see the papers by Leckey, Webber, and Eberts.

5 *R. v. Daviault* [1994] 3 SCR 62; Sarah Burningham, "Notwithstanding Extreme Intoxication," *Policy Options*, 22 March 2022, https://policyoptions.irpp.org/magazines/notwithstanding-extreme-intoxication/.

6 *R. v. Sullivan*, 2022 SCC-19 (13 May 2022).

7 Lawrence Baum, *The Puzzle of Judicial Behavior* (Ann Arbor: University of Michigan Press, 1997), 57. See C. Herman Pritchett, *The Roosevelt Court: A Study in Judicial Politics and Values 1937–1947* (New York: Macmillan, 1948).

8 Baum, *Puzzle of Judicial Behavior*, 64, 69.

9 Jeffrey Segal, "Separation-of-Powers Games in the Positive Theory of Congress and Courts," *American Political Science Review* 91 (1997): 30.

10 See: Walter F. Murphy, *Elements of Judicial Strategy* (Chicago: University of Chicago Press, 1964); Jack Knight and Lee Epstein, "On the Struggle for Judicial Supremacy," *Law & Society Review* 30 (1996): 92. These institutional provisions include security of tenure and judicial independence. Although subject to much less systematic study than the US court, there is evidence that similar forms of strategic behaviour are present on the Canadian court. See: Lorne Sossin, "The Sounds of Silence: Law Clerks, Policy Making and the Supreme Court of Canada," UBC *Law Review* 30 (1996): 294–97; Carl Baar, "Using Process Theory to Explain Judicial Decision Making," *Canadian Journal of Law and Society* 1 (1986): 57–79; Douglas Sanders, "The Bill of Rights and the Indian Act," in *Equality Rights and the Charter*, ed. Anne Bayefsky and Mary Eberts (Toronto: Carswell, 1985), 534–7; Peter H. Russell, "The *Anti-Inflation* Case: The Anatomy of a Constitutional Decision," *Canadian Public Administration* 20 (1977): 632–65.

11 Lee Epstein and Jack Knight, *The Choices Justices Make* (Washington: CQ Press, 1998), xiii.

12 Baum, *Puzzle of Judicial Behavior*, 97.

13 Ibid., 59–107.

14 Malcolm M. Feeley and Edward L. Rubin, *Judicial Policy Making and the Modern State: How the Courts Reformed America's Prisons* (Cambridge: Cambridge University Press, 1998), 5.

15 Ibid., 148.

16 Ibid., 210.

17 *Vriend v. Alberta* [1998] 1 SCR 493; *M. v. H.* [1999] 2 SCR 3.

18 Feeley and Rubin, *Judicial Policy Making*, 161.

19 *A.-G. Quebec v. Irwin Toy* [1989] 1 S.C.R. 927, 993–4. See also Christopher M. Dassios and Clifton P. Prophet, "Charter Section 1: The Decline of Grand Unified Theory and the Trend Towards Deference in the Supreme Court of Canada," *Advocates' Quarterly* 15 (1993): 289–91.

20 Kent Roach has noted that there is a reasonable justification underlying the criticism that the Supreme Court is not always consistent about when it should defer to legislative limits on rights. See Kent Roach, "Judicial Activism in the Supreme Court of Canada," in *Judicial Activism in Common Law Supreme Courts*, ed. Brice Dickson (Oxford: Oxford University Press, 2007), 77.

21 RJR *Macdonald v. A.-G. Canada* [1995] 3 S.C.R. 199, para. 136.

22 *Morgentaler, Smoling and Scott v. The Queen* [1988] 1 SCR 30.

23 [1988] 1 SCR at 51.

24 *Ford v. Quebec (Attorney General)* [1988] 2 SCR 712.

25 Allyson Jeffs, "About Face: Massive Outcry Forces Klein to Back Down on Controversial Move to Limit Sterilization Settlements," *Edmonton Journal*, 12 March 1998.

26 Andrew Heard, *Canadian Constitutional Conventions: The Marriage of Law and Politics* (Toronto: Oxford University Press, 1991), 147.

27 Segal, "Separation-of-Powers Games," 42.

28 House of Commons Debates, (6 April 1989) at 153 (Brian Mulroney).

29 See Dennis Baker, *Not Quite Supreme: The Courts and Coordinate Constitutional Interpretation* (Montreal: McGill-Queen's University Press, 2010).

30 Christopher Manfredi, *Judicial Power and the Charter* (Toronto: McClelland and Stewart, 1993), 207–8.

31 Manfredi, *Judicial Power*, 208–9. Although one could argue that pre-emptive use of the notwithstanding clause at least has the virtue of providing legal certainty, I would counter that this is not sufficiently beneficial to short-circuit the process of constitutional supremacy.

32 Manfredi, 209.

33 Christopher Manfredi and James Kelly, "Six Degrees of Dialogue: A Response to Hogg and Bushell," *Osgoode Hall Law Journal* 37, no. 3 (1999): 513–27; Christopher Manfredi and James Kelly, "Dialogue, Deference and Restraint: Judicial Independence and Trial Procedures," *Saskatchewan Law Review* 64, no. 2 (2001): 323–46; Christopher Manfredi, "The Unfulfilled Promise of Dialogic Constitutionalism: Judicial-Legislative Relationships Under the Canadian Charter of Rights and Freedoms," in *Protecting Rights Without a Bill of Rights: Institutional Performance and Reform in Australia,* eds. Tom Campbell, Jeffrey Goldsworthy, and Adrienne Stone (Aldershot, UK/Burlington, VT: Ashgate, 2006), 239–59; Christopher Manfredi, "The Day the Dialogue Died: A Comment on *Sauvé v. Canada,*" *Osgoode Hall Law Journal* 45, no. 1 (2007): 105–23.

34 Sujit Choudhry, "Review of *Judicial Power and the Charter, 2d ed.*" in *International Journal of Constitutional Law* 1 (2003): 384.

35 See the papers by Newman, Pelletier, St-Hilaire, Sigalet, Rousseau, and Cote.

36 See, for example: Robert Leckey and Eric Mendelsohn, "The Notwithstanding Clause: Legislatures, Courts, and the Electorate," *University of Toronto Law Journal* 72, no. 2 (2022): 189–215; Grégoire Webber, Eric Mendelsohn, and Robert Leckey, "The Faulty Received

Wisdom around the Notwithstanding Clause," *Policy Options*, 10 May 2019, policyoptions.irpp.org/magazines/may-2019/faulty-wisdom-notwithstanding-clause.

37 *Reference Re Public Service Employee Relations Act (Alta.)* [1987] 1 SCR 313; *Saskatchewan Federation of Labour v. Saskatchewan* [2015] 1 SCR 245.
38 Kent Roach, "Constitutional and Common Law Dialogues Between the Supreme Court and Canadian Legislatures," *Canadian Bar Review* 80 (2001): 524.
39 *House of Commons Debates*, 20 November 1981, 13042–3.

PART FOUR

Quebec

Without doubt, Quebec has been the predominant living labora-
tory for our experiment with and study of the notwithstanding
clause (NWC). Quebec was the first jurisdiction in which it was
invoked and was also the first to do so pre-emptively and in
omnibus fashion. It is also in Quebec that the political discourse
has been richest on the relationship between general political will,
as expressed by the National Assembly, and judicial review on
constitutional grounds, and on the tension between individual
and collective rights and interests. It is therefore not surprising
that within the federation, it is in Quebec that the tradition of
liberal constitutionalism has found both its most articulate
expression and its greatest challenge and setbacks.

In the first two essays in this section, the authors provide not
only a full-throated defence of the NWC, explaining that it is a legitimate political device that enables legislatures to give expression to
popular will within a constitutional, democratic framework, but
also that it is, in Quebec's case, an absolutely necessary instrument
through which Quebec's distinct character can find both political expression and legal protection. Benoît Pelletier identifies and
endeavours to dismantle the "myths" associated with the NWC:
first, that its invocation produces a high political price for the government invoking it, and second, that its invocation amounts to an
admission, implicit or otherwise, of a denial of rights or freedoms.
Guillaume Rousseau and François Côté argue that the NWC has
given rise to a distinct Quebec theory which "holds that legislative

overrides can be legitimately made, even pre-emptively, in order to promote social justice or national identity."

In the last two essays in this section, Marion Sandilands and Jonathan Montpetit push back strongly, arguing that Quebec's invocation of the NWC, especially in the contexts of Bills 21 and 96, effectively subordinates fundamental rights and freedoms – especially as expressed in the Canadian and Quebec Charters of Human Rights and Freedoms – to a nationalist conception of Quebec. The effect, Sandilands argues, is rendering nugatory the enumerated rights and freedoms in both Charters, in favour of a constitutionalized French language charter given supremacy over all other laws and given moral justification by way of a declaration of Quebec nationhood.

Montpetit makes the broader argument that the result of Quebec's use of the NWC in these particular ways is to jeopardize, if not altogether terminate, Quebec's relatively short-lived – though rich and enthusiastic – experiment with liberal constitutionalism which began with the Quiet Revolution.

9

The Notwithstanding Powers and Provisions:
An Asset for Quebec and for Canada

Benoît Pelletier

Canadian federalism is based on the originality of its components, that is, on the particularism of the federated states (the provinces). The Supreme Court of Canada has recognized this in the past, in eloquent and unequivocal terms: "The principle of federation recognizes the diversity of the component parts of Confederation, and the autonomy of provincial governments to develop their societies within their respective spheres of jurisdiction."[1]

In this chapter, we will argue, among other things, that one of the ways in which the Canadian constitutional framework allows each component of the Canadian federation to express its uniqueness is through the notwithstanding power in section 33 of the Canadian Charter of Rights and Freedoms.[2] This is even more true for Quebec, since it has a duty to uphold, defend, preserve, and develop its distinctiveness – based on, among other things, its national characteristics, including language, culture, civil law, social values, institutions, and a general way of life – within the Canadian federation.

In support of this thesis, we will examine the nature of overriding powers and provisions and their place in the basic structure of the Canadian state (part I), their compatibility with federalism and constitutionalism and with the recognition of rights and freedoms (part II), the myths regarding their use (part III), and the legal-political context in which they are occurring and evolving (part IV).

I. THE NATURE OF OVERRIDING POWERS AND
PROVISIONS[3] AND THEIR PLACE IN THE BASIC
STRUCTURE OF THE CANADIAN STATE

Within a state, there must be a healthy balance between the legislative and executive branches on the one hand, and the judiciary on the other. This balance is at the heart of constitutionalism, or at least essential to it.

Constitutional democracy is somewhat different from the general principle of democracy. The latter is essentially based on the will of the majority in a given political situation or unit. Constitutional democracy, however, is much more complex. It involves the interaction of the legislative, executive, and judicial branches of government in the pursuit of two objectives: one is the implementation of what might be called the "collective will," and the other is the protection of minority groups. The legislature,[4] the government, and the courts each have a role to play in achieving these two objectives. As a matter of fact, constitutional democracy involves both respect for the majority will of the community and respect for the rights of minorities, particularly their constitutional rights. It exists when the authority of the majority is limited by legal and constitutional rules in a way that the right of individuals and minorities are preserved. Constitutional democracy does not, however, prevent the state from making certain societal choices that are necessary for its continuation.

One cannot speak of societal choices or the promotion of collective rights and interests without also speaking of appreciation for minority rights. In fact, minorities are part of the community and the interests of the minority are intertwined or added to those of the majority group.

However, it comes as a surprise to us that the notwithstanding powers are being questioned as inconsistent with the very principle of constitutional democracy. After all, notwithstanding powers and provisions are far more democratic – being exercised by the elected house of the people, among others – than decisions made by unelected judges on the basis of their own understanding of the law, or even their own ideology.

With the patriation of the Canadian Constitution in 1982, the constituent authorities saw fit to include a notwithstanding power in section 33 of the Canadian Charter. Indeed, this power allows Parliament and provincial legislatures to override fundamental freedoms, legal rights, and equality rights.[5] However, this provision cannot be applied to democratic rights, mobility rights, and linguistic rights.[6] Moreover, the question of equality rights between men and women remains unanswered,[7] and the question of whether the override power can apply to regulations or other delegated legislation also remains unresolved at this time.[8]

Canada only officially incorporated a notwithstanding power into its new constitutional charter on 17 April 1982, with the patriation of the Canadian Constitution. However, such a provision was previously discussed and agreed upon, in November 1981, as part of a political agreement on the adoption of the Charter between the federal minister of justice, Jean Chrétien, and the attorneys general of Saskatchewan and Ontario, Roy Romanow and Roy McMurtry, which the prime minister and the premiers – with the exception of the premier of Quebec – accepted.[9]

To date, the Canadian government has never invoked the override power in the Charter. A notwithstanding power is found in section 2 of the Canadian Bill of Rights,[10] a federal statute that is quasi-constitutional in nature. The Supreme Court of Canada has paid so little attention to this statute in its jurisprudence that Parliament has never needed to use a "notwithstanding" clause to override the legislative primacy of the bill.

Section 33 has, nonetheless, been used on occasion by provincial governments, in particular by Quebec in 1982 in the context of the enactment of an omnibus legislation repealing all laws passed before the Charter came into force and re-enacting them after adding a standard provision declaring that the legislation applies without regard to section 2 and sections 7 to 15 of the Charter.[11] Quebec has also used notwithstanding provisions more recently, in the context of the Act Respecting the Laicity of the State[12] and Bill 96, An Act Respecting French, the Official and Common Language of Quebec.[13] A notwithstanding power is also found in section 52 of the Charter of Human Rights and Freedoms.[14] Saskatchewan, the Yukon, Ontario, Alberta, and New Brunswick have also made use of section 33 of the Charter or have ever expressed the intention to do so.[15]

Under the notwithstanding power, "The elected legislative branch of government may make important policy decisions and isolate them from review by the unelected judicial branch of government."[16]

While it is useful and highly beneficial for the courts to play a role in the elaboration and interpretation of the rights and freedoms that Canadians should enjoy, they must refrain from acting as legislators. If judges were to play a greater "political" role, their non-accountability to the electorate might well be a course of controversy. This would undermine the independence and impartiality of the courts, and ultimately politicize them.[17] Put differently, allowing political decisions to be made by the elected representatives mitigates the politicization of the courts.[18] In this sense, the absence of a notwithstanding power in the Charter would go against the principles of constitutional democracy, as the courts would be the final arbiters of social values.

In *Ford v. Quebec (Attorney General)*,[19] the Supreme Court of Canada determined that section 33 sets out formal requirements only and that, in invoking it, Parliament or a legislature must specify the provisions it intends to override. More specifically, the court states that if the Parliament or a legislature wishes to override part of a provision, section, or subsection of the Charter, there must be a precise, explicit mention of the number of the section, subsection, or paragraph of the Charter that contains the provision or provisions exempted.[20] One of the purposes of this is to ensure that the decision to invoke section 33 of the Charter is made with full knowledge of the facts and that the public itself is well informed of the existence and scope of the exemption.

In the *Ford* case, the Supreme Court of Canada has examined the legitimacy of the override power in section 33 of the Charter.[21] The word "legitimacy" is important here because it implies an examination of the policy as well as the legal aspects of the section 33 provisions in question. Legitimacy is a hard concept to define. It is based on both significant popular support and respect for the established constitutional order, unless it allows the creation of a new constitutional order based on the will of the people. The Supreme Court concluded that the use of section 33 of the Charter was constitutional in itself, as part of the constitutional order and as a matter of strict law, as well as politically legitimate.[22] The use of the notwithstanding power is only framed in terms of undemanding rules of form, in order to give the legislature the maximum possible leeway in this matter.

In the *Devine*[23] case, the Supreme Court of Canada confirmed the previous *Ford* decision.[24]

In the *Ontario (AG)* v. *G*[25] case, Karakatsanis J., on behalf of five of her colleagues,[26] reiterated that the override power in section 33 of the Charter can be invoked even for "purely political reasons."[27]

Côté and Brown J.J., dissenting in part, held that section 33 of the Charter allows Parliament and provincial legislatures to suspend the effect of a declaration of invalidity.[28] They further argued as follows: "S. 33(1) suggests that, in cases to which it applies, *legislatures*, and *not courts*, are best positioned to know when a suspended declaration is desirable and if so, for how long."[29]

In the *Hak*[30] case, Marc-André Blanchard J., of the Superior Court of Quebec, among other things, stated that there should be a connection between the notwithstanding provisions and the objectives pursued by the legislature.[31]

As can be seen from the foregoing, the jurisprudence of the Supreme Court of Canada has so far been very light on the exercise of the override power. Blanchard J. would like to see at least a *prima facie* case that the suspension of a right or freedom is in furtherance of the legislature's objective.[32] Clearly, on the legal side, we are not there yet.

II. THE COMPATIBILITY OF OVERRIDING POWERS AND PROVISIONS WITH FEDERALISM AND CONSTITUTIONALISM AND WITH THE RECOGNITION OF RIGHTS AND FREEDOMS

Overall, it can be said that section 33 of the Charter is not necessarily inconsistent with the rights and freedoms guaranteed by the Charter. Rather, it prevents the courts from assuming a political role, that is, the courts do not make decisions on certain sensitive matters that are more appropriately made by the legislative or executive branches of the government.[33] In other words, section 33 places certain policy decisions about the application of rights and freedoms themselves in the hands of legislators and governments. It modulates the application of those rights and freedoms, but the intention of the institutions using them being to necessarily restrict or violate them.

Since it flows directly from it and is a part of it, the notwithstanding power in section 33 of the Charter is not inconsistent with the Constitution of Canada. Indeed, the overriding power in section 33, the supporting provision (justification provision) in section 1 of the Charter, and the various rights and freedoms set out in the Charter are all part of the same constitutional package, which seeks to accommodate the rights and freedoms of each individual, the rights and freedoms of others, the general welfare, the collective will, and the separation of powers in the state.

The notwithstanding power in section 33 of the Charter is not inconsistent either with the federal principle itself, considering the latter postulates respect for the particular identity of federated political entities (the provinces, in the case of Canada) as well as the expression of the diversity intrinsic to a country. This "expression of diversity" is permitted and encouraged by the notwithstanding power in section 33.

Federalism presupposes respect for the intrinsic diversity of a country. More specifically, it is a flexible way of organizing power in a state. This flexibility allows federalism to adapt to the different socio-political and socio-demographic contexts to which it is exposed. The power of exemption easily fits into this dynamic, considering it allows political entities to make collective choices that differ from those of its federative partners.

As for constitutionalism, it is consistent with the idea of the superiority or predominance of the constitutional order in a state. But the power to override is part of the constitutional framework itself. It is intended to ensure that collective interests are not ignored.

The notwithstanding power does not weaken the Charter. Rather, it is part of it.[34] It is intended to ensure that collective interests are given fair consideration in a context where a culture of individual rights and freedoms prevails.

III. THE APPLICATION OF THE OVERRIDING POWERS AND PROVISIONS AND THEIR ROLE IN JUDICIAL INTERPRETATION

It is worth remembering that section 33 of the Charter and the overriding power it contains have their own intrinsic limits, which makes their exercise even more legitimate and justified from the outset. Indeed, section 33 in question relates only to some of the rights and freedoms of the Charter and is valid only for a period of five years, subject however to one or more successive renewals of the same duration. This time limit is often put forward by proponents of the notwithstanding power, who argue that in this sense the rights of individuals are not seriously threatened.[35] Indeed, it is claimed that any override provision will be subject to public debate when it is enacted and re-enacted, especially since only some – not all – rights can be affected by such a provision.

As previously mentioned, section 33 of the Charter does not apply to democratic rights, mobility rights, language rights, or Indigenous rights. All these are either linked to Canadian citizenship (democratic rights) or to the socio-political and socio-demographic context of Canada (mobility rights, language rights, and Indigenous rights). This choice was not made at random by the constituent. It was clearly the intention of the framers that those rights and freedoms that are, arguably, universal – such as the fundamental rights and freedoms in section 2, the legal rights in sections 7 to 14, and the equality rights in section 15 of the Charter – should be covered by the notwithstanding power. This is the true meaning of article 33 of the Charter.

It is also important to note that the general rule of construction regarding the non-retroactivity of a statute applies to section 33, which has been interpreted by the Supreme Court of Canada, in *Ford* and *Irwin Toy Ltd.*,[36] as permitting prospective override only. If the enactment of a statute is intended to give retroactive effect to the overriding provisions of the Charter, said statute is, to that extent, of no force and effect.[37]

Legislation that is covered and protected by a notwithstanding clause is effective in spite of a provision. This does not, however, prevent the courts from scrutinizing the measures in question and even declaring them unconstitutional on the grounds, for example, that they violate or limit Charter rights and freedoms and are not justified under its section 1. All that the courts are prevented from doing is to sanction such unconstitutionality by declaring the measures in question invalid or inoperative. We will circle back to this point later.

According to the Supreme Court, in the case *Toronto v. Ontario*:[38]

We add this. Were a court to rely on unwritten constitutional principles, in whole or in part, to invalidate legislation, the consequences of this judicial error would be of particular significance given two provisions of our Charter ... [S.] 33 preserves a limited right of legislative override. Where, therefore, a court invalidates legislation using s. 2(b) of the Charter, the legislature may give continued effect to its understanding of what the Constitution requires by invoking s. 33 and by meeting its stated conditions ... Were, however, a court to rely not on s. 2(b) but instead upon an unwritten constitutional principle to invalidate legislation, this undeniable aspect of the constitutional bargain would effectively be undone, since s. 33 applies to permit legislation to operate "notwithstanding a provision included in section 2 or sections 7 to 15" only.[39]

In the various judgments they render, the courts are influenced by the existence of section 33 of the Charter, in the sense that they might not come to the same conclusions in their judgments were it not for the presence of section 33 at issue. For example, in the *Ford* case, the Supreme Court uses a necessity test to apply section 1 of the Canadian Charter, which is more stringent than the *Oakes* test.[40] More specifically, the court mixes the minimal impairment test ("should impair as little as possible the right or freedom in question") with the necessity test.[41] The Supreme Court might not have applied the necessity test if section 33 of the Charter had not applied.

Moreover, the Supreme Court of Canada has, on a number of occasions, held that restrictions imposed by any law on rights and freedoms not covered by the overriding power of section 33 of the Charter – such as section 3 of the latter concerning the right to vote, or section 23 concerning minority official language education rights – must be reviewed under a strict standard of justification.

Thus in the *Sauvé*[42] case, McLachlin C.J. pointed out that the 1982 Constitution intended to emphasize the privileged nature of the right to vote by excluding it from the scope of section 33 of the Charter.[43]

A few years later, in the *Frank*[44] case, Wagner C.J. reiterated this view.[45]

In *Conseil scolaire francophone de la Colombie-Britannique*,[46] Wagner C.J. reiterated his opinion and held, more specifically, that the decision of the framers to exclude rights and freedoms from the ambit of section 33 of the Charter reflected the importance they attached to those rights and freedoms and their intention to provide a strict framework for derogations from it.[47]

This may come as a surprise, considering the opposite should be true. Indeed, a right or freedom covered by section 33 of the Charter should be subject to a stricter test by the courts, since the parliaments concerned can always override the courts' findings and sanctions if they see fit. This was the view taken by Côté and Brown J.J. in *Frank*.[48]

If there is to be any caution on the part of the courts, it is in respect of anything outside the scope of section 33 of the Charter, for then Parliament does not have the ability to respond – by way of a notwithstanding clause – to the findings and decisions of a court. In fact, the exemption allows the court to go further in the normal way. The fundamental freedoms are within the scope of 33. Does this make them less important?

Subsection 33(1) of the Charter allows Parliament or a legislature to enact legislation that expressly declares that the legislation or any of its provisions has effect notwithstanding a particular provision of section 2 or sections 7 to 15 of the Charter. As aforementioned, in *Ford*, the Supreme Court of Canada made it clear that the provision in question must be referred to. The idea that Parliament (and government) must justify to the courts the exercise of the override power is ludicrous. In such a scenario, section 33 of the Charter would duplicate section 1 of the Charter. Courts would be required to test the proportionality between the reasons given by Parliament – or the objectives it seeks – and the means it uses to achieve them, including in particular the use of the notwithstanding clause. This would lead the courts to an examination of the merits of the exercise of the notwithstanding power that would be completely contrary to the spirit of the power, as well as being counterproductive.[49]

Subsection 33(2) of the Charter provides that a law or provision that is the subject of an exemption power has effect notwithstanding a particular provision of section 2 or sections 7 to 15 of this Charter. The key word here, in our view, is "effect." In the English version of section 33 of the Charter, the word "operation" is used instead, in the context of stating that the law or provision of the law that is the subject of the declaration referred to in section 33 in question "shall have such operation as it would have but for the provision of this Charter referred to in the declaration." It is clear to us that, if we look at the law or the provision of the law referred to in the section 33 declaration in question, its effects persist even if it could be invalid under the Charter. This is similar to the difference between constitutional validity and constitutional inoperability. In the case of validity, it appears that a statute is invalid and void if, by its very nature and the extent of its encroachment on the jurisdiction of the other level of government, it is not within the jurisdiction of the legislature that passed it. In the case of inoperability, a provincial statute is suspended to the extent that it conflicts with a federal statute. This does not mean that the law is invalid. Rather, its effects are suspended to the extent of the conflict and for as long as the conflict continues. The same reasoning applies with respect to the doctrine of interjurisdictional immunity, under which a statute may be declared inapplicable to a particular situation or context without being declared invalid.

In the case of the override power in section 33 of the Charter, the law to which the override power is applied has full force and effect even though it may be invalid or potentially invalid. Subsection 33(3) of the Charter provides that a declaration under section 1 shall cease to have effect no later than five years after it comes into force. This is, of course, subject to renewal of the declaration under subsection 33(4), although successive renewals are possible. At the time that the above declaration ceases to have effect – under subsection 33(3) of the Charter – a legislative provision that has already been declared invalid would automatically lose all its effect.

In other words, the notwithstanding power in section 33 of the Charter allows a piece of legislation to have full effect despite its invalidity, for the period of time provided by the Constitution.

IV. THE MYTHS REGARDING THE USE OF OVERRIDING POWERS AND PROVISIONS

There are a number of myths associated with the use of the notwithstanding power. One is that there is a high political price to pay for its use. Another is that it implicitly involves an admission of denial of rights or freedoms. Let's look at each of these myths.

1. The Political Cost

Many public commentators believe that there is a political cost to the use of an exemption power, since, they say, few citizens appreciate a government that infringes the rights and freedoms of its people.[50] It can have a significant impact on an election. As the attorney general of Ontario stated in *Ford*, when challenging the constitutionality of the standard override provision, "There must be a 'political cost' for overriding a guaranteed right or freedom."[51]

The political price that elected officials, or more specifically a government, have to pay for their use of overriding provisions is very relative; it depends essentially on the objective they pursue in doing so.[52] In Quebec itself, the use of overriding provisions is generally seen by the population as a good thing, especially when it has an identity-based purpose.[53]

For example, as a protest against the patriation of the Canadian Constitution and the imposition of the Charter, every law passed between 1982 and 1985 under René Lévesque's government made reference to the notwithstanding clause.[54] This systematic use did not seem to affect the premier's popularity.

For his part, Robert Bourassa's popularity increased in the wake of the adoption of Bill 178, An Act to Amend the Charter of the French Language,[55] in 1988. This law, which included an overriding provision, was essentially aimed at imposing French on commercial signage (signs, posters, and advertisements) outside businesses and at making French prevail inside them.

This "political cost" thesis is also unsound considering that the current Quebec government led in the polls throughout its first term and was re-elected with an overwhelming parliamentary majority in the 3 October 2022 election.[56]

The fact is that a government's determination to pursue collective goals – social, identity, or otherwise – is often appreciated by the general public, even if it sometimes involves the limitation of individual rights or freedoms. In Quebec, the population has long understood that there are societal objectives that sometimes go beyond individual concerns. This is certainly the case when the objectives in question contribute to the strengthening of the French language and the culture on which it is based. The population of Quebec usually applauds government initiatives that tend toward the achievement of such objectives.

2. Admission

Furthermore, it is frequently argued by commentators in the public arena that the exercise of the notwithstanding power necessarily implies an admission by the legislature and government concerned that some right and freedom is being violated. We reject this view, because the use of a notwithstanding clause may have no other purpose than to give the legislative and executive branches the last word on important social issues.[57] This is not to say, however, that there cannot be cases in which the legislature and government are aware that they are limiting rights and freedoms beyond what is permitted by supporting provisions such as section 1 of the Charter, but the notwithstanding power allows them to do so if they believe it is required by the public interest. In short, it is normal for legislators and governments to make collective choices, which in some cases override the judgments of the courts.

The question obviously arises as to how one can, in good conscience, wish to violate or otherwise restrict human rights and freedoms. The answer simply lies in the fact that no right or freedom is absolute and that rights and freedoms evolve and develop in a given socio-political context. It is precisely this context that the overriding power allows to be taken into account, which the courts do not always do fully or properly.

In any case, it is our view that the use of a notwithstanding power does not involve any admission that a right or freedom has been infringed, but rather an affirmation of Parliament's desire to have the final say on certain social issues that are both critically important and highly sensitive.

In any event, the potential limitation of rights and freedoms depends fundamentally on the interpretation of those rights and freedoms by the courts. If the courts had not applied a particularly strict and rigorous test when implementing section 1 of the Charter, the use of the notwithstanding power would not have been so necessary when the interests of the state and the community are at stake.

Courts should not be tempted to usurp the function of the legislature – let alone that of the constituent. The override power acts as such a reminder. It puts the legislative power and, by extension, the executive power, back in the forefront of societal decisions, especially when Quebec's originality is at issue. All this in a context where Canadian federalism has great difficulty in taking this originality into account, leaving it to the Quebec National Assembly alone to affirm it.

V. THE LEGAL-POLITICAL CONTEXT IN WHICH OVERRIDING POWERS AND PROVISIONS ARE OCCURRING AND EVOLVING

In society in general, and the legal community in particular, many people are concerned with the Quebec government's propensity to resort to the notwithstanding clauses when identity issues are concerned. However, it is important to understand the context in which this is made. This context is marked by the increasingly obvious judicialization of our political system, the non-adherence of Quebec to the patriation of 1981–82, the prevailing crisis of values between

Quebecers and other Canadians, and a certain insensitivity of the courts to the specificity of Quebec.

1. The Strong Judicialization of the Canadian System

We live in a context of strong judicialization. This has, of course, been accentuated by the coming into force of the Canadian Charter. Since then, the state has been required to demonstrate the reasonableness of its measures and to draw inspiration from what is done in other free and democratic societies around the world.

Considering the adoption of the Charter, the courts have been called upon to rule on a host of philosophical and even ideological questions. Whether it is about the life of the fetus, same-sex marriage, prostitution, or medical assistance in dying, the courts are making fundamental choices about the evolution of society. They are not to blame for this, as this was the original intent of those who drafted the Constitution. However, the increasingly creative way in which judges conceive and interpret the law, and their obvious bias in favour of individual rights and freedoms as opposed to collective rights or interests, allows them to set benchmarks regarding our societal progress.

Among other things, in constitutional matters, the Supreme Court of Canada regularly appeals to the principles of broad, dynamic, teleological, and evolutionary interpretation of the law to justify its conclusions in a given case. The court even invokes concepts such as underlying constitutional principles or the fundamental structure or architecture of Canada – concepts that are as vague as one could wish – to colour the interpretation of constitutional texts.

The good thing about exemption powers is that they limit the state's propensity for judicialization and restore or at least consolidate the separation of powers.

2. The Need for Quebec to Assert Its Specificity, the Relative Insensitivity of the Courts to Quebec's Specificity, and the Unnecessarily Unifying Interpretation of the Charter

Professor Guillaume Rousseau invokes, in the following excerpt, the sovereignty of Parliament and of the legislatures in support of the legitimacy of the notwithstanding clause, both in the Canadian Charter and in the provincial charters of rights:

[Our translation] The theoretical aspect of this study reveals that from Henri Brun to Jacques Gosselin to André Binette, not to mention Guy Tremblay and Eugénie Brouillet, a coherent vision emerges in Quebec's thinking on the notwithstanding clause, as several elements are often repeated. The main elements are that, even before a judgment declaring a law to be inconsistent with a charter, the use of the notwithstanding clause may be justified, particularly in the name of parliamentary democracy and sovereignty. According to these authors, this is particularly true if the purpose of the use of the notwithstanding clause is to protect Quebec's identity or to achieve social progress.[58]

In their book *Droit constitutionnel*,[59] authors Henri Brun, Guy Tremblay, and Eugénie Brouillet put forward the idea that the exemption power allows for the restoration of parliamentary democracy. They state: [Our translation] "It is indeed particularly important for Quebec society to preserve the right to the final word that it had until now in certain matters that are vital for it given its singular cultural situation in North America and in Canada. The express derogation allows it to regain this right to the final word."[60]

The use of the notwithstanding power by Quebec is particularly justified when it comes to the defence of its language and culture, as these issues are intimately linked to its collective future. Quebec, as a society with a weakened identity, is perfectly entitled to resort to the notwithstanding power to assert, loudly and clearly, its specificity and originality within the Canadian context.

For Quebec, the great challenge is to reconcile the expression of its national dimension and its special identity with respect to the constitutional rights of individuals and minority groups. This challenge may only be met if, in certain cases, the Quebec state has the power to make fundamental identity choices, choices that it deems necessary to affirm its specificity. This is precisely what the notwithstanding powers allow.

In its various decisions on the Charter of the French Language (Bill 101),[61] the Supreme Court of Canada has consistently issued declarations of unconstitutionality. Sometimes, it was in the name of freedom of expression. Sometimes, it was because of the application of section 133 of the Constitution Act, 1867.[62] At other times, it was under section 23 of the Canadian Charter, with respect to minority language education. In the *Solski*[63] case, the Supreme Court skillfully, but unfortunately, substituted the criterion of "significant part of the instruction" of section 23 for that of "the major part of the instruction," which ultimately resulted in a dilution of Bill 101. In the *Nguyen*[64] case, the Supreme Court authorized the use of "bridging schools" in order to circumvent the strict application of section 23. In our view, a strict application would undoubtedly have been more in keeping with the original intention of the constituent.

More recently, the Act Respecting the Laicity of the State was to be invalidated in part by the Quebec Superior Court. It might have been struck down in its entirety had it not been for the use of override provisions.

Although the Canadian Charter is now more accepted by Quebecers than it was at its outset, its unifying effect potentially jeopardizes the expression of Quebec's singular identity, whether it be in terms of language, culture, purely legal matters, or in terms of identity in general.

Quebec's specificity is an asset and an added value for Canada, and it must be promoted as such. It is only natural that it should be expressed, manifested, within the Canadian federal link. One way for Quebec to assert its own deep identity within Canada is to use the notwithstanding power when it feels that collective interests must take precedence over individual interests.

In the name of its uniqueness, Quebec makes collective choices that are different from those of its federative partners. These choices are often challenged by the courts. They are also widely denounced or denigrated by the "rest of Canada." If it wants to preserve its originality, Quebec has no choice but to persist in asserting its identity and signing on.

Federalism itself is a mode of organizing state powers that authorizes and promotes the exercise of the right to be different for each of its components or political units. By claiming this right, Quebec is simply putting its particularism at the service of both itself and a certain Canadian ideal.

We believe that the Canadian judicial system lacks sensitivity to Quebec's specificity and that it too often espouses a unitary rather than a truly federal vision of the country.[65] This leaves Quebec with little choice but to exercise its overriding power to express and promote its distinctiveness within Canada.

The relative insensitivity of the courts to Quebec's distinctiveness is manifested in the generally uniform, unchanging, and all-encompassing interpretation that the courts typically give to the Charter and the rights and freedoms that flow from it. This interpretation of the Charter is unnecessarily unifying. While it may be intended to draw out of the Charter values that are common to all Canadians, it has the significant drawback of gradually eroding, judgment after judgment, Quebec's unique identity and threatening the diversity inherent in this country.

The courts' insensitivity to Quebec's uniqueness is also accompanied by the principle that Charter rights and freedoms are to be interpreted broadly and purposively, when in our view they would be better interpreted contextually, that is, with particular reference to the particular context of Quebec.

Added to this is the fact that section 1 of the Charter – which, it should be recalled, allows the rights and freedoms it confers to be restricted under certain conditions – is applied by the Supreme Court of Canada in a manner that is too narrow and too obtuse.[66] This strict interpretation and application of section 1 makes the existence and exercise of the waiver power even more relevant.

The Supreme Court's premise is that human rights and freedoms are to be interpreted broadly and purposefully, as well as in an evolutionary fashion. On the other hand, it imposes a rigorous test at the stage of the application of the justificatory provision set out in section 1 of the Charter. This creates a clear imbalance between individual rights and freedoms, on the one hand, and collective interests on the other. This imbalance can only encourage legislators to use the notwithstanding power in section 33 of the Charter. Because of the stringent test imposed by section 1 of the Charter, legislators cannot assume that the courts will agree with them at all, even if they believe that they were right to enact the legislation containing notwithstanding provisions. In this context, the use of the notwithstanding power by legislatures becomes a real "safety valve," a protection against judicial interventionism or activism, a guarantee that their legislation won't be undermined by the courts.

It is true that the implementation of section 1 of the Charter does not prevent the courts from showing deference to the legislature and its legislative choices and other decisions.[67] However, one must admit that this deference is not found in all cases in the case law. Indeed, why should the same deference not be shown to Parliament's use of the notwithstanding power in section 33 of the Charter? The answer is in the question.

In any event, it would be wrong to view section 1 of the Charter as a substitute for the override power in section 33 of the Charter. The two provisions do not serve the same purpose, nor do they have the same scope (section 33 being much broader). As the Supreme Court of Canada stated in *A.G. (Que.) v. Quebec Protestant School Boards*:[68] "Whatever their scope, the limits which s. 1 of the Charter allows to be placed on the rights and freedoms set out in it cannot be equated with exceptions such as those authorized by s. 33(1) and (2) of the Charter."[69]

It is not surprising that Quebec has a distinct practice or theory with regards to the use of the notwithstanding power. Quebec does resort to this power to achieve various societal and identity objectives, as well as purely state objectives, that its federal partners do not consider useful or necessary to pursue.

3. Quebec's Non-Adherence to Patriation and to the Constitution Act, 1982 and the Crisis of Values between Quebecers and Other Canadians

It should be remembered that Quebec never subscribed to the project of patriating the Constitution.[70] In 1982, the patriation of the Canadian Constitution was not considered acceptable to the then-premier of Quebec, nor has it been considered so by his successors, regardless of party affiliation. On the one hand, the patriation was not acceptable because of what it contained: a Charter that limited the powers of Quebec's National Assembly and a constitutional amendment procedure that provided only for financial compensation limited to certain matters and that gave Quebec no right of veto. On the other hand, it was also unacceptable because of what it did not contain: reform of the division of legislative powers and central institutions and measures to promote greater decentralization and flexibility in Canadian federalism.

The exclusion of Quebec from the patriation process is based in part on the highly questionable decision of the Supreme Court of Canada on 28 September 1981, in the now famous *Re: Resolution to Amend the Constitution*. In this decision, the court upheld a constitutional convention that had no precedent, meaning that it did not exist. In the name of this convention, the court set aside the unanimity rule that had previously been applied by political actors in matters that, like patriation, went to the heart of federal-provincial relations. Quebec's exclusion also stems in part from the duplicity and surreptitious scheming of the then-political actors.

It is quite understandable, in our opinion, that Quebec should seek to limit the effect of the patriation of the Canadian Constitution. After all, the Constitution applies to Quebec against its will. This is a very good reason for Quebec to resort to the notwithstanding power in section 33 of the Charter when it believes that the public interest requires it.

Though the Charter is now widely accepted, even cherished, by Quebecers, there are cases where the best interests of Quebec must prevail over it. These are cases where its identity, or even its collective future, is at stake. In short, Quebec is asserting its right to make distinctive choices within Canada. The notwithstanding power is one of the instruments or tools it has at its disposal to do so.

Speaking of distinctive choices, it should be noted that the specificity of Quebec does not only include language, culture, and civil law. It is also based on institutions, a way of life, and values. It encompasses the secularity of the state and interculturalism.

With regards to the secular nature of the state, it should be noted that it is one of the main components of religious freedom. Indeed, the separation of church and state has been a well-established principle in Canadian law for a very long time.[71] In the Act Respecting the Laicity of the State, the National Assembly of Quebec and, by extension, the Quebec government, resolutely opted for the establishment of a stricter duty of reserve in religious matters with regards to persons exercising certain functions placing them in a position of authority. It is a balanced law, despite appearances, and of relatively limited application.

Quebec advocates for interculturalism over multiculturalism. The latter is included in section 27 of the Charter – as a principle of constitutional interpretation[72] – and in the Canadian Multiculturalism Act.[73] It postulates, among other things, that every individual has the right to have his or her own cultural life, to profess and practice his or her own religion or to use his or her own language.[74] Multiculturalism also implies that the diversity of the Canadian population in terms of race, ethnic origin, colour, national origin, and religion is a fundamental characteristic of Canadian society.

As for interculturalism, it is seen in Quebec as one of the main values that forge the identity of this society. This concept is essentially based on the idea that all Quebecers – regardless of their language,

race, colour, nationality of origin, religion, or ethnic origin – share a
common cultural and linguistic core, which is itself the result of the
fusion and osmosis of the diverse contributions – Indigenous, francophone, anglophone, allophone, etc. – that have shaped Quebec's
identity over the years.

Many people see multiculturalism and interculturalism as contradictory in every respect. We see them as complementary. The fact
remains that Quebec's choices regarding the secular nature of the
state and interculturalism are strongly denounced by a segment of
the Canadian population. In other words, there is a profound lack of
understanding in Canada of the values promoted by Quebecers and
of their conception of life in society.

This leads us to assert that there is a real crisis of values in Canada
and a growing gap between the way Quebecers, on the one hand,
and other Canadians, on the other, perceive the country and deal
with its social dynamics.

This crisis of values can only encourage Quebec to use its overriding power to assert and even impose its own collective choices
within the Canadian context.

4. Quebec's Political Impasse

Politically speaking, Quebec is in a bind at the moment. On the one
hand, Quebec independence is no longer on the radar. This option
would only get the support of 32 per cent of the Quebec population.[75] Young people themselves no longer believe in it.

On the other hand, Canadian federalism is, to say the least, hard
to reform through constitutional means. Quebec's demographic and
political weight within Canada is steadily declining. The federal
government continues to harbour centralizing and unnecessarily
paternalistic ambitions.

Indeed, the centralization of the Canadian system is likely to
increase in the years ahead, especially with the exercise of federal
spending power in provincial jurisdictions, as well as a constitutional jurisprudence that is decidedly Ottawa-friendly.

In addition, there is not enough respect across Canada for
Quebec's profound identity. Too many Canadians feel that Quebec's
specificity is an obstacle to Canadian unity rather than an added
value for the country. This is highly regrettable. In this context,
one of the only avenues available to Quebec to assert its originality

is the notwithstanding power of section 33 of the Charter. This section is, for Quebec, a spearhead of its identity affirmation in the Canadian context.

The truth is that Canadian federalism has had great difficulty in formally recognizing and accommodating Quebec's distinct character. Certainly, the House of Commons recognized in 1995 "that Quebec is a distinct society within Canada."[76] It also recognized, in 2006, "that the Québécois form a nation within a united Canada."[77] In 2014, it was the Supreme Court of Canada's turn to recognize that Quebec has special social values.[78] Nevertheless, there is nothing in the country's constitutional structure that makes Quebec unique, except, of course, the constitutional autonomy it enjoys, and a few constitutional provisions that, here and there, confirm its uniqueness.[79]

At a time when a number of Canadians are denying the singular character and national dimension of Quebec's identity, it is important that the exercise of the notwithstanding power be revalued and even rehabilitated in the eyes of those who question it.

Denying Quebec's deep identity and challenging the means by which it asserts that identity – such as the notwithstanding power – can only serve to undermine Canadian unity and to propagate a negative and pejorative image of Quebec.

CONCLUSION

All the above context demonstrates, in our opinion, the usefulness of notwithstanding provisions in a federal state which, like Canada, is also multinational, if only because of the existence of the Quebec nation, the Indigenous peoples, and the Acadian people.

Still, in the context described above, it is only natural that notwithstanding provisions be used preventively and somewhat more frequently than in recent years. Indeed, even if they were used only as a preventive measure, the notwithstanding provisions would not avoid litigation. They would, it seems, only prevent the sanction of unconstitutionality.

To condemn the use of notwithstanding provisions is to deprive Quebec, consciously or not, of one of the only instruments or mechanisms at its disposal to assert its distinct and unique character and its national traits in the Canadian federation, a federation which sometimes tends toward absorbing its intrinsic diversity.

The Quebec nation has a number of unique characteristics, including language, culture, social values, civil tradition, and even historical background. The notwithstanding power allows for the expression of these characteristics in the Canadian political and constitutional system. In this sense, it is an asset to Quebec and to Canada as a whole.

NOTES

1 *Reference re Secession of Quebec* [1998] 2 SCR 217 at para 58. See also *Reference re Securities Act*, 2011 SCC 66 at para 73.

2 Canadian Charter of Rights and Freedoms, Part I of the Constitution Act, 1982, being Schedule B to the Canada Act 1982 (UK), 1982, c 11 [Charter] or [Canadian Charter].

3 In this text, we will make a distinction between an overriding power and an overriding provision. Thus, the overriding power will refer to the constitutional measure that authorizes an exemption to a charter, while the override provision will refer to the exercise of that power in a particular statute. In this vein, the reader is asked to note that the word "exemption" will be used in the sense of derogation. Therefore, rather than speaking of "derogatory power," which is a bit pejorative, we will speak occasionally of "exemption power."

4 In this article, the word "legislature" will sometimes be used to refer to legislatures or parliaments in general, including the Canadian Parliament, and not just provincial legislatures. This will depend on the context.

5 It should be remembered that the provisions of section 33 of the Charter apply not only to the Canadian Parliament and provincial legislatures, but also to the legislative authorities of the Yukon, the Northwest Territories, and Nunavut. That conclusion comes from section 30 of the Charter.

6 See, for example: *Frank v Canada (AG)*, 2019 SCC 1 at para 25 [*Frank*]; *Conseil scolaire francophone de la Colombie-Britannique v British Columbia*, 2020 SCC 13 at para 148 [*Conseil scolaire*].

7 *Hak c Procureure générale du Québec*, 2019 QCCA 2145 at paras 39–52.

8 With respect to the application of the notwithstanding power in section 33 of the Canadian Charter to regulations, we can only look to section 52 and subsection 56.1(3) of the Charter of Human Rights and Freedoms, CQLR c C-12, for guidance at this time. These provisions make statutes, regulations, orders, ordinances, and orders in council subject to the legislative primacy of the latter. This suggests that these rules of law are also

covered by the overriding authority of section 52 of that charter. The same would normally be true of section 33 of the Canadian Charter.

9 Pierre Elliott Trudeau accepted the derogatory power only against his will, but he nevertheless accepted it with full knowledge.

10 Canadian Bill of Rights, SC 1960, c 44.

11 The omnibus law in question was the Act Respecting the Constitution Act, 1982, CQLR, c L-4.2.

12 Act Respecting the Laicity of the State, CQLR c L-0.3.

13 Bill 96, An Act Representing French, the Official and Common Language of Québec, 2nd Sess, 42nd Leg, Québec, 2022, c 14, sponsored by Simon Jolin-Barrette, Minister Responsible for the French Language.

14 Charter of Human Rights and Freedoms, CQLR c C-12.

15 See text.

16 David Johansen and Philip Rosen, *The Notwithstanding Clause of the Charter* (Library of Parliament, 1989).

17 Geoffrey Sigalet explains that the notwithstanding clause allows legislatures to control judicial decisions without directly affecting the independence of judges: "In contrast with other court curbing measures, such as highly polarized appointments processes, court packing, jurisdiction stripping, etc., the notwithstanding clause does not directly interfere with the judicial decision-making processes, nor with the composition of the judiciary." This volume, chapter 7.

18 Ibid.

19 *Ford v Québec (AG)*, [1988] 2 SCR 712 [*Ford*].

20 Ibid., para 33.

21 Ibid., paras 23 and 27 in the French version.

22 The fact that the use of a notwithstanding clause is considered legitimate by the Supreme Court of Canada, as a matter of policy, does not preclude it from also being legal, even constitutional. In our view, the exercise of the notwithstanding power in section 33 of the Charter is both legal in the strict sense of the law and legitimate in the political sense.

23 *Devine v Quebec (AG)*, [1988] 2 SCR 790.

24 Ibid., 812.

25 *Ontario (Attorney General)* v. *G*, 2020 SCC 38.

26 And Judge Rowe submitted concurring reasons.

27 *Ontario (Attorney General)* v. *G*, para 137.

28 Ibid., para 239

29 Ibid., para 240. See also para 241.

30 *Hak c Procureur général du Québec*, 2021 QCCS 1466.

31 Ibid., para 770. See also para 777.
32 See *Hak c Procureur général du Québec*, para 777.
33 On the "political role" of the courts, see Manfredi, this volume, chapter 8.
34 Dwight Newman explains the importance of an holistic reading of the Canadian Constitution: "It is important to see the notwithstanding clause as part of Canada's Constitution and to let it live as part of the Constitution rather than taking the view that there should be special restrictions put upon it based on the rest of the Constitution or views about what the rest of the Constitution would have meant without the notwithstanding clause." Furthermore, in the same paper, Newman emphasizes that notwithstanding powers and provisions are a practical support for democratic participation, which is itself a structuring principle of our constitutional order. He adds that following the path of putting more and more power in the hands of judges is simply not a substitute for the political responsibility of individuals. Finally, he concludes that over-riding powers and provisions facilitate the ongoing coordination of different approaches to the protection and enforcement of rights and freedoms, and allow for the enhancement of the various political or sociological identities within Canada. This volume, chapter 3.
35 Ibid.
36 *Irwin Toy Ltd c Québec (Procureur général)*, [1989] 1 RCS 927 [Irwin Toy]; *Ford*.
37 *Irwin Toy*, 966; *Ford*, para 36.
38 *Toronto (City) v. Ontario (Attorney General)*, 2021 SCC 34.
39 Ibid., para 60. However, see the dissident opinion in particular at para 182.
40 [1986] 1 SCR 103 [*Oakes*].
41 *Oakes*, para 70.
42 *Sauvé v. Canada (Chief Electoral Officer)*, 2002 SCC 68.
43 Ibid., paras 11, 14, and 44. This view is strongly contradicted by Gonthier J., dissenting, at paras 95 and 96 of the case.
44 *Frank*.
45 Ibid., para 25.
46 *Conseil scolaire*.
47 Ibid., para 148. Chief Justice Wagner spoke on behalf of six of his colleagues.
48 *Frank*, para 141. Côté and Brown J.J. were dissidents.
49 If the courts were to impose substantive conditions on the exercise of the derogatory power, they would usurp the function of the legislature and place an unduly onerous burden of proof on the latter.

50 Mark Mancini, "Political Costs as Control on the Notwithstanding Clause," *Advocates for the Rule of Law* (blog), 24 October 2018, www.ruleoflaw.ca/political-costs-as-control-on-the-notwithstanding-clause/; Chris Hall, "The House: Will Doug Ford Pay a Price for Deploying the Notwithstanding Clause?" CBC News, 12 June 2021, www.cbc.ca/radio/thehouse/doug-ford-notwithstanding-section-33-constitution-1.6062167.

51 *Ford*, para 30.

52 Without going so far as to discuss the political cost that can be derived from the use of overriding powers and provisions by parliaments and governments, Christopher Manfredi speaks of the "political" role of judges, "How does the notwithstanding clause affect the strategic relationship between courts and legislatures? Its inclusion in the Charter initially made it more difficult for the Court to assert final authority over the articulation and enforcement of constitutional rights because it provided a clear institutional mechanism for legislatures to resist assertions of judicial power. The clause generated uncertainty about the locus of constitutional supremacy, which encouraged strategic moderation of judicial review to avoid a political confrontation that might undermine the Court's long-term institutional status." On another note, in the same paper, Manfredi essentially argues that section 33 of the Charter is a positive contribution to the liberal constitutionalism that prevails in Canada. In particular, it allows legislatures to play an important – and legitimate – role in interpreting the constitutional framework and adapting it to the changing circumstances of society. According to Manfredi, there is no reason why the courts in general, and the Supreme Court in particular, should have a monopoly on the adjudication and arbitration of cases that may involve important legal and even moral principles. Such a monopoly could only make the Constitution more rigid in its interpretation and implementation, as stated by Manfredi. We can only agree with these statements. However, we do not share Manfredi's concerns about the pre-emptive use of the notwithstanding provisions. We also disagree with his conclusions about what he identifies as other deficiencies of overriding powers and provisions. This volume, chapter 8.

53 For example, the political price to be paid for the use of a notwithstanding provision appears to be much higher in Ontario than in Quebec. This is evidenced by the Ontario legislature's repeal of Bill 28, An Act to Resolve Labour Disputes Involving School Board Employees Represented by the Canadian Union of Public Employees, 1st Sess, 43rd Leg, Ontario, 2022, c 19. See Bill 35, An Act to Repeal the Keeping Students in Class Act, 1st Sess, 43rd Leg, Ontario, 2022, c 19.

54 That omnibus law was discussed above.

55 An Act to Amend the Charter of the French Language, SQ 1988, c 54.

56 Coalition avenir Québec won 90 of 125 seats. On this point, see Élections Québec, "Results of October 3, 2022 General Election," www.electionsquebec.qc.ca/en/results-and-statistics/general-election-results/2022-10-03/.

57 As previously discussed, the intention of the legislator in using a notwithstanding clause may simply be to avoid having the courts decide a matter that is essentially one of collective choice.

58 Guillaume Rousseau, "La disposition dérogatoire des chartes des droits : de la théorie à la pratique, de l'identité au progrès social," *Institut de recherche sur le Québec*, (March 2016): 5.

59 Henri Brun, Guy Tremblay, and Eugénie Brouillet, *Droit constitutionnel*, 6th ed. (Cowansville, Québec: Yvon Blais, 2014).

60 Brun, Tremblay, and Brouillet, *Droit constitutionnel*, para XII–2.21.

61 Charter of the French Language, CQLR c C-11.

62 Constitution Act, 1867 (UK), 30 & 31 Vict, c 3, s 91, reprinted in RSC 1985, Appendix II, No 5 [1867 Act].

63 *Solski (Tutor of) v Quebec (Attorney General)*, 2005 SCC 14.

64 *Nguyen v Quebec (Education, Recreation and Sports)*, 2009 SCS 47.

65 It was the case in the *Re: Resolution to amend the Constitution, 1981*, [1981] 1 SCR 753, where the majority on the issue of strict legality relied heavily on Canada's unitary features to support its conclusions and even went so far as to speak of federal primacy in the Canadian context.

66 *Oakes*. The Supreme Court of Canada has tended in recent years to relax the *Oakes* test. It is now looking for means that, among a range of means, infringe as little as reasonably possible on rights and freedoms.

67 On this point, see in particular the case *Carter v Canada (AG)*, 2015 SCC 5 at paras 97 and 98.

68 *A.G. (Que.) v. Quebec Protestant School Boards* [1984] 2 SCR 66.

69 Ibid., 86.

70 Marie Paré, "La légitimité de la clause dérogatoire de la Charte canadienne des droits et libertés en regard du droit international," *Le Revue juridique thémis* 29, no. 3 (1995).

71 See: *SL v Commission scolaire des Chênes*, 2012 SCC 7; *R v Big M Drug Mart Ltd* [1985] 1 RCS 295; See also *Loyola High School v Quebec (AG)*, 2015 SCC 12.

72 Section 27 of the Charter does not confer substantive rights that can be limited, but rather is used to interpret other provisions of the Charter. It

was notably used to define the content of freedom of conscience and religion under section 2(a) of the Charter to include indirect coercion (*Big M Drug Mart Ltd.* [1985] 1 SCR 295). It was also applied to support a non-denominational approach to governing (*R. v. Edwards Books and Art Ltd. et al.* [1986] 2 SCR 713). Furthermore, this section was used to connect multiculturalism to the state duty of religious neutrality (*Mouvement laïque québécois v. Saguenay (City)* [2015] 2 SCR 3) and to define the right to an interpreter under section 14 of the Charter to include services in languages other than French and English (*R. v. Tran* [1994] 2 SCR 951).

73 Canadian Multiculturalism Act, RSC 1985, c 24. See also *Department of Canadian Heritage Act*, SC 1985, c 11.

74 These assumptions stem in part from the *International Covenant on Civil and Political Rights*, art 27.

75 Philippe Fournier, "La souveraineté tient bon," *L'actualité*, 25 February 2021, lactualite.com/politique/la-souverainete-tient-bon/.

76 *House of Common Debates*, 35-1, vol. 133, No. 267 (29 November 1995) (The Honourable Gilbert Parent).

77 *House of Common Debates*, 39-1, vol. 141, No. 086 (24 November 2006) (The Honourable Peter Milliken).

78 *Reference re Supreme Court Act, ss 5 and 6*, 2014 SCC 21 at paras 18, 49, 56, 57, 59, 69, and 145.

79 We are referring to provisions such as section 133 of the 1867 Act, section 94 of the 1867 Act (*a contrario*), section 93(A) of the 1867 Act and section 59 of the Constitution Act, 1982, being Schedule B to the Canada Act 1982 (UK), 1982, c 11.

10

Bill 21 and Bill 96 in Light of a Distinctive Quebec Theory of the Notwithstanding Clause: A Distinct Approach for a Distinct Society and a Distinct Legal Tradition

Guillaume Rousseau and François Côté

On 3 October 2022, the Coalition Avenir Quebec got re-elected with a larger majority, after using the notwithstanding clause of the Canadian Charter of Rights and Freedoms[1] on eight occasions in three different acts.[2] What can we learn from that about the Quebec theory and practice of the notwithstanding clause?

In this chapter, we set out the latest developments in our reflections on that theory and practice and we attempt to respond to some of the points raised by colleagues at the conference. In this context, we will first explain why the uses of the notwithstanding clause in Bill 21 (Act Respecting the Laicity of the State[3]) and Bill 96 (Act Respecting French, the Official and Common Language of Quebec[4]) are in line with the idea that Quebec law espouses a distinctive theoretical and practical conception of the notwithstanding mechanisms, and also why the overrides featured in these bills are in line with another approach to that mechanism as well, an approach that promotes the use of the clause in order to better protect human rights (part 1). In the second, briefer part of this chapter, we will then address why Quebec's distinctive approach to the notwithstanding clauses falls in line with its distinctive civil law legal tradition,[5] and why, in that respect, the notwithstanding mechanism can be seen and used as a shield to protect it from a standardized and standardizing common law judicial construction of charter rights by Canadian tribunals (part 2).

1. BILL 21, BILL 96, AND A DISTINCTIVE QUEBEC
THEORY OF THE NOTWITHSTANDING CLAUSE

In our 2017 paper,[6] we demonstrated that there is a distinctive and coherent theoretical approach to the notwithstanding clause approved by a substantial number of leading Quebec constitutional law authors and academics, including Henri Brun and Guy Tremblay, two of the founding fathers of Quebec's constitutional law doctrine. As we wrote in that paper, "Even if it is neither unanimous nor single-minded, it is still a dominant vision with substantial cohesiveness."[7] And that is even more true today, since Benoît Pelletier recently proposed a vision of the notwithstanding clause largely in line with that approach in a report which draws on our 2017 paper.[8]

Basically, that theory holds that legislative overrides can be legitimately made, even pre-emptively, in order to promote social justice or national identity. To define social justice, we refer to Jacques Gosselin,[9] who mentions human rights that bear a collective or community value, such as those enshrined in the International Covenant on Economic, Social and Cultural Rights,[10] and André Binette, who mentions progressive measures, the protection of minorities or vulnerable groups, and gives the example of provisions protecting victims of sexual assault that are mostly women.[11] When it comes to national identity, we refer to Henri Brun, Guy Tremblay, and Eugénie Brouillet, and therefore mostly to culture and language.[12]

Our paper also demonstrated, through an empirical study, that the National Assembly did use the notwithstanding mechanism on numerous occasions between 1975 and 2017: over sixty times to override the Canadian Charter of Rights and Freedoms and over forty times to override Quebec's own Charter of Human Rights and Freedoms.[13] This is a *sharp* contrast with the rest of the federation, where the total sum of times the override of the Canadian Charter was employed in the same time period can be counted on a single hand, all other provinces and the federal government combined. More interestingly, in the overwhelming majority of cases, in Quebec the clause was invoked in the name of collective issues of social justice or national identity[14] – such as when it was invoked to allow more advantageous pension plans for female workers than their male counterparts to advance women's condition, or in matters of linguistic rights to specifically protect the crucial vitality of French language in Quebec and curtail the free-market English expansionism to its detriment (two small examples among legions).

Our study also revealed that the National Assembly's practical use of the override does largely align with that theory, although it has been invoked less by elected officials for matters of national identity and more for matters of social justice, while the main doctrinal attention goes the other way around.

These empirical data and conclusions are contested by maître Marion Sandilands, who represents the Quebec Community Groups Network, an organization that strongly oppose new measures to protect the French language in Quebec, such as Bill 96, but also the very moderate Bill C-13[15] put forward by the Trudeau government. Sandilands mentions and then overlooks the uses of the notwithstanding clause related to social progress, does not consider the numerous cases where the clause is used many times in a single act (therefore putting on the same level an act with one use of the clause and an act with five uses of it), does not calculate the proportion of collective identity-related cases out of all cases, and then concludes that the Quebec practice of the Charter overrides bears little resemblance to the theory.[16] Since the theory is about both social progress and national identity, this does not fully make sense to us. If her point is to underline the fact that the clause is more frequently used to promote social progress than to promote national identity, then we would agree with her on this specific point since it was one of the findings of our 2017 paper in which we considered all uses of the clause, including those related to social progress and those included in acts with many such uses, to conclude that an important proportion of these uses were related to national identity and an even larger proportion to social progress. But we find it hard to reconcile our empirical conclusions with the rest of her other opinions on our thesis, nor, more broadly, do we agree with several of her reasoning premises when it comes to Quebec and Quebec law. And those conclusions we have reached after an in-depth analysis of thousands of pages of parliamentary archives related to acts that use the clause, an in-depth analysis that Sandilands seemingly did not consider useful to make before contradicting our findings. It is on the basis of an incomplete analysis that she concludes that Bills 21 and 96 are not in line with the Quebec theory and practice of the notwithstanding clause. Sandilands is certainly entitled to her own political opinions. She suggests that the use of the notwithstanding mechanism in Bill 96 to protect the French language in Quebec borders on the establishment of police-state powers despite the absence of evidence to that effect, imagining that Bills 21 and 96 are discriminatory pieces of legislation fuelled by an us-versus-them mentality aimed at creating second-class citizens, despite them applying the same formally and universally equal rights and protections to literally everyone in Quebec with no distinction whatsoever. She seems reluctant to recognize the Quebec people as a distinct founding nation within the Canadian federation that could legitimately defend its own distinct conception of law and fundamental rights according to distinct legal parameters and values other than those of the Anglo-Canadian hegemony. We respectfully fail to see her criticism as rationally affecting the core validity of our findings and conclusions as a matter of legal science.

On the contrary, in the present chapter we will demonstrate that these bills fall squarely in line with that theory, as both do invoke the override mechanism in the name of national identity and, to a lesser extent, social progress (1.1). In addition, both these overrides can also be construed as in line with the idea that notwithstanding clauses could be used to better promote human rights and affirm parliamentary sovereignty (section 1.2 below).

1.1 Invoking the Notwithstanding Clause in the Name of National Identity and, to a Lesser Extent, Social Progress

In light of our previous demonstrations, we now argue that the uses of the notwithstanding clause in Bill 21 and Bill 96 are in line with that theory, and that they bring the practice even more in line with the theory, as their purposes are more closely linked to national identity than to social justice.

For Bill 21, the demonstration is easy as references to the nation and national objectives are clearly enunciated in the legislation. The very first recital of its preamble reads as follows: "As the Quebec nation has its own characteristics, one of which is its civil law tradition, distinct social values and a specific history that have led it to develop a particular attachment to State laicity." Two paragraphs later, another recital adds that, "In accordance with the principle of parliamentary sovereignty, it is incumbent on the Parliament of Quebec to determine the principles according to which and manner in which relations between the State and religions are to be governed in Quebec." The word "nation" is used again in the fifth and the eighth paragraphs: "As the Quebec nation attaches importance to the equality of women and men ... As State laicity should be affirmed in a manner that ensures a balance between the collective rights of the Quebec nation and human rights and freedoms." On top of that, during the hearings on Bill 21, the minister responsible for the bill said this: "*Notwithstanding clauses are introduced in the Bill ... Quebec has used these provisions more than 100 times since 1975. Almost always, it has done so to promote its distinct character or to allow social progress. With Bill 21, we are entering into this tradition and we are fully embracing it*"[17] (emphasis added). The national identity imperative is self-evident here. So is the social progress imperative, since the equality of women and men is a social progress objective that is promoted by Bill 21, a bill that aims to reduce the influence of religions in the state sphere, which are often hostile to this equality.

It is also strongly present in Bill 96, another piece of legislation focused on another core element of Quebec's national identity: French language. In our 2017 paper, we predicted that the notwithstanding clause would one day be used by the National Assembly to protect the entire Charter of the French Language in the name of national identity.[18] Five years later, our prediction turned out to be correct. Section 118 of Bill 96 does now indeed invoke the notwithstanding mechanisms of both the Canadian and the Quebec charter. To protect the new and reforged version of the Charter of the French Language, the bill sets in place[19] as much as possible from judicial scrutiny (in addition to Bill 96's sections 199 and 200, invoking the overrides to protect the bill itself as an amending statute). In this context, Bill 96's overrides are justified in the name of the same goals as those of that charter, whose first recital could not be clearer about national identity: "Whereas the French language, the distinctive language of a people that is in the majority French-speaking, is the instrument by which that people has articulated its identity." Let us also note that its second recital is related to the right of workers to carry on their activities in French entrenched in section 4, and therefore to social progress: "Whereas the National Assembly of Quebec recognizes that Quebecers wish to see the quality and influence of the French language assured, and is resolved therefore to make of French ... the normal and everyday language of work." Its fifth recital is relevant as well, since it states the following: "Whereas these observations and intentions are in keeping with a new perception of the worth of national cultures in all parts of the earth, and of the obligation of every people to contribute in its special way to the international community." In addition to those already standing recitals, Bill 96 added the following paragraphs in the Charter of the French Language's preamble:

Whereas the National Assembly recognizes that French is the only common language of the Quebec nation and that it is essential that all be aware of the importance of the French language and Quebec culture as elements that bind society together, and whereas it is resolved therefore to ensure that everyone has access to learning French and to perfecting knowledge and mastery of that language, and to make French the language of integration.

Whereas, in accordance with parliamentary sovereignty, it is incumbent on the Parliament of Quebec to confirm the status of French as the official language and common language in the territory of Quebec and to enshrine the paramountcy of that status in Quebec's legal order, while ensuring a balance between the collective rights of the Quebec nation and human rights and freedoms.

The objectives to protect Quebec's national identity (through French as its official and common language) and to promote social progress manifestly encompasses the Charter of the French Language, Bill 96, which includes dozens of sections implementing the right to work in French, and the notwithstanding clauses the latter will add to the former – all falling in line with the distinctive Quebec theory of the notwithstanding clause. In coherence with this reasoning, such employs of the notwithstanding mechanism were justified by Bill 96's responsible minister during the recent parliamentary hearings in terms that clearly indicate why the legislator do not blindly trust a Supreme Court that rendered many judgments against the Charter of the French Language, when it could have otherwise (notably under section 1) but chose not to:

The parliamentary sovereignty provisions that are used are to ensure that ... In the course of history, the Charter of the French Language has been cut up, if I may say so. And, in a subject that is so important to the Quebec nation, it is important to ensure that it is the will of the National Assembly, the will of parliamentarians, based on parliamentary sovereignty, to define the legislative regime applicable to the protection of French. Because for the Quebec nation, for the Quebec state, for the perpetuation of the French language, all the necessary measures must be put in place to protect the French language, the Charter of the French Language, and it is up to the elected representatives to choose how the relationship with respect to the French language will be defined.[20]

Marion Sandilands argues that the uses of the clause in Bill 21 and Bill 96 are different and broader compared to previous past uses of the clause, since the notwithstanding clauses in these bills are set to a universal level, protecting entire legislations from the entire content of the Canadian or Quebec Charter that can theoretically be over-ridden (section 2 and 7 to 15 of the Canadian Charter and section 1 to 38 of the Quebec Charter). This is in contrast with more specific and targeted uses of the mechanism Quebec made in the past to protect only certain sections of a protected legislation from certain sections of either Charter. To her, it would seem erroneous to claim that the new overrides made in those bills are in line with the distinctive Quebec theory of the notwithstanding mechanism because they would go so far above and beyond what she perceives as a usual practice of targeted overrides that they should not be construed as anchored in precedents.

To this argument, we can first reply that while it has indeed been a while since Quebec made such all-encompassing universal derogations (most of them in the 1980s), it's far from new or unheard of. As a matter of fact, Quebec *did* use the notwithstanding clause to protect entire laws (and not just targeted sections) from judicial scrutiny, and it *did* use the mechanism to derogate to the maximum possible extent of a charter and not just specific charter sections. Indeed, Quebec did use an omnibus derogation to the Canadian Charter from 1982 to 1985[21] to protect the entire content (and not just targeted sections) of all laws in Quebec from Canadian Charter scrutiny.[22] This use of the mechanism, not unlike those in Bill 21 and Bill 96, was deemed valid by the Supreme Court in *Ford*. As we enumerated in our 2017 paper,[23] Quebec did make several derogations to the entire content of the Quebec Charter. It did so eleven times from the late 1970s to the 2000s, and now again twice more with Bill 21 and Bill 96. Therefore, out of forty-four distinct pieces of legislation mentioning either notwithstanding clause carried over forty-seven years, Quebec made global overrides of either charter on fourteen occasions.[24] And on four occasions (at the time of our paper; now six with Bills 21 and 96), there was a global derogation to both charters. We mention this last data because Sandilands underlines the importance of the simultaneous override of both charters in Bill 21 and 96. But she also mentions that the notwithstanding clauses of the two charters should not be conflated because it banalizes the overrides (even though, since *Ford*[25] the Supreme Court of Canada itself conflates the interpretations of both charters and their overrides). In other words, Sandilands seems to argue that it should be necessary to take notwithstanding references to the Quebec Charter into consideration if it might assist in criticizing Bills 21 and 96, but not when such accounts hamper her argument that the notwithstanding mechanism should be reserved for absolutely exceptional uses.

That being said, it also remains that the compatibility of the uses of the override clause made in Bill 21 and Bill 96 with the distinctive Quebec theory just does not depend on these previous uses. It depends on the theory itself, which is to say the statements of the authors at its origin. These statements suggest that there is nothing wrong with a broad use of the clause. Brun, Tremblay, and Brouillet mention that the clause allows, "simply put, to restore parliamentary democracy with respect to certain rights and freedoms."[26] They add that, "The founding provinces wanted to retain the power to decide freely on certain matters for themselves in contrast to a Canadian Charter that aims at standardizing and centralizing law in Canada," and that "it is indeed vital for the Quebec society to have the last word on some subjects that are essential to its survival, given its specific cultural situation ... The express derogation procedure allows, to some degree, to keep this power to have a final say on some subjects."[27] Brun, Tremblay, and Brouillet use expressions like "certain rights and freedoms," "certain matters," and "some subjects" instead of expressions like "precise right" or "specific issues" that would indicate a preference for a restricted and targeted use of the clause. To us, these first three expressions are broad enough to open the door to broad uses of the clause, such as uses that would cover rights and freedoms related to sections 2 or 7 to 15 of the Canadian Charter and matters or subjects such as language or laicity.

During the hearings on Bill 21, Brun, Tremblay, and several other jurists[28] signed a brief to the parliamentary commission that clearly approves the broad use of the clause proposed in this bill with the following words:

In order to establish parliamentary sovereignty over such an important societal issue, the Government is pre-emptively using the notwithstanding clauses, which allow the Act respecting the laicity of the State to be exempted from the application of the Canadian and Quebec Charters of Rights. These so-called notwithstanding provisions are explicitly provided for in each of the two charters themselves. They are, by definition, not subject to any legal control. Moreover, the use of the express exemption is not subject to any substantive conditions, as the Supreme Court of Canada has recognized.

After 15 years of mobilization of civil and political society on this societal issue, we believe that the legislator's willingness to use the notwithstanding provisions is fully legitimate, both from the point of view of a social truce on this issue, at the end of a democratic decision, and from the point of view of a preventive approach aimed at protecting the direct validity of the legislation. The Government is acting within its full jurisdiction in relation to legislation with a secular purpose which falls within section 92(13) of the Constitution Act, 1867, dealing with property and civil rights in the province. In doing so, it affirms the Quebec difference in relation to this kind of issue, which is intimately linked to the civil law conception of the province, which stems from its unique historical trajectory within the federation and which is intimately linked to the Quebec reality that underlies it.

...

If Canada preaches so much for diversity, we submit that it should primarily accept Quebec's diversity in the pursuit of a major social interest (similar to the national margin of appreciation granted to Member States before the European Court of Human Rights with respect to their sovereign legislative action in such societal issues).[29]

Here as well the wording reflects an approval of the broad use of the clause, as those uses of the notwithstanding mechanism are about allowing "the Act respecting the laicity of the State," and not just parts of this act, to be exempted "from the application of the Canadian and Quebec Charters of Rights," and not just from a limited number of sections of these charters. Not to mention that the references to civil law, history, diversity, major social interest, and the national margin of appreciation indicate that the use of the clause is linked to national identity and social progress and therefore in keeping with the Quebec theory of the clause.

1.2 The Notwithstanding Clause as an Instrument to Better Promote Human Rights and Affirm Parliamentary Sovereignty

While we find obvious that the overrides made in Bill 21 and in Bill 96 are aligned with a desire to protect Quebec's collective national identity and promote social progress – and thus in line with our distinct Quebec theory of the notwithstanding clause. We also happily concede that national identity and social progress are not the *only* reasons that can justify invoking the charters' notwithstanding mechanisms.

Quebec's Human Rights Commission suggests that the overrides should be used only to better promote human rights,[30] a suggestion that echoes both Allan Blakeney's understanding of the clause as a mechanism to promote social rights[31] and the theory of "coordinate interpretation" espoused recently by Sun, Sérafin, and Foccroule-Ménard, according to which the legislator might have some say in determining the content of charter rights.[32] While we don't necessarily agree with the exclusivist view of the Human Rights Commission, we can and do agree with it to the extent that an override can, in fact, be employed to better promote human rights – albeit in a broader sense. And we wholeheartedly agree with Sun, Sérafin, and Foccroule-Ménard when they hold that the legislator can legitimately have his say as to how a society construes what human rights are, what they cover, and how they should work within the borders of its own jurisdiction. Such positions are in our opinion entirely coherent and complementary with the distinctive Quebec theory of the not-withstanding clause.

In the case of the Act Respecting the Laicity of the State, it is obvious since the second part of its section 4 reads as follows: "State laicity also requires that all persons have the right to lay parliamentary, government and judicial institutions, and to lay public services, to the extent provided for in this Act." Such wording can only mean that Bill 21, including its prohibition to wear religious symbols and the obligation to have one's face uncovered, are related to that fundamental right to secular public institutions and services provided to everyone in Quebec. Of course, one can disagree with the National Assembly and affirm that there is a right for civil servants to wear religious symbols and cover their face while on duty and that this right should quash the rights of children and recipients of public services – but that is not the point. The point is that the National Assembly has created a human right to secular public services and has decided that this right, its scope, and limits, shall be protected from being quashed or rerouted in the name of other human rights claims by invoking the notwithstanding clause. Therefore, whether one agrees or not with the National Assembly, the fact is that it used the override to promote a human right, and more generally human rights in the plural sense, since the right to secular public services is linked to freedom of conscience. Some will say that the National Assembly's conception of human rights is different from the Supreme Court's conception. But again, whether this is true or not does not matter for the argument, since said argument is that the clause should be used to promote human rights as the legislator conceives them. There can be many different theoretical approaches to the clause, although any serious one has to take into account that its *raison d'être* is to give the last word to the legislator and to make sure that his conception prevails if he wants it to prevail, whether or not his conception is more or less aligned with that of the Supreme Court.

The same holds true for Bill 96 and more generally for Bill 101, the Charter of the French Language. In fact, section 4 of Bill 21, about the right to secular public services, is inspired by sections 2 to 6 of Bill 101. Theses sections enshrined five fundamental language rights, such as the right to work in French. And just as all of Bill 21 aims at protecting the right to secular public services, almost all of Bill 101 aims at protecting these fundamental language rights. That is why the Charter of the French Language includes dozens of sections about labour relations or inspections and inquiries, notably in workplaces. Again, one can agree or not with these fundamental language rights. Some could prefer that the right to work in French and in English be protected, or that the employer's management power be more respected. These are legitimate political opinions. But in no way do they contradict the fact the Bill 101 and Bill 96, which add new fundamental language rights and reinforce the right to work in French, promote human rights as conceived by the National Assembly. Therefore, the inclusion of notwithstanding clauses in these bills is linked to human rights in general and to social rights in particular.

Of course, opponents to Bill 21 and Bill 96 would like to suggest that these bills promote only the human rights of the majority to the detriment of those of the minorities, and that the Quebec theory and practice of the clause ignore minorities. To that, we can first reply that this theory and practice do not ignore minorities, since our 2017 paper quotes Binette, who mentions the protection of minorities and the Juror Act,[33] which uses the clause to protect certain rights of Indigenous peoples. Secondly, we can also reply that such a suggestion is simply false, since section 4 of the Act Respecting the Laicity of the State and sections 2 to 6 of the Charter of the French Language confer rights to *all* Quebecers, regardless of any personal distinction. We can also reply, as a third rebuttal, that the state of Quebec exists precisely to defend the rights of its population, sociologically characterized by a large French-speaking local majority that defines it as a group which constitutes, in fact, a minority in Canada.[34] Therefore, those opposing Bill 21 and Bill 96 in the name of minorities' rights, while at the same time saying that the Anglo-Canadian majority embodied by the Supreme Court should impose its will on the French minority embodied by the state of Quebec, are in a contradiction. In other words, we agree with Sandilands when she says that minorities cannot control the will of the majority, but we don't understand why she so resolutely insists that this majority should dominate that minority.

2. THE NOTWITHSTANDING MECHANISM AS A
SHIELD TO PROTECT A DISTINCT LEGAL TRADITION

In and of themselves, these previous findings, we contend, are sufficient to uphold the validity of our theoretical and empirical conclusions: there effectively *is* a distinctive theory and practice of the notwithstanding clause in Quebec. But let's open the reflection one step further and ask: how come? How is it that Quebec adopts such a distinct approach to the override that so sharply contrasts with the theoretical and practical approaches the issue receives in English Canada? Part of the answer resides in the distinctive conception of parliamentary sovereignty that is unique to Quebec in Canada. As we demonstrated in our 2017 paper, only in Quebec is the legislative assembly named "National Assembly" and perceived as the legal embodiment of a distinct people and the guardian of its collective rights, in a historical and cultural perspective.[35] Part of it resides in the distinctive civil law legal tradition of Quebec – a legal tradition that is not only a different set of positive rules and jurisprudence from Anglo-Canadian common law, but is also, indeed, a systemically different way to *comprehend and apply law as a science.* The civilist legal tradition does not *think* law the same way the common law legal tradition does. And for Quebec, the notwithstanding clause thus also works as a shield to protect this crucial socio-legal distinction from being negated in the name of an Anglo-Canadian common law understanding of human rights that stems from a centralized, standardized, and standardizing Supreme Court jurisprudence, which – not always but (too) often, especially in matters of public law or when "politically sensitive" cultural issues are raised – seemingly sets aside the originality of the civilist worldview to read, review, and quash Quebec's laws as if they were common law statutes subject to common law parameters.[36]

Indeed, when all is said and done, and once all the technical questions have been answered, the entire issue at hand regarding Quebec's use of charter overrides to protect its legislation from judicial scrutiny and invalidation really boils down to one simple question: does Quebec have any right, as a people and as a nation state, to be different than the rest of English Canada and to preserve that difference, or is it duty-bound to organize its culture, its society, and the intricate normative mesh of its interpersonal and collective relationships only as dictated by Anglo-Canadian standards? With history as our constant witness for almost 250 years since the Quebec Act[37] of 1774, Quebec has systematically embraced the first idea and rejected the second. This reality has been recognized since the earliest days of British rule, was reconducted at the birth of the Confederation, and still holds true to this day. We hold this as self-evident: Quebec is a distinct society within Canada – linguistically, culturally, and more importantly, legally. And a particular element of that recognized societal distinction, one which cannot be denied without denying Quebec itself or rewriting history, is its distinctive civil law legal tradition.

As a matter of fact and of law, Quebec's entire civilist legal system functions according to different structures, different sources, and different methods than those of Anglo-Canadian common law. While common law lauds remedy-oriented judicial powers of intervention *a posteriori* through individual grievances, civil law embraces a generalist legislation-oriented conception of law where *a priori* legal certainty and stability is paramount. Common law analyzes matters of equality and discrimination through the lens of the substantive effects an individual may subjectively feel from the legal norm or a factual situation regardless of form or intent. For the civil law, however, it's the other way around: equality and discrimination *are* formal and intent-based as a matter of law and the question of its "felt" effects, especially when it involves subjective issues of personal identity, choices or beliefs, is a matter almost entirely left for the streets and the urns in the political domain, not for the judicial sandbox. While common law is focused on the rights of the concrete individual as a trump card against the state and everyone else to protect its infinitely variable personal interests, civil law is more focused on the right of a people to govern itself as a whole through the enactment of abstract generalist rules that tell everyone, as abstract persona and regardless of individual distinctions, what to do or not to do in abstract contexts and situations, expecting the concrete individual to adapt to the norm rather than the other way around. The list goes on and on; the two legal traditions are not the same and do not function the same way.[38]

Yet, since the imposition of the Canadian Charter of Rights in 1982, and exponentially since the late 1990s/early 2000s, there is an observable and troubling tendency for Canadian tribunals, especially those of federal nomination – the Supreme Court of Canada leading the charge – to ignore or deny Quebec's different, civilist approach to questions of human rights in the name of Anglo-Canadian common law individualism when it comes to collective or identity matters. This is especially true in the domains of language and religion, which are of paramount importance to Quebec society as a collective whole. It happened time and time again through the decades, from *Ford* to *Bergevin*,[39] *Boisbriand*,[40] *Multani*,[41] and *Amselem*,[42] to name but just a few cases. Many authors – Brun, Tremblay, Brouillet, Pelletier, Popovici, Morel, and Taillon, among others – have pointed out and criticized this negationist tendency, largely collectively perceived in Quebec as the unwanted imposition of an alien legal model to reform Quebec's civilist social choices in the name of an incompatible common law worldview. And this criticism is far from recent. Premier Daniel Johnson, Sr was already worried about the issue as far back as 1968, when the Canadian Charter was just a theoretical project, calling the idea of a standardized interpretation of human rights in Quebec by the Supreme Court a "grave political mistake" given the "considerable differences" between the legal traditions on this matter.[43] Quashing section after section of the Charter of the French language, imposing one "reasonable accommodation" – a common law judicial construct largely unrecognized by the civilist tradition[44] – after the other, rejecting formalism to embrace substantively subjective conceptions of equality, considering religion not as a choice but akin to an intrinsic personal characteristic of the individual, to name only a few examples; for Quebec, these judicial constructions are *imposed* by the Supreme Court and while compliance is *enforced* by judicial powers, it is certainly not generally *accepted* as a genuine representation of the social contract. Some international observers, such as Sujit Choudry,[45] have even suggested that this decried tendency from the Supreme Court (since the constitutional patriation of 1982) to conduct Charter control of Quebec civilist law through an Anglo-Canadian common law standard when it comes to politically sensitive issues is leading to a fracture of the trust and confidence Quebec's legislature and people can maintain toward Canadian tribunals in matters of collective interests and national identity. On far too many occasions for the last four decades, Canadian tribunals have invoked the Canadian Charter (or the Quebec Charter, which they have shackled to the former in such occasions) to reform Quebec's political choices made law in the name of a common law interpretation of human rights in which, simply put, Quebec does not recognize itself nor its legal tradition.

In this perspective, recourse to Charter overrides take an entirely different tone. Not only is it entirely in line with the distinctive Quebec theory of the notwithstanding clause (as Quebec's distinct legal tradition is historically part of its national identity[46]) – it is also a strong and formal reminder that Quebec is a civilist jurisdiction and that this paramount consideration *must* be respected judicially if public and legislative confidence in the courts is to be preserved. This entails two things. First off, it serves as a reminder that, from a civilist perspective, pre-emptive uses of overrides are perfectly logical as the civilist validity of legal norms is not fact-dependent – the legislator is under no obligation whatsoever to first wait for a tribunal to strike down its law in the name of a factual situation before deciding to uphold it anyway through an override. It can do so beforehand as a matter of rational logistics and principles because, in itself, the whole legal norm is an *a priori* abstraction. Moreso, such *pre-emptive* uses of the overrides also convey a particular meaning for Quebec within the Canadian federation: it is a formal statement by the National Assembly that *it* and *it only* is the true sovereign arbiter of social relationships in Quebec[47] and that, in collective matters of high importance linked to social progress or national identity, it simply can no longer *blindly* trust that the Supreme Court will effectively recognize and respect its civilist tradition and resist the temptation to quash it in the name of a standardized Anglo-Canadian common law approach. It is not because the common law tradition sees something as "wrong" or "discriminatory" that a civilist perspective will necessarily arrive at the same conclusion – or vice-versa. Imposing an Anglo-Canadian common law solution to a human rights issue in civilist Quebec is thus tantamount to an unacceptable form of judicial imperialism purporting that English Canada and the common law tradition are better and know better than Quebec and its civilist tradition when it comes to human rights.

In this perspective, invoking charter overrides becomes a shield against this possibly. It is not for nothing that several references, as we've seen above, were made to Quebec's civilist tradition in Bill 21 and Bill 96, both protected by the override and shielded from invalidation by Canadian tribunals whose effective respect of the traditional distinction is more than questionable. In other words, through such uses of the notwithstanding mechanism, the National Assembly is saying that, "According to our civilist interpretation of the law, we think that this measure is valid and not discriminatory, but we simply cannot take the risk that Canadian tribunals could review and quash it under a common law worldview unaligned with Quebec's societal and legal values, that may or may not see things differently – and given the highest social importance of these issues, we will use the notwithstanding mechanism pre-emptively to avoid that risk in the first place." The very first recital of Bill 21's preamble – "As the Quebec nation has its own characteristics, one of which is its civil law tradition, distinct social values and a specific history that have led it to develop a particular attachment to State laicity" – is here highly indicative of such a perspective. And as for Bill 96, while it does not yet feature an explicit reference to the civilist tradition *per se*, it does propose to add no less than five references to the "Quebec nation" in the Charter of the French Language – heavily implying the civilist tradition, especially when referring to "Quebec's legal order" and explicitly mentioning the "balance between the collective rights of the Quebec nation and human rights and freedoms" in the last recital it will add to its preamble.

The importance of such issues also justifies why, in the name of legal coherence and self-determination, the National Assembly employs the override in the broadest sense possible to pre-emptively and entirely subtract such legislative works from judicial scrutiny as widely as possible. This is a method which has been analyzed and deemed valid by the Supreme Court, even from what can be seen as a common law standpoint, since *Ford*, and one that has been recognized as valid at trial level in the ongoing *Hak*[48] case, one may add as well.

And in that perspective, it is also important to underline the fact that section 120 of Bill 96 modifies the preamble of the Civil Code[49] to mention that this code governs persons, relations, and property not only in harmony with Quebec's Charter of Human Rights, but also in harmony with the Charter of the French Language. Personally, we believe that this section should have mentioned Bill 21, but the main point is that the conception of Quebec constitutional law behind this section is that the Charter of Rights is neither more nor less important than our fundamental language rights or our civil law tradition. They are all equally important in their own ways and must be treated in coherent harmony on the greater canvas of the civilist legal tradition.

Quebec is asserting its legitimate right to regulate social affairs through its own legitimately distinct civilian legal worldview. The notwithstanding clause, in that respect, is a means to that end. In furtherance of that perspective – and it will be a very interesting venue to evaluate for Quebec in the near future – the National Assembly could very well consider introducing, and periodically renewing, omnibus overrides to cover the entire Quebec Civil Code. Just as our argument about national identity led us to predict in our 2017 paper that the clause was going to be used in the Charter of the French Language, our argument about the civil law tradition now leads us to predict that one day it could be used to protect the Civil Code.

Some could argue that it would be a radical move with tremendous effects on human rights. We believe that it would not be against human rights; it would be for another conception of human rights. And foremost, it would be about Quebec's self-determination, a blind spot for Sandilands and many other commentators of the notwithstanding clause. After the failures of referendums and attempts at reforming Canadian federalism in a way that would accommodate Quebec's identity, the time has come for Quebec to fight for self-determination by using unilateralism, whether it be by modifying the Constitution Act, 1867,[50] as Bill 96 did, or by using the notwithstanding clause. Notably.

NOTES

1 Canadian Charter of Rights and Freedoms, Part I of the Constitution Act, 1982, being Schedule B to the Canada Act 1982 (UK), 1982, c. 11.
2 See Bill 21, Bill 96, and Act Amending Certain Acts Establishing Public Sector Pensions Plans, 2019, c. 25, s. 1, 2, 3, 4, and 9.
3 Act Respecting the Laicity of the State, C.Q.L.R. c. L-0.3.
4 Act Respecting French, the Official and Common Language of Québec, 2022, c. 14.
5 In contrast with the common law legal tradition systematically applying everywhere else in Canada.
6 Guillaume Rousseau and François Côté, "A Distinctive Quebec Theory and Practice of the Notwithstanding Clause: When Collective Interests Outweigh Individual Rights," *Revue générale de droit* 47 (2017): 343.
7 Ibid., 372.
8 Benoît Pelletier, "La théorie du fédéralisme et son application au contexte multinational canadien," in *La laïcité : le choix du Québec. Regards pluridisciplinaires sur la Loi sur laïcité de l'État*, eds. Marc-André Turcotte

and Julie Gagnon (Québec, QC: Secrétariat à l'accès à l'information et à la réforme des institutions démocratiques, 2021), 373, 464, 467.

9 Jacques Gosselin, *La légitimité du contrôle judiciaire sous le régime de la Charte* (Cowansville, QC: Yvon Blais, 1991), 241–6.

10 *International Covenant on Economic, Social and Cultural Rights*, 19 December 1966, 999 UNTS 171 (entered into force 23 March 1976).

11 André Binette, "Le pouvoir dérogatoire de l'article 33 de la Charte canadienne des droits et libertés et la structure de la Constitution du Canada," *Revue du Barreau*, Special Issue (2003): 139, 146.

12 Henri Brun, "La *Charte des droits et libertés de la personne*: domaine d'application," *R du B* 37, no. 2 (1977): 199; Henri Brun, Guy Tremblay, and Eugénie Brouillet, *Droit constitutionnel*, 6th ed. (Cowansville, QC: Yvon Blais, 2014), 970.

13 Charter of Human Rights and Freedoms, C.Q.L.R. c C-12.

14 As opposed to invoking the notwithstanding mechanism to pursue state imperatives of administrative efficiency or individualistic identity issues.

15 Bill C-13, An Act to Amend the Official Languages Act, to Enact the Use of French in Federally Regulated Private Businesses Act and to Make Related Amendments to other Acts, First Session, Forty-fourth Parliament, 70–71 Elizabeth II, 2021–22.

16 Marion Sandilands, this volume, chapter 11.

17 Québec, Assemblée Nationale, *Journal des débats. Commissions parlementaires*, Commission des institutions, 1st sess., 42nd legis., 4 June 2019 (Simon Jolin-Barette). Quotation translated directly from French to English by the authors, who bear the sole responsibility for any mistranslation. See also François Côté and Guillaume Rousseau, "From Ford v. Québec to the Act Respecting the Laicity of the State: A Distinctive Quebec Theory and Practice of the Notwithstanding Clause," *The Supreme Court Law Review* 94 (2020), 482.

18 Rousseau and Côté, "Distinctive Quebec Theory," 405.

19 From a technical standpoint, Bill 96 is an amending statute; its purpose is to enact a wide series of amendments to the already standing Charter of the French Language (and to a myriad of accessory statutes that also interact with it) to enhance its capacity to effectively protect and promote French as Quebec's national language and to formally respond to the Supreme Court's jurisprudence regarding this Charter. Bill 96's section 118 thus purports to create new sections (213.1 and 214) in the Charter of the French Language, that will, themselves, protect the latter Charter with notwithstanding clauses references.

20 Québec, Assemblée Nationale, *Journal des débats. Commissions parlementaires*, Commission des institutions, 2nd sess., 42nd legis., 14 April 2022 (Simon Jolin-Barette), http://www.assnat.qc.ca/fr/travaux-parlementaires/commissions/cce-42-2/journal-debats/CCE-220414.html. Quotation translated directly from French to English by the authors, who bear the sole responsibility for any mistranslation.

21 Act Respecting the Constitution Act, 1982, SQ 1982, c. 21.

22 At that time, the omnibus notwithstanding clause did not refer to Quebec's Charter. That was before the ruling in *Ford* v. *Québec* [1988] 2 S.R.C. 712, where the Supreme Court conflated the evaluation of rights limitation under the *Oakes* test (*R.* v. *Oakes* [1986] 1 S.R.C. 103) for both charters, even though the wording of section 9.1 of Quebec's Charter is completely different from the wording of section one of the Canadian Charter.

23 Rousseau and Côté, "Distinctive Quebec Theory," 423 (Appendix).

24 Here counting the acts themselves and not the individual references contained therein – we include Bills 21 and 96 in this count.

25 *Ford v. Quebec* [1988] 2 S.R.C. 712.

26 Brun, Tremblay, and Brouillet, *Droit constitutionnel*, 968, para XII–2.15. Quotation translated directly from French to English by the authors, who bear the sole responsibility for any mistranslation.

27 Brun, Tremblay, and Brouillet, *Droit constitutionnel*, 970, para XII–2.20 and XII–2.21. Quotation translated directly from French to English by the authors, who bear the sole responsibility for any mistranslation.

28 Eugénie Brouillet was by then vice-president at the Université Laval and therefore not active in the debate on Bill 21. One of the authors of the present paper, Côté, participated in the drafting of this brief (which mobilized, amongst other things, our distinct Quebec theory of the notwithstanding clause), co-signed by Brun and Tremblay, and was one of its lead speakers during the formal hearings in front of the National Assembly.

29 Juristes pour la laïcité de l'État, "Mémoire présenté à la commission des institutions. Projet de loi 21," *Assemblée nationale*, (2019): 18–19. References omitted.

30 Commission des droits de la personne, *L'utilisation de la clause dérogatoire de l'article 52 de la Charte des droits et libertés de la personne par le législateur*, résolution COM-270-9.1.2 du 16 septembre 1986.

31 Dwight Newman, this volume, chapter 3.

32 Kerry Sun, Stéphane Séraphin, and Xavier F. Ménard, "Notwithstanding the Courts? Directing the Canadian Charter Toward the Common Good,"

Ius et Iustitium (blog), 1 July 2021, iusetiustitium.com/notwithstanding-the-courts-directing-the-canadian-charter-toward-the-common-good/.

33 Jurors Act, SQ 1976, c 9, s 58, today CQLR c J-2, s 52.

34 "The principle of federalism facilitates the pursuit of collective goals by cultural and linguistic minorities which form the majority within a particular province. This is the case in Quebec, where the majority of the population is French-speaking, and which possesses a distinct culture. This is not merely the result of chance. The social and demographic reality of Quebec explains the existence of the province of Quebec as a political unit and indeed, was one of the essential reasons for establishing a federal structure for the Canadian union in 1867." *Reference re Secession of Quebec* [1998] 2 SCR 217, par. 59. It is also of interest to note that this view has been confirmed in international law. According to the United Nations Human Rights Committee, the local French-speaking majority in Quebec is indeed a minority when considering that Quebec is a non-sovereign state within the Canadian federation – while the Quebec English-speaking community in its borders are, in fact, not a minority (rather being members of the federation's broader English-speaking majority). *Ballantyne, Davidson, McIntyre v. Canada*, Communications Nos. 359/1989 and 385/1989, U.N. Doc. CCPR/C/47/D/359/1989 and 385/1989/Rev.1 (1993), para 11.2.

35 Rousseau and Côté, "Distinctive Quebec Theory," 408–13.

36 The following arguments are largely inspired by Côté's pending and unpublished law doctorate thesis. François Côté, "Code civil, Chartes des droits et traditions juridiques: entre subjugation et résistance du droit civil québécois face à la common law canadienne en matière privée" (PhD diss., Université de Sherbrooke and Université Laval, 2022).

37 Quebec Act, 1774, 14 Geo. III, c. 83. Section VIII of this act recognizes that Quebec law operates according to a different *system* of laws and rules than those of English common law, barring certain fields of exception such as criminal law. Of course, several legal constructs in Quebec were and are *inspired* by common law sources, but are adapted to function according to civilist principles and reasonings.

38 In addition to Côté's upcoming thesis, the interested reader will want to consult the dual comparative works of Aline Grenon and Louise Bélanger-Hardy: Aline Grenon and Louise Bélanger-Hardy, eds., *Éléments de common law canadienne : comparaison avec le droit civil québécois* (Montreal: Thompson-Carswell, 2008); Aline Grenon and Louise Bélanger-Hardy, eds, *Elements of Quebec Civil Law: A Comparaison with*

the Common Law of Canada (Toronto: Thompson-Carswells, 2008). See also David Gilles' in-depth historical study on the matter: David Gilles, *Essais d'histoire du droit – De la Nouvelle-France à la Province de Québec* (Sherbrooke: Revue Droit Université Sherbrooke, 2014).

39 *Commission scolaire régionale de Chambly v. Bergervin* [1994] 2 S.C.R. 525.

40 *Québec (Commission des droits de la personne et des droits de la jeunesse) v. Montréal (Ville); Québec (Commission des droits de la personne et des droits de la jeunesse) v. Boisbriand (Ville)*, [2000] 1 S.C.R. 665.

41 *Multani v. Commission scolaire MargueriteBourgeoys* [2006] 1 S.C.R. 256.

42 *Syndicat Northcrest v. Amselem* [2004] 2 S.C.R. 551.

43 Secrétariat aux affaires intergouvernementales canadiennes, *Positions du Québec dans les domaines constitutionnel et intergouvernemental* (Quebec: Ministère du Conseil exécutif, 2001), 35–6.

44 Tatiana Gründler, *Aménagements raisonnables et non-discrimination* (Ardis, 2016).

45 Sujit Choudry, "Rights Adjudication in a Plurinational State: The Supreme Court of Canada, Freedom of Religion and the Politics of Reasonable Accommodation," *Osgoode Hall Law Journal* 50, no. 3 (2013): 575.

46 Sylvio Normand, "Le Code civil et l'identité," in *Du Code civil du Québec : contribution à l'histoire immédiate d'une recodification réussie*, ed. Jean-Guy Belley, Nicholas Kasirer, and Serge Lortie (Montreal: Themis, 2005), 619.

47 This approach, we remark, is also consistent with the parliamentary sovereignty perspective of the override mentioned above.

48 *Hak v. Procureur général du Québec*, 2021 QCCS 1466 (currently under appeal).

49 *Civil Code of Québec*, C.Q.L.R. c CCQ-1991.

50 *Constitution Act, 1867*, 30 & 31 Victoria, c. 3 (U.K.).

11

Quebec's Bills 21 and 96: An Underwater Eruption

Marion Sandilands

Legally speaking, the use of the notwithstanding clause in Bill 96 is the most sweeping override of human rights charters in Canada since patriation. How did we get here, and where, exactly, is "here"?

This chapter is in four parts. First, it describes how the notwithstanding clause is used in Bill 96, and sets out the legal effects and implications. Second, it puts this moment into the context of Quebec's history of using overrides, responding directly to the work of Guillaume Rousseau and François Côté. Third, it argues that Bills 21 and 96 are in fact a constitutional project – the underwater eruption of a constitutional volcano. Fourth, the chapter explains why anyone outside Quebec should care.

It is important to note that one can accept that Quebec's distinct language and culture should be protected in law, yet insist that this protection has not, does not, and ought not require the ousting of human rights charters.

I. THE NOTWITHSTANDING CLAUSE IN BILL 96

In Quebec, there are actually two "overrides" because there are two human rights charters. In Quebec, the Quebec Charter is a quasi-constitutional statute. Its paramountcy clause is also its so-called notwithstanding clause.[1] In this way, the National Assembly can declare that legislation applies notwithstanding the Quebec Charter and/or the Canadian Charter.[2]

Where this chapter refers to a *targeted* override, this means an override of *selected* provisions of a human rights charter. Where the chapter refers to a *total* override, this means an override of *every* provision of a human rights charter.

Of all provinces, Quebec has indeed made the most use of section 33 of the Canadian Charter. Most notably, in 1982, Quebec used section 33 in an omnibus fashion to shield *all* of its legislation from the operation of the entire Canadian Charter (a total override).[3] Of great note, however, there was no simultaneous override of the Quebec Charter at that time. Quite the opposite, in fact: in 1982, the Quebec Charter was amended to strengthen and entrench it as Quebec's paramount statute.[4] Thus, until 2019, there had never been a total override of both the Quebec and Canadian Charters.

In 2019, the National Assembly adopted Bill 21, An Act Respecting Laicity of the State. This bill included a legal first in Quebec: a total and pre-emptive override of both the Quebec and Canadian Charters.[5]

Bill 96, An Act Respecting French, the Official and Common Language of Quebec, was introduced in the National Assembly on 13 May 2021, and adopted on 24 May 2022. Bill 96 is a wide-ranging and complex piece of legislation. It amends the Charter of the French Language, twenty-five other provincial statutes, two regulations, and the Constitution Act, 1867.

Bill 96 transforms the Charter of the French Language. Through 119 amendments to that statute, it significantly enhances the law's requirements as to the use of French, as well as its monitoring, search, complaints, and penal provisions. Bill 96 also brings in a suite of changes to other key statutes in Quebec, including the preliminary provisions of the Civil Code and Code of Civil Procedure, and amends the Charter of Human Rights and Freedoms ("Quebec Charter") itself. Finally, Bill 96 adds a paramountcy clause into the Charter of the French Language. This statute will now be paramount over any conflicting law enacted after Bill 96.[6]

Bill 96 ousts Quebec and Canadian charters the same novel way as Bill 21: totally and pre-emptively, to the full extent possible. Bill 96 ousts both charters in two respects. First, it amends the Charter of the French Language to provide that the *entire* Charter of the French Language has effect notwithstanding sections 2 and 7–15 of the Canadian Charter (the full ambit of section 33 of the Canadian Charter) and despite sections 1 to 38 of the Quebec Charter (the full ambit of section 52 of the Quebec Charter).[7] Second, it provides that the remainder of Bill 96 – all the amendments to the twenty-five other provincial statutes, two regulations, and the Constitution Act, 1867 – is similarly immunized from the application of the Canadian Charter and Quebec Charter.[8]

What is the effect of the Charter overrides in a statute of this size and scope?

The Charter of the French Language affects so many aspects of life within the province, such as commerce, employment, education, access to public services, expression in a range of contexts, and the legal system. Because the override is applied in such wide-ranging legislation, and in the Charter of the French Language as a paramount statute, it effectively creates a Charter-free zone with respect to a wide range of interactions between individuals and the state in Quebec.

Bill 96 also creates a large state apparatus to monitor and enforce the law, including a swath of new administrative powers, all immune from Charter scrutiny. These include new ministerial discretionary powers, warrantless search powers broader than those struck down in *Hunter v Southam*, disclosure protections that explicitly enable privacy breaches,[9] and some very draconian penal provisions. Thus, the legal effects of the Charter overrides in Bill 96 are even more far-reaching than those of Bill 21.

This also raises a novel question in Canadian law: does the pre-emptive use of section 33 immunize the *exercise* of the statutory powers from judicial review on Charter grounds? For instance, can a search carried out under these powers be challenged on the basis that the search violates section 8 of the Canadian Charter?[10] If not, then this arm of the administrative state would be created and operate entirely outside the constitutional constraints that have become the norm in Canada.

The complete and pre-emptive use of the override has some unique legal and constitutional effects. These effects were present with Bill 21, but they come into greater focus with Bill 96.

Which provisions of Bill 96 actually "need" the override, in the sense that the override would shield provisions that obviously violate Charter rights? There is no clear answer to this question. Various Charter rights are engaged – and likely infringed – in various provisions of Bill 96, but not every provision of Bill 96 obviously violates Charter rights. If the total pre-emptive override is not "needed" to protect every provision of Bill 96, what is it for? The total overrides are serving a constitutional purpose.

The use of total pre-emptive override in this fashion rearranges the hierarchy of laws in Quebec. This is most obvious with the Quebec Charter: prior to Bill 21, the Quebec Charter was at the top of the hierarchy.[11] With its total and indefinite override of the Quebec Charter, Bill 21 effectively demoted the Quebec Charter to second place. Using the same mechanism, Bill 96 effectively places the Charter of the French Language at the top and demotes the Quebec Charter to third place.

This reversal is significant. The Quebec Charter was enacted two years before the Charter of the French Language. The first version of the Charter of the French Language attempted to override the Quebec Charter, but after strong opposition, this proposal was withdrawn.[12] The National Assembly maintained the primacy of the Quebec Charter over the Charter of the French Language. The Quebec Charter has great legal and symbolic value in Quebec.[13] With Bills 21 and 96, this value is diminished.

What about the Canadian Charter? Does this use of section 33 attempt to rearrange the hierarchy of the Canadian Constitution? In my view, it does. The override in Bill 21 effectively places the entire Laicity Act above sections 2 and 7–15 of the Canadian Charter for five years. Bill 96 does the same thing for the entire Charter of the French Language. As a result, sections 2 and 7–15 of the Canadian Charter are effectively no longer the Supreme Law of Canada in the province of Quebec.

2. QUEBEC'S HISTORY OF THE NOTWITHSTANDING CLAUSE: RESPONSE TO ROUSSEAU

This section responds directly to the work of Guillaume Rousseau and François Côté.[14] They posit a distinctive theory and practice in Quebec around the use of the overrides of both the Canadian and Quebec Charters. Rousseau and Côté argue that the distinct theory and practice of the overrides in Quebec can ground the practice of pre-emptively using the override to protect language and culture.[15] The response is as follows: While there are undeniably distinct theories in Quebec literature of the nature of the notwithstanding clause and its appropriate uses, the so-called "distinctive Quebec theory" is not nearly as coherent or monolithic as Rousseau and Côté make it appear. Moreover, the theory has no relation to Quebec's past practice of using the overrides. And, even if there is both a distinct theory and practice, the use of the overrides in Bills 21 and 96 is manifestly and categorically different from any past practice.

a. Theory: Neither Monolithic nor Universal

In Quebec, the theoretical literature on derogations predates the Canadian Charter: the theories first came about before in the late 1970s, the early days of the Quebec Charter. There seem to be two currents. First, in certain instances, collective interests may prevail over individual rights and interests. In Quebec, these collective interests include social progress and the survival of Quebec's unique language and collective identity.[16] Second, the theories posit that a Charter override is an expression of parliamentary sovereignty. On these views, the override gives the Quebec National Assembly "the last word" on matters of social progress or matters essential to the survival of Quebec society.[17] On some theories, this justifies the pre-emptive use of the clause.[18]

One well-developed and nuanced variation on these theories is Benoît Pelletier's, in this volume. According to Pelletier's view, the Canadian Charter – which was brought in without Quebec's consent – created constraints on legislative power and a unifying effect across Canada, and thereby removed some of Quebec's ability to pursue its distinctive collective interests. In this context, section 33 is one important and legitimate tool for Quebec to assert and protect its distinctiveness within the Canadian federation.[19]

A few comments can be made on Rousseau and Côté's methodology and approach. While Rousseau and Côté purport to uncover a "distinct Quebec theory," the theory is neither coherent nor singular in Quebec.

First, as Maxime St-Hilaire points out, Rousseau and Côté conflate the theory about the Quebec and Canadian charters.[20] As St-Hilaire notes, there are several important differences between the two charters, and the conflation of the two charters is misleading. First, the two charters are of a fundamentally different nature: one is constitutional while the other is quasi-constitutional legislation. Further, the Quebec Charter's justification clause does not apply to all provisions of the Quebec Charter – most notably the equality clause.[21] Thus, a derogation from the Quebec Charter might save legislation that might well be a justifiable limit on rights to which the justification clause does not apply. Third, the Quebec Charter guarantees a much broader set of rights than the Canadian Charter. For all these reasons, the theory of these two derogation clauses should not be conflated. Further, one might expect to see a larger number of derogations from the Quebec Charter than from the Canadian Charter. By treating the two charters together in articulating their "distinct Quebec theory" and in cataloguing past practice, Rousseau and Côté find a banality in overrides to the Canadian Charter that would not exist if one looked at the Canadian Charter by itself.

Further, the presentation of the theory as a "distinctive Quebec theory" is problematic. The theory is not universal in Quebec.[22] Nor is it entirely distinct to Quebec. The theory takes elements from other theories of derogation, most notably in its emphasis on parliamentary supremacy. More fundamentally, St-Hilaire notes that Rousseau's theory creates an opposition between "Canadian" scholars and "authentically Quebec" scholars, and attempts to paint "Quebec" scholarship with a monolithic brush in order to minimize the gravity of overriding fundamental constitutional rights:

C'est une forme d'opération particulière de « biais de confirmation » (confirmation bias) qui voit Rousseau faire une distinction entre, d'une part, les « juristes canadiens » et « certains juristes québécois proches de ces derniers » et, de l'autre, les juristes qui, pour penser « l'inverse » de ceux-ci, seraient authentiquement québécois, « au point où il y aurait une théorie de la disposition dérogatoire proprement québécoise » ...

En somme, non seulement Rousseau prétend-il à tort pouvoir inférer la légitimité d'une pratique à partir de son effectivité, mais encore faut-il se rendre compte que, cette effectivité, il la fabrique en partie, et ce dans le but simultané de lui faire justifier la théorie qu'il a choisie sur une base existentialiste. Par conséquent, je ne vois rien de valide dans l'argumentaire au moyen duquel il veut défendre la thèse selon laquelle il aurait déboulonné quelque mythe de la gravité de la dérogation aux droits constitutionnels fondamentaux.

Rousseau himself is not a neutral observer of the changes occurring in Quebec's legal order, but rather an active participant. Rousseau first published on this topic in 2016 for the Institut de recherche sur le Quebec,[23] where he is the current research director.[24] Rousseau served as special counsel to the government of Quebec leading up to the adoption of Bill 21.[25] This research also provided the basis for Côté and Rousseau's 2020 *Supreme Court Law Review* article defending the use of the overrides in Bill 21.[26] Rousseau is also counsel to Mouvement laïque Québécois, a party defending Bill 21 in the constitutional challenge.[27]

b. Practice: Does Not Align with the Theory

In any event, assuming there is a "distinctive Quebec theory," is there also a "Quebec practice" that can be explained by this theory? The answer is no.

There is no doubt that section 33 has been used more in Quebec than any other province.[28] Rousseau and Côté have meticulously categorized each override of both the Quebec Charter and Canadian Charter since 1975, the advent of the Quebec Charter. For the reasons articulated by Maxime St-Hilaire above, the derogations from the Quebec Charter and Canadian Charter should not be conflated. There is understandably a higher number of derogations from the Quebec Charter than the Canadian Charter, and the inflated total number of derogations creates the impression that derogations from either charter are numerous and trivial. For this reason, the analysis in this chapter focuses only on the overrides of the Canadian Charter.

Rousseau and Côté's work clearly shows which overrides are targeted and which are total. They categorize the purposes of the overrides: "state imperative," "social objective," "identity issues," or none of these.

Rousseau and Côté's own categorizations disprove their own theory: there are very few examples of the use of section 33 to protect language and culture in Quebec.

The Canadian Charter overrides fall into four categories. First, pension legislation that overrides section 15 to shield provisions that essentially protect women and former clerics.[29] This is categorized as having a "social progress" objective. Second, there is education legislation that overrides section 2(a) and section 15 in order to protect certain privileges of Catholics and Protestants with respect to religious education.[30] This is categorized as having either a "collective identity" objective or no categorization. The third category is one piece of agriculture legislation to assist young farmers, which overrode section 15 to counter the prohibition on discrimination on the basis of age – categorized as a "social progress" objective.[31] Fourth and finally, there was the override of section 2(b), following the Supreme Court's decision in *Ford*, to protect the specific provision of the Charter of the French Language found to be unconstitutional.[32] Rousseau and Côté categorize this as having a "collective identity" purpose.

Thus, according to Rousseau and Côté's own categories, there have been eight instances of overrides of the Canadian Charter to protect "collective identity," and seven of these were in education, to protect denominational and confessional school rights, not language. The eighth is the *Ford* override, dealing with language. This was a *post facto* override of two *specific* Canadian Charter provisions to shield two *specific* provisions of the Charter of the French Language.

Thus, if there is a distinct Quebec practice of Charter overrides, it bears very little resemblance to the so-called "distinct Quebec theory."

c. Neither the Theory nor Practice Grounds the Use of the Overrides in Bills 21 and 96

Further, Rousseau and Côté's work clearly shows that there is no precedent for the use of the overrides in Bills 21 and 96. With one exception, *all* prior uses of section 33 are targeted overrides. Prior to Bill 21, the Canadian Charter had been totally overridden only once before, in 1982.[33] This was the spectacular omnibus override to shield all of Quebec's legislation from the operation of the Canadian Charter. However, as mentioned above, there was no simultaneous override of the Quebec Charter.[34] Thus, although the Canadian Charter would not apply in Quebec, the same rights became justiciable under the Quebec Charter. As a result, the *Ford* case itself, which was started during the period of the 1982 override, was brought under the Quebec Charter as well as the Canadian Charter.

Also of note, Rousseau and Côté do not code the 1982 override as being related to identity issues – they give it no categorization at all. Other scholars have characterized the 1982 override as a political protest against the patriation of the Canadian Charter without Quebec's consent.[35] This will be discussed further in the third part of this chapter.

The *only* use of the override to protect language – namely the *Ford* override – was specific, targeted, and post facto (after a decision of the Supreme Court). While Rousseau and Côté state that the override has been used pre-emptively in 98 per cent of instances,[36] the *Ford* override was, exceptionally, *not* pre-emptive. Thus, Quebec's only instance of overriding the Canadian Charter for the purposes of protecting language was targeted, specific, and post facto. The overrides in Bills 21 and 96 do not share any of those characteristics.

The use of overrides in Bills 21 and 96 is categorically different from any prior use of the overrides. In the superior court decision in the constitutional challenge to Bill 21, the trial judge (Blanchard J.) noted that Bill 21 was the first time the notwithstanding clauses had been used to suspend *all* provisions in *both* the Canadian and Quebec charters.[37] Bill 96 is the second.

Ironically, Rousseau and Côté's research reveals that, rather than being consistent with past practice, the use of section 33 in Bills 21 and 96 is a complete break from past practice.

To respond directly to the conclusion of their *Supreme Court Law Review* paper, calling upon Canadian courts to recognize Quebec's distinct theory and practice of the clause[38]: there is no singular "Quebec theory" of section 33, and this theory does not align with past practice. In any event, courts could well accept the presence of a distinct theory and practice in Quebec, and nonetheless easily find that the use of the overrides in Bills 21 and 96 is not grounded in that theory and practice.

Finally, a few additional comments on Rousseau and Côté's analysis.

First, from Rousseau and Côté's review of the theory, it is not clear why the justification clause in the Canadian Charter cannot adequately take into account cultural or identity-based considerations. For example, the Supreme Court in *Ford* recognized that the protection of the French language is a pressing and substantial objective capable of justifying a Charter infringement.[39] Why is this not a sufficient mechanism? The only answer is that the core of Rousseau's theory is simply parliamentary sovereignty: the true focus is not *what* is to be decided, but rather *who* gets to decide. In this, the theory is indistinguishable from other (non-Quebec) theories supporting the existence and use of section 33 based on an expression of parliamentary will.[40]

Second, in Côté and Rousseau's analysis, there is no mention whatsoever of minorities within Quebec. The "collective identity" interests protected in these theories are explicitly those of the majority in Quebec, which is undeniably a minority within Canada.[41] The "collective identity" is treated as monolithic, and the cultural and linguistic minorities within Quebec are simply not discussed. By definition, minorities cannot control the democratic will of the majority; this is precisely when they call upon the courts to uphold their rights. It is not clear whether any of the scholars cited by Rousseau and Côté would support the use of the overrides when used in legislation that explicitly harms minority groups in the interests of the "collective identity."

3. BILL 21 AND 96: A CONSTITUTIONAL ERUPTION?

In this volume, the notwithstanding clause has been variously described as a "pistol," a "dagger," and a "sword of Damocles." At the beginning of their paper in *Supreme Court Law Review*, Côté and Rousseau describe the notwithstanding clause as a "volcano" that has been dormant but has recently erupted: "Legal theories and practices can sometimes be compared to volcanoes. Formed in the past and remaining quiet for ages, these peaceful giants in the background scenery appear dormant, taken for granted, uninteresting even, save for a few experts – until one day they erupt in the most spectacular fashion in a sudden torrent of heated activity that changes the entire landscape."[42]

What exactly *is* the volcano, and what landscape has been changed?

As argued above, Rousseau and Côté's thesis of a distinct theory and practice is an edifice and does not explain Bills 21 and 96. What theory does explain the current eruption?

In its 1965 preliminary report, the Royal Commission on Bilingualism and Biculturalism famously stated that Canada, without knowing it, was "passing through the greatest crisis in its history." The commission stated that "the source of that crisis lies in Quebec" and that "if it should persist and gather momentum it could destroy Canada."[43]

The year 2022 marked the fortieth anniversary of the notwithstanding clause, and indeed of patriation itself. By and large, the constitutional discussions leading up to patriation were an attempt to resolve this crisis. As Peter Russell noted, the Canadian Charter had a political purpose: as an entrenched bill of rights, it was to be an instrument of Canadian unity – a source of common values and identity, to counter any decentralizing tendencies of provinces. In particular, it was to counter Quebec nationalism.[44] However, the patriation of the Constitution in 1982, which brought with it the Canadian Charter, was done without Quebec's consent.

In Sujit Choudhry's account, the Canadian Charter created real obstacles to Quebec's linguistic nation-building.[45] He argues the distinct society clause in the Meech Lake Accord would have palliated this effect: it would have been the first constitutional recognition of the two-nation theory of Canada, which is of central importance to many in Quebec. However, the clause faced opposition from the rest of Canada on the basis that it might interfere with the universal application of the Charter. According to Choudhry, this "set up the Charter as an obstacle to, rather than as a central component of, how many Quebecers understood the nature of their relationship with Canada."[46]

In short, the Charter's political project backfired.

The constitutional wounds from patriation have never healed. Guy Laforest termed this wound "the internal exile of Quebecers in the Canada of the Charter."[47] According to Laforest, the adoption of the Meech Lake Accord would have rectified the problem.

Subsequent constitutional reforms aimed at bringing Quebec back into the fold failed. After the eruptions in Meech, Charlottetown, and the 1995 referendum, Canada entered a constitutional stalemate. The volcano went dormant.

In 2009, Guy Laforest wrote, "One day in the future, the question will resurface, and it will be part of the constitutional doctrine of a future government of Quebec."[48]

The question has now resurfaced. The volcano is erupting. What is the constitutional doctrine of Bill 21 and Bill 96?

The constitutional project is revealed in a number of novel features in both bills. First and most obviously, both bills use the overrides in the same way: pre-emptively and totally. As explained above, this is unprecedented in Quebec, and by extension, in all of Canada.

Second, both bills employ a legal concept of the "Quebec nation" enshrined into law. Aside from one water conservation statute, the first appearance of this term in Quebec legislation was Bill 21 itself.[49] With Bill 96, the term "Quebec nation" is inscribed into the Charter of the French Language, the Quebec Charter, and the Constitution Act, 1867.[50] Both Bills 21 and 96 refer to the "collective rights of the

Quebec nation," although these rights are not defined. Membership in the "Quebec nation" is not defined; it is not clear whether it is coextensive with residency in Quebec.

Third, both bills expressly reference parliamentary sovereignty. The preamble of Bill 21 explicitly employs this concept for the first time ever in Quebec legislation. Bill 96 does as well.

Parliamentary sovereignty is the corollary of the Charter overrides. The use of the overrides removes to the greatest extent possible any constraints on the National Assembly to legislate as it sees fit and advance the interests of the "Quebec nation."

The pairing of the two novel features – "Quebec nation" and the unprecedented Charter overrides – bears some reflection. Does one have anything to do with the other?

In 2009, Sujit Choudhry reviewed the nation-building purposes of the Canadian Charter. He characterizes Canada as a plurinational place, and he characterizes the Canadian Charter as an attempt to create a pan-Canadian political identity. He concludes that, "Had the Charter been effective at combatting Quebec nationalism and serving as the glue of a pan-Canadian national identity, the last twenty-five years of constitutional politics would not have happened."[51] In a plurinational context with competing national narratives, "There is a danger that rather than transcending those national narratives, a bill of rights will be drawn back into it. This what has happened in Canada."[52] For many in Quebec, the Canadian Charter is seen as an *obstacle* to the interests of the "Quebec nation."

Because patriation was done without Quebec's consent, for many in Quebec the Canadian Charter is viewed as an externally imposed constraint on Quebec's ability to advance its national interests. On *some* versions of this view, the assertion of the "Quebec nation" is synonymous with the rejection of the Canadian Charter. It is important to stress that the assertion of the "Quebec nation" does not *require* the rejection of constitutional human rights protections; however, this is the path chosen in Bills 21 and 96.

And what of the Quebec Charter? One of the authors of the Quebec Charter, Jacques-Yvan Morin (deputy premier under Réné Lévesque), would have liked to see the Quebec Charter become more entrenched and harder to amend or override.[53] The opposite has occurred. In its demotion in Quebec's legal order, the Quebec Charter has been thrown out with the bathwater.

This outcome was not inevitable. As Jonathan Montpetit notes, during the Quiet Revolution, Quebec developed a tradition of liberal constitutionalism based in the universal acceptance of the Quebec Charter as a nationalist and quasi-constitutional human rights instrument intended to constrain state power.[54] This tradition is now ending. As Gregory Bordan states, "What we are now witnessing is a protest against the very concept of entrenched rights and freedoms."[55]

With Bills 21 and 96, we see the emergence of a new legal order in Quebec, with a new orientation and theoretical basis. Quebec becomes the only Canadian province where human rights charters are not supreme.[56] The Charter overrides remove a constraint on the state's power: the National Assembly's power is increased (some would say reclaimed), with a corresponding decrease in power of the courts to adjudicate rights. Insofar as human rights run up against the interests of the "Quebec nation" as determined by the government in power, human rights are no longer justiciable.

This is nothing short of constitutional change – for all of Canada. It is a change in confederation.

This constitutional change is being done by way of regular legislation and the regular legislative process. It is a major change, but without the broad public discussion that came with previous constitutional changes. By contrast to the all-consuming public dialogue during patriation, Meech, Charlottetown, and the referendums, very little public dialogue on the constitutional aspects of Bill 96 has taken place, even within Quebec. Of course, this is happening during a pandemic and a war, where world events and daily struggles justifiably consume public attention.

In some sense, this is an underwater eruption: it will radically change the landscape, but its true nature is not apparent. Its effects may not be revealed until the next seismic event. Canadians will realize one day that the ocean floor is no longer where they thought it was.

4. WHY SHOULD ANYONE OUTSIDE QUEBEC CARE?

There are at least three reasons for the Rest of Canada to care. First, this change affects the Canadian political community. Second, it affects minorities adversely. Third, it affects the integrity of the Canadian Constitution.

a. The Charter and Canadian Political Community

First, the ousting of the Canadian Charter breaks the Canadian political community. If the project of the Canadian Charter was to create a Canadian political community, we are witnessing the failure of this project.

As Choudhry notes, one of the main sticking points around the "distinct society" clause in the Meech Lake Accord was the concern that courts might interpret the Charter differently in Quebec as a result of that clause. If the Canadian Charter is meant to be pan-Canadian, this means Canadians should have the same charter rights no matter where they are. On this view, it is an affront for it to apply unequally in one province: it was "an assault on a basic, non-negotiable term of the Canadian social contract and the very identity of the country."[57]

This has now happened. With Bills 21 and 96, we have the emergence not of a differentiated *interpretation* of the Charter in Quebec, but of a differentiated *application* of the Charter in Quebec. Quebecers have fewer charter rights than other Canadians. In some sense, this is Meech on steroids. Or asymmetrical charter federalism. Or perhaps one country, two systems.

b. Adverse Impacts on Minorities

Second, Bills 21 and 96 have clear detrimental impacts on minorities within the province.[58] In the case of Bill 21, Canadians coast to coast have noticed and this has sparked outrage and frustration. Many Canadians (including Quebecers) are not comfortable with the idea that a province can remove the human rights protections of minorities in order to advance majority interests. It is causing division not only within Quebec, but across Canada.

c. Integrity of the Constitution

Third, this affects the integrity of the Canadian Constitution. The Constitution is more than a text; it is practice and convention.

To quote from Blanchard J., the total override in Bill 21 "trivializes" the use of human rights overrides generally and shows "indifference" toward the true scope of the derogation.[59] This kind of override is now being used again, two years later in Bill 96, with even farther-reaching consequences. The taboo against the use of section 33 has been lifted. The overrides in Quebec right now set a precedent for future legislatures in any province, or even federally, to override fundamental rights.[60] This is especially worrying in a world with liberal democracies under threat and rising populism everywhere, including in Canada.

Strong constitutions protect against the vagaries of populism and abuses of power. The stakes cannot be any more stark than this: these uses of the override weaken Canada's Constitution when it is needed the most.

NOTES

1 Charter of Human Rights and Freedoms, CQLR c C-12, s 52 ["Quebec Charter"].
2 While an override under section 33 of the Canadian Charter has a five-year limit, an override of the Quebec Charter is indefinite.
3 An Act Respecting the Constitution Act, 1982, S.Q. 1982, c. 21. This use of section 33 of the Canadian Charter was upheld in *Ford v Quebec (Attorney General)* [1988] 2 SCR 712 [*Ford*].
4 See Michèle Rivet, "*La Charte québécois des droits et libertés* hier, aujourd'hui et demain: Entretien avec Jacques-Yvan Morin," *Quebec Journal of International Law* Special issue (2015): 18. By operation of section 52 of the Quebec Charter, as amended by section 16 of An Act to Amend the Charter of Human Rights and Freedoms, S.Q. 1982, c. 61, the fundamental freedoms in the Quebec Charter (sections 1–8) took precedence over any subsequent statute. See *Ford*, paras 9–10, 38.
5 Act Respecting Laicity of the State CQLR c L-0.3, see ss 33-34 ["Bill 21"].
6 Bill 96, An Act Respecting French, the Official and Common Language of Québec, 42nd leg, 1st sess, s 63, modifying Charter of the French Language, s 88.15 ["MCFL"].
7 Bill 96, s 118, MCFL s 213.1, 214.
8 Bill 96, ss 199 and 200.
9 Search: Bill 96, s 111, MCFL s 174; disclosure protection: Bill 96, s 107, MCFL s 165.22.
10 In some ways, this is the extension of the Leckey/Webber-St-Hilaire debate in this volume. According to St-Hilaire, because there is no remedy for legislation protected by section 33, likewise there is no remedy for the *exercise* of legislation protected by section 33. For the times section 33 is invoked, there cannot be any judicial review of the protected legislation in

relation to these inapplicable provisions, and as a consequence, there cannot be any remedy for a non-existent charter rights violation, be it a "mere" declaration of "inconsistency."

11 By virtue of the Quebec Charter's paramountcy clause, section 52.

12 See Jonathan Montpetit, this volume, chapter 12.

13 Ibid.

14 See: Guillaume Rousseau and François Côté, "A Distinctive Quebec Theory and Practice of the Notwithstanding Clause: When Collective Interests Outweigh Individual Rights," *Revue générale de droit* 47 (2017): 342; François Côté, "From Ford v. Québec to the Act Respecting the Laicity of the State: A Distinctive Quebec Theory and Practice of the Notwithstanding Clause," *The Supreme Court Law Review* 94 (2020): 463–89.

15 Côté and Rousseau, "From Ford v. Québec," para 42–43.

16 Ibid., para 28.

17 See Côté and Rousseau, especially para 16, quoting from the leading textbook Henri Brun, Guy Tremblay, and Eugénie Brouillet, *Droit constitutionnel*, 6th ed. (Cowansville, Québec: Yvon Blais, 2014).

18 See, for example, Côté and Rousseau, para 19, referring to Jacques Gosselin.

19 See Benoît Pelletier, this volume, chapter 9.

20 See Maxime St-Hilaire, "Les Leçons de Jordan, III : à quelles conditions est-il légitime de déroger aux droits constitutionnels fondamentaux?" *Constitutional Forum constitutionnel* 26, no. 3 (2017): 21–3.

21 The justification provision (section 9.1) only applies to fundamental rights (sections 1–9), and does not apply to equality rights (sections 10–20), political rights (sections 21–22), judicial rights (sections 23–28), and economic and social rights (sections 39–48).

22 See, for example, St-Hilaire himself, who argues that a derogation from the Canadian Charter is justifiable only in circumstances of emergency or otherwise exceptional circumstances. St-Hilaire, "Leçons de Jordan," 19.

23 See Guillaume Rousseau, "La disposition dérogatoire des chartes des droits : de la théorie à la pratique, de l'identité au progrès social," *Institut de recherche sur le Québec* (March 2016): 5. Noted in St-Hilaire, "Leçons de Jordan," n 26.

24 See "Guillaume Rousseau – Directeur de la Recherche," *Institut de recherche sur le Québec*, http://irq.quebec/team/guillaume-rousseau/.

25 See author's acknowledgments at the end of Côté and Rousseau, "From Ford v. Québec."

26 See Côté and Rousseau.

27 See *Hak c Procureur general du Québec*, 2021 QCCS 1466, list of counsel [*Hak*].

28 For a list of all uses, see Caitlin Salvino, "A Tool of Last Resort: A Comprehensive Account of the Notwithstanding Clause Political Uses 1982–2021," *Journal of Parliamentary and Political Law* 16, no. 1 (2022).

29 Rousseau and Côté, "Distinct Quebec Theory," List item 21, 28, 35, 37, 39, 41.

30 Ibid., List item 23, 26, 27, 29, 31, 33, 34, 38.

31 Ibid., List item 22.

32 Ibid., List item 25.

33 Ibid., 425, List item 13.

34 Quite the opposite: the Quebec Charter was amended to strengthen and entrench it as Quebec's paramount statute. See Michèle Rivet, "*La Charte Québécois*," 18.

35 See, for example, Janet L. Hiebert, "Notwithstanding the Charter: Does Section 33 Accommodate Federalism?" in *Canada at 150: Federalism and Democratic Renewal*, ed. Kyle Hanniman and Elizabeth Goodyear-Grant (Institute of Intergovernmental Relations, 2019), 69.

36 Côté and Rousseau, "From Ford v. Québec," para 54.

37 *Hak*, paras 767–768.

38 Ibid., para 60.

39 *Ford*, 777–8.

40 See, for example, Dwight Newman, "Canada's Notwithstanding Clause, Dialogue, and Constitutional Identities," in *Constitutional Dialogue: Rights, Democracy, Institutions*, ed. Geoffrey Sigalet, Gregoire Webber, and Rosalind Dixon (Cambridge: Cambridge University Press, 2019), 209.

41 Rousseau and Côté, "Quebec Theory," 395.

42 Côté and Rousseau, "From Ford v. Québec," para 1.

43 A. Davidson Dunton and André Laurendeau, eds, *A Preliminary Report of the Royal Commission on Bilingualism and Biculturalism* (Ottawa: Roger Duhamel, 1965), 13.

44 Peter Russell, "The Political Purposes of the Canadian Charter of Rights and Freedoms," *Canadian Bar Review* 61 (1983) 30; Sujit Choudhry, "Bill of Rights as Instruments of Nation Building," in *Contested Constitutionalism*, eds. James Kelly and Christopher Manfredi (Toronto: UBC Press, 2009), 233.

45 Choudhry, "Bill of Rights," 233.

46 Ibid., 244.

47 Guy Laforest, "The Internal Exile of Quebecers in the Canada of the Charter" in *Contested Constitutionalism*, ed. James Kelly and Christopher Manfredi (Toronto: UBC Press, 2009), 252.

48 Ibid., 256.

49 Bill 21 inscribed this term into the Act Respecting Laicity of the State and the Quebec Charter. The only other mention of "Quebec nation" in legislation is in the preamble of a water conservation statute enacted in 2009. Act to Affirm the Collective Nature of Water Resources and to Promote Better Governance of Water and Associated Environments, CQLR c C-6.2.

50 Bill 96, section 159, amending Constitution Act, 1867, adding ss 90.Q.1 and 90.Q.2.

51 Choudhry, "Bill of Rights," 246.

52 Ibid., 247.

53 See Rivet, "*Charte québécois.*" See also discussion of Morin by Montpetit, this volume, chapter 12.

54 See Jonathan Montpetit, this volume, chapter 12.

55 See Gregory B. Bordan, this volume, chapter 14.

56 Gregoire Webber or Robert Leckey might argue that the Charter remains supreme in the face of pre-emptive and sweeping use of section 33 because courts can declare that a law violates the Charter even if they cannot declare the law inoperative. However, until this argument is accepted by a Canadian court, we are left with the received wisdom that section 33 effectively insulates laws from Charter oversight. As such, the pre-emptive and sweeping use of section 33 effectively places those laws above the Charter in the hierarchy of laws.

57 Choudhry, "Bill of Rights," 243.

58 See discussion of adverse impacts of Bill 21 in Bordan, this volume, chapter 14.

59 *Hak*, para 754 ("banalise") (author's translation), 768.

60 As Gregory Bordan notes, the use in Ontario's Bill 307 (2021) is similar to uses in Quebec. Ontario invoked the clause again in 2022, in Bill 28, Keeping Students in Class Act, 2022. This bill was later repealed after public outcry. Both governments who invoked the clause – in Ontario and Quebec – were returned with strong majority governments in the 2022 provincial elections. Bordan, this volume, chapter 14.

12

The Rise and Fall of Liberal
Constitutionalism in Quebec

Jonathan Montpetit

When the Coalition Avenir Quebec (CAQ) government wrote notwith-standing clauses into legislation aimed at regulating religious symbols (Bill 21) and protecting the French language (Bill 96), Premier François Legault and his ministers insisted the decision respected long-standing norms in the province.[1] Simon Jolin-Barrette, the minister who spon-sored both bills, argued the notwithstanding clause in the Canadian Charter of Rights and Freedoms had already been used hundreds of times by previous Quebec governments, a figure that requires import-ant qualification but is not wholly inaccurate.[2] The government's justification was based, in part, on research conducted by Guillaume Rousseau and François Côté, who catalogued and categorized each instance in Quebec when the notwithstanding clauses in the federal and provincial charters of rights were invoked.[3] They argued there is a distinctive Quebec understanding of the legitimacy of notwith-standing clauses, which explains why governments in the province have been more inclined to use them than elsewhere in Canada. Other notable jurists, including Benoît Pelletier, maintained using the clauses was simply part of Quebec's approach to federalism.[4]

These justifications tended to focus on the notwithstanding clause in the federal charter; the use of the override clause in the Quebec charter was discussed less frequently. When focus is on the federal clause, the CAQ government's legislative strategy with Bills 21 and 96 appears in line with long-standing grievances about the patri-ation process and Quebec's ongoing quest for more autonomy from Ottawa. This narrow view, I will argue, obscures what was path-breaking about the legislative strategy. By seeking to override not simply the Canadian charter, but the Quebec charter as well, the CAQ government made a definitive break from the province's own tradition of liberal constitutionalism. This tradition gave birth to the Quebec Charter of Human Rights and, until recently, conditioned how politicians used its notwithstanding clause. With the rise of a new conservative nationalist movement in Quebec, though, the province's liberal constitutional tradition was marginalized and its future is now uncertain.

I. THE RISE OF LIBERAL CONSTITUTIONALISM

Quebec underwent a period of intensive modernization in the 1960s. At the outset of this period, Jacques-Yvan Morin, a law professor at the Université de Montréal, argued the province needed to join the global human rights movement, which had begun in 1948 with the Universal Declaration of Human Rights. In a 1963 article published in the *McGill Law Journal*, Morin wrote that the need for a provincial charter of rights arose from two sociological developments in Quebec. First, a rapidly expanding state apparatus was becoming increasingly involved in people's lives, and so its administrative power needed to be balanced with individual liberty. And second, Quebec's cultural majority was being confronted with greater religious and ethnic pluralism. Morin concluded that as a modern society, Quebec required a specific set of laws to protect the "political liberties of its citizens, no matter how unpopular, against the majority of the population."[5]

At this juncture, the future of the Canadian rights revolution was still in the balance. Of the provinces, only Saskatchewan and Ontario had bills of rights; Alberta's had been tossed out by the Supreme Court in 1946. The federal government, under Prime Minister John Diefenbaker, had passed a bill of rights in 1960, but as Morin pointed out in his article, it didn't have a paramountcy clause and could easily be abridged. Morin was identifying here the central obstacle to efforts to codify human rights in Canada: parliamentary sovereignty.[6] Inherited from the British constitutional tradition, parliamentary sovereignty – in the words of A.V. Dicey – "means neither more nor less than this, that Parliament ... has the right to make or unmake any law whatever."[7] But if lawmakers could simply pass legislation overriding previously established limits on their power, then the protection of individual rights would always be at

the whim of the governing party. Modern liberal constitutionalism thus holds that there needs to be entrenched legal limitations
on government.[8] Broadly understood, liberal constitutionalism is a
commitment to ensure that "administrative and adjudicative functions operate autonomously from, and potentially limit, powerful
factions or leaders."[9]

In sketching the range of rights to be included in an eventual
Quebec charter, Morin drew heavily on the guarantees in the UN
declaration and the European Convention on Human Rights. As
such, the rights are a mix of the negative rights associated with liberal constitutionalism, as well as the positive rights – economic and
social rights – associated with republican thought. But the content of Morin's hypothetical charter is arguably secondary to his
vision of the broader role it should play in Quebec's constitutional
framework, namely that it should provide lasting restrictions on
state power. A lengthy section of the 1963 article is devoted to
the problem of reconciling the need for hard-and-fast limits on
government, on the one hand, with the British tradition of parliamentary sovereignty on the other. In order to give the charter
constitutional (rather than mere statutory) features, he proposed
requiring a two-thirds majority to amend fundamental individual
rights.[10] There is a tendency, he noted, for national groups to be
overly concerned with collective rights when their political des-
tiny is uncertain. The modernizing Quebec state was in the process
of removing these concerns by actively empowering the francophone majority through a vast array of reforms. At the same time,
though, greater and greater administrative power was at the disposal of legislators, making the rigorous protection of individual
rights "indispensable."[11]

It was roughly a decade before the Quebec government, under
Liberal premier Robert Bourassa, tabled legislation to create a provincial charter of rights. But the influence of Morin's thinking on
this process is undeniable. His proposed charter was championed
by the newly formed *Ligues des droits de l'homme*, an influential
civil rights organization in the 1960s and 1970s. Morin himself
was tasked with drawing up a list of civil rights to be included in
a revised version of Quebec's Civil Code, another precursor to the
charter. When Bourassa's government finally presented its draft of
the charter, it contained most of the basic elements that Morin had
suggested in 1963.[12] In the meantime, Morin had become involved

in nationalist organizations, including the Parti Québécois (PQ). He was elected in 1973 and was the party's parliamentary leader when the charter, then known as Bill 50, was tabled in the National Assembly.

As leader of the PQ caucus, Morin initially expressed lukewarm support for the bill. Even though Bill 50 contained many of the articles he had proposed in 1963, the government did not include the two-thirds majority rule, and nor did the proposed charter contain a paramountcy clause. The Liberal justice minister, Jérôme Choquette, was worried about relinquishing parliamentary sovereignty and creating legislative instability.[13] But without these provisions, Morin said in a 1974 speech to the National Assembly, the charter would be nothing more than a "regular law," unable to offer sustained protection to individual rights.[14] He reiterated the dangers that a growing bureaucratic state posed to members of an industrializing society who suddenly found themselves rent from traditional social bonds. Morin also noted that Quebec was no longer a monolithic society, and again underscored that unpopular political and social views needed protecting. This line of criticism against the bill was echoed by civil society groups, including the *Ligues des droits de l'homme*, as well as influential political observers. An editorial in the Sherbrooke newspaper *La Tribune* said that without a paramountcy clause, the rights laid out in the charter were nothing but "sterile prose."[15] In *Le Devoir*, an editorialist said Choquette hadn't yet chosen whether to protect human rights or the rights of the state. The paper called for "concrete mechanisms and protections" for the rights of individuals and groups.[16] Faced with widespread opposition, the Bourassa government struck a compromise. It agreed to gradually phase in a paramountcy clause, but also added an override clause that could be invoked with express intent. With these concessions, the bill passed unanimously in 1975.

The history of the Quebec Charter of Human Rights illustrates there was a general willingness among political elites in the province to accept a strong, if not absolute, check on state power and the potential excesses of majority government, one of the central features of liberal constitutionalism. Even if the override clause was used frequently in the early years of the Quebec Charter, politicians and civil society were nevertheless aware that new norms around parliamentary supremacy had been established.

The first version of the Charter of the French Language to be tabled in the National Assembly, Bill 1, invoked the override clause of the

Human Rights Charter.[17] This provoked significant criticism. The provincial human rights commission, in a submission to legislators, said using the clause was "inadmissible" given Bill 1 would significantly increase the administrative powers of the state.[18] The Quebec Bar Association, business groups, and unions all publicly called for section 172 to be dropped from Bill 1.[19] Claude Ryan, who was *Le Devoir*'s publisher at the time, wrote, "In a democratic society, the Charter of Human Rights and Freedoms has to come first."[20] One of the few significant differences between Bill 1 and Bill 101 was the absence of a human rights override clause in the latter. Camille Laurin, the PQ minister who sponsored both language bills, said the override wasn't needed because "the [new] bill doesn't infringe on the Charter of Human Rights."[21]

When Lévesque invoked the notwithstanding clause in the Canadian Charter of Rights and Freedoms to protest the 1982 constitutional repatriation process, he assured Quebecers they would still have access to the Quebec Charter of Human Rights. But the following year, he invoked the notwithstanding clauses in both charters to override the rights of striking public teachers in back-to-work legislation. Lévesque was roundly criticized in the media, though less for suspending elements of the federal Charter than for suspending elements of the Quebec Charter. "In the future we should give our rights a more solid grounding, with no easy loopholes for politicians," an editorialist wrote in Quebec City's *Le Soleil* newspaper.[22]

Until recently, perhaps the most controversial use of Charter overrides in Quebec was Robert Bourassa's decision to invoke the federal and provincial notwithstanding clauses following the 1988 Supreme Court ruling in *Ford v. Quebec*.[23] Bourassa – whose government, recall, passed the Quebec Human Rights Charter in 1975 – expressed deep ambivalence about using the override clauses. In a lengthy speech to the National Assembly in December 1988, Bourassa said he had "much reticence" about his decision, adding (with some hyperbole), "There is no precedent in Quebec or elsewhere for a premier or government who finds themselves suspending fundamental freedoms."[24] Bourassa, of course, paid a political price for using the notwithstanding clauses. It caused a major rift in his cabinet and voter base, and weakened support for the Meech Lake Accord outside of Quebec. Ultimately, the Liberal government reformed Bill 101 in order to comply with the Supreme Court decision.

These examples demonstrate that while Quebec's tradition of liberal constitutionalism didn't preclude the use of the notwithstanding clause, its use was circumscribed by widely held political norms about the limits of legislative power, and the importance of safeguarding individual rights. These norms, it's worth noting, were shared by federalists and sovereigntists alike.

2. THE FALL OF LIBERAL CONSTITUTIONALISM

The loss of the 1995 referendum, narrow though it was, fragmented the sovereigntist movement in Quebec. Following Premier Jacques Parizeau's infamous referendum night speech, in which he blamed the loss on "money and ethnic votes," there was a sense among many sovereigntists that the movement needed to show a more inclusive face. Led by intellectuals such as Gérard Bouchard and Alain-G. Gagnon, they put forward an open conception of the Quebec nation, defined principally as a community where French is the common language but is otherwise pluralistic in its ethnic and cultural makeup. Despite the challenge this pluralistic nationalism posed to Quebec's status in the federation, it was nevertheless compatible with the commitments of constitutional liberalism. This progressive wing of the movement, however, was gradually marginalized by a conservative and republican nationalist sensibility, which argued instead for a robust defence of the culture and values of Quebec's historical francophone community.[25] As this conservative-republican ideology came to dominate the political establishment in Quebec, the roles of democratic institutions started to be reimagined.

The emergence of this ideology coincided with the so-called reasonable accommodation crisis, the acrimonious debates about minority cultural practices that erupted in the early 2000s. At the time, intellectuals such as Jacques Beauchemin, Eric Bédard, and Marc Chevrier, among others, contributed articles to small-circulation literary magazines (*Argument* and *L'Action nationale*), offering strident critiques of federal multiculturalism policies, liberal individualism, and the excesses of consumerist society.[26] Within this nationalist intellectual circle, there were notable differences between those drawing from Quebec's own conservative tradition and those influenced by the republican current that originated in France.[27] But at a general level these two streams have similar conceptions of the Quebec nation, whose essence is understood to lie in the cultural practices that French-speaking Quebecers have shared across time. They see this as the source of all political legitimacy in Quebec and believe preserving the continuity of the nation should be the state's priority. Policies that empower identities other than a narrowly defined conception of the Québécois are considered existential threats to the nation's survival. Laicity, Quebec's house brand of secularism, serves multiple purposes within this context. It represents a continuation of the modernization project that began during the Quiet Revolution, when the francophone majority emancipated itself from both anglophone capital and the Catholic Church. Laicity is also seen as the only appropriate response to the reasonable accommodation crisis because it introduces limits on minority cultural expression in the public sphere. It is considered to be a bulwark against an Anglo-Canadian liberalism intent on prioritizing individual rights of minorities over the collective rights of the Quebec nation.

Despite modest beginnings, this intellectual movement eventually found a powerful patron in Pierre Karl Péladeau, whose Quebecor media empire provided an important platform for conservative nationalists, turning some into media personalities in their own right. Their cause was aided too by the collapse of PQ support under liberal-leaning leader André Boisclair, twinned as it was with the brief success of the conservative Action démocratique du Quebec. Prominent conservative nationalists were given key advisory roles in the PQ by Boisclair's successor, Pauline Marois. Her short-lived minority government tried unsuccessfully to pass a sweeping ban on ostentatious religious symbols in 2013. Ahead of the 2018 election, François Legault's relatively new political party, the Coalition Avenir Quebec, embraced conservative nationalist identity politics, promising to reduce immigration levels and impose more limits on religious symbols in the public sphere. This helped broaden the party's appeal among sovereigntist voters and was a key factor in its historic victory that year.

Once in power, the CAQ pursued a legislative agenda that exposed the tensions between the party's ideological orientation and Quebec's tradition of liberal constitutionalism. Nowhere was this more evident than in the Laicity Act (Bill 21) and the reforms to the French-language charter (Bill 96). As Marion Sandilands points out, the two pieces of legislation effectively marked the first time that the term "collective rights of the Quebec nation" appeared in law.[28] Both acts also pre-emptively invoked the notwithstanding clauses in the federal and provincial charters of rights.[29] And in each, the clauses are used to maximum effect, that is, all eligible rights are subject to the override. This, as Superior Court Justice Marc-André Blanchard noted in his April 2021 judgment in *Hak v. Quebec*, is unprecedented.[30]

By using the notwithstanding clauses in this way, the Legault government sought to claim greater autonomy for the legislature from the courts. The government was unambiguous about its motivations. When Simon Jolin-Barrette, serving then as Immigration, Diversity, and Inclusiveness minister, tabled Bill 21 in 2019, he explained his decision to invoke the overrides by saying, "It's up to Quebec's parliament, and not the courts, to decide on a matter so fundamental to society."[31] Two years later, tabling Bill 96, Premier Legault described the original French-language charter as having been "cut up" by the courts. Using the notwithstanding clauses, he said, would limit court challenges to his proposed reforms.[32]

The CAQ government was claiming, in effect, that judicial oversight of its flagship legislation amounted to unjustified interference in the legislature's prerogative. Legault and his supporters mounted two distinct arguments for making this claim, one with potentially more far-reaching implications than the other. The first was an updated version of a familiar argument about the need for Quebec to protect its distinct identity within the federation. As Benoît Pelletier asserts in his contribution to this volume, and as he did in his testimony before the court in *Hak v. Quebec*, the notwithstanding clause in the Charter of Rights allows provinces to resist the centralizing tendencies of the federal government and assert a measure of independence by ensuring provincial legislators have the final say on matters within their jurisdiction. This is especially important for Quebec, given it never signed the Constitution.[33]

To these observations, conservative nationalists often added that the federal charter upholds an Anglo-American version of liberal individualism that is foreign to the collectivist mindset supposedly native to Quebec.[34] But this line of argumentation could only justify the derogation from the federal Charter, not the provincial one. Surely the rights protected by the Quebec Charter of Human Rights can't be considered an alien legal invention; they were approved unanimously by the National Assembly in 1975. Justifying use of the Quebec override provision, therefore, must entail a more substantive claim about the role of the National Assembly.

Within the liberal constitutional tradition, democracy necessitates a range of checks and balances on the administrative power of the state. Executive power can be justifiably limited by a judiciary interpreting the constitutional limits set out in the first place by legislators themselves. Civil society groups are, moreover, enabled by liberal rights to represent diverse interests before the state.[35] And in a federal context, different levels of government give voice to different publics, which acts as a further check on the power held by any one executive or representative body.

For Quebec nationalists, though, the National Assembly isn't seen simply as one branch of a network of institutions that compose democratic government. The Quebec legislature, and by extension the Quebec government, is seen rather as the one and only institutional voice able to speak for the public. In an argument plan submitted to the superior court in *Hak v. Quebec*, the Quebec attorney general stated: "It falls to the National Assembly of Quebec, as the privileged site of important debates in Quebec society and as the organ expressing the sovereignty of the people, to decide on the model for organizing relations between the Quebec state and religions."[36]

Rousseau, commenting on the parliamentary sovereignty principle written into the Laicity Act's preamble, argues its scope ought to be larger in Quebec "because Parliament is considered to be the incarnation of a distinct people."[37] According to Rousseau, this enlarged conception of parliamentary sovereignty justifies the legislature's ability to derogate from the charters. This, though, resembles less a claim about parliamentary sovereignty in the liberal constitutional tradition than it does a claim about popular sovereignty in the republican sense. The emphasis is on a legislative body that represents the indivisible and inviolable will of the people, as opposed to the system of checks and balances that forestalls the excesses of majoritarianism. Republicanism, in the classic form inherited from Jean-Jacques Rousseau, is wary about constraints on the people's ability to govern themselves.[38] In Quebec's parliamentary context, where the executive is not wholly distinct from the legislative branch, such a view of the National Assembly can easily translate into a transfer of unchecked power to the government.

This more republican interpretation of the legislature's role changes the locus of political freedom for Quebecers. Whereas in the liberal constitutional tradition freedom is enabled via checks and balances meant to protect the individual from arbitrary state power,

in the republican tradition freedom requires some form of membership or participation in the public that is governing itself. But under
the conservative-republican bent of recent Quebec politics, the people, or nation, has been articulated as a homogeneous community
defined by both language and historically held cultural values. This
raises barriers of entry for Quebecers who don't (or can't) identify
with this narrow definition of the nation. Cultural minorities are
thus excluded from the self-governing demos, exposed to the will of
the legislative majority and, in the case of the Laicity Act and Bill 96,
have diminished recourse to Charter safeguards. It was the danger
of such arrangements that concerned Morin nearly sixty years ago
when he began to advocate for a charter of human rights in Quebec.

3. CONCLUSION: QUEBEC'S UNSETTLED
DEMOCRATIC ECOSYSTEM

In order to fully appreciate the challenge to the existing constitutional
paradigm in Quebec, it is worth considering Bills 21 and 96 within
the broader context of the first CAQ government. As Bill 21 made
its way through the courts, the independence of the judiciary came
under sustained attack by conservative nationalist pundits.[39] A series
of complaints were filed with the Canadian Judicial Council alleging
judges involved in the case were biased.[40] While the complaints were
ultimately rejected, the campaign nevertheless prompted the Quebec
division of the Canadian Bar Association to take the unusual step
of issuing a press release to reiterate its belief in the impartiality of
the judiciary.[41] In the meantime, Jolin-Barrette, who became justice
minister in June 2020, engaged in a public dispute with the chief
justice of the Court of Quebec, Lucie Rondeau, who had expressed
reservations about government overreach.[42] When Jolin-Barrette
sought to end the court's practice of looking for bilingual judges
in certain jurisdictions, Rondeau objected and brought the matter
before the superior court, which ruled against the government, citing the independence of the judiciary.[43] Jolin-Barrette responded by
adding an amendment to Bill 96 allowing the government to bypass
the ruling.[44]

Other associational and adjudicative institutions were also desta-
bilized by CAQ government policy in its first term. The government,
for instance, was reluctant to relinquish the additional powers it had
accumulated under the emergency measures provision of the Public

Health Act, invoked at the outset of the COVID-19 pandemic.[45] Opposition parties and jurists criticized Legault for choosing to renew the emergency provisions without debate in the National Assembly.[46] In 2020, the CAQ government abolished school boards, removing an elected level of government that had routinely questioned provincially imposed policies. Notably, the English Montreal School Board successfully argued in *Hak v. Quebec* that section 23 of the Canadian Charter of Rights should prevent the Laicity Act from applying to English boards.[47] In a separate case, English school boards argued that section 23 also protects them from being eliminated by the Quebec government.[48] And in June 2022, the government passed "academic freedom" legislation, which among other things protects professors who use offensive language in the classroom and bars universities from requiring so-called "trigger warnings" before difficult material is broached.[49] The law should be seen as a response to the perception, shared by many conservative nationalists, that racial justice groups wield too much influence on administrative decisions.[50]

The CAQ was re-elected with another majority in the October 2022 election. Their first term was characterized by a tug-of-war between the legislature and the judiciary, by an expansion of executive prerogative, and by policies that delegitimized forms of minority representation. At the outset of the party's second term in government, Quebec's democratic institutions were at a critical juncture. It was the broad commitment to liberal constitutional norms, which began in the Quiet Revolution, that allowed an ecosystem of civil society groups and rights-based advocacy to thrive alongside the modernizing state. Moving away from this constitutional tradition does not, by itself, signal democratic backsliding. Other modes of constitutionalism, republican or otherwise, are perfectly compatible with democracy, and liberal constitutionalism's own democratic shortcomings have been well documented. But by seeking a break from liberal constitutionalism, the CAQ government unsettled the institutional ecosystem that supported democratic life in the province. In the ensuing transitional period, minority groups in Quebec are liable to feel an added sense of vulnerability, one that is unlikely to diminish until the CAQ government, or a successor, communicates where the new boundaries of state power lie.

NOTES

1 Act Respecting the Laicity of the State, CQLR c l-0.3, ss 33-34; Bill 96, An Act Respecting French, the Official and Common Language of Québec, 1st Sess, 42nd Leg, 2021, cl 118.

2 Quebec, National Assembly, *Journal des débats de l'Assemblée nationale*, 42-1, No 45-58 (16 June 2019). There is significant debate around how to count instances when section 33 of the Canadian Charter of Rights and Freedoms has been used. See Caitlin Salvino, "A Tool of Last Resort: A Comprehensive Account of the Notwithstanding Clause Political Uses 1982–2021," *Journal of Parliamentary and Political Law* 16, no. 1 (2022).

3 Guillaume Rousseau and François Côté, "A Distinctive Quebec Theory and Practice of the Notwithstanding Clause: When Collective Interests Outweigh Individual Rights," *Revue générale de droit* 47 (2017): 343–431.

4 Pelletier, a former Liberal cabinet minister, provided testimony in support of the CAQ government in *Hak v. Quebec*. His expert report is reprinted as "La théorie du fédéralisme et son application au contexte multinational canadien," in *La laïcité: le choix du Québec. Regards pluridisciplinaires sur la Loi sur laïcité de l'État*, ed. Marc-André Turcotte and Julie Gagnon (Québec, QC : Secrétariat à l'accès à l'information et à la réforme des institutions démocratiques, 2021), 373–528. See also his contribution to this volume, chapter 9.

5 Jacques-Yvan Morin, "Une Charte des droits de l'homme pour le Quebec," *McGill Law Journal* 9, no. 4 (1963): 273.

6 Dominique Clément, *Canada's Rights Revolution: Social Movements and Social Change, 1937-82* (UBC Press, 2009), 18–23.

7 Ibid., 19–20.

8 Thomas M.J. Bateman, "Rights Application Doctrine and the Clash of Constitutionalisms in Canada," *Canadian Journal of Political Science* 31, no. 1 (1998).

9 Tom Ginsburg, Aziz Z. Huq, and Mila Versteeg, "The Coming Demise of Liberal Constitutionalism?" *University of Chicago Law Review* 85, no. 2 (2018): 239.

10 Morin, "Charte des droits," 304.

11 Ibid., 289.

12 Clément, *Canada's Rights Revolution*, 121.

13 Ibid., 123.

14 "Projets de loi 50 - Loi concernant les droits et libertés de la personne," deuxième lecture, Quebec National Assembly, *Journal des débats* 30-2, no. 79 (12 November 1974): 2741–64.

15 Jean Desclos, "Nos libertés sur papier," *Sherbrooke La Tribune*, 12 November 1974, 4.

16 Jean-Claude Leclerc, "La Charte des droits et sa Commission," *Le Devoir*, 2 November 1974, 4.

17 Section 172 of Bill 1 reads, "*L'article 52 de la Charte des droits et libertés de la personne (1975, chapitre 6) est modifié par l'addition à la fin, après le mot "Charte," des mots "ou à moins qu'il ne s'agisse de la Charte de la langue française au Québec."* See Bill 1, *Charte de la langue française au Québec*, 2nd Sess, 31st Leg, Quebec, 1977, cl 172.

18 Rodolphe Morissette, "Une "charte" qui n'en est pas une: La commission des droits de la personne réclame divers adoucissements au projet," *Le Devoir*, 17 June 1977, 1.

19 See Michel Vastel, "Le Board of Trade craint un gouvernement totalitaire," *Le Devoir*, 31 May 1977, 1; Louis Farladeau, "La FTQ recommande d'utiliser la souplesse qu'offre la loi," *La Presse*, 22 June 1977, C6; "De Bellefeuille suggère le retrait de l'article 172," *La Presse*, 24 June 1977, A8; "Le CPQ et la loi 101: un certain progrès mais loin de l'acceptable," *La Presse*, 22 July 1977, A7.

20 Claude Ryan, "Politique linguistique et droits humains," *Le Devoir*, 14 May 1977, 4.

21 Raymond Giroux, "Laurin a fait plusieurs changements mineurs," *Le Soleil*, 13 July 1977, 1.

22 Raymond Giroux, "Deux chartes n'auront pas suffi," *Le Soleil*, 17 February 1983, A14.

23 *Ford v. Quebec (Attorney General)* [1988] 2 SCR 712.

24 Quebec, National Assembly, *Journal des débats*, 33-2, vol 30, no. 83 (20 December 1988), at 4425.

25 Mathieu and Laforest speak of a "republican-conservative nexus" in Quebec. See Félix Mathieu and Guy Laforest, "Uncovering National Nexus's Representations: The Case of Québec," *Studies in Ethnicity and Nationalism* 16, no. 3 (2016). See also Chedly Belkhodja, "Le discours de la 'nouvelle sensibilité conservatrice' au Québec," *Canadian Ethnic Studies* 40, no. 1 (2008): 79–100; Jean-Marc Piotte and Jean-Pierre Couture, *Les Nouveaux Visages du nationalism conservateur au Québec* (Montreal: Québec Amérique, 2012).

26 Belkhodja, "nouvelle sensibilité conservatrice."

27 I am grateful to Guillaume Rousseau for stressing the importance of this distinction. See his "Philosophies et laïcité, liberalisme pluraliste et républicanisme" in Guillaume Rousseau, *Loi sur la laïcité de l'état commentée et annotée: philosophie, genèse, interprétation et application* (Sherbrooke: Éditions R.D.U.S., 2020), 23–60. See also Guillaume Lamy, *Laïcité et valeurs québécoises: Les sources d'une controverse* (Montréal: Québec Amérique, 2015).

28 Marion Sandilands, this volume, chapter 11. Sandilands makes the further important observation that collectively Bill 21 and Bill 96 alter the hierarchy of laws in Quebec. With their broad charter overrides, Quebec became "the only Canadian province where human rights Charters are not supreme."

29 See notes 1 and 2.

30 *Hak c Québec (Procureur général du Québec)* 2021 QCCA 1466 at para 768.

31 Quebec, National Assembly, *Conférence de presse de M. Simon Jolin-Barrette, leader parlementaire du gouvernement et ministre de l'Immigration, de la Diversité et de l'Inclusion,* 28 March 2019.

32 Quebec, National Assembly, *Conférence de presse de M. François Legault, premier ministre, et M. Simon Jolin-Barrette, ministre responsable de la Langue française,* 13 May 2021.

33 Pelletier, "Théorie du fédéralisme."

34 See, for example: Mathieu Bock-Côté, "La loi 21: un choc Canada-Québec," *Le Journal de Montréal,* 15 December 2021, https://www.journaldemontreal.com/2021/12/15/la-loi-21-un-choc-canada-quebec; François Côté, "Laïcité et Charte canadienne: le Québec n'y a jamais consenti," *Le Journal de Québec,* 29 November 2019, https://www.journaldequebec.com/2019/11/29/laicite-et-charte-canadienne-le-quebec-ny-a-jamais-consenti.

35 Aziz Huq and Tom Ginsburg, "How to Lose a Constitutional Democracy," UCLA *Law Review* 65 (2018): 78.

36 *Hak c Québec* (Procureur général du Québec), [2021] QCCA 1466 (Argument plan of the Respondent at para 61). [*Hak*].

37 Rousseau, *Loi sur la laïcité de l'état,* 98.

38 For a contemporary republican account of the case against judicial review see Richard Bellamy, *Political Constitutionalism: A Republican Defence of the Constitutionality of Democracy* (Cambridge: Cambridge University Press, 2007).

39 See, for example: Antoine Robitaille, "Il faut parler de l'impartialité des juges," *Le Journal de Québec,* 20 March 2021, https://www.journal

dequebec.com/2021/03/20/il-faut-parler-de-limpartialite-des-juges-1;
Jean-François Lisée, "Les trudeauistes à la cour," *Le Devoir*, 19 December
2020, https://www.ledevoir.com/opinion/chroniques/592014/les-trudeauistes-
a-la-cour.

40 See generally: "Laïcité : une plainte pour impartialité contre la juge en chef
du Québec suscite le débat," Radio-Canada, 2 December 2019, https://
ici.radio-canada.ca/nouvelle/1414756/laicite-plainte-impartialite-
juge-chef-quebec-debat; "Le groupe PDF Québec porte plainte contre la
juge en chef du Québec," *La Presse Canadienne*, 5 December 2019,
https://www.ledevoir.com/societe/568476/plainte-d-un-groupe-contre-la-
juge-en-chef-du-quebec-nicole-duval-hesler; "Frédéric Bastien remet
encore en cause le processus judiciaire entourant la loi 21," *Agence QMI*,
23 February 2020, https://www.journaldequebec.com/2020/02/23/frederic-
bastien-remet-encore-en-cause-le-processus-judiciaire-entourant-la-loi-21.

41 L'Association du Barreau canadien – Division du Québec, News Release,
"Processus de nomination à la magistrature," 16 November 2020.

42 See "Bilinguisme des juges : différend entre le ministre de la Justice et la
Cour du Québec," Radio-Canada, 9 March 2021, https://ici.radio-canada.
ca/nouvelle/1776015/cour-quebec-lucie-rondeau-ministre-jolin-barrette-
selection-juge-bilingue-bilinguisme; Jean-François Racine, "Le torchon
brûle toujours entre la juge en chef et le ministre," *Le Journal de Québec*,
6 November 2021, https://www.journaldequebec.com/2021/11/06/le-
torchon-brule-toujours-entre-la-juge-en-chef-et-le-ministre. See generally
Luis Millán, "Quebec justice minister, judiciary locked in 'power struggle,'
says law prof," *The Lawyer's Daily*, 18 February 2022, https://www.
thelawyersdaily.ca/articles/33659/quebec-justice-minister-judiciary-locked-
in-power-struggle-says-law-prof.

43 *Conseil de la magistrature c. Ministre de la Justice du Québec* [2022]
QCCS 266.

44 Hugo Pilon-Larose, "Québec légifère pour interdire le bilinguisme exigé
chez les juges," *La Presse*, 21 March 2022, https://www.lapresse.ca/
actualites/politique/2022-03-21/quebec-legifere-pour-interdire-le-
bilinguisme-exige-chez-les-juges.php.

45 Public Health Act, CQLR c S-2.2, s 119.

46 See generally: Jean-François Parent, "L'état d'urgence, 351 actions
législatives plus tard," *Droit-inc*, 10 March 2022, https://www.droit-inc.
com/article35571-L-etat-d-urgence-351-actions-legislatives-plus-tard;
Fanny Lévesque, "'Trois, quatre' décrets resteront en vigueur, promet
Dubé," *La Presse*, 17 March 2022, https://www.lapresse.ca/covid-
19/2022-03-17/fin-de-l-urgence-sanitaire/trois-quatre-decrets-resteront-

en-vigueur-promet-dube.php; David Rémillard, "Modifier la Loi sur la santé publique : la CAQ 'ouverte aux propositions,'" Radio-Canada, 18 March 2022, https://ici.radio-canada.ca/nouvelle/1870001/urgence-sanitaire-modification-loi-sante-publique-caq-ouverture.

47 *Hak*, at 939–1003.

48 The Quebec Superior Court granted the school boards an injunction in August 2020. See *Quebec English School Boards Association c. Procureur général du Québec* [2020] QCCS 2444.

49 See sections 3 and 4 of Bill 32, An Act Respecting Academic Freedom in the University Sector, 2nd Sess, 42nd Leg, 2022.

50 See generally: "François Legault appelé à reconnaître le racisme systémique," Radio-Canada, 9 October 2020, https://ici.radio-canada.ca/nouvelle/1739937/francois-legault-appele-reconnaissance-racisme-systemique; Fanny Lévesque, "Anglade veut des excuses, Legault en remet," *La Presse*, 29 September 2021, https://www.lapresse.ca/actualites/politique/2021-09-29/debats-houleux-sur-le-racisme-systemique/anglade-veut-des-excuses-legault-en-remet.php; Marc-André Gagnon, "Legault exclut déjà une conclusion du rapport attendu cet automne," *Le Journal de Québec*, 13 October 2020, https://www.journaldequebec.com/2020/10/13/groupe-daction-contre-le-racisme-legault-exclut-deja-le-racisme-systemique; Marie-Hélène Proulx, "La gauche qui dérange," *L'actualité*, 5 May 2021, https://lactualite.com/societe/la-gauche-qui-derange/.

PART FIVE

Legitimacy, Justification, Democracy

The use of the notwithstanding clause (NWC) raises profound questions about the nature of, and criteria for, justification, not merely of its invocation, but also for legislated limitations on rights and freedoms generally. The matter of justification is, of course, textually enshrined in section 1 of the Charter, which sanctions those "reasonable limits" found to be prescribed by law and "demonstrably justified in a free and democratic society."

In this section, our contributors entertain arguments about the line between justification and legitimacy, given the conventional wisdom that the NWC precludes altogether the formal exercise of justification under section 1. Notwithstanding this accepted orthodoxy, in the context of the court challenge to Quebec's Bill 21, Gregory Bordan offers a bold and creative argument for looking to section 1 for guidance on the substantive elements of a proposed section 33 threshold test, one that supplies a framework that tolerates limits only when they can be demonstrably justified in a free and democratic society. At bottom, the question arises as to whether the NWC can be employed for ends or in a manner not consistent with the core values and principles of a "free and democratic society."

In his chapter, Tsvi Kahana, using Quebec's Bill 96 as case study, considers whether some uses of the NWC are not legitimate in a free and democratic society when they are "tyrannical" in nature, that is, simply inconsistent with democratic purposes, processes, or methods. Kahana argues that invocation of the NWC is tyrannical "when a given use of the mechanism is motivated by a desire to disadvantage minorities or silence opposition, or when it results in exceptionally severe rights violations such that it offends universal liberal values and is unacceptable in a democracy." Because of the possibility of the NWC's facilitation of legislated authorization of the "abhorrent violation of rights," and, therefore, that its use may – and has, on occasion – crossed the line into tyrannical use, it should never be used pre-emptively, thereby giving society the benefit of considered judicial review prior to the invocation.

In her chapter, Mary Eberts argues that although equality rights protected under section 15 of the Charter may be limited by the invocation of the NWC, the equality rights of women and men expressly codified in section 28 are independently protected and are not subject to the same override. In advancing this argument, Eberts underscores the importance of confining section 33 analysis to those rights and freedoms to which the NWC applies, and not to preclude impugning legislation which touches rights and freedoms protected in and covered by the Charter provisions other than sections 2 and 7 to 15.

Both Cara Zwibel and Jamie Cameron extend this analysis to democratic rights and freedoms (sections 3–5 of the Charter). In the context of Ontario's *Working Families* case, they argue that democratic rights, while overlapping in certain obvious respects with section 2 rights and freedoms – especially, but not exclusively, freedom of expression – are independently enshrined and protected in sections 3–5, which are not subject to the application of the NWC. Zwibel lays out what both authors refer to as the "accountability principle," explaining that "section 33 is intended to function as a mechanism of democratic accountability. Ultimately, it places a decision about the operation of a law in the hands of legislators who, in turn, represent their constituents." That decision must be used responsibly and with regard to those rights and freedoms not touched by the NWC's use, be it a general or a targeted use. The other categories of rights not expressly subject to the NWC include mobility rights (section 6), official language rights (sections 16–20), and minority language rights (section 23). While acknowledging the NWC empowerment of legislatures to override section 2(b)'s rights of democratic participation, Cameron points to "its carve-out for section 3" which, she argues, "expresses textual intolerance for derogations from ballot-box rights that are guaranteed by the Charter." She notes that section 3 enshrines not only the rights of democratic participation, but those of "meaningful participation" which must be protected, and which ought not to be restricted by way of NWC invocation.

Caitlin Salvino considers the legitimacy of NWC use in a different context, namely that of minority rights. She argues that "minority groups are uniquely vulnerable to the attempted or actual invocation of the NWC," and that the formal conditions for its invocation "are inadequate and ill-suited for the unique vulnerability of minority groups." This, along with what she sees as the lack of political consequence for the invocation of the NWC, has broader repercussions for our democracy, particularly in an age of rising populism.

Sabreena Delhon closes out the section, and the volume, with a consideration of the influence that the NWC might have, as much symbolically as practically, on the quality of democratic culture broadly. But Delhon does not begin by looking at the NWC itself. Instead, her focus is our civic culture. She draws attention to the pervasiveness of the challenges to effective democratic engagement. Of particular concern is what Delhon sees as the toxicity in our political discourse, especially in online activity, and the ways that this inhibits and discourages constructive, healthy, and meaningful civic engagement. In such an environment, citizens are less able or less likely to effectively hold politically accountable those governments that invoke the NWC. So, while operating as an instrument through which rights and freedoms may be lawfully restricted, against a backdrop of toxicity and democratic backsliding, it may also act to structurally impede meaningful democratic participation and psychologically impair the electorate's sense of agency.

13

The Notwithstanding Clause, Bill 96, and Tyranny

Tsvi Kahana

There has been much controversy about Bill 96, An Act Respecting French, the Official and Common Language of Quebec, which become law in June 2022. In this chapter, I seek to evaluate Bill 96 in terms of the notion of a tyrannical use of the notwithstanding clause (NWC), a notion I introduced in previous work.[1] I conclude that Bill 96 is indeed tyrannical in its use.

Part I of this chapter introduces the notion of the tyrannical use of the NWC, which I developed in previous work. According to my definition, tyrannical use occurs when a given use of the mechanism is motivated by a desire to disadvantage minorities or silence opposition, or when it results in exceptionally severe rights violations such that it offends universal liberal values and is unacceptable in a democracy. Part I also introduces the factors for evaluating the extent to which a given use of the NWC may be characterized as an instance of tyranny, also found in my previous work. Part II evaluates Bill 96 based on these criteria. Part III concludes the chapter. In part III, and throughout the chapter, I also highlight some similarities and differences between the four times Quebec used the NWC in relation to Quebec's identity – the omnibus use in 1982,[2] the sign law in 1988, the religious symbols law in 2020, and the broad language law in 2022. The chapter ends with three lessons we may learn from the use of the NWC in relation to Quebec's identity.

I. THE NWC AND TYRANNY

A. *The* NWC *and Rights Protection*

Aside from its roots in political compromise, several justifications have been offered in support of including an NWC in a constitutional bill of rights based on parliamentary sovereignty,[3] democratic principles,[4] separation of powers,[5] or rights principles.[6] Whatever the justification is, the NWC brings with it an obvious rights-based concern whereby it may be used by legislatures to authorize abhorrent violations of rights.[7]

To better understand this concern, we should distinguish between opponents and supporters of the NWC. For opponents of the NWC, the tyranny concern is obvious and does not merit special analysis. For them, every use of the mechanism is inappropriate and represents the tyranny of the majority. Such approach implies two assumptions. First, the rights that are susceptible to section 33 represent the bare minimum required in a liberal democracy such that their violation is by definition tyranny. Second, judicial interpretations of rights and limits should always prevail – either because they are always right, or because overriding judicial decisions are harmful vis-à-vis the rule of law.

Under this approach, a use of the NWC will be either unnecessary or an instance of tyranny. If the NWC is used to protect from judicial review an act that is constitutional, then the use of the NWC is unnecessary. If, on the other hand, it is used to shield from judicial review an unconstitutional act, or to re-enact an act that was struck down by the court – it is tyrannical.

If one supports the NWC and believes that an NWC-bearing bill of rights represents a nuanced and better form of constitutionalism, then the tyranny concern requires explanation. This approach rejects one or both of the assumptions. Most commonly, supporters of the NWC do not accept the second assumption. For them, the legislature may be able to use the NWC when it disagrees with the judicial interpretation or application of rights and limits. Under this approach, whereby the NWC itself is ideal, the concern is not that the legislature will use the NWC to enact laws that the court did or may strike down. That is bound to happen, and it may be a good thing – it is the whole point of the NWC. Rather, to make sense of the concern for NWC supporters who also believe in constitutional rights protection, it must be based on the following argument.

Judges have formulas for striking down legislation. In Canada, for example, they strike down legislation when it limits a right in the Canadian Charter of Rights and Freedoms (Charter) in a way that is not justified under section 1, the "limitations clause." I will call a limit on a right that is not justified under the limitations clause a "violation of a right."

The judicial formula for striking down legislation does not require that the rights violation be tyrannical. It is sufficient that the limit on a right is not justifiable under the limitation clause to make it a violation of rights.[8] In other words, there is a realm of limits on rights that judges may view as violations, but those limits are not necessarily tyrannical. For NWC supporters, if a court strikes down a law within this realm, the legislature may legitimately override its decision because the judge's limit is only one of several acceptable limits. The concern is that legislatures may misuse the NWC by authorizing rights violations that are *outside* that realm of legitimacy.

If the legislature crosses the line of legitimacy, I say that it engages in a tyrannical use of the NWC. How do we delineate this line of legitimacy? This is the topic of the next section.

B. Delineating the Legitimacy of NWC Uses

In previous work, I developed the notion of tyrannical uses of the NWC based on lessons learned from rights theory, constitutional theory, and constitutional doctrine. I argued that the use of the NWC may be deemed tyrannical if it is motivated by a desire to target minorities or to silence political opposition,[9] or if its impact on rights is exceptionally severe such that it is unacceptable in a liberal democracy. In this section, I briefly discuss each of these elements — the motivation and the impact – and also add a third element necessary for their fine-tuning. That element is the legal effect of the legislation.[10]

I. MOTIVATION FOR THE NOTWITHSTANDING LEGISLATION[11]
Legislation enacted based on the desire to target minorities is tyrannical under my definition, even if the legislation itself seems benign.[12] When an NWC use is motivated by the desire to cause harm to individuals or groups, to exclude for the sake of exclu-

sion, to effectuate hate, or to silence political opposition, it may be characterized as tyranny. If the legislation is motivated by other objectives, I do not deem the motivation tyrannical, even if the objective is not constitutional. For example, religious convictions are not a pressing and substantial objective under the *Oakes* test. However, religious motivation for legislation, on its own, does not render the legislation tyrannical.

2. IMPACT OF THE NOTWITHSTANDING LEGISLATION ON RIGHTS

Even if a law is enacted for benign reasons, its substantive content may affect rights so severely that we may say it offends universal liberal values and hence is tyrannical. Of course, it is impossible to pinpoint the exact point when a given law enters the realm of tyranny as opposed to merely violating rights. But we can say that the more severe a limit is, the more likely it is to be tyrannical. Factors that affect severity are the proximity of the limit to the core of the right, whether the law involves criminalization or confinement, whether the law prohibits (even if not criminalizes) a certain behaviour, the law's impact on minorities generally and on disadvantaged minorities specifically, the breadth of the law's application across population, time, and place, and the degree to which the legislation is unjustified in terms of these factors.

3. FINE-TUNING: THE LEGAL EFFECT OF THE NOTWITHSTANDING LEGISLATION AND OF THE USE OF THE NWC

Ordinarily, the motivation and impact factors should suffice to assess whether a given use of the NWC is tyrannical. However, the operation of constitutional principles or mechanisms may skew the motivation and impact analyses in three ways.

First, the fact that not the entire Canadian Constitution is subject to the NWC means that an act may be unconstitutional even with the use of the NWC. That would be the case, for example, if a provincial legislature used the NWC to protect its legislation from judicial scrutiny a provision that is *ultra vires* under the division of powers. When a legislature uses the NWC to enact an act that is unconstitutional anyway, even if the impact on rights is exceptionally severe, the legal effect of the act significantly reduces the impact on rights. I say that the impact is reduced rather than disappears for two reasons. First, the act may not be challenged in a court or may be challenged only after a period during which it was enforced, so the impact on rights would take place until a court declared that act to be unconstitutional. Second, even an unconstitutional act has expressive impact.[13]

The ultimate unconstitutionality of the notwithstanding legislation may also skew the motivation analysis. Suppose a bill with a notwithstanding declaration is introduced for the clear purpose of discriminating a non-patriotic minority. Now, take a patriotic, moderate legislator, who would never vote for actual discrimination against a minority. That legislator may nevertheless support a bill that he or she knows has no legal impact in order to mobilize support within his or her ultra-patriotic constituents.[14] Again, motivation that is deemed by members of the minority to be targeting them sends a message of exclusion and silencing even if the legislation is invalid in the end. However, as a matter of fact, it is difficult to infer tyrannical motivation for legislation when the makers of the legislation know it is not valid.

Second, in Canada it is possible to have legislation pass but nevertheless not be in force. This may be done, for example, by not proceeding to submit the legislation for royal assent or by proscribing in the bill that it comes into force on proclamation rather than on receiving royal assent. When a law passes but is never brought into force, it has no legal effect and hence has only expressive impact. Moreover, unlike an act that was brought into force but that is ultimately unconstitutional even with the use of the NWC, an act that was not brought into force will not be enforced even for a limited period of time.

Third, section 33's text allows for pre-emptive use of the NWC, that is, a legislature may use the mechanism to prevent judicial review rather than to respond to a judicial decision striking down the law and re-enacting it.[15] Indeed, most uses of the NWC were not made in direct response to a judicial decision.[16] This means that legislatures may use the NWC to enact a law that would have been found constitutional by a court (or that would later be found constitutional if the notwithstanding declaration were removed). If the NWC is used tyrannically to protect such a law, we cannot say that it was the NWC that brought it about because that instance of tyranny would have taken place even without the NWC. Since my inquiry seeks to evaluate the impact of the use of the NWC compared to a situation in which the NWC did not exist, we should consider the constitutionality of the act had it not been for the NWC.

When looking at the legal effect of the legislation, I consider whether the law was brought into force, whether there is a basis for attacking the constitutionality of the law even as a notwithstanding law, and whether it is likely that the law would be upheld without invoking the NWC (including, of course, any actual subsequent finding of constitutionality).

Based on the foregoing, we can say that an NWC use has ordinary legal effect when three conditions are met: (1) the notwithstanding act is brought into force; (2) the notwithstanding act, with the NWC declaration, is constitutional; and (3) the notwithstanding act would likely be unconstitutional without a notwithstanding declaration.

A very weak legal effect occurs when the first condition is not met, and the act is not brought into force (such that the act has only expressive impact). A weak legal effect occurs when the second condition is not met, such that the act will be ultimately unconstitutional, even given the use of the NWC (in such a case, there is both expressive impact, and the act may be enforced until struck down by a court).

A strong legal effect occurs when the use of the NWC takes place in response to a judicial decision, such that we know – rather than surmise – that the third condition is met; that is, without the NWC, the statute would be unconstitutional. A very strong legal effect occurs when the NWC is used to re-enact a law that was struck done by the final court, namely, the Supreme Court of Canada (SCC), because then the legal effect applies throughout the country, and the precedent concerning unconstitutionality may not be changed by the highest court in a province.

4. THREE POINTS OF CLARIFICATION

To conclude, it will be useful to clarify three points. The two main factors of the analysis are motivation and impact. For a use of the NWC to be deemed tyrannical, it is sufficient that either the motivation behind its enactment or its impact on rights is tyrannical. The legal effect analysis serves only as a secondary tool which may amplify a finding of tyranny (when there is a strong or very strong legal effect) or soften a finding of tyranny (when there is a weak or very weak legal effect).

Second, unconstitutionality and tyranny are not identical. Many tyrannical laws will also be unconstitutional, but a law can be constitutional and tyrannical, or unconstitutional and not tyrannical. For example, a law that allows a province to confiscate property without any justification would be tyrannical. However, in Canada such a law would be constitutional since the right to property is not protected by the Constitution. Similarly, a law that creates a tax for passage between provinces would be unconstitutional but not tyrannical. It would be unconstitutional for violating section 6 of the Charter. However, it would be difficult to characterize this law as tyrannical as it does not offend a universal human value. The criterion for constitutionality is Charter compliance, whereas the criterion for tyranny is a violation of universal liberal values.

Third, my argument in this chapter does not imply that a non-tyrannical use of the NWC is a good thing or is always legitimate. The argument is that a tyrannical use of the NWC is a bad thing and is never legitimate. To address the question of whether and when a use of the NWC is a good thing, one must have a theory about the role of the NWC as a good thing and explain which types of uses fall under this theory. In the next part of this article, I evaluate Bill 96 based on motivation, impact, and legal effect.

II. IS BILL 96 TYRANNICAL?

A. Introduction

The preservation of the French language has been a major element in Quebec's identity since confederation. Since the birth of the Charter in 1982, giving priority to one language has been subject to constitutional scrutiny as a potential violation of freedom of expression and equality. Generally speaking, Quebec governments have been accepting such scrutiny. In 2022, however, the Quebec legislature passed the very broad Bill 96 and immunized it from judicial scrutiny by invoking the NWC. The political agenda of Quebec's governing party, the Coalition Avenir Quebec (CAQ), has long been to strengthen Quebec elements of identity and governance over Canadian or universal elements. Among other things, Bill 96 prescribes that:

· public signs must be predominantly in French;[17]
· organizations with twenty-five or more employees must undergo a "francization" program and communicate in French with employees[18] and consumers;[19]
· the minister of justice may prohibit the Court of Quebec and municipal courts from requiring bilingualism (French and

English) to qualify for appointment as a provincial judge;[20]
- as of May 2023, immigrants who have been settled in Quebec for more than six months will receive services from the government exclusively in French;[21]
- the Office québécois de la langue française[22] will be conferred more significant powers of investigation and inspection;
- all contracts negotiated with the government must be exclusively in French;[23]
- contracts between private parties and some of the related documents (except for employment contracts) must present a French version and can be entered in English only if the parties have expressed their wish to do so.[24]

B. Evaluation of Bill

I. MOTIVATION

The motivation for NWC legislation is tyrannical if it is aimed at excluding minorities for the sake of exclusion or at silencing political opposition. Neither motivation is detected in relation to Bill 96. Based on the statements of members of Parliament and participants during parliamentary proceedings, we can conclude that the motivation for the act was the survival of the French language as a common language in Quebec. The decline of French and the marginalization of the use of French within Québécois society warranted government action.[25]

It is true that the legislation passed a few months before an election and was used in the election campaign to demonstrate the CAQ's commitment to Quebec nationalism. It may even be that part of the motivation of the bill was to mobilize political power by invoking majoritarian sentiment. However, as long as the motivation behind the legislation was benign, the mere fact that it likely deepened the political divide between majority and minority does not render it tyrannical.

Bill 96 is a good opportunity to note two motives that are not tyrannical, even though they seem inappropriate at a first glance. These are the desire to protest the Charter and the desire to block judicial review. I will introduce these motives and explain why they are not tyrannical.

The Minister of Justice explained, concerning the use of the NWC:

The parliamentary sovereignty clauses are ... a very concrete way for Quebec to affirm that it does not adhere to the 1982 repatriation project, which was carried out despite its formal opposition.

We can express our disagreement with the interpretation given
to the Canadian Charter of Rights and Freedoms. The future of
Quebec is decided in Quebec and nowhere else.[26]

For a subject as important as the protection of the French language, it must be up to the elected representatives of the Quebec
nation to determine how to protect the French language.[27]

We can detect the two motives here. The first is "to affirm" that
Quebec does not accept the 1982 creation of the Charter, and that
Quebec, not Canada and its Charter, decide about Quebec. Here,
the culprit is not the court – it is the Charter itself. The second
motive has to do not with the Charter itself, but with "the interpretation given to the Canadian Charter" by judges. Without the use of
the NWC, the risk is that "the National Assembly finds itself under
the supervision of judges appointed by the federal government who
sometimes make good decisions, but historically often took decisions that have harmed French in Quebec."[28]

Both of these motives are benign. While I support the entrenchment of rights and judicial review, a lack thereof does not imply
tyranny. The motives I deem to be tyrannical are those that relate to
rights, namely the desire to target minorities or to silence opposition.
It is possible not to have judicial review or entrenched rights while
still respecting minorities. For the same reason, I deem political protest against the acceptance of the Charter to be a benign motive.[29]

2. IMPACT ON RIGHTS

The legislation impacts three Charter rights: freedom of expression,
equality, and privacy (the legislation also impacts the right to receive
government services, but that is not an independent Charter right,
and I analyze it as part of equality). The impact on freedom of
expression and equality is not tyrannical. However, the impact on
privacy is tyrannical.

FREEDOM OF EXPRESSION (SECTION 2(B))

Freedom of expression guarantees the right to express oneself in the
language of one's choice,[30] and protects against forced expression.[31]
The legislation does not go so far as to prohibit other languages, but
the requirement that French must always be used in communications is a requirement for forced expression. In addition, it will have
a silencing effect on other languages since it will increase the cost

for speaking those languages. For example, if a francized corporation wishes to keep English communications, it will have to maintain bilingualism in all communications. Requiring that all signs are predominantly in French means that other languages are somewhat silenced and creates forced expression.

That said, because other languages are not prohibited, I do not believe that this legislation is tyrannical. In the *Ford* case,[32] the Supreme Court ruled that the preservation of French in Quebec is a pressing and substantial objective for the sake of which freedom of expression may be limited. The question is one of proportionality: how far can the preference of French go for the sake of its preservation, at the expense of other languages? While the policies created by Bill 96 may be disproportionate and hence unconstitutional, I do not believe that they reach the level of tyranny.

EQUALITY (SECTION 15)

The law does not make a direct distinction and is neutral on its face, but it creates adverse effect discrimination. The law stipulates that government services will be provided only in French. This means that anyone who does not speak French may not be able to receive government services. This policy will not affect the majority of Quebec residents, as they speak French. It will greatly affect immigrants to Quebec who do not speak French. The legislature was aware of this effect, and therefore, this provision does not apply to immigrants during the first six months following their arrival in Quebec.

To examine whether this discriminatory result is tyrannical, we should look at the grounds for discrimination, the social good to which the discrimination relates, and the potential justification for the legislation. The grounds for discrimination and the nature of the social good bring this legislation close to tyranny; however, the potential justification for the legislation renders it non-tyrannical (even if it is disproportionate and unconstitutional).

The grounds for discrimination here are a mastery of a language. Indirectly, the grounds are national origin because there is a correlation between not speaking French and being an immigrant to Quebec. Discrimination based on national origin is at the core of the right to equality. The good in question is the receipt of government services. That good itself is known to be a right under political liberalism (albeit not a constitutional right in Canada).[33]

Nationality-based discrimination in relation to the good of receiving social services may render the discrimination tyrannical.

That said, the justification for the legislation distances it from being tyrannical. A state – or a province – cannot be expected to give services to immigrants in every language. Beyond the need to protect the French language, efficiency considerations also support providing services in one language. Moreover, six months is not long enough to learn a language, but it is certainly long enough to acquire an initial vocabulary.[34] The expectation that Quebec is fully bilingual is an important matter of Quebec's identity, Canadian federalism, and Canadian identity, but it is not a matter of universal human rights. Therefore, while it is possible that the violation of equality legislation is unconstitutional, it cannot be said that it amounts to a tyrannical violation of human rights.

By comparison, Quebec's religious symbols act forced some of its residents to choose between wearing religious symbols and working in government. Such a choice is not required here. Learning French does not conflict with having another language as one's first and main language.

PRIVACY (SECTION 8)

The invasion of privacy authorized by Bill 96 is extremely serious. The law confers significant powers of inspection and investigation on the Office québécois de la langue française (Office)[35] that are akin to powers given to the government in dictatorial regimes and that render this legislation tyrannical. For the purpose of enforcing the Act, section 174 of the amended Charter of the French Language authorizes *the Office to enter almost any place, excluding private dwellings but including other private property, and take photographs of the place and of the property located there. Furthermore, the Office may require information or documents from relevant people and "cause" them to access this information, including data contained in a computer system.*[36] In some senses, the powers given to the Office québécois de la langue française are broader than the powers given to the police. Such powers are akin to powers given to the government in dictatorial regimes and render this legislation tyrannical.[37]

Here, too, the comparison to the enactment of the omnibus bill, the sign law, and the religious symbols law is illuminating. These three laws did not deal with enforcement powers at all.

3. LEGAL EFFECT

The legal effect of most of the provisions of Bill 96 is ordinary, as the three conditions are met: Bill 96 was brought into force; if it were not for the use of the NWC, some portions of the legislation would surely be found unconstitutional; and with the use of the NWC, these portions are constitutional.

With regard to the infringement of freedom of expression and equality, it is hard to predict what the courts would have ruled. On the one hand, the Supreme Court ruled that the preservation of the French language is a pressing and substantial objective that justifies limiting rights. On the other hand, the court may have found them too broad and hence disproportionate.

However, the infringement on privacy is not justified at all. For example, there was no need for a provision that allows intrusion into the computers of institutions that are captured by the law. There is no doubt that the courts would have struck these powers down as disproportionate to the purposes of the legislation.

That said, the Quebec Superior Court did suspend the constitutionality of sections 9 and 208.6 of the Charter of the French Language, as amended by Bill 96.[38] These provisions require that "a French translation certified by a certified translator shall be attached to any pleading drawn up in English." The court ruled that these provisions were in violation of section 133 of the Constitution Act, 1867, whereby both French and English "may be used by any Person or in any Pleading or Process in or issuing from any Court of Canada established under this Act, and in or from all or any of the Courts of Quebec." Section 133 is not subject to section 33.

As sections 9 and 208.6 were found to be unconstitutional, even given the use of the NWC, the legal effect of the use of the NWC with regard to these provisions was weak. As the legal effect is generally ordinary and not weak, the conclusion about the tyrannical nature of the legislation remains mostly intact.

CONCLUSION:
TYRANNY, QUEBEC IDENTITY, AND THE NWC

In this chapter, I presented the notion of tyrannical use of the NWC and came to the conclusion that Bill 96 constitutes such tyrannical use. To conclude the chapter, it is worth comparing Bill 96 to the other three uses of the NWC in the service of Quebec's identity.

The motive behind Bill 96 is like the motive behind the omni-bus use (political protest and prevention of judicial review) and the motivation behind the sign law (protection of the French language). These motives are benign.

The impact on rights of Bill 96 is tyrannical, but an important difference emerges between this bill, on the one hand, and the other two tyrannical uses of the NWC in Quebec – the sign law and religious symbols law, on the other. In the case of the sign law, the substance of the law was tyrannical because the law prohibited the use of a language. In the case of the broad language law, the substance of the law was not tyrannical, but the enforcement mechanism was tyrannical, as the sweeping powers given to the Office québécois de la langue française are of the type seen in despotic regimes.

Looking at the use of the NWC in the context of Quebec's identity from a bird's-eye view reveals three lessons – one good, one bad, and one ironic.

The good lesson is that a dialogue between courts and legislatures is possible even when the NWC is used. In 1988, the Supreme Court struck down Quebec's French-only sign policy, ruling that only a predominantly French sign requirement would be constitutional. In 1988, the Quebec legislature refused to accept this notion and re-enacted the French-only policy for outdoor signs via the NWC. Thirty-four years later, the Quebec legislature accepted the Supreme Court's view, even in a bill that uses the NWC – the broad language law accepts the predominantly French principle.

The bad lesson is that tyranny is possible, even in 2022. In the two years that Quebec used the mechanism tyrannically, it twice provided an argument for doing away with the mechanism.

The ironic lesson is that Quebec had the potential to become an exemplar of appropriate NWC uses. Most supporters of the NWC support it for institutional reasons – the need to allow the legislature a say in constitutional issues. Quebec makes an additional argument: unlike other provinces, it did not sign onto the patriation project.

Even if this argument is only partially valid, it is a powerful addition to the institutional argument and makes the use of the NWC more legitimate in Quebec. Therefore, had Quebec used the NWC reasonably, each use would have allowed a national seminar about courts and legislature in Canada and Quebec. However, because

Quebec has been using the mechanism tyrannically, it is impossible to have this debate; instead, one must protest against the tyranny.

The story of Bill 96 strengthens the argument, made by this writer and others, that the NWC should only be used in response to a final judicial decision by the Supreme Court.[39] Even if the majority of Quebecers (putting aside the question of whether the legislature does indeed represent the majority) believe that harsh and sweeping measures are necessary in order to preserve the French language in Quebec, it is crucial that a judge approves this policy if challenged. Judicial analysis would explain what rights are violated, to what extent, and the justification for the infringement. Such an analysis would have allowed for a more rights-oriented public debate than the one we have witnessed so far. And perhaps the time that will pass from the initial enactment of the policy to its striking down by the Supreme Court will allow politicians and the public a sober second thought that would prevent the use of the mechanism tyrannically.

NOTES

1 Tsvi Kahana, "The Notwithstanding Clause in Canada: The First Forty Years," *Osgoode Hall Law Journal* (forthcoming 2023).

2 See Lorraine Eisenstat Weinrib, "Learning to Live with the Override," *McGill Law Journal* 35 (1990): 541.

3 See, for example, Guillaume Rousseau and François Côté, "A Distinctive Quebec Theory and Practice of the Notwithstanding Clause: When Collective Interests Outweigh Individual Rights," *Revue générale de droit* 47 (2017): 343–431.

4 See, for example, Paul C. Weiler, "Rights and Judges in a Democracy: A New Canadian Version," *University of Michigan Journal of Law Reform* 18, no. 1 (1984): 51–80.

5 See, for example, Peter H. Russell, "Standing Up for Notwithstanding," *Alberta Law Review* 29, no. 2 (1991): 293, https://doi.org/10.29173/alr1563.

6 See, for example, Lois G. Macdonald, "Promoting Social Equality through the Legislative Override," *NJCL* 4 (1994): 1. See also Allan Blakeney, "The Notwithstanding Clause, the Charter, and Canada's Patriated Constitution: What I Thought We Were Doing" *Constitutional Forum constitutionnel* 19, no. 1 (2010): 1–9, https://doi.org/10.21991/C9KD4W.

7 See: John Whyte, "On Not Standing for Notwithstanding," *Alberta Law Review* 28, no. 2 (1990): 355; Tsvi Kahana, "Legalism, Anxiety and Legislative Constitutionalism," *Queen's Law Journal* 31 (2006): 536; Leonid Sirota, "Flipping the Line: Has the Supreme Court really become more activist?" *The Line*, 15 November 2015, https://theline.substack.com/p/flipping-the-line-has-the-supreme.

8 For example, the Oakes test, which establishes the test for striking down legislation, does not mention the matter of tyranny. Furthermore, Oakes lists several constitutional concepts and values for Canada but does not directly mention the need to prevent the tyranny of the majority. See *R v Oakes* [1986] 1 SCR 103, 26 DLR (4th) 200 [*Oakes*] at para. 63–71.

9 While I consider silencing political opposition a tyrannical motivation, the same is not true for the motivation of preventing judicial review and thus arguably silencing the courts. Some theories of the NWC explicitly allow for pre-emptive use of the mechanism when the legislature is certain that law it creates via the NWC is constitutional. See, for example, Brian Slattery, "A Theory of the *Charter*," *Osgoode Hall Law Journal* 25 (1987): 701.

10 For the full analysis, see Kahana, "Notwithstanding Clause in Canada," part II.

11 By "notwithstanding legislation," I refer to legislation invoking the NWC. I refer to the declaration stating that the act shall operate notwithstanding certain provisions of the Charter as a "notwithstanding declaration."

12 Because of the psychological and expressive effects of legislation, it is actually difficult to imagine legislation that is motivated by the desire to target minorities that will not have the impact of targeting minorities. Even if the subject matter of the law is trivial, the fact that the minority members know that they are excluded or burdened – even trivially – would result in targeting. Nevertheless, it is possible to think of such an example when the majority hides its motivation from the minority. Suppose, for example, that the majority legislates an exemption from income tax for a certain minority. That policy in itself seems benign. However, if the motivation behind this legislation is contempt, or the view that the minority is not worthy of participating in the funding of government, I deem this legislation tyrannical based on motivation alone, even if the minority is happy with the exception.

13 See: Cass R. Sunstein, "On the Expressive Function of Law," *University of Pennsylvania Law Review* 144 (1996): 2021; Elizabeth S. Anderson and Richard H. Pildes, "Expressive Theories of Law: A General Restatement," *University of Pennsylvania Law Review* 147, no. 5 (2000): 1503. While

the literature discusses the expressive function of law in the context of enforceable law, the rationale behind this expressive function does not depend on enforceability. This rationale is based on the message sent by the institution creating the laws. But institutions are made of people. When the legislature does something as important as legislating, that very action sends a message, even if, eventually, the message is dimmed, or even outweighed by the striking down of the law in court.

14 The use of the NWC in the Alberta anti-same-sex marriage legislation is a case in point. As I show, this legislation was based on homophobic sentiment. However, it may be that legislators allow themselves to vote for a tyrannical act because they know it will not be enforceable. See Kahana, "Notwithstanding Clause in Canada," part III(B)(4).

15 For analysis, see Donna Greschner and Ken Norman, "The Courts and Section 33," *Queen's Law Journal* 12, no. 2 (1987): 155.

16 Kahana, "Notwithstanding Clause in Canada," part IV(E).

17 Sections 48–49.

18 Division II.

19 Section 99; Catherine Jenner, Anna C. Romano, and Romy Proulx, "Bill 96 and the Charter of the French Language: The Language of Business in Québec," *Stikeman Elliott*, 12 August 2022, https://www.stikeman.com/en-ca/kh/corporations-commercial-law/business-impacts-of-quebecs-language-law-changes-an-update-on-bill-96.

20 Sections 8–9.

21 Section 22.3.

22 Sections 167–169.

23 Section 21.

24 Sections 29 and 49; Jenner, Romano, and Proulx, "Bill 96 and the Charter."

25 See: Québec, National Assembly, *Journal des débats (Hansard of the National Assembly)*, 42-2, vol. 45, No 7 (2 November 2022) at 375 (Mathieu Lévesque); Tommy Chouinard, "Le Québec risque de devenir une 'Louisiane,' dit Legault," *La Presse*, 29 May 2022, https://www.lapresse.ca/actualites/politique/2022-05-29/congres-de-la-caq/le-quebec-risque-de-devenir-une-louisiane-dit-legault.php; "Québec adopte la réforme de la Charte de la langue française," Radio-Canada, 24 May 2022, https://ici.radio-canada.ca/nouvelle/1885719/loi-96-vote-pq-plq-opposition.

26 See Québec, National Assembly, *Journal des débats (Hansard of the National Assembly)*, 42-2, vol 45, No 7 (12 May 2022), http://www.assnat.qc.ca/fr/travaux-parlementaires/assemblee-nationale/42-2/

journal-debats/20220512/325503.html#_Toc103852173 (Simon Jolin-Barette) [Translation].

27 Ibid. [Translation].

28 See Québec, National Assembly, *Journal des débats (Commission de la Culture et de l'Éducation)*, 42-1, vol 45, No 92 (21 September 2021), http://www.assnat.qc.ca/fr/travaux-parlementaires/commissions/cce-42-1/journal-debats/CCE-210921.html (Guillaume Rousseau) [Translation].

29 See Kahana, "Notwithstanding Clause in Canada," III(A)1.

30 *Ford v Québec (AG)* [1988] 2 SCR 712 at para 40 [*Ford*].

31 RJR-MacDonald Inc v Canada (AG), [1995] 3 S.C.R. 199.

32 RJR-MacDonald Inc v Canada (AG), para 72-3.

33 See Erin Kelly, ed., *Justice as Fairness: A Restatement* (Harvard University Press, 2001), 58.

34 Compare to the following position, expressed by the president of the Commission des droits de la personne et des droits de la jeunesse: "Such a requirement is also likely to pose difficulties for immigrants in obtaining essential administrative services, especially when they are still in the francization process. Moreover, the very short deadline set by the bill does not seem to take into account the many factors that can influence the success and duration of a francization and integration process. The Commission therefore recommends amending Bill 96 to remove this condition." See Québec, National Assembly, *Journal des débats (Commission de la Culture et de l'Éducation)*, 42-1, vol 45, No 100 (6 October 2021), http://www.assnat.qc.ca/fr/travaux-parlementaires/commissions/cce-42-1/journal-debats/CCE-211006.html (Philippe-André Tessier). [Translation]

35 See sections 174-5 of the Act: "174. A person making an inspection for the purposes of this Act may:
(1) enter at any reasonable hour any place, other than a dwelling house, where an activity governed by this Act is carried on, or any other place where documents or other property to which this Act applies may be held;
(2) take photographs of the place and of the property located there;
(3) cause any person present who has access to any computer, equipment or other thing that is on the premises to use it to access data contained in an electronic device, computer system or other medium or to verify, examine, process, copy or print out such data; and
(4) require any information relating to the application of this Act or the regulations as well as the communication, for examination or reproduction, of any related document.

Any person who has custody, possession or control of documents referred to in this section must communicate them to the person making an inspection and facilitate their examination by that person."

175. A person making an inspection for the purposes of this Act may, by notification of a notice, require any person to communicate to him, within a reasonable time determined by the notice, any information or document relating to the carrying out of this Act."

In addition to these provisions, fines for a violation of the act may be *up to $30,000 and may be doubled and then tripled if the violation continues.* See section 207.

36 See sections 174-5 of the Act. 174. "A person making an inspection for the purposes of this Act may:

(1) enter at any reasonable hour any place, other than a dwelling house, where an activity governed by this Act is carried on, or any other place where documents or other property to which this Act applies may be held;

(2) take photographs of the place and of the property located there;

(3) cause any person present who has access to any computer, equipment or other thing that is on the premises to use it to access data contained in an electronic device, computer system or other medium or to verify, examine, process, copy or print out such data; and

(4) require any information relating to the application of this Act or the regulations as well as the communication, for examination or reproduction, of any related document.

Any person who has custody, possession or control of documents referred to in this section must communicate them to the person making an inspection and facilitate their examination by that person.

175. A person making an inspection for the purposes of this Act may, by notification of a notice, require any person to communicate to him, within a reasonable time determined by the notice, any information or document relating to the carrying out of this Act."

37 "Why francophone Quebeckers should worry about Bill 96," Campbell Clark. The government tried to deny the power reinforcement: https://www.quebec.ca/gouvernement/politiques-orientations/langue-francaise/pl96. But the fact is supported by different sources. See: Jenner, Romano, and Proulx, "Bill 96 and the Charter"; "The Main Impacts of Québec's Bill 96 on Companies," *Dentons*, 23 June 2022, https://www.dentons.com/en/insights/articles/2022/june/22/the-main-impacts-of-quebecs-bill-96-on-companies; Marco Bélair-Cirino and François Carabin, "Cinq craintes – fondées ou non? – au sujet de la loi 96," *Le Devoir*, 21 May

2022, https://www.ledevoir.com/politique/quebec/713883/cinq-craintes-fondees-ou-non; Robert Leckey, "Loi 96: une atteinte à la justice et aux droits fondamentaux," *Policy Options Politiques*, 20 May 2022, https://policyoptions.irpp.org/fr/magazines/may-2022/loi-96-droits-fondamentaux/.

38 *Mitchell c Procureur général du Québec*, 2022 QCCS 2983 at para 78 [*Mitchell, 2022*].

39 See, for example: Greschner and Norman, "The Courts and Section 33"; Tsvi Kahana, "Understanding the Notwithstanding Mechanism," *University of Toronto Law Journal* 52 (2002): 221.

14

Are There Constitutional Limits on the
Use of the Notwithstanding Clause?

Gregory B. Bordan

There is much debate over that peculiar feature of Canadian constitutional law, section 33 of the Constitution Act, 1982 (Canadian
Charter), the so-called notwithstanding clause or legislative override: Why was it included? What is its purpose? When, if ever, is it
politically legitimate to invoke it? What conditions are required for
recourse to it to be legally effective?

Speaking broadly, there are two approaches to understanding the
clause. One approach understands it as the fruit of a purely political
compromise, a compromise which, from a principled perspective,
introduced a clause which is irreconcilably at odds with the concept
of entrenched fundamental rights embodied in the remainder of the
Canadian Charter. For proponents of this view, legislative recourse
to the notwithstanding clause may be constitutionally valid, but it is
always morally and politically suspect.

A second approach argues that the notwithstanding clause fulfills
a useful constitutional function, although a diversity of functions are
posited by writers.[1] On this approach, the notwithstanding clause
should be understood as conceptually integrated into the Charter,
part of the balance which the framers of the Constitution struck
between the legislative and judicial branches of government. For
proponents of this approach, legislative recourse to the notwithstanding clause can be legitimate and justified in some, or many,
circumstances.

In *Ford v. Quebec (Attorney General)*,[2] the leading case on the
notwithstanding clause, the Supreme Court of Canada declared that
the differing views argued before the court "as to the constitutional

perspective from which the meaning and application of s. 33 ... should be approached" were not "particularly relevant or help-ful."[3] It refused the urgings of parties to read into section 33 requirements of legislative form beyond those expressly required under the terms of section 33, viz. that "the override declaration ... be an express declaration that an Act or a provision of an Act shall operate notwithstanding a provision included in s. 2 or ss. 7 to 15 of the Charter."[4]

A case currently before the courts in Quebec and likely to reach the Supreme Court of Canada may offer the court an opportunity to explore whether, apart from the issue of section 33's minimal requirements of form, there are any substantive restrictions on a legislature's capacity to override fundamental rights and freedoms through recourse to the notwithstanding clause.

I will begin with a brief discussion of the political context which makes this issue particularly timely. I will then elaborate on an argu-ment raised before the Quebec courts, although not developed at length. I intend only to sketch out the broad outlines of an approach which, to date, has not been considered by the courts. While I ref-erence a number of doctrinal authors to help frame and situate the argument, I make no pretence at a complete literature review. My aim is to draw attention to an issue which has gone largely undis-cussed to date. The proposal I advance is that in Canada, as a free and democratic society, there are necessarily certain inherent con-stitutional limits on how section 33 can be used. I will argue that section 33 was not conceived by the framers of the Constitution as a means for shielding rights violations which attack the very core of guaranteed right or freedom, and that it should not now be interpreted as permitting such violations. The proposed approach leaves room for broad use of section 33, but posits that fundamental constitutional principles establish guardrails around its use which ensure judicial protection of the core of constitutionally entrenched rights and freedoms.

CONTEXT: QUEBEC'S BILL 21

The Act Respecting the Laicity of the State,[5] popularly known as Bill 21, is the 2019 Quebec statute which prohibits broad categories of persons "from wearing religious symbols in the exercise of their functions." Bill 21 is presently the subject of four court challenges that were joined for trial. A single first instance judgment was rendered on 20 April 2021 for all four cases (the Trial Judgment).[6] For the most part, it upheld the law. At the time of writing, the case is pending before the Quebec Court of Appeal.

The prohibition on religious symbols is often described by the Quebec government as applying to persons in authority. This is a rather loose description, as the ban includes persons who cannot reasonably be said to occupy positions of authority, such as research lawyers employed by a government ministry, and does not include many persons who do exercise considerable authority, such as the minister of finance or the president of the Treasury Board.[7] Most of those targeted are state employees, but this is not universally true. The largest targeted group are principals, vice principals, and teachers in public schools. Lawyers and notaries are also a prime target of Bill 21. Any lawyer or notary working for a Quebec government department in any capacity, or for numerous other bodies and commissions, is subject to the ban, as well as private sector lawyers and notaries retained by those same departments, bodies, and commissions if their function requires them to appear before a court or to interact with third parties. The prohibition makes no distinction between a visible symbol and a religious symbol worn under an employee's clothing. It is the very act of wearing a religious symbol which triggers the prohibition, not the fact that it can be seen by others.[8]

However, Bill 21's declared purpose is much broader than its ban on religious symbols. Its purpose as set out in its preamble is to firmly establish "laicity" as one of the state's core values alongside Quebec's "civil law tradition, distinct social values and ... specific history."[9] Section 1 declares that Quebec is a lay state. Section 2 defines laicity as being based on the following principles:

(1) the separation of State and religions;
(2) the religious neutrality of the State;
(3) the equality of all citizens; and
(4) freedom of conscience and freedom of religion.

While many might immediately see the ban on wearing a religious symbol as being at odds with some or all of these principles, Bill 21 expressly declares that state laicity *requires* compliance with the ban. Indeed, the Trial Judge notes that one can speak of Bill 21 aiming to create a lay state, but in reality it aims simply to remove rights from persons who wear religious symbols.[10] So courts will ultimately be left to try to figure out how, or whether, the ban on religious symbols can be squared with the aforementioned principles on which state laicity are said to rest.

In any event, this conception of state laicity, which is said to *require* prohibiting the wearing of religious symbols by broad categories of persons working for or connected in some way to the state, is further entrenched as a quasi-constitutional principle by being incorporated into Quebec's Charter of Human Rights and Freedoms[11] (Quebec Charter). Laicity is now included in the Quebec Charter as one of the core values which, together with "democratic values ... public order and the general well-being of the citizens of Quebec," may limit the exercise of the rights and freedoms protected by that Charter.[12]

Most importantly for present purposes, Bill 21 expressly declares that it, and the amendments it made to the Quebec Charter and other legislation, have effect notwithstanding sections 2 and 7 to 15 of the Canadian Charter. It also invokes the equivalent provision in the Quebec Charter to override sections 1 to 38 of that Charter as well.[13]

JUSTIFICATIONS FOR RECOURSE TO THE NOTWITHSTANDING CLAUSE IN THE CANADIAN CHARTER

While the notwithstanding clause has often been seen as being at odds with the guaranteed rights and freedoms set out in the Canadian Charter, a number of writers have sought a theoretical foundation for it, that is, a rationale for when it is justified and legitimate to override the rights and freedoms which are said to be guaranteed by the Constitution.

Some writers support legislative recourse to the notwithstanding clause only after the courts have had the opportunity to deliberate on legislation, for example where the legislature uses the clause to correct perceived errors committed by a court. Others support its pre-emptive use to pursue certain social interests which may require displacing rights in circumstances in which the legislature considers itself better placed than the judiciary to make the necessary trade-offs.[14] Guillaume Rousseau posits the widest grounds of which I am aware on which to legitimate the pre-emptive use of the notwithstanding clause. He considers recourse to the notwithstanding clause to be legitimate when used to protect Quebec's collective identity, to advance its collective interests, or to advance "social progress."[15]

There has been wide agreement that use of the notwithstanding clause should be exceptional,[16] although in recent years there has been some whittling away at this view. For example, Dwight Newman criticizes what he calls "excessive deference to judicial interpretation of rights."[17] Yet he too writes, "[Obviously], the use of the notwithstanding clause is not meant to be entirely routine. If it were inserted in every bill that potentially affected sections 2 or 7 through 15 of the Charter, it would amount to a rejection of those sections of the Charter as part of Canada's Constitution ... It would not be appropriate to have legislators excessively involved in second-guessing judicial decisions on an everyday basis. Doing so would effectively subvert a proper institutional division."[18] However, both those who oppose the notwithstanding clause and those who see it as having a legitimate role within our constitutional order appear to assume that the only restrictions on its use are moral or political, not constitutional.

NORMALIZING RECOURSE TO THE NOTWITHSTANDING CLAUSE

Until recently, the nearly universal assumption was that recourse to the notwithstanding clause was an exceptional measure that would be accompanied by political debate and would carry political consequences, an assumption which has largely proven true over the past forty years.[19] This can no longer be assumed to be true. Indeed, the reality on the ground may already have changed.

The Trial Judgment was rendered on 20 April 2021, upholding Bill 21's use of the notwithstanding clause. Less than a month later, on 13 May 2021, the Quebec government tabled Bill 96, An Act Respecting French, the Official and Common Language of Quebec. Bill 96's scope is vast. It introduced numerous and profound changes to Quebec's Charter of the French Language[20] and to thirteen other statutes, including the Constitution Act, 1867. Like Bill 21, Bill 96 invokes the notwithstanding clauses in both the Canadian and Quebec Charters. Bill 21 and Bill 96 are the two keystones of the present Quebec government's cultural and linguistic policy.

In his judgment, the Trial Judge noted the historical departure that Bill 21's use of the notwithstanding clause represents:

[768] However, in a more remarkable and relevant way for our purposes, Bill 21 represents the first legislative text which simultaneously overrides sections 1 to 38 of the Quebec Charter and sections 2 and 7 to 15 of the Canadian Charter. Therefore, we are forced to note that in so doing, the legislator has suspended, in relation to Bill 21, nearly the entirety of the rights and freedoms in the province of Quebec. Regardless of one's perspective on Bill 21, it must be emphasized that this is not a trivial matter, quite the contrary. This is why the Court earlier noted a certain trivialization and indifference as to the real scope of the exercise of the override.[21]

Bill 96 also invokes the notwithstanding clauses in both Charters to the fullest extent possible even though there seems to be less need to "protect" Bill 96 from Charter scrutiny than there is for Bill 21. Bill 96 may be controversial from certain perspectives, yet most of it is clearly less violative of the Canadian and Quebec Charters than is Bill 21. Nonetheless, Quebec opted to invoke the notwithstanding clause in Bill 96 to the maximum extent possible.

While the Trial Judge's concern about the maximal override of basic rights is understandable from the perspective of constitutionally entrenched fundamental rights and freedoms, use of the override should not come as a surprise from a broader political perspective. Supporters of both bills, such as Rousseau, are strong proponents of the view that the notwithstanding clause is an important tool for protecting Quebec's collective identity and advancing its collective interests. They frequently associate the notwithstanding clause with democracy and parliamentary sovereignty. Rousseau presents it as a means for giving expression to the popular will of Quebecers expressed through the majority vote of the elected members of the legislature, unconstrained by an unelected judiciary.[22] As an advisor to the Quebec government on Bill 21, Rousseau's views have clearly been influential in shaping the policy of the current government.

It appears likely that recourse to the notwithstanding clause in both bills was not only designed to allow them to achieve their specific legislative objectives. As the Trial Judge noted, the scope of the override clearly exceeds any conceivable requirement from that perspective.[23] Rather, I suggest, invoking the notwithstanding clauses was itself an *objective*, designed to normalize their use.

It is crucial to distinguish this current situation from the period following the coming into force of the Canadian Charter when Quebec systematically invoked the notwithstanding clause in all its legislation as a political protest against the patriation of the Constitution without Quebec's consent. At that time, Quebec did not override the Quebec Charter because it was protesting the unilateral action taken by Ottawa and the other provinces, not the enshrinement of basic rights per se. The current use of the notwithstanding clause is categorically different. Its very purpose is to assert the pre-eminence of the legislature in defining which rights will be respected and which will have to cede in the face of the so-called "popular will" expressed through a majority vote of elected representatives. Therefore, we are now witnessing a protest against the very concept of entrenched rights and freedoms.

These two instances of the use of the notwithstanding clauses likely constitute a significant step toward normalizing the practice. Recourse to the notwithstanding clauses attracted some opposition in the case of Bill 21, less in the case of Bill 96, and both those ministorms have largely passed. Future use of the override power is likely to attract even less attention. So the political price which was widely assumed would attach to their use will likely be largely blunted in the future.

Furthermore, Bill 21's amendment to the Quebec Charter, which introduces laicity as one of the core values permitted to limit the exercise of the rights and freedoms protected by that Charter, could give Quebec greater latitude to extend the ban on religious practices in the future, without having to invoke the notwithstanding clause in the Quebec Charter. Quebec will be able to argue that future bans are part of ensuring a lay state, itself justification for restricting religious practices according to the government's view of laicity, now embedded in the Quebec Charter. This would attenuate whatever residual opprobrium might still be associated with use of the notwithstanding clause.[24]

There is also no reason to believe that this phenomenon will remain limited to Quebec. We have already seen Ontario's Ford government invoke the notwithstanding clause in Bill 307, the Protecting Elections and Defending Democracy Act, 2021, which was tabled in the Ontario legislature on 10 June 2021, and enacted on 14 June 2021. Bill 307 re-enacted third party spending rules and other rules related to the conduct of Ontario elections only two days after those rules had been declared unconstitutional by the Superior Court of Justice. The very name of the act suggests that in tabling Bill 307, rather than appealing the first instance judgment or modifying the spending law to take account of the judgment, the Ontario government was adopting a view of the notwithstanding clause similar to the one propounded by Rousseau and seemingly by the present Quebec government that equates democracy with unconstrained parliamentary sovereignty and majority rule, a view which at its core is antithetical to entrenched rights and freedoms.[25]

These uses of the notwithstanding clause are not just a political or symbolic protest. If use of the notwithstanding clause is successfully normalized – and we appear to have moved a long way down that road – we seriously risk neutering the constitutional protection of rights and freedoms afforded by both the Canadian and Quebec Charters.[26]

ADDRESSING THE LIMITS OF THE
NOTWITHSTANDING CLAUSE[27]

In the Bill 21 case, the attorney general of Quebec argues that legislation which invokes the notwithstanding clause is thereby shielded from all judicial scrutiny. In this section, I will propose two roles that courts should retain notwithstanding the presence of an override clause in impugned legislation. The first is the use of their power to issue declarations. The second is through a residual ability to undertake a substantive threshold review of legislation containing an override to determine whether its purpose, and therefore the purpose of the override, is constitutionally illegitimate, as discussed below.

Courts' Declaratory Function[28]

In the Bill 21 case, the attorney general of Quebec begins from the premise that a declaration under section 33 effectively nullifies the overridden Charter rights. On that view, there is no violation of the rights or freedoms in the presence of an override declaration. Consequently, there is no basis for a judicial declaration that a right has been unjustifiably violated. I suggest that this is a misconception of the effect of an override.

The effect of a legislative declaration of an override pursuant to section 33(1) of the Canadian Charter is set out in section 33(2), which provides that the legislation "in respect of which a declaration made under this section is in effect shall *have such operation as it would have but for the provision of this Charter* referred to in the declaration" (emphasis added). The plain meaning is that the legislation *shall continue to operate* as long as the declaration enacted pursuant to section 33(1) remains in force.[29] In other words, an override enacted pursuant to section 33 temporarily suspends *the effect of section 52* of the Canadian Charter which otherwise would render the legislation "of no force or effect" to the extent of any inconsistency between the legislation and the Charter-guaranteed rights and freedoms enumerated in the override.[30] This does not support the assertion that recourse to section 33 suspends or nullifies rights or freedoms themselves. It merely suspends the normal sanction of a violation which is to render the legislation without force or effect pursuant to section 52.[31] As a result, recourse to section 33 should not be a bar to a court adjudicating a claim of a rights violation. Should the court find that basic rights have been violated and that the violation is not justified under section 1 of the Canadian Charter, it should remain open to the court to issue a declaration to that effect.

By issuing a declaration, the court would fulfill an important judicial function, one which only it can fulfill. The court would provide a reasoned opinion on whether, and why, the prohibitions either do or do not violate Charter rights. Regardless of the court's conclusion, the law would continue to operate due to the override (assuming the override is validly invoked). However, public debate could proceed, properly informed of the judicial position. This would be part of the dialogue between the legislative and judicial branches, one which should not be pre-empted by use of the override.

Take Bill 21 as an example. Should the court conclude and declare that Bill 21 constitutes an unjustified limit on rights, the declaration would itself be a partial remedy for those affected by the law. The declaration itself would be a public vindication of Charter rights because it would be an authoritative statement that those claiming the right to wear a religious symbol had been acting consistently with a constitutional conception of basic rights and freedoms guaranteed by the Canadian Charter. That said, the public debate concerning the propriety of the law could continue, properly focused on whether countervailing interests justify overriding the Charter rights. That is precisely the debate which proponents of recourse to the notwithstanding clause should welcome: are there collective interests advanced by the legislation which justify violating the rights of certain individuals? Absent a judicial declaration, nothing prevents a government from arguing that Bill 21 does not violate individual rights. Debate then proceeds either on a wrong premise or on a premise which, at best, remains murky.[32]

John Rawls's views on the courts' role in advancing public reason seems particularly a propos here: "In the midst of any great constitutional change, legitimate or otherwise, the Court is bound to be a center of controversy. *Often its role forces political discussion to take a principled form so as to address the constitutional question in line with the political values of justice and public reason. Public discussion becomes more than a contest for power and position. This educates citizens to the use of public reason* and its value of political justice by focusing their attention on basic constitutional matters."[33]

Judicial Review: A Threshold Determination of the Legitimacy of the Legislation's Purpose

Proponents of the override propose a variety of circumstances in which they consider it to be politically legitimate or appropriate to invoke section 33.[34] However, they argue, in law the decision to invoke section 33 is at the legislature's unfettered discretion and recourse to the override is not subject to any substantive constitutional constraints.

At first blush, this position may seem to find support in *Ford* where the Supreme Court declared that, "[Section] 33 lays down requirements of form only, and there is no warrant for importing into it grounds for substantive review of the legislative policy in exercising the override authority in a particular case."[35]

However, interpreting this as support for the "no-restrictions" position is, I suggest, an unnecessarily broad reading of the court's statement. Respondents in *Ford* contended that the legislative override was of no force or effect because the override provision was not in conformity with section 33. Some argued that the legislative provision invoking section 33 did not sufficiently specify the rights or freedoms which the legislation intended to override. They argued that it was necessary to refer to the rights to be overridden in words, not merely by section or paragraph number.[36] One of the Court of Appeal justices also suggested that to invoke section 33, the legislature must identify the provision in the law which the legislature contemplates as possibly infringing a specified right or freedom.[37] Arguments were also raised about whether an override can be included in an "omnibus" law which simultaneously inserts an override into multiple statutes.[38]

In response to all these contentions, the court held "that a s. 33 declaration is sufficiently express if it refers to the number of the section, subsection or paragraph of the Charter which contains the provision or provisions to be overridden."[39] Hence, a provision which declares that, "This Act shall operate notwithstanding the provisions of sections 2 and 7 to 15 of the Constitution Act, 1982" validly invokes section 33 of the Canadian Charter. "There is no reason why more should be required under s. 33. A reference to the number of the section, subsection or paragraph containing the provisions or provisions to be overridden is a sufficient indication to those concerned of the relative seriousness of what is proposed. It cannot have been intended by the word 'expressly' that a legislature should be required to encumber a s. 33 declaration by stating the provision or provisions to be overridden in the words of the Charter, which, in the case of the standard override provision in issue in the appeal, would be a very long recital indeed."[40]

Ford did not address, let alone settle, the question of whether there are any limits on the purpose for which section 33 can be validly invoked, arising not from the text of section 33, which addresses only the formal requirements for invoking an override, but from basic principles which must inform all constitutional interpretation.[41]

The innovation of the Canadian Charter was not so much the creation of new rights, as their entrenchment in the country's Constitution. In the early Charter case of *Quebec Protestant School Boards,* the Supreme Court wrote the following to distinguish the language rights of section 23 from the other enumerated rights:

Section 23 of the Charter is not, like other provisions in that constitutional document, of the kind generally found in such charters and declarations of fundamental rights. It is not a *codification of essential, pre-existing and more or less universal rights that are being confirmed and perhaps clarified, extended or amended, and which, most importantly, are being given a new*

primacy and inviolability by their entrenchment in the supreme
law of the land. The special provisions of s. 23 of the Charter
make it a unique set of constitutional provisions, quite peculiar
to Canada.[42]

This is clear recognition that the rights to which a section 33 override can apply are "essential, pre-existing and more or less universal
rights." Yet, at the same time, the drafters of the Canadian Charter
recognized that the entrenched rights could not be absolute; they
had to be subject to limits. The principle of limits on the enumerated
rights and freedoms is incorporated in the very provision that guarantees those rights and freedoms, section 1. In section 1's oft-cited
words, the Canadian Charter "guarantees the rights and freedoms
set out in it subject only to such reasonable limits prescribed by law
as can be demonstrably justified in a free and democratic society."
However, while the principle of reasonably limited rights is declared
in section 1, it was left to the jurisprudence to flesh out that principle
by defining the parameters of those limits and a methodology for
determining them.

In the relatively sparse jurisprudence which refers to section 33 of
the Canadian Charter, the Supreme Court has distinguished limits
placed on Charter rights and freedoms which are adjudicated through
the prism of section 1, from exceptions authorized by section 33.[43]
Section 33 is an exception, and operates differently from section 1, in
two key ways alluded to previously. First, and most importantly, it
allows a legislature to determine that a law will continue to have full
force and effect notwithstanding that it may infringe fundamental,
legal, or equality rights. Second, as a corollary of the first, it removes
from the judiciary the balancing task involved in determining whether
a legislated limit on a guaranteed right or freedom is reasonable, giving the final word on that to the legislature.

However, there remains a question which has not been addressed
by the Supreme Court: are there any limits to the power granted legislatures under section 33? *Ford* addressed the formal requirements
of section 33. It did not consider whether there are substantive limits
on the purpose for which section 33 may be invoked.

It would not be surprising to find that a power granted under the
Constitution is subject to limitations arising from the character of
the Constitution in which it is embedded. The Constitution exists in
a context and that context unavoidably implies assumptions about

the meaning of terms, the behaviour of the relevant actors, and the scope of rights or powers that are granted. These assumptions serve to delimit the scope of a constitutional provision. Such implicit limits are repeatedly recognized in Canadian jurisprudence.[44]

If the power granted legislatures under section 33 were without limits, it would mean that the drafters of the Canadian Charter granted legislatures the power to entirely supplant, without restriction, the very same rights which the drafters so eloquently declared in section 1 to be guaranteed in the Charter. That guarantee is given legal form by being entrenched through the Charter's onerous amending formula, which erects significant legislative barriers to any modification of those rights. It should give us pause before accepting that the same drafters simultaneously authorized the override of key rights and freedoms, without restriction, by ordinary laws adopted by simple legislative majorities. The inherent contradiction between the guarantee of rights and the override power would be most acute if the latter may be used to deny the very core of what is said, in section 1, to be constitutionally guaranteed.

The history of section 33 militates against the rather radical view that the power granted by section 33 is without limits other than the modest formal requirement of clarity imposed by the terms of the provision itself. That history is often presented as a last-minute compromise forced on then-Prime Minister Trudeau to gain the agreement of several recalcitrant provincial premiers.[45] Dwight Newman offers a more refined history in which he argues that the view of a simple last-minute compromise is incomplete. Rather, he argues, the notwithstanding clause had roots in careful and consistently espoused arguments by Premiers Blakeney and Lougheed.[46] Premier Blakeney was concerned that an overly absolutist interpretation of the enumerated rights could make it impossible to legislate other basic social and economic rights, which he called "moral rights," such as a right to basic health care.[47] Premier Lougheed was concerned that an unconstrained judiciary, which rendered decisions with which the legislatures could not agree, could end up undermining the judiciary itself by triggering a political response such as court-packing. On this view, section 33 was intended to be part of mutual checks and balances between the legislature and judiciary: "One key theme of his defence is that it [section 33] permits a certain responsiveness to interpretations of rights with which there is ultimate democratic disagreement."[48]

What emerges is that the proponents of including an override contemplated its use in the context of the *protection* of rights while safeguarding the integrity of constitutional institutions, including the independence of the judiciary itself. They did not conceive of it as authorizing the undermining of the core of what they had entrenched.

This context should point to substantive limitations on the purpose for which section 33 may be used. By context, I am referring to the fact that section 33 is placed within the Canadian Charter, whose primary purpose is to guarantee and safeguard the enumerated rights and freedoms, bolstered by the history of section 33, which shows that the original proponents of an override viewed it as part of a larger *rights-protecting* system. To jump immediately to my conclusion, it should be outside the power of a legislature to use section 33 to enact and enforce a law whose very purpose or object is incompatible with a liberal, democratic society respectful of the entrenched rights and freedoms. Such a law would be aimed at undermining the very structure of the Canadian Charter through a direct attack on the core of the guaranteed rights and freedoms themselves. It is an interesting question whether an attack on the foundation of the Constitution adopted through a formal constitutional amendment would, per force, be constitutional. However, it is submitted that it should clearly be outside the power of a legislature to co-opt section 33 for such a purpose.

This issue was raised by Slattery as early as 1983.[49] He proposed a hypothetical scenario of a severe economic downturn accompanied by a swing in popular sentiment against a particular racial group, leading a legislature to enact a law confiscating that racial group's property. He suggested that such a blatantly racist law would be so inimical to the foundations of the Charter that it could not be constitutional to enact it through section 33. Slattery's solution was to argue that section 33 should be understood as subject to section 1, but section 1 suitably interpreted and adapted to section 33.

Slattery wrote before the development of section 1 jurisprudence, notably *Oakes*. In light of that jurisprudence and the treatment of section 33 since *Oakes*, I do not believe it is open to us to simply adopt the Slattery position. As well, section 1, as we have seen, addresses *limits* on rights while section 33 creates an *exception* to the application of section 52. Nonetheless, section 1, particularly its two-step analysis, can be instructive in considering the limits that may apply to the power granted by section 33.

The overwhelming majority of Canadian Charter cases requiring a section 1 analysis are decided at the second step, the proportionality test. The proportionality test is used to assess whether the means chosen by the legislature to pursue its objective are reasonable and demonstrably justified. It is at this second step that courts are required to balance the interests of society with those of individuals and groups.[50]

Only rarely are cases decided at the first step of the section 1 analysis, which requires assessing whether the impugned legislation's objective is "of sufficient importance to warrant overriding a constitutionally protected right or freedom."[51] In *Oakes*, this is described as requiring "at a minimum, that an objective relate to concerns which are pressing and substantial in a free and democratic society before it can be characterized as sufficiently important."[52]

This first step acts as a threshold test which legislatures rarely fail to satisfy. The phrase "of sufficient importance" might suggest a *quantitative* assessment of the objective along some scale of importance. This may just be an unhappy choice of phrase, as an examination of the few cases in which a law has failed at this first step suggests that what is at issue is a *qualitative* assessment of whether the character of the impugned law's objective is such as to exclude it as a constitutionally legitimate objective.

Big M, a pre-*Oakes* case, was the first Canadian Charter case in which a law failed at this first step.[53] It was also among the early cases to elaborate a systematic approach to assessing the constitutional acceptability of a legislative limit on a guaranteed right or freedom. *Big M* considered the constitutionality of the Lord's Day Act, a law which prohibited various commercial activities on Sunday, the "Lord's Day." It is clear in *Big M* that the court was considering a threshold question of whether the character of the law qualified it to restrict rights:

81. Moreover, consideration of the object of legislation is vital if rights are to be fully protected. The assessment by the courts of legislative purpose focuses scrutiny upon the aims and objectives of the legislature and ensures they are consonant with the guarantees enshrined in the Charter. The declaration that certain objects lie outside the legislature's power checks governmental action at the first stage of unconstitutional conduct ... It will also allow courts to dispose of cases where the object is clearly improper, without inquiring into the legislation's actual impact.

...

85. If the acknowledged purpose of the Lord's Day Act, namely, the compulsion of sabbatical observance, offends freedom of religion, it is then unnecessary to consider the actual impact of Sunday closing upon religious freedom.[54]

Significantly for our purpose, the assessment of the legislation's objective is presented as being prior to the section 1 analysis.[55] This had been clearly stated in *Quebec Protestant School Boards* in a passage cited with approval in *Big M*:

An Act of Parliament or of a legislature which, for example, purported to impose the beliefs of a State religion would be in direct conflict with s. 2(a) of the Charter, which guarantees freedom of conscience and religion, and would have to be ruled of no force or effect *without the necessity of even considering whether such legislation could be legitimized by s. 1.*[56]

The significance of this is that this first step of the analysis is based on an underlying constitutional logic. It is not derived from the words of section 1.

Big M held that in view of the history of the Lord's Day Act, the unavoidable conclusion was that the act's primary purpose was to compel sabbatical observance. Compelling a religious observance was held to offend freedom of religion, similar to the hypothetical discussed in *Quebec Protestant School Boards*. Consequently, the act was held unconstitutional without the court having to even consider whether its impact or effects might be justified under the proportionality test. Stated otherwise, a law enacted for the purpose of violating the core of a guaranteed right is "in direct conflict" with that right and is, therefore, inimical to the Charter. This determination ends the analysis.

The fact that this first step of the constitutional analysis was subsequently, in *Oakes*, integrated into the section 1 analysis is a formal change which does not affect the underlying logic that the purpose test is based on a compelling constitutional logic, rather than being dictated by the words of section 1.

A similar conclusion emerges from *Zundel*, one of the few other cases to hold a law unconstitutional based on its illegitimate purpose.[57] *Zundel* challenged the false news provision of the Criminal Code under which he had been charged for spreading Holocaust denial. The Crown conceded that the government's purpose in enacting (or maintaining an ancient prohibition) was to restrict expressive activity. The majority noted that Parliament had not identified any social problem justifying the prohibition and concluded that no specific purpose was disclosed on the face of the provision. In the absence of an identified objective sufficient to justify overriding freedom of expression, the provision had to be declared unconstitutional.[58] In other words, the law restricted a protected freedom for no clearly identifiable purpose. Therefore, all the law could be said to do was to deny a fundamental right. That, concluded the majority, cannot be constitutionally acceptable.[59]

Without seeking to be necessarily exhaustive, the same limitation should be recognized in the power granted legislatures under section 33. It seems a reasonable, if not necessary, assumption that in granting that power, the drafters of the Canadian Charter took as given that the override would be used for purposes consonant with the entrenchment of fundamental, legal, and equality rights. Legislatures may differ with the courts on what is the proper balance between the protected individual rights and freedoms and collective interests. That is an issue weighed under the second step of the *Oakes* test, unless a legislature has declared, by recourse to section 33, that it is making the final determination.[60] However, a law whose objective is categorically illegitimate within the Canadian constitutional framework should not be able to be shielded by recourse to section 33 any more than it could be justified under section 1. In other words, a law which would fail at the first step of the *Oakes* test should not be capable of being "saved" by section 33.[61]

Take, as an example, a law imposing a state religion, the hypothetical considered in *Quebec Protestant School Boards* and frequently cited since then as an archetype of a categorically unconstitutional law. Such a law would be in direct conflict with the very core of freedom of religion. Section 33, conceived as part of a legitimate dialogue between the legislature and the judiciary regarding an appropriate balancing of rights and collective interests, could never have been designed to allow such a blatant denial of the very rights said to be protected by the Canadian Charter.[62]

A law enacted for the purpose of overriding the core of a protected right or freedom does not merely limit that right. It directly attacks the very existence of that right. There may be a legitimate disagreement between the courts and legislature over the extent to which, and circumstances in which, a right may be limited. However, a legislative attack directed against the right itself is more akin to a back-door attempt to amend the Canadian Charter to abrogate the right than it is a limit on the right. It is incompatible with the structure and underpinnings of the Canadian Charter to conceive of section 33 as permitting legislation to effectively override a guaranteed right in a manner which could not, on any reasonable conception of the right, be reconciled with the legislation.

Recall that section 1 declares that the rights and freedoms set out in the Canadian Charter are "*subject only* to such reasonable limits prescribed by law as can be demonstrably justified in a free and democratic society," and section 33 does not declare that it operates notwithstanding section 1. It is consistent with the language of sections 1 and 33 for the latter to be interpreted in a manner which does not allow it to be used for purposes which are incompatible with those fundamental values. It is one thing for courts and legislatures to disagree on how a basic right should be applied in given circumstances. That is a constitutionally legitimate dispute. Section 33 provides the mechanism by which the legislature may take upon itself the burden of having the final word in the dispute, even where the courts consider that the law in question unjustifiably (under section 1) infringes a guaranteed right. In such cases, the debate is over reasonable limits, on drawing lines between competing rights and purposes.

However, it is quite another thing to hold that section 33 allows a legislature to effectively abrogate a guaranteed right by shielding a law which has as its purpose a direct attack on the very core of that right. If that is allowed, then the rights and freedoms set out in the Canadian Charter cannot be said to be "*subject only* to such reasonable limits prescribed by law as can be demonstrably justified in a free and democratic society."

We can expect that few laws would fail this threshold review, just as there are few instances of laws failing at the first step of a section 1 analysis. However, it is possible to conceive of such laws. Sadly, examples can even be found within Canadian history, so this is not a purely theoretical issue.[63]

Returning to Bill 21, the Trial Judge acknowledged that the act has the declared purpose of establishing a "lay state." However, he sharply observed that laicity implies an absence of religion and that, in fact, Bill 21 does nothing other than remove rights from persons who wear religious symbols, without doing anything else to promote laicity.[64] A law whose purpose, indeed whose essence, lies in prohibiting a religious practice attacks the very core of freedom of religion as well as freedom of conscience and expression. It does so not as an incidental effect of the pursuit of another good. In and of itself, the suppression of the targeted expressions of religion is the "good" which is sought.[65] As a law whose purpose is to ban religious practice, Bill 21 should not be able to be shielded through the use of an override.

In *Oakes*, Dickson C.J. wrote: "Canadian society is to be free and democratic. The Court must be guided by the values and principles essential to a free and democratic society which I believe embody, to name but a few, respect for the inherent dignity of the human person, commitment to social justice and equality, accommodation of a wide variety of beliefs, respect for cultural and group identity, and faith in social and political institutions which enhance the participation of individuals and groups in society."[66] He wrote this in relation to the section 1 analysis the court was being called upon to undertake. However, the guiding principles he sets out are fundamental ones. There is little reason, I suggest, that they are not guideposts for constitutional interpretation more broadly.

The limits on section 33 proposed in this chapter leave considerable scope for legislatures to use section 33 to shield legislation which might otherwise be declared inoperative by the courts. Supporters and opponents of section 33 would continue to debate the legitimacy and wisdom of recourse to section 33, a debate that would fall to be decided in the political, not judicial, arena. However, the thesis of this chapter is that there are certain outer guardrails around the powers granted by section 33 which rest on fundamental constitutional principles, particularly a constitution with entrenched rights and freedoms.[67] The residual power of judicial review which flows from this thesis, even if little used, represents an important rampart protecting core values of Canada as a constitutional democracy in which the rights of minorities are not left to depend solely on the shifting goodwill of legislative majorities.

CONCLUSION

It is unnecessary to look beyond Canada's own history for examples of how it is precisely when there is a groundswell of public support for discriminatory action that the danger of the tyranny of the majority is at its greatest and the need for entrenched rights is most acute.[68] How is this danger addressed by those who contend that there are, and should be, no constitutional constraints whatsoever on the use of the override?

This question was put to Rousseau at *The Notwithstanding Clause at 40* conference. He provided two responses. The first was based on his historical review of the Quebec legislature's use of the notwithstanding clause since the 1970s. He argued that it shows that the override has only been used for "legitimate purposes in the collective interest." Therefore, misuse of the power is not a real concern. Yet, the 1970s is when Quebec first gained the benefit of a charter of rights, the Quebec Charter in 1975 and later the Canadian Charter. Prior to that, Quebec's history of respecting basic rights was, indeed, a spotty one. Significantly, as the Trial Judge pointedly noted, relying on Rousseau's own analysis, Bill 21 is the first time that Quebec has simultaneously overridden all the basic rights in both the Canadian and Quebec Charters. So, Bill 21 is now the prime example of how the legislature can treat minorities when unconstrained by any charter, especially minorities disfavoured in the public eye.

Rousseau's second response was particularly revealing. He argued that should a legislative majority choose to act "autocratically" against a minority, the proper remedy is to go door to door at the next election and convince the majority to vote differently. This extreme concept of unconstrained parliamentary sovereignty leaves minorities at the mercy of the majority. To remind ourselves how deeply rooted a popular view can be and how ingrained it can become against a minority, it is useful to recall the words of Chief Justice Taschereau, dissenting in the famous 1953 case of *Saumur v. City of Quebec.*[69] The City of Quebec had prohibited the distribution of pamphlets in public streets through an ostensibly neutral bylaw which, in fact, was found to have been aimed at preventing the distribution of materials by the Jehovah Witnesses, who were the repeated victims of harassment by the Quebec government for their beliefs. The Supreme Court, in a split decision, held that the bylaw could not be used to prevent the Witnesses from distributing their pamphlets. The chief justice dissented on the ground that the pith and substance of the bylaw was to control and regulate the usage of streets, but added that even if the city's motive was to prevent Jehovah's Witnesses from distributing their literature in the streets, that was not reason to declare the bylaw illegal or unconstitutional. To underscore his position, he quoted from a portion of the pamphlets' attacks on religion and the Vatican, and commented as follows: "Decency, moreover, would demand that I not quote more. And it seems to me unnecessary to do so to demonstrate that a municipality, 90 per cent of whose population is Catholic, has not only the right, but the duty, to prevent the dissemination of such infamies."[70] In other words, the chief justice supported the legislation because the expression was offensive to the majority's religion.

The idea that minorities' rights should not be at the mercy of the goodwill of the majority, lies at the heart of the revolution notably led by the majority in *Saumur* and followed by subsequent political developments during Quebec's Quiet Revolution, of which one of the notable events was the enactment of the Quebec Charter. The push to normalize the use of the notwithstanding clauses in both the Canadian and Quebec Charters, and to maximally invoke the override of fundamental rights and freedoms to make those rights depend on the "will of the majority," risks turning the clock back to the pre-*Saumur* era, to an approach rooted in a time prior to Quebec's Quiet Revolution.[71] In this context, it is all the more pressing that we consider whether our constitutional order allows the section 33 override to be used for any and all purposes or whether some purposes are constitutionally excluded.

NOTES

The author wishes to thank Professor Peter Benson for his thoughtful contributions. He also wishes to thank Mtre Christine Carron, Mtre Alexandra Belley-Mckinnon, and Mtre Jérémy Boulanger-Bonnelly for their comments on earlier drafts of this chapter. Of course, any errors or shortcomings in this chapter are those of the author alone.

1 See discussion in body of the chapter.
2 *Ford v. Québec (Attorney General)* [1988] 2 SCR 712.
3 Ibid., 740 (para. 33).
4 Ibid.
5 Act Respecting the Laicity of the State, CQLR c L-0.3 (Bill 21).
6 *Hak c. Procureur général du Québec*, 2021 QCCS 1466 (CanLII), rendered by Marc-André Blanchard J.C.S. (Trial Judge). The Trial Judgment declared Bill 21 constitutional on all but two points. The prohibition on members of the National Assembly exercising their function with their face covered (the act's other substantive prohibition) was held an unconstitutional infringement of section 3 of the Canadian Charter, and the ban

on wearing religious symbols and on exercising one's function with one's face covered and related provisions in the act, in so far as they apply to teachers, principals, and vice principals, were held to unjustifiably infringe the section 23 language rights of the English minority in Quebec and, therefore, to be of no force and effect in so far as they affect anyone who may benefit from the rights guaranteed by that section of the Charter. The author of this paper is a member of the Board of the Coalition Inclusion Québec, a public interest plaintiff in *Lauzon et al. c. Procureur général du Québec*, one of the four cases joined for trial.

7   The full list of persons subject to the prohibition is set out at Schedule II of Bill 21.

8   See the definition of "religious symbol" in section 6 of Bill 21, in particular the "subjective" criterion set out in section 6(1) and the apparently "objective" criterion set out in section 6(2). The fact that the definition draws no distinction between external, visible symbols and ones which are not visible was expressly asserted by the minister responsible for Bill 21, Simon Jolin-Barrette, at a 28 March 2019 press conference (Exhibit P-16 at the trial at first instance), and acknowledged by the attorney general at trial. See Trial Judgment, para. 320–6.

9   Preamble to Bill 21.

10 Trial Judgment, para. 379.

11 CQLR c C-12.

12 Section 9.1 of the Quebec Charter. Section 9.1 is usually treated by the courts as the equivalent of section 1 of the Canadian Charter in that it is the provision under which a court must weigh a violation of a protected right or freedom against the listed values to determine whether the violation is justified. The Quebec Charter governs the broad realm of private relations in addition to government action. Therefore. it will not be surprising if we find parties using the principles set out in Bill 21 to seek to justify discriminatory actions in private relations not covered by Bill 21, for example in hiring of staff at daycares. If the principles of equality and freedom of religion *require* teachers not to wear religious symbols in schools, is it not justified for a daycare to demand the same of its staff? Such arguments are invited by the lack of clarity in the logic underlying who is targeted by Bill 21. It remains to be seen whether courts will allow the prohibitions in Bill 21 to seep into relations beyond those specifically enumerated in the act. However, it is predictable that there will be pressures to extend the scope of the prohibitions.

13 Bill 21, section 33. The override is found at section 52 of the Quebec Charter. Its reach is broader than the reach of section 33 of the Canadian

Charter, as it covers sections 1 to 38, which include the chapters on
Fundamental Freedoms and Rights, Right to Equal Recognition and
Exercise of Rights and Freedoms, Political Rights, and Judicial Rights.
As well, there is no automatic sunset clause under the Quebec Charter. In
this chapter, I refer to the notwithstanding clause or override without distinction to refer to section 33 of the Canadian Charter and section 52 of
the Quebec Charter according to the context.

14 For a useful presentation of the early approaches to the notwithstanding
clause, see Tsvi Kahana, "Understanding the Notwithstanding
Mechanism," *University of Toronto Law Journal* 52 (2002): 221.

15 Guillaume Rousseau and François Côté, "A Distinctive Quebec Theory
and Practice of the Notwithstanding Clause: When Collective Interests
Outweigh Individual Rights," *Revue générale de droit* 47 (2017):
343–431.

16 This is clear throughout Kahana's review, "Understanding the
Notwithstanding Mechanism," and explicit at p. 268. This was also the
view expressed by the Trial Judge at para. 754: "However, by definition,
in a society concerned with respecting the fundamental rights it grants to
its members, use of the override clause must be done in a parsimonious
and circumspect manner." (author's translation)

17 Dwight Newman, "Canada's Notwithstanding Clause, Dialogue, and
Constitutional Identities," in *Constitutional Dialogue: Rights, Democracy,
Institutions*, eds. Geoffrey Sigalet, Gregoire Webber, and Rosalind Dixon
(Cambridge: Cambridge University Press, 2019), 209–25.

18 Ibid., 223–4.

19 The introduction of an automatic sunset clause at section 33(3), timed to
correspond to the maximum term of Parliament or a provincial legislature
under the Constitution, was designed to repeatedly force reconsideration
of the use of the override back on the public agenda at intervals at which
elections will be held. Peter Hogg and Wade K. Wright, *Constitutional
Law of Canada*, 5th ed. Supplemented (Toronto: Thomson Reuters, loose
leaf), ch. 39.

20 CQLR c C-11.

21 Trial Judgment, para. 768, author's translation, footnotes omitted.
Original:
*"Cependant, de façon plus remarquable et pertinente pour notre propos,
la Loi 21 constitue le premier texte législatif qui déroge simultanément
aux articles 1 à 38 de la Charte québécoise et 2 et 7 à 15 de la Charte
canadienne[538]. Donc, on ne peut que constater qu'en agissant ainsi le
constituant suspend, à l'égard de la Loi 21, presque l'ensemble des droits*

et libertés dans la province de Québec. Peu importe la perspective que l'on entretient face à la Loi 21, il faut souligner qu'il ne s'agit pas là d'une mince affaire, bien au contraire. Voilà pourquoi le Tribunal évoquait plus haut une certaine banalisation et indifférence quant à la portée réelle de l'exercice de dérogation. [Footnote 538: *Pour un tableau des lois utilisant les clauses dérogatoires, voir* Guillaume Rousseau *et* François Côté, "A distinctive Quebec Theory and Practice of the Notwithstanding Clause: When Collective Interests Outweigh Individual Rights," (2017) 47 *R.G.D.* 343, p. 423]."

22   Rousseau and Côté, "Distinctive Quebec Theory." In that work, Rousseau and Côté present an empirical analysis of Quebec writers and Quebec legislation. However, their own view is apparent notably in their concluding paragraph, at 422, which bears quoting in full: "And in the end, one thing remains certain. In the name of national democracy and parliamentary sovereignty, the final say in many crucial matters resides in the hands of the highest source of power: the people and its elected representatives ... which are precisely the objective that the notwithstanding clause – and the Quebec theory and practice of it that we exposed – aims to achieve."

23   The Trial Judge noted the existence of legislative precedent for targeted overrides, designed to be no wider than required. Trial Judgment, para. 772.

24   Even though it would still be necessary for the government to invoke the notwithstanding clause in the Canadian Charter, being able to publicly defend the ban as consistent with the Quebec Charter would lessen opprobrium associated with use of the override and also serve the political purpose of highlighting Quebec's distinctiveness.

25   On 3 November 2022, Ontario adopted Bill 28, An Act to Resolve Labour Disputes Involving School Board Employees Represented by the Canadian Union of Public Employees, SO, c. 19, which included an override of sections 2 and 7–15 of the Canadian Charter, as well as an override of Ontario's Human Rights Code. That act removed teachers' right to strike and provided steep fines for contraventions. The act, and particularly its recourse to the override, triggered strong protest from many sectors of society, including from the federal government, unlike the milder response to Quebec's uses of the notwithstanding clause and to the Ontario government's previous use of the notwithstanding clause. In the face of this political backlash, the government quickly chose to repeal the Act (Bill 35, An Act to Repeal the Keeping Students in Class Act, 2022, SO c. 20, enacted on 14 November 2022).

26 A generalized use of the override might be said, on Rousseau's logic, to be the ultimate expression of the principles of representative democracy and parliamentary sovereignty. It is worth recalling that Quebec was the first Canadian jurisdiction to enact a comprehensive charter of rights and freedoms and that the Quebec Charter preceded the Canadian Charter by seven years.

27 The present section focuses on the notwithstanding clause of the Canadian Charter. The equivalent clause in the Quebec Charter might raise somewhat different issues, given the law's quasi-constitutional status.

28 I do not address the source of the judicial power to issue declarations, only the rationale for doing so where the override has been invoked. Suffice to note that declaratory relief is among the types of relief which a court can grant pursuant to section 24 of the Canadian Charter. As well, in Quebec a court can issue a declaration pursuant to art. 142 of the Code of Civil Procedure, CQLR c C-25.01. See *Gosselin v. Québec (Attorney General)*, 2002 SCC 84 [2002] 4 SCR 429, para. 96.

29 Recall that pursuant to section 33(3), such a declaration automatically ceases to have effect after five years. Absent re-enactment of the override (section 33(4)), upon its lapse, the legislation is immediately subject to full Charter scrutiny.

30 The correlation between the effect of an override as provided in section 33 and the normal effect of a violation of a guaranteed pursuant to section 52 of the Canadian Charter is even clearer from the French version of section 52 which reads, "*Elle rend inopérantes les dispositions incompatibles de toute autre règle de droit.*" (emphasis added)

31 One finds a number of statements in Supreme Court jurisprudence which might be taken as asserting that recourse to section 33 overrides the rights and freedoms themselves. Perhaps the strongest is found in *Reference re Secession of Quebec* [1998] 2 S.C.R. 217 at para. 47, where the court wrote: "Moreover, it is to be remembered that s. 33, the 'notwithstanding clause,' gives Parliament and the provincial legislatures authority to legislate on matters within their jurisdiction in derogation of the fundamental freedoms (s. 2), legal rights (ss. 7 to 14) and equality rights (s. 15) provisions of the Charter." However, I am unaware of any case in which the court has explored or specifically scrutinized the mechanism by which section 33 operates and its implications. On the other hand, this issue has been subject of lively doctrinal debates: Robert Leckey and Eric Mendelsohn, "The Notwithstanding Clause: Legislatures, Courts and the Electorate," *University of Toronto Law Journal* 72, no. 2 (2022): 189, 195–6, 201–3, 206–8; Grégoire Webber, "Notwithstanding Rights,

Review, or Remedy? On the Notwithstanding Clause on the Operation of Legislation," *University of Toronto Law Journal* 71 (2021): 15; Maxime St-Hilaire and Xaiver Foccroulle Ménard, "Nothing to Declare: A Response to Grégoire Webber, Eric Mendelsohn, Robert Leckey, and Léonid Sirota on the Effects of the Notwithstanding Clause," *Constitutional Forum* 29, no. 1 (2020): 38–9.

32 There may also be practical reasons for a declaration. A declaration issued while the override is in effect could avoid a lengthy trial after the lapse of the override, a process which could unnecessarily, and avoidably, delay a remedy to a violation of Charter rights.

33 John Rawls, *Political Liberalism* (New York: Columbia University Press, 1996), 239 (emphasis added). This position is also akin to the "deliberative disagreement" approach proposed by Kahana in "Understanding the Notwithstanding Mechanism," 248.

34 See, for example, the following, as well as the authors referred to therein: Newman, "Canada's Notwithstanding Clause," 224–30; Rousseau, "Distinctive Quebec Theory," 359–73; Kahana, "Understanding the Notwithstanding Mechanism," 226–37, 248–50; Lorraine Eisenstat Weinrib, "Learning to Live with the Override," *McGill Law Journal* 35 (1990): 565–9.

35 *Ford v. Québec (Attorney General)*, para. 33.

36 Ibid., para. 25, 28–30, 32.

37 Ibid., para. 32.

38 Ibid., para. 35.

39 Ibid., para. 33.

40 Ibid.

41 Indeed, the court's conclusion striking down the retroactive application of the statute was not based on the text of section 33, which was indeterminate in that regard, but on general rules of statutory construction. *Ford*, para. 36. Underlying that rule of construction is the principle that individuals are entitled to know the law at the time they choose to act. Therefore, this brings to bear a principle of general application in the court's recognition of a restriction on legislature's use of section 33. It should also be noted that the discussion of section 33 in *Ford* is *obiter dictum*.

42 *A.G. (Que.) v. Quebec Protestant School Boards* [1984] 2 SCR 66 at p. 79 (emphasis added).

43 For example: *A.G. (Que.) v. Quebec Protestant School Boards*, p. 86; *R. v. Oakes* [1986] 1 S.C.R. 103 at para. 63; *Corp. Professionnelle des Médecins v. Thibault* [1988] 1 S.C.R. 1033 at para. 28 (referring to the override as the "exception clause"); *Vriend v. Alberta* [1998] 1 S.C.R. 493

at para. 139 (referring to "even overarching laws under s. 33 of the Charter").

44 For example: *Reference re Alberta Statutes* [1938] SCR 100 at 134–5; *Manitoba (A.G.) v. Metropolitan Stores Ltd.* [1987] 1 S.C.R. 110 at para. 50; *R. v. Big M Drug Mart Ltd.* [1985] 1 S.C.R. 295 and *R. v. Oakes* [1986] 1 S.C.R. 103, discussed below, seminal cases in the development of section 1 jurisprudence, which both rest their analysis on certain a priori understanding of the principles underlying what it means for Canada to be a free and democratic society and on the place of individuals, conceived as free persons with an inherent dignity, within that society; *Re Manitoba Language Rights* [1985] 1 S.C.R. 721, grounded on an understanding that our constitutional order as based on the continuing operation of an actual order of positive laws governing society.

45 See, for example, Kahana, "Understanding the Notwithstanding Mechanism," 223, and the sources cited there.

46 Newman, "Canada's Notwithstanding Clause," 214–19.

47 It seems that, using section 1, Canadian courts have done a better job at leaving room for such rights than Blakeney apparently feared, but this is beside the point.

48 Newman, "Canada's Notwithstanding Clause," 218.

49 Brian Slattery, "Canadian Charter of Rights and Freedoms – Override Clauses under Section 33 – Whether Subject to Judicial Review Under Section 1," *Canadian Bar Review* 61 (1983): 393.

50 *Oakes*, para. 70.

51 Ibid., 69.

52 Ibid.

53 See *R. v. Big M Drug Mart Ltd.*, note 44.

54 Ibid, para. 81, 85. See also para. 139.

55 Ibid, notably para. 81, 84, 142.

56 *A.G. (Que.) v. Quebec Protestant School Boards* [1984] 2 S.C.R. 66 at p. 88 (emphasis added).

57 *R. v. Zundel* [1992] 2 S.C.R. 731.

58 The majority, in *obiter*, did pursue the section 1 analysis based on a posited objective in order to meet the dissenting justices' arguments. This does not alter the conclusion that its own analysis was completed at the first step.

59 The dissenting justices did not contest this principle. Rather, they saw the act as pursuing a legitimate purpose, an analysis rejected by the majority.

60 Weinrib, "Learning to Live," usefully points to the different perspective which the judiciary and legislature should bring to the weighing process. It

is not necessary for the purposes of this chapter to dwell on that distinction. However, the approach proposed in this chapter seems to me to be consistent with the one propounded by Weinrib as long as her statement that section 33 allows denials of guaranteed rights (p. 567) is understood to mean that it allows denials of rights to have effect notwithstanding the violation of the rights.

61 Recall that prior to *Oakes*, this step was conceived as conceptually prior to the section 1 analysis. See notes 55 and 56 and accompanying text.

62 A somewhat analogous argument was raised by Beetz J. in a concurring opinion in *National Bank of Canada v. Retail Clerks' International Union et al.*, 1984 CanLII 2 (SCC), [1984] 1 S.C.R. 269 at p. 296: "*This type of penalty is totalitarian and as such alien to the tradition of free nations like Canada*, even for the repression of the most serious crimes. I cannot be persuaded that the Parliament of Canada intended to confer on the Canada Labour Relations Board the power to impose such extreme measures, even assuming that it could confer such a power bearing in mind the Canadian Charter of Rights and Freedoms" (Emphasis added).

63 Consider, for example, Canada's internment of Japanese Canadians, or even the prohibition on the distribution of tracts of Jehovah Witness' literature in Quebec on the ground that their religious content made it contrary to public order to allow them, a law eventually struck down by the Supreme Court in *Saumur v. City of Quebec* [1953] 2 S.C.R. 299.

64 Trial Judgment, para. 379, 367.

65 It is worth noting that the internal logic of Bill 21 does not dictate that the present ban on wearing religious symbols is necessarily limited to only the specific positions now targeted. There is no inherent reason that the logic underlying the law as it is now could not be extended to embrace other public positions. Indeed, Bill 21's amendment to imbed the principle of "laicity," undefined, in the Quebec Charter suggests that the principle can apply more broadly, even to relations between individuals. Therefore, if section 33 can constitutionally shield Bill 21 from judicial review, there would be no impediment to extending the ban to any, or every, public display of religion, a position which should not be inconceivable given the broad bans on public displays of religious symbols instituted in France.

66 *Oakes*, at para. 64.

67 To be clear, once the formal requirements of section 33 are met, the burden would have to rest on those contesting a law to demonstrate that it fails to meet the rather low threshold constitutional standard required of any legislation. This is different from a section 1 review.

68 See note 66.

69 Ibid.

70 Ibid., 318, author's translation. Original French: "*La décence, d'ailleurs, me commanderait de ne pas en citer davantage. Et cela ne me paraît pas nécessaire pour démontrer qu'une municipalité, dont 90 pour cent de la population est catholique, a non seulement le droit, mais le devoir, d'empêcher la dissémination de pareilles infamies.*"

71 Ironically, Bill 21 is frequently presented by its proponents as completing the Quiet Revolution. This is the position of the attorney general of Quebec set out in his appeal factum in the Bill 21 case and also adopted by several of the government's expert witnesses in that case. The minister responsible for Bill 21, Simon Jolin-Barette, described the bill at a press conference held on 28 March 2019, soon after the bill's introduction in the National Assembly, as "*la suite logique de la Révolution tranquille et de la déconfessionnalisation du système scolaire Québécois*" [the logical continuation of the Quiet Revolution and the deconfessionalization of – the Quebec school system].

15

Notwithstanding v. Notwithstanding: Sections 28 and 33 of the Canadian Charter of Rights and Freedoms

Mary Eberts

Often called the notwithstanding or *non obstante* clause, or even the override, section 33 of the Charter of Rights and Freedoms[1] provides that Parliament or the legislature of a province may expressly declare in legislation that it, or a provision of it, shall operate notwithstanding a provision included in section 2 or sections 7 to 15 of the Charter. This declaration lasts only five years, but it can be renewed.

Section 28 provides: "Notwithstanding anything in this Charter, the rights and freedoms referred to in it are guaranteed equally to male and female persons."

This chapter explores the relationship between section 33 and section 28 of the Charter, a relationship which has not yet been the subject of a judgment of a court of appeal in Canada, nor of the Supreme Court itself. As *Hak*,[2] the Bill 21[3] case in Quebec, shows, section 28 of the Charter may be particularly important when invocation of section 33 is done with respect to legislation presenting a potential violation of the equality rights of women.

Bill 21, passed in 2019, is the latest expression of Quebec's desire to laicise government services and activities. Legislation introduced in 2017 by the Liberal government[4] was tied up in litigation launched by the National Council of Canadian Muslims[5] until the Liberals lost the election in 2018 to François Légault and the Coalition Avenir Quebec. Légault promised during the campaign that his government would introduce the law once again, containing a notwithstanding clause,[6] and Bill 21 was the result.

Bill 21 forbids the wearing of religious symbols by those providing government services, ranging from members of the legislature to crown attorneys and classroom teachers. The legislation has had a particularly severe impact on Muslim women who wear the hijab or the burka. Since the adoption of the legislation, "every documented case of a person denied employment or having lost their job because they wear religious symbols is of a Muslim woman who wears the hijab."[7] The uncontested evidence on the trial record in *Hak* also shows that every documented case of a person who has had to remove their religious symbol in order to work is a Muslim woman who wears the hijab.[8] Further, uncontested statistics regarding Quebec's religious demographics and religious symbols worn show that Muslims constitute the second largest religious group in Quebec after Christians, and the hijab is worn by around 50 per cent of Muslim women in Quebec.[9]

The Supreme Court of Canada recognizes that a law which is neutral on its face will violate equality guarantees when the law has a disproportionate negative impact on a vulnerable group.[10] The statistics about the impact of Bill 21 on Muslim women who wear the hijab or burka support the argument that the bill constitutes indirect or impact discrimination, and is a violation of the women's right to substantive equality. Invoking section 33 to protect the bill squarely raises the question of whether section 15 or section 28 of the Charter can be successfully invoked to challenge that discrimination.

The Court of Appeal of Quebec authorized the claimants in *Hak* to add a section 28 claim to their pleadings, following a case conference in which they were, in effect, invited to do so.[11] The case, with the section 28 claim, was decided at first instance in 2021.[12] The Court of Appeal has now heard argument on the appeal in *Hak* and reserved judgment.[13]

In this chapter, I examine the relationship between sections 28 and 33 within the context of the kind of discrimination suggested by the facts in *Hak*. I draw substantially on the events leading to the inclusion of these sections in the Charter. The language of section 28, particularly its use of the word "persons," also brings into play the significance of that term in the history of Canadian women's long struggle for equality. Landmark cases in that struggle have focused on the meaning of the term "persons," making it both legally and constitutionally significant. Section 28 is only one of two places in the Charter where the term "person" is used.[14]

THE ARCHITECTURE OF THE CHARTER

I begin with a brief overview of the architecture of the Charter. In section 1, the Charter provides that it guarantees the rights and freedoms set out in it subject only to such reasonable limits prescribed by law as can be demonstrably justified in a free and democratic society. Section 28 provides that notwithstanding anything in this Charter, the rights and freedoms referred to in it are guaranteed equally to male and female persons.

Section 24(1), entitled "Enforcement of Guaranteed Rights and Freedoms," provides that anyone "whose rights and freedoms, as guaranteed by this Charter, have been infringed or denied may apply to a court of competent jurisdiction to obtain such remedy as the court considerers appropriate and just in the circumstances." Section 52(1) of the Constitution Act, 1982 provides that the Constitution of Canada is the supreme law of Canada and any law that is inconsistent with the provisions of the Constitution is, to the extent of the inconsistency, of no force or effect. The term "law" in this provision would include any law passed under the protection of section 33, because section 33 does not oust the operation of section 52.

The reach of section 33 includes those rights and freedoms in sections 2 and 7 to 15 of the Charter. Charter provisions excluded from the ambit of section 33 configure the Canadian democratic state. The democratic rights in section 3 affirm that every citizen has the right to vote and to run for office in parliamentary and legislative elections, sets a term length for Parliament and the legislatures requires annual sittings, and makes provision for emergencies.[15] Section 6 provides to every citizen of Canada mobility rights and the right to gain a livelihood in any part of Canada.

Sections 16 to 20, dealing with the official languages of Canada and New Brunswick, combine declarations of the status of English and French with specific language rights dealing with the courts, legislatures, and government of either jurisdiction. Section 23 provides for minority language educational rights. The protection of language and minority language rights, along with the provision of mobility rights, reflect Pierre Trudeau's vision of a country where a francophone person could be comfortable anywhere, even outside Quebec.

Section 28 thus shares with some fundamental features of our democratic state the freedom from section 33. One may also observe that a counterpart to section 28, dealing specifically with the equality of Indigenous women, is also outside the reach of section 33, by reason of its location in section 35 of the Constitution Act, 1982. Section 35(4) was added as a result of the First Ministers' Conference on Aboriginal and Treaty Rights in 1983.[16] It provides that "notwithstanding any other provision of this *Act,* the aboriginal and treaty rights referred to in subsection (1) are guaranteed equally to male and female persons." It is significant that both of these fundamental statements about the equality of women and men are beyond the reach of the notwithstanding clause.

ORIGINS OF SECTIONS 33 AND 28

Section 33

Section 33 was added to the Charter after the Supreme Court of Canada determined that legally Canada could on its own seek patriation of the Charter, but constitutional conventions require that it seek agreement of the provinces.[17] The provincial argument in this case had focused to a large extent on the fact that the proposed Charter of Rights would limit or suppress provincial legislative power. This ruling in *Re Resolution to Amend the Constitution* effectively ended the plan Trudeau had pursued since 1980 of Canada on its own seeking patriation in the face of provincial opposition. The need for provincial support for the patriation effort, and the provinces' concern about the Charter's limitation on their power to legislate, were the essential drivers behind section 33. The agreement on section 33 broke the impasse between the federal and provincial governments and allowed the patriation project to proceed. Section 33 did, however, have origins in earlier stages of the patriation process; it was not an overnight creation.

The premiers opposed to Canada's unilateral patriation of the Constitution included a notwithstanding clause in the materials they brought to the November 1981 Federal-Provincial First Ministers' Conference, held 2 to 5 November in Ottawa.[18] Adams and Bower point out that a notwithstanding clause had featured not only in common law but also in Canadian constitutional history, and argue that the one created in November 1981 was not an innovation.[19] They refer in particular to the clause inserted into the 1960 Canadian Bill of Rights.[20] They point out that in the era of parliamentary sovereignty, a subsequent legislative enactment was taken to amend a prior one.

In such circumstances, the notwithstanding clause in the Bill of Rights was meant to ensure that any future derogations from the protected rights and freedoms would not arise by operation of law alone, or be in doubt, but "would need to be explicit, deliberate, transparent, and subject to the exposed debate and criticism of the democratic process."[21]

What became section 33 was part of the famous "Kitchen Accord,"[22] forged in the late hours of 4 November between Jean Chrétien, Roy Romanow, and Roy McMurtry.[23] All the provinces still present at the conference on 5 November agreed with the Kitchen Accord; Quebec had left the meeting on 4 November, before it was arrived at.

Of those involved in framing the Kitchen Accord, Alan Blakeney posits perhaps the most broadly based purpose for the notwithstanding clause. His point of view is set out in response to John Whyte's suggestion that the clause allows the legislature or executive to decide that a rights breach is not as important as a particular government policy, or to legislate pursuant to its disagreement with the court's interpretation of rights.[24] In challenging Whyte's description as under-inclusive, Blakeney states that some rights were included in the Charter because infringements of those rights were best addressed by judicial action, while others are best enforced by legislative executive or administrative action and so were not included in the Charter.[25] Use of the notwithstanding clause would allow governments to protect those rights not included in the Charter; in that sense, section 33 as well as section 1 are capable of mediating between rights.[26]

Roy McMurtry has described section 33 as "a form of balancing mechanism between the legislators and the courts in the unlikely event of a decision of the courts contrary to the public interest."[27] Jean Chrétien referred to the section as a "safety valve which is unlikely ever to be used except in non-controversial circumstances." That safety valve can be used to "correct absurd situations without going through the difficulty of obtaining constitutional amendments."[28] McMurtry and Chrétien reiterated this understanding of the purpose of section 33 in a statement they issued with Roy Romanow in 2018, responding to Premier Ford's intention to use the override in Ontario for the first time: "The clause was designed to be invoked by legislatures in exceptional situations, and only as a last resort after careful consideration. It was not designed to be used by governments as a convenience or as a means to circumvent proper process."[29]

Not just the "framers" of section 33, quoted above, but legal scholars, take the view that section 33 is to be exercised responsibly.[30] Dwight Newman's review of the context of the adoption of section 33, including the remarks of Premiers Blakeney and Lougheed, leads to his conclusion that section 33 "was not an incoherent compromise and was not a rights override, but adopted to permit legislatures to protect unenumerated rights and to engage in reasonable disagreements with courts about rights."[31] He posits that the notwithstanding clause has two key purposes. First, the text of section 33 creates a means by which legislatures may act in light of rights beyond those enumerated in the Charter when Charter rights interfere with those rights. Secondly, the text creates a means by which legislatures may engage with and disagree with judicial interpretations of rights.[32]

The Supreme Court of Canada has held, however, that the language of section 33 "imposes requirements of form only and there is no warrant for importing into it grounds for substantive review of the legislative policy in exercising the override authority."[33] Such a minimalist approach seems to leave available and potentially valid, at least for now, all the various reasons for using the notwithstanding clause mentioned above.

Section 28

SIGNIFICANCE OF THE WORD "PERSON"

For almost two centuries, women's struggle for equality in Canada and Britain included cases aimed at establishing that in law, the term "person" includes the female as well as the male.[34] The exclusion of women from the term "person" was a major form of systemic discrimination against them, which took over 150 years of litigation and legislative reform to overcome.

In Canada, an early focus of this effort was establishing the right of women, as "persons," to practice law and to become members of the Senate, both of which are essential to full citizenship. Clara Brett Martin, the first woman called to practice law in Ontario and the commonwealth, was able to enter the legal profession only after legislation was passed to establish her eligibility as a woman to be admitted as a solicitor[35] and as a barrister.[36]

The Law Society of New Brunswick and the province's supreme court refused to authorize Mabel Penery French to practice law on the ground that she was not a "person" as required by the profession's governing statute,[37] and legislation was required to secure her admission.[38] When she later applied for admission to the bar in British Columbia, the British Columbia Supreme Court rejected her argument that she was a person entitled to practice law,[39] and legislation was again required to secure her admission to the bar.[40]

In 1915, the Quebec Superior Court refused Annie Langstaff MacDonald the opportunity to take the provincial bar examination on the grounds of public order, good morals, and public decency.[41] The Quebec Court of Appeal refused her appeal.[42] Legislation was finally passed by Quebec in 1941[43] allowing women to be called to the bar in Quebec, after eleven other women had tried unsuccessfully to do so. In 1956, women became eligible to be notaries in Quebec. When women entered legal academia in the 1970s, they wrote about these struggles, which became part of Canadian women's growing understanding of the link between personhood and their full equality.[44]

The most famous of the "persons" line of cases was brought by women arguing that they were "persons" eligible to be called to the Senate pursuant to section 24 of the Constitution Act, 1867. The Supreme Court of Canada ruled against the arguments of the "Five Persons" (Henrietta Muir Edwards, Nelly McClung, Louise McKinney, Emily Murphy, and Irene Parlby).[45] On appeal, the Judicial Committee of the Privy Council determined that women are "persons," and thus within the terms of section 24.[46]

The enduring systemic discrimination against women in public life confronted in the Persons case has been described as follows: "Legal precedent stretching back to Roman law was cited for the proposition that women had always been considered 'unqualified' for public life, and it was argued that this common understanding in 1867 was incorporated in s. 24 of the Constitution Act, 1867, and should continue to govern Canadians in succeeding ages."[47]

In response to such arguments, Viscount Sankey formulated the observation that the Constitution "planted in Canada a living tree capable of growth and expansion within its natural limits."[48] The Supreme Court has held that the living tree doctrine requires that narrow technical approaches are to be eschewed, and that the past plays a critical but non-exclusive role in determining the content of the rights and freedoms in the Charter.[49]

The *Persons* case has become a Canadian symbol of women's progress against centuries of inequality. The Five Persons are recognized with a sculpture on Parliament Hill, and Canada has declared 18 October "Persons Day." On Persons Day in 2021, the prime minister recognized the progress in women's equality brought about by the "landmark" *Persons* case, but said, "We have much to do ... we cannot leave half the country behind as we move forward."[50] Being recognized as a person under law, equal to male persons, is for Canadian women a powerful signal of their triumph over centuries of systemic discrimination against them.

WOMEN BECOME INVOLVED IN PATRIATION PROCEEDINGS
It had become clear to many women's rights advocates by the 1970s that the equality guarantees of the Canadian Bill of Rights were ineffectual against entrenched inequality based on sex.[51] The difficulty of overcoming the resistance of courts and legislatures with the tools available to women under Canadian law gave rise to an interest in the entrenched rights protections of the US Bill of Rights and in the campaign by American women for an equal rights amendment.

Even before Canada took definite steps toward repatriating the Constitution in 1980, Canadian women had also begun to realize how closely their hopes for equality were associated with the project of constitutional renewal, which had been underway for the previous decade. The first Canada-wide Divorce Act[52] had been passed in 1968. Only ten years later, Prime Minister Trudeau announced his government's willingness to cede divorce jurisdiction to the provinces. There had been no prior consultation with women about this initiative. Concerned that this step would mean a return to a patchwork of provisions and difficulty in enforcing orders from province to province, Canadian women strongly opposed it. By 1980, women's lobbying had derailed the federal proposal. After this experience, women seeking equality gave a high priority to constitutional matters.[53]

On 2 October 1980, Prime Minister Trudeau presented to the House of Commons a "Proposed Resolution for a Joint Address to Her Majesty the Queen Respecting the Constitution of Canada," which contained the government's desired constitutional amendments, including the draft Canadian Charter of Rights and Freedoms. A Special Joint Parliamentary Committee on the Constitution established by the prime minister then had several months of hearings, during which it received over a thousand submissions by groups and individuals.[54] Among the submissions were those from the National Association of Women and the Law (NAWL),[55] the National Action Committee on the Status of Women (NAC),[56] and the Canadian Advisory Committee on the Status of Women (CACSW)[57] commenting on the draft Charter.[58]

These submissions covered a range of topics,[59] including the unseemly breadth of the draft section 1, argument against the delay of three years in the coming into force of section 15, and the need to use the term "person" uniformly throughout the Charter. The recommendations with respect to the draft of section 15 included changing the title from "Anti-Discrimination Rights" to "Equality Rights," and adding the phrase "equality under the law" to make it clear that the section guaranteed substantive equality not just equality in enforcement and administration of the law. The submissions also advocated that the guarantee encompass not only the equal protection of the law, but also equal benefit of the law. These specific recommendations were aimed directly at the disappointing Supreme Court rulings in the *Bedard*, *Lavell*, and *Bliss* cases.[60]

The grounds of discrimination listed in the draft of section 15 were critiqued not only on the basis that the list was under-inclusive. Jurisprudence on the Fourteenth Amendment considered certain legislative classifications, like race, to be inherently suspect, and subjected them to strict scrutiny. Legislation based on such classifications could be justified only by a compelling state interest. At the opposite extreme, classifications not seen as inherently suspect could be justified if there was a reasonable basis for them. At that time, the American jurisprudence seemed to place the ground of sex somewhere in between those two categories, and strict scrutiny was not applied to sex-based distinctions. CACSW and NAWL argued that under the Charter's equality guarantees, sex should be treated as a suspect classification and subject to strict scrutiny, like race.[61] Beverley Baines, legal advisor to both CACSW and the Ad Hoc Committee of Canadian Women on the Constitution during the patriation process, identifies the basic point of submissions like these: "To challenge the prevailing hierarchy that treated sex discrimination as less heinous than some other forms of discrimination."[62]

Importantly, even at this stage, prior to the inclusion of section 33 in the Charter, the submissions of the National Association of Women and the Law recommended that the Charter include a "purpose clause" to guarantee the equal right of men and women to the enjoyment of civil political and economic rights set forth in the Charter. This would be "an over-riding statement of principle" to be used in the interpretation of the Charter.[63] Although the NAWL submission used the word "interpretation," it was clear that the purpose clause was to be more than a simple interpretive provision. It was meant to make the equality of men and women a guiding principle of the Charter.

When it introduced a new draft of the Charter on 12 February 1981, the government of Canada acknowledged the role of women's group submissions in the changes it made to sections 1 and 15.[64] In the first Supreme Court decision dealing with section 15, *Andrews v. Law Society of B.C.*,[65] Justice McIntyre specifically acknowledged that the expanded array of equality rights in section 15 was "deliberately chosen" to remedy some of the perceived deficits in the Canadian Bill of Rights.[66] He referred directly to the *Bedard*, *Lavell*, and *Bliss* cases.[67] His reasons for judgment also clearly establish that the impact of a law must be considered in order to assess whether it perpetuates inequality.[68] He stated: "Every difference in treatment between individuals under the law will not necessarily result in inequality ... and identical treatment may frequently produce serious inequality."[69] The reasons make clear that the language changes advocated by women in 1980 and accepted by government had indeed ensured that section 15 protects "substantive equality," not just equality in process and administration. The Supreme Court has recognized substantive equality as the "animating norm" of section 15.[70]

THE AD HOC CONFERENCE

Some key recommendations made by women's groups to the Special Joint Committee were not taken up by government. The three-year delay in the coming into force of section 15 remained in the draft legislation. The government did not accept that "person" should be used throughout the Charter, and the amended Charter did not include a purpose clause affirming women's equality. Women's equality advocates were alarmed by these omissions. They were also concerned by the addition to the January 1981 version of the Charter a new section (now 27) directing interpretation of the Charter to be consistent with the preservation and enhancement of the multicultural heritage of Canadians. This, they considered, might bring into Charter interpretation practices inimical to the safety and equality of women.[71]

An immediate concern was that Canada seemed to be sabotaging plans by the Canadian Advisory Council on the Status of Women to promote further discussion of the Charter by Canadian women. Under what many considered to be pressure from the federal government, the council cancelled its national conference on the Charter scheduled for 14 February 1981. Relations between the organized women's movement and the government of Canada had not been smooth since the tabling of Canada's Charter proposals, but they had reached a crisis point by the end of January 1981. Noted Canadian journalist Doris Anderson resigned as chair of the advisory council, and the opportunity to discuss the government's January 1981 draft Charter seemed to have been lost.[72]

However, a group soon to be known as the Ad Hoc Committee of Canadian Women on the Constitution rapidly organized a huge national conference of women on 14 February 1981, the date originally intended for the cancelled CACSW conference. Over 1,200 women[73] attended the Ad Hoc conference, which produced a suite of recommendations for further Charter reform.[74] The very first item on the list of required changes was the addition of a statement of purpose providing that the rights and freedoms set out in the Charter are guaranteed equally to men and women with no limitations. The proposed wording of the Purpose Clause was, "The Canadian Charter of Rights and Freedoms guarantees to men and women equally the rights and freedoms set out in it."[75]

The Ad Hoc Committee began lobbying efforts on 16 February, right after the close of the conference, with particular focus on the Purpose Clause; they sought to have it included in section 1 of the Charter.[76] By 18 March 1981, all political parties had pledged their support for the Purpose Clause, and on that day, representatives of the Ad Hoc Committee met for a drafting session with federal officials. They brought with them a draft of the Purpose Clause,[77] which by then included the notwithstanding language.

At the 18 March meeting, though reluctant, the government officials accepted the Ad Hoc Committee's insistence on inclusion of the "notwithstanding" language.[78] In the 18 March meeting, Ad Hoc representatives also explained their use of the term "persons" (which was accepted for inclusion in the section) by reference to the *Persons* case.[79] The Ad Hoc delegation did not succeed in having the clause inserted in section 1. A compromise was reached that saw it inserted where it now appears as section 28. Beverley Baines, the legal advisor in the delegation, later wrote: "This clause was understood by all present as having the same effect as if the provision had appeared in s. 1."[80]

Kerri Froc concludes that the core language of section 28 was "virtually unchanged" from the words proposed by NAWL to the Special Joint Committee and the language of the Purpose Clause resolution at the Ad Hoc Conference.[81] Sandra Burt states that in this drafting session, the Ad Hoc Committee had succeeded in "demanding and obtaining what they felt was an iron-clad guarantee" of the equality rights of women.[82]

On 23 April 1981, the NDP motion in the House of Commons to include section 28 in the draft Charter that formed part of the Patriation Resolution was accepted unanimously.[83] The next stage in the development of section 28 occurred after the Kitchen Accord agreed on section 33 of the Charter in early November 1981.

ESCAPING SECTION 33

Initially, there was uncertainty about whether section 33 would apply to section 28, but on 9 November the prime minister announced in the House of Commons that it would.[84] There began a vigorous two-week campaign to have section 28 released from section 33,[85] involving women and their allies across the country, and focused to a large extent on provincial premiers. During that time, NDP leader Ed Broadbent stated in the House of Commons, "We must restore the original positive wording of section 28, which ensures the paramountcy of the principle that men and women are equal."[86] Conservative Leader Joe Clark described section 28 as "another step forward" in guaranteeing the equality of status of male and female persons, "similar in importance to the *Persons* case."[87]

After Premier Alan Blakeney of Saskatchewan signified his consent (the last premier to do so), Joe Clark made a motion in the House of Commons to amend the draft Charter in the Patriation Resolution so as to remove section 28 from section 33. It passed unanimously on 24 November 1981.[88] Both sections use the term "notwithstanding," and as de Jong argues, there is nothing in the text of the Charter to suggest that "notwithstanding" would have a different, or less powerful, meaning in section 28 than it does in section 33.[89] This linguistic equivalency makes decisive the fact that section 28 was specifically removed from the effect of section 33 after November 1981.

LESSONS FROM THE HISTORY OF SECTION 28

Because Canada declined the recommendation to use "person" throughout the Charter, its appearance in section 28 is significant. Its uniqueness gives it meaning. That meaning lies in its association with the *Persons* case, and women's history of seeking their full personhood at law. Historically the full "person" was the male person. That section 28 guarantees the rights and freedoms in the Charter equally to male and female persons means that women have reached a significant milestone. They are full rights holders under the Constitution of Canada. In that, they are equal to men, long the apex rights holders in Canadian and British law. There can be no more powerful guarantee of women's substantive equality with men.

The section's history shows that making women full rights holders, and fully equal to men, was its purpose. The pathway from the "purpose clause" recommended by NAWL, to the resolution of the Ad Hoc Committee, and then on to the language of section 28, makes that clear. The history of the section also shows that government accepted that purpose. Motions to include section 28 in the Charter, and then to pull it out from under section 33, were unanimously passed by the House of Commons. The Charter, with section 28 in it, was successfully patriated from the United Kingdom.

Section 28 is, therefore, an equality "guarantee," both by its explicit language and also by its intent. To say that it is merely an interpretive provision is to adopt a narrow technical approach to its language, contrary to the intent of the *Persons* case itself. As Cee Strauss contends, section 28 can be both an interpretive provision and a declaration of substantive equality.[90] Moreover, the language of section 28 differs greatly from section 27, which is explicitly stated to be an interpretive provision. Section 28 uses the term "guarantee," crucial and rarely used rights-conferring language in this Charter. As de Jong points out, the term "guarantee" is used in both declaratory and directive capacities to command those to whom the Charter applies to obey and enforce the rights and freedoms so guaranteed.[91]

INTERPRETATION OF SECTION 28 ... SO FAR

Elmer Driedger stated of section 28, "This section means and accomplishes nothing."[92] While somewhat kinder, Peter Hogg seems equally dismissive. In a passage referred to by Chief Justice Duval Hesler in *Hak*, he says that the language of section 28 "falls short of a requirement of the equal treatment of 'male and female persons' presumably because that objective is attained by the general equality clause of s. 15. All that s. 28 seems to require is that the other provisions of the Charter be implemented without discrimination between the sexes. To the extent that the other provisions of the Charter would apply equally to male and female persons anyway, s. 28 has very little work to do."[93]

Strauss observes that since at least the mid-1990s, courts have primarily perceived section 28 as redundant or ineffectual. The usual position has been that section 28 is an interpretive provision only.[94]

In *Boudreau v. Lynch*,[95] the Appeal Division of the Nova Scotia Supreme Court rejected an argument that section 28 could be used as a stand-alone sex equality guarantee during the three-year hiatus in the coming into force of section 15, in order to support a male plaintiff's argument that the Family Benefits Act discriminates against him on the basis of sex.[96] Rather, Hart J.A. observed that the attorney general of Nova Scotia had argued that section 28 was only intended to counter the legislative override provision of section 33 with respect to any form of sexual discrimination.[97] He observed that the framers of the Constitution "have treated sexual discrimination as the most odious form of discrimination" and prevented it from being carried on under the legislative override provision.[98]

The relationship between sections 28 and 33 was considered by the Quebec Superior Court in *Syndicat de la function publique du Quebec Inc. c Quebec (Procurateur General)*.[99] Julien J. of the superior court asked what is the purpose of section 28, given that section 15 protects the equality between the sexes. She concludes: "*L'article 28 protégerait de façon particulière le droit à l'égalité des sexes. Le législateur ne pourrait y déroger par application de l'article 33.*"[100]

SECTIONS 28 AND 33 ADDRESS IMPACT DISCRIMINATION AGAINST MUSLIM WOMEN

Sections 15 and 28 Together

Section 33 provides for a declaration that legislation or a provision thereof "shall operate notwithstanding a provision included in section 2 or sections 7 to 15" of the Charter. Section 33 does not repeal any provision of sections 2 or 7 to 15. Section 33 merely suspends the operation of the targeted right or freedom with respect to the legislation in which the section 33 invocation appears. That right remains in full operation vis-à-vis all other legislation. Nor does invocation of section 33 eliminate the jurisprudence interpreting the targeted right or freedom. It remains in existence to be used in cases where section 33 is not a barrier to its application, and to inform analysis of particular equality problems.

All that being said, however, it is still no easy matter to determine the most effective way of deploying sections 15 and 28 together to address inequality like that visited by Bill 21 upon Muslim women who wear the burka or hijab. Two remedial avenues present themselves. To obtain a remedy pursuant to subsection 24(1) of the Charter, applicants must establish that their rights or freedoms are "guaranteed" by the Charter, and that they have been infringed or denied. Section 52 of the Charter provides that "any law which is inconsistent with the provisions of the Constitution is, to the extent of the inconsistency, of no force or effect." A claimant can seek a declaration under either section 24 or section 52. Section 24 offers the possibility of other remedies like injunctions or damages.

The question of the relationship between sections 15 and 28 becomes important in a case like *Hak* because the effect of section 33 is to suspend the operation of section 15. Does suspension mean that the section 15 right is no longer "guaranteed" as required by section 24? Can a suspended right be "infringed or denied," as required by section 24, if suspension means it does not afford the litigant any protection in the first place? It can be argued, I suggest, that section 15 is still a right "guaranteed" by the Charter as required by section 24, even if its operation is suspended by section 33.

However, it is difficult to conceive how to argue that a suspended right has been infringed or denied; the question seems too close to an abstract issue of law upon which an advisory opinion is being sought. It has been argued that there is no impediment to claiming infringement or denial of section 15 rights which have been made subject to section 33. The argument on the merits of section 15's application to a statute like Bill 21 could proceed, but invocation of section 33 means that the court would not be able to grant a remedy.[101] Whether this is possible remains a question for a court to decide, in the exercise of its discretion.

In *Hak*, it was argued that section 28 could be invoked in aid of the guarantees of equality in section 15, to take those guarantees beyond the reach of section 33. The immunity of section 28 from application of section 33 would, under this argument, be somehow transferred, or lent, to section 15, thus invigorating it to resist the suspensive effect of a section 33 invocation. A remedy could then be sought under section 24(1) for the denial or infringement of the invigorated section 15.

To accept that a section 24(1) application depends for its viability and success on the invocation of section 15 (however invigorated that section needs to be by section 28) is to make the assumption that section 28 is not a stand-alone guarantee, but rather takes its meaning and effectiveness from its relationship with one of the guarantees in sections 2 or 7 to 15. If one accepts that assumption, it may be more correct to say that section 28 is in need of the support of section 15, in order to be a genuine rights "guarantee," rather than to say that section 15 is being assisted or invigorated by section 28.

In *Hak*, it was the latter argument, made on behalf of the procureur général du Quebec, which prevailed. It was argued that because section 33 applies to section 15, there no longer exists the required substrate of "right" upon which the language of section 28 can operate to guarantee the equality of women and men.[102]

It may be that the main lesson from this discussion is that section 28 and section 15 taken together *should* be able to support a remedy for the egregious violation of Muslim women's substantive equality caused by the impact of Bill 21. Whether section 28 is assisting section 15, or section 15 is the necessary underpinning for the operation of section 28, should make no difference.

Proceeding under section 52 of the Constitution Act, 1982, becomes an attractive option in such circumstances. One can argue that Bill 21 is inconsistent with "the provisions of the Constitution" which are found in sections 28 and 15, taken together, whether section 28 is taken to be supporting 15 or section 15 is providing the substrate for the operation of section 28. Use of the plural "requirements" in section 52 provides the opportunity to consider the combined effect of sections 15 and 28. Establishing inconsistency is a more general requirement than establishing infringement or denial. It is certainly inconsistent with the combined effect of sections 15 and 28 for Bill 21 to place so substantial a burden on Muslim women who wear the burka or hijab. Section 33, applying only to section 15, is an incomplete protection against the application to Bill 21 of section 52 of the Constitution Act, 1982.

Section 28 on Its Own

The history of section 28, in my view, provides strong support for the argument that section 28 is a free-standing guarantee of the equal rights of women. Declaring that women are equally entitled with men to the rights and freedoms in the Charter is a sound means of establishing women's equality as a purpose and principle of the Charter. If a woman is equal in basic constitutional rights to a man, historically the apex rights holder of Canadian and British law, then she has full equality, and it is guaranteed by the Charter.

The language of section 28 is confined to the traditional terms "women" and "men." Its presupposition of a gender binary reflects legal understandings at the time it was inserted into the Constitution. The challenge of Bill 21 does not require that a more extended or nuanced interpretation of section 28 be deployed; the discriminatory impact of the bill has been pleaded to be, and demonstrated to be, on women. Whether the language of section 28 can be broadened to include others does not arise on the facts of *Hak*. The case does, however, squarely raise the question of whether section 28 on its own can provide the basis for an application under either section 24(1) or 52 for a remedy addressing Muslim women's systemic inequality.

Section 28 is a guarantee of rights within the meaning of section 24(1). The term "guarantee" is expressly used in the section, and there is no justification for treating that use of "guarantee" any differently from its use in section 1. Some might argue that section 28 does not appear in a section of the Charter dedicated to rights-conferring provisions. This contention, in my view, can carry little or no weight. Location alone cannot overcome the powerful indications that section 28 was meant to confer rights. The history of the provision shows that it was treated throughout its development as a substantive *and* rights-conferring Purpose Clause, a close cousin to section 1. Its language is markedly stronger than an explicitly interpretive provision, section 27, which does appear in the same segment of the Charter. It should also be noted that section 28 and section 35(4), both immune from section 33 (albeit for different reasons),[103] both state that women are equal rights holders.

The treatment of Muslim women in Bill 21 infringes or denies the right to equality guaranteed by section 28. It is also "inconsistent" with section 28 within the meaning of section 52 of the

Constitution. The inequality in Bill 21 is not permitted or protected by section 33, because section 33 cannot suspend the operation of the section 28 guarantee. What remains, then, is for a court to examine whether the imposition of discrimination on Muslim women is justified within section 1 of the Charter. In any such analysis, the presence of section 33 cannot be used as a justificatory factor. I agree with Premier Blakeney that section 1 and section 33 are two separate ways of mediating between the power of the legislature and the commands of the Charter, as interpreted by the courts. They cannot be doubled up.

CONCLUSION

Since patriation, section 28 has often been dismissed as merely interpretive, or even meaningless. However, when examined in detail vis-à-vis legislation purportedly protected by section 33, it is clear that while it may be useful as an interpretive provision, it is also without doubt a rights-conferring provision. It is immune from suspension pursuant to section 33. It is long past time for the substantive worth of section 28 to be recognized, so that its strength can be deployed against blatant systemic discrimination like that facing the Muslim women of Quebec.

NOTES

1 Part I of the Constitution Act, 1982, Schedule B to Canada Act, 1982 (UK) 1982, c.11.

2 *Hak v. Procureur Général du Québec*, 2021 QCCS 1466. For commentary on the impact of section 28 on Bill 21, see: Samir A. Alam and Kerri A. Froc, "Quebec's Secularism Bill Violates Canada's 'Equal Rights Amendment,'" CBA/ABC National, 17 April 2019; Rebecca James et al., "Contesting Discrimination in Quebec's Bill 21: Constitutional Limits on Opting Out of Human Rights," *Directions* (November 2019): 1; Cee Strauss, "Section 28's Potential to Guarantee Substantive Gender Equality in *Hak v. Procureur Général du Québec*," CJWL/RFD 3 (2021), 84; Kerri A. Froc, "Shouting into the Constitutional Void: Section 28 and Bill 21," *Constitutional Forum constitutionnel* 28, no. 4 (2019), https://doi.org/10.21991/cf29391.

3 *La loi sur la laïcité de L'Etat*, L.Q. 2019, c.L-0.3.

4 Bill 62, S.Q. 2017, c.19, passed 18 October 2017.

5 The Quebec Superior Court granted two stays in the coming into effect
   of section 10 of the act, which stated that providers and seekers of
   government services covered by the act's schedules should have their faces
   covered. *National Council of Canadian Muslims (NCCM) et al. v. Attorney
   General of Quebec*, 2017 QCCS 5459 and 2018 QCCS 2766. In an
   unrelated case, the Quebec Court of Appeal ruled that a lower court judge
   had wrongly denied a woman wearing a hijab the right to be heard on a
   Highway Safety Code matter, because she was acting from a sincerely held
   religious belief and wearing the hijab does not conflict with overriding
   public interest. *El-Alloul v. Procureur Général du Québec*, 2018 QCCA
   2611.

6 Lucy Uprichard, "What Is Quebec's Secularism Law – And How Does It
   Affect Women?" *Chatelaine*, 6 November 2018, https://chatelaine.com/
   news/quebec-secularism-bill-21-women/.

7 Brief of the Incidental Appellants English Montreal School Board,
   Mubeenah Mughal and Pietro Mercuri, 2 December 2021, in *Attorney
   General of Quebec et al. v. Hak et al.*, Court of Appeal of Quebec, on
   appeal from a judgment of the Superior Court, District of Montreal,
   rendered 20 April 2021 (*"English Montreal School Board CA Factum"*)
   at paras. 11 and 16.

8 *English Montreal School Board CA Factum*, para. 16.

9 Ibid., para. 16.

10 *Fraser v. Canada (Attorney General)* 2020 SCC 28, at 40, 30 (*"Fraser"*).

11 *Hak v. Procureur Général du Québec*, 2019 QCCA 2145 at paras. 3,
   27–39, 50–9.

12 Ibid.

13 The case was heard in the Court of Appeal in November 2022.

14 The other is section 11, which protects a "person" charged with a crime.

15 The principle of democracy (and its attributes in Canada) were not dealt
   with in the Constitution Act, 1867 itself. To have done so, suggested the
   Supreme Court in the *Secession Reference*, "might have appeared redundant, even silly, to the framers." *Reference re Secession of Quebec* [1998]
   2 SCR 217 at para. 62.

16 By means of the Constitutional Amendment Proclamation, 1983
   (31/84-102).

17 *Re Resolution to amend the Constitution* [1981] 1 SCR 753, 772–808.
   The court stated that the federal houses have "untrammeled" authority at
   law to adopt and submit to Her Majesty for action by the UK Parliament
   the proposed resolution about patriation, and are not subordinated to
   provincial assent, although the legislative powers of the provinces would

be limited by the Charter of Rights. In response to the provincial argument that constitutional conventions requiring provincial consent when their powers were being affected would be "crystallized" into law, the court emphasized that what is desirable as a political limitation does not translate into a legal limitation without expression in imperative constitutional text or statute: 779, 784, 788.

18 John D. Whyte, "Sometimes Constitutions are Made in the Streets: The Future of the Charter's Notwithstanding Clause," *Constitutional Forum constitutionnel* 16 (2007): 79–80.

19 Eric M. Adams and Erin R.J. Bower, "Notwithstanding History: The Rights-Protecting Purposes of Section 33 of the Charter," *Review of Constitutional Studies* 26, no. 2 (2022): 126–8, https://dx.doi.org 10.2139/ssrn.4185044.

20 S,C, 1960, c.44.

21 Adams and Bower, "Notwithstanding History."

22 So nicknamed because it was arrived at in the kitchen of the premises where the premiers were meeting.

23 Marc-André Roy and Laurence Brosseau, *The Notwithstanding Clause of the Charter: Background Paper* (Ottawa, ON: Library of Parliament Research Paper, 2018), 4. The agreement was reached after Prime Minister Trudeau had agreed to the application of the clause to fundamental freedoms in return for the five-year limitation and re-enactment clause.

24 Allan Blakeney, "The Notwithstanding Clause, the Charter, and Canada's Patriated Constitution: What I Thought We Were Doing," *Constitutional Forum constitutionnel* 19, no. 1 (2010): 6, referring to Whyte, "Sometimes Constitutions," 79–80.

25 Blakeney, 1. He says at 6 that such rights might include the right to food and shelter, the right to care for one's family, and basic medical care.

26 Ibid.

27 Roy McMurtry, "The Search for a Constitutional Accord – A Personal Memoir," *Queen's Law Journal* 8 (1982): 65, quoted in Roy and Brosseau, *The Notwithstanding Clause*, 6. Interestingly, Mike Harris and Preston Manning also endorse the idea of using section 33 in response to a judicial decision, not pre-emptively. They also accept the idea that the proposed use of section 33 should be referred to the electorate in a referendum. Mike Harris and Preston Manning, *Vision for a Canada Strong and Free* (Montreal, QC: The Fraser Institute, 2007), 236–7.

28 Both quotations from Chrétien are from House of Commons, *Debates*, 20 November 1981, 13042–13043, quoted in Roy and Brosseau,

The Notwithstanding Clause, 6. This paper contains extracts from the writings of others present at the First Ministers' Conference, pp. 5–7 and fns. 17–27.

29 Reported in "Chrétien, Romanow, McMurtry Condemn Ford's Use of Notwithstanding Clause," *The Canadian Press,* 14 September 2018. Ford proposed to pass Bill 31, Efficient Local Government Act, 2018, 1st Sess., 42nd Leg., Ontario 2018 (second reading, 17 September 2018), adding section 33 protection to the earlier Bill 5, the Better Local Government Act, 2018, S.O. 2018, c.11, which had been declared contrary to section 2 of the Charter by the Ontario Supreme Court. *City of Toronto et al. v. Ontario (Attorney General),* 2018 ONSC 5151. Ontario counsel undertook to the Court of Appeal that if it granted a stay of the Ontario Supreme Court judgment, the government would not proceed with Bill 31. In granting the stay, the court stated that Ontario's undertaking had nothing to do with its decision. *Toronto (City) v. Ontario (Attorney General),* 2018 ONCA 761 para. 8. Ontario also passed The Protecting Elections and Defending Democracy Act, 2021, S.O. 2021, c.31, adding override protection to the earlier Protecting Ontario Elections Act, 2021, S.O. 2021 c.5, which had been declared contrary to the Charter by the Ontario Supreme Court. *Working Families Ontario v. Ontario,* 2021 ONSC 4076. The Court of Appeal ruled against this approach in 2023 ONCA 139.

30 Tsvi Kahana speaks of three conditions: 1. The clause should never be used simply to opt out of the Charter, but only on the ground that judicial interpretation of the Charter in a particular case is not optimal; 2. The clause should not be used to interfere with the judicial process; 3. Legislative debates should receive more adequate time and culminate in a free vote. Kahana, "Standing Up for Notwithstanding," *Globe and Mail,* 19 September 2002. In the 20 January 2020 issue of *Policy Options,* Marc Mancini and Geoffrey Sigalet argue that the legislation should set out a reasonable legislative definition of what rights mean, and not simply try to override rights in the name of majoritarian preference, and that invoking the clause should always involve a discussion of how the proposed law relates to Charter rights. Mark Mancini and Geoffrey Sigalet, "What Constitutes the Legitimate Use of the Notwithstanding Clause?" *Policy Options Politiques,* 20 January 2020, https://policyoptions.irpp.org/magazines/january-2020/what-constitutes-the-legitimate-use-of-the-notwithstanding-clause/.

31 Dwight Newman, "Canada's Notwithstanding Clause, Dialogue, and Constitutional Identities," in *Constitutional Dialogue: Rights, Democracy,*

Institutions, ed. Geoffrey Sigalet, Gregoire Webber, and Rosalind Dixon (Cambridge: Cambridge University Press, 2019), 209–14.

32 Ibid., 219.

33 *Ford v. Quebec (Attorney General)* [1998] 2 SCR 712 at para. 33.

34 See: *The King v. Alice Stubbs and Others* (1788) 2 T.R. 395; *The Queen v. Crossthwaite* (1867) Ir. Com. L.R. 463; *Chorlton v. Lings* (1868) L.R. 4 (C.P.) 374; *The Queen v. Harrald* (1872) L.R. 7 Q.B. 361; *Jex-Blake v Senatus of University of Edinburgh* (1873) 11 M.784; *Beresford-Hope v. Lady Sandhurst* (1889) 23 Q.B.D.79; *De Sousa v. Cobden* (1891) 1 Q.B. 687; *Nairn v. University of St Andrews* (1909) A.C.147; *Viscountess Rondda's Claim* (1922) 2 A.C. 339; and discussion at pp. 33–8 in Beverley Baines, "Women, Human Rights and the Constitution" in *Women and the Constitution in Canada*, ed. Audrey Doerr and Micheline Carrier (Ottawa, ON: CACSW and Minister of Supply and Services Canada, 1981), 31–63.

35 An Act to Provide for the Admission of Women to the Study and Practice of Law, S.O. 1892, c. 32.

36 S.O.1895, c. 27.

37 *In Re Mabel P. French* (1905), 37 N.B.R. 359 (S.C.). She was called only after passage of An Act to Remove the Disability of Women So Far As Relates to the Study and Practice of Law, S.N.B. 1906, c.3.

38 S.N.B. 1906, c.3.

39 *In Re Mabel P. French* (1912) 17 BCR 1; [1912] 1 WWR 488 (CA).

40 SBC 1912, c18.

41 *Dame Langstaff v. The Bar of the Province of Quebec* (1915), 47 QSC 131 at 139–40.

42 *Dame Langstaff (Annie MacDonald) v. The Bar of the Province of Quebec* (1915) 15 Que. K.B. 11 (CA).

43 An Act Respecting the Bar, S.Q. 1941, c. 56.

44 An Act to Amend the Notarial Act, S .Q. 1955–56, c. 62. See: Gail Brent, "The Development of the Law Relating to the Participation of Canadian Women in Public Life," *University of Toronto Law Journal* 25 (1975): 358; Mary Eberts, "The Rights of Women" in *The Practice of Freedom: Canadian Essays on Human Rights and Fundamental Freedoms*, ed. R. St.J. MacDonald and John P. Humphrey (Toronto: Butterworths, 1979). The details of these women lawyers' legal battles are set out in M. Elizabeth Atcheson et al., *Women and Legal Action: Precedents, Resources and Strategies for the Future* (Ottawa, ON: Canadian Advisory Council on the Status of Women, 1984), 8–12. That book was published before the coming into force of section 15 in 1985 as a resource to aid women doing litigation under the new Charter.

45 *In the Matter of a Reference as to the Meaning of the Word "Persons" in Section 24 of the British North America Act, 1867* [1928] SCR 276.

46 (U.K.) 30 & 31 Vict., c. 3, reprinted in RSC 1985, Appendix II, no. 5, s. 24.

47 As described in the reasons of *Reference re Same Sex Marriage*, 2004 SCC 79 at paragraph 22.

48 *Edwards v. Canada* [1930] AC 124 at 136–7.

49 *Reference re Prov. Electoral Boundaries (Sask.)* [1991] 2 SCR 158 at 180.

50 Canada, Prime Minister, Statement by the Prime Minister on Persons Day, 18 October 2021. A small but important connection illustrates the lineage from the *Persons* case to the women's movement for equality guarantees in the 80s. Counsel for the Five Persons before the Privy Council was Newton Wesley Rowell, Toronto lawyer. His daughter and granddaughter made substantial contributions to the establishment of the Women's Legal Education and Action Fund, a national organization founded to litigate cases for women's equality under the Charter of Rights.

51 Two decisions of the Supreme Court, in particular, demonstrated its weakness: *Attorney-General Canada v. Lavell; Isaac et al. v. Bedard* [1974] SCR 1349 and *Bliss v. Attorney-General of Canada* [1979] 1 SCR 183.

52 S.C. 1968–69, c.24.

53 See: Mary Eberts, "Women and Constitutional Renewal," in *Women and the Constitution in Canada*, ed. Audrey Doerr and Micheline Carrier (Ottawa, ON: CACSW and Minister of Supply and Services Canada, 1981), 15–17; Chaviva Hosek, "Women and Constitutional Process," in *And No One Cheered: Federalism, Democracy and the Constitution*, ed. Keith Banting and Richard Simeon (Toronto: Methuen Publications, 1983), 284; Katherine K. de Jong, "Sexual Equality: Interpreting Section 28," in *Equality Rights and the Canadian Charter of Rights and Freedoms*, ed. Anne F. Bayefsky and Mary Eberts (Toronto, Calgary, Vancouver: Carswell, 1985), 497–500.

54 de Jong, "Sexual Equality," 500. This unilateral approach to patriation precipitated the provinces' reference case discussed above in the history of section 33.

55 National Association of Women and the Law, *Presentation to the Joint Committee on the Constitution*, November 1980. Copy in possession of the author.

56 National Action Committee on the Status of Women, *Presentation to the Senate House of Commons Special Joint Committee on the Constitution of Canada*, 20 November 1980. Copy in possession of the author.

57 Canadian Advisory Council on the Status of Women, *Women, Human Rights & the Constitution.* Submission of the Canadian Advisory Council on the Status of Women to the Special Joint Committee on the Constitution, 18 November 1980. Copy in possession of the author.

58 In addition to de Jong, "Sexual Equality" and Hosek, "Women and Constitutional Process," see also Kerri A. Froc, "The Untapped Power of Section 28 of the Canadian Charter of Rights and Freedoms," (PhD diss., Queen's University, 2015). Froc provides a detailed account of women's group presentations at the Special Joint Committee and the subsequent Ad Hoc Committee of Canadian Women efforts to secure the text of section 28 of the Charter. See particularly pages 134–228.

59 de Jong, "Sexual Equality," 501–4.

60 See note 51.

61 Canadian Advisory Council on the Status of Women, *Women, Human Rights*, 6–14. The application of section 1 to all Charter breaches made the consideration of a grounds hierarchy in section 15 unnecessary, as it turned out, but the groups making these arguments had proposals for section 1 that differed considerably from what it eventually became.

62 Beverley Baines, "Section 28 of the Canadian Charter of Rights and Freedoms: A Purposive Interpretation," *Canadian Journal of Women and Law* 17 (2005): 51–2.

63 Froc, "Untapped Power," 139–41. See also National Association of Women and the Law, *Presentation to the Joint Committee*, 22:54.

64 de Jong, "Sexual Equality," 504.

65 [1989] 1 SCR 143 ("*Andrews*").

66 *Andrews*, 170.

67 Ibid., 167–8, 170.

68 Ibid., 165.

69 Ibid., 164.

70 *Fraser*, paragraphs 41–2.

71 Froc, "Untapped Power," 143, 148. She points out that no "purpose clause" had been included in the draft Charter recommended by the Special Joint Committee when it reported to Parliament 13 February 1981. See 150.

72 The most well-known account of this protest, and other actions leading to the inclusion of section 28 in the Charter and its release from the override, is Penney Kome, *The Taking of Twenty-Eight: Women Challenge the Constitution* (Toronto: Women's Educational Press, 1993).

73 Froc, "Untapped Power," 152.

74 See: Anne F. Bayefsky and Mary Eberts, eds., *Equality Rights and the Canadian Charter of Rights and Freedoms* (Toronto, Calgary, Vancouver: Carswell, 1985), 634–44; Appendix VII, *Summary of those Resolutions Passed* at the Ad Hoc Conference on Women and the Constitution.

75 Bayefsky and Eberts, *Equality Rights*, 645.

76 Froc, "Untapped Power," 190–2.

77 Ibid., 200–3.

78 Ibid., 203, 205.

79 Ibid., 204.

80 Baines, "Section 28," 51; Froc, 205.

81 Froc, 201; See also de Jong, "Sexual Equality," 519.

82 Sandra Burt, "The Charter of Rights and the Ad Hoc Lobby: The Limits of Success," *Atlantis* 14, no. 1 (1988): 79.

83 Froc, "Untapped Power," 208–9.

84 Hosek, "Women and Constitutional Process," 291.

85 Froc, "Untapped Power," 211, 216.

86 *House of Commons Debates*, 32nd Parliament, 1st Sess. No. 11, 20 November 1981, at 13056, quoted in Froc, 218.

87 *House of Commons Debates*, 32nd Parliament, 1st Sess. No. 11, 20 November 1981, at 13050, quoted in Froc, 208.

88 Ibid., 219.

89 de Jong, "Sexual Equality," 522.

90 Strauss, "Section 28's Potential," 100.

91 de Jong, "Sexual Equality," 522–3.

92 Quoted in de Jong, 516, fn. 86.

93 Quoted in 2019 QCCA 2145 at para. 51.

94 Baines, "Section 28," 52. This was the position taken by the judge of first instance hearing the *Hak* case: 2021 QCCS 1466 at para. 820.

95 1984 CanLII 3055 (NSSCAD). See also "Section 28 – Gender Equality Rights," *Government of Canada*, https://www.justice.gc.ca/eng/csj-sjc/rfc-dlc/ccrf-ccdl/check/art28.html: "With respect to section 33, section 28 may mean that, even where a legislature or Parliament passes legislation allowing abrogation or infringement of section 2 or sections 7–15 of the Charter, it will not be able to do so in a way which disproportionately affects people on the basis of gender."

96 *Boudreau v. Lynch*, para 12.

97 Ibid., para. 9.

98 Ibid., para. 12.

99 *Syndicat de la function publique du Quebec Inc. v. Quebec (Procurateur General)* [2004] RJQ 524 204 CanLII 76338 as discussed in Kerri A. Froc,

"Shouting into the Constitutional Void: Section 28 and Bill 21," *Constitutional Forum constitutionnel* (2019) 28:4.

100 Ibid.

101 As suggested in Grégoire Webber, Eric Mendelsohn, and Robert Leckey, "The Faulty Received Wisdom around the Notwithstanding Clause," *Policy Options*, 10 May 2019, policyoptions.irpp.org/magazines/may-2019/faulty-wisdom-notwithstanding-clause; and Leonid Sirota, "Concurring Opinion," *Double Aspect*, 23 May 2019, https://doubleaspect.blog/2019/05/23/concurring-opinion/; and contra: Maxime St-Hilaire and Xaiver Foccroulle Ménard, "Nothing to Declare: A Response to Grégoire Webber, Eric Mendelsohn, Robert Leckey, and Léonid Sirota on the Effects of the Notwithstanding Clause," *Constitutional Forum* 29, no. 1 (2020): 38–9.

102 2021 QCCS 1466 at para. 820.

103 Section 28 is protected by its introductory language "notwithstanding anything in this Charter" and section 35(4) is not named in section 33 as a right to which section 33 may be applied. Nor could it be: section 35 is not in the Charter itself.

16

Section 33, the Right to Vote, and Democratic Accountability

Cara Faith Zwibel

I. INTRODUCTION: THE NOTWITHSTANDING CLAUSE AND DEMOCRATIC ACCOUNTABILITY

The Canadian Charter of Rights and Freedoms includes a relatively unique mechanism in section 33's "notwithstanding clause." Some view the notwithstanding clause as fundamentally undermining the Charter, arguing that the entrenchment of rights means little if they can simply be ousted by ordinary legislation. Others take the view that the clause is what makes the Charter legitimate, claiming that ultimate determinations about rights should be left to those we elect to represent us. Regardless of the view one takes of the clause, there seems to be little controversy about the notion that section 33 is intended to function as a mechanism of democratic accountability. Ultimately, it places a decision about the operation of a law in the hands of legislators who, in turn, represent their constituents.

There has been a recent surge in legal academic attention to the notwithstanding clause, much of which focuses on how courts should interpret section 33 and whether there is scope to move beyond the purely formalistic approach adopted by the Supreme Court of Canada in *Ford v. Quebec.*[1] Some of this literature quite clearly comes out of an underlying sense of discomfort with the clause (or at least the ways in which it has been used most recently)[2] and an attempt to minimize or mitigate its impact as much as possible. As Dwight Newman points out elsewhere in this volume,[3] section 33 can be used for rights-protecting purposes, but recent uses in Quebec and Ontario[4] appear to undermine rather than protect fundamental rights.

My contribution in this chapter is to join the calls for a purposive understanding of section 33, but also to consider the impact that the section might have on how certain Charter rights are themselves interpreted. In particular, I want to examine and hypothesize about what the exclusion of the Charter's democratic rights from section 33's scope might say about the extent and reach of those rights. Since there is broad consensus that section 33 is a tool of democratic accountability, close scrutiny of some of the other Charter tools we use to preserve our democracy is a worthwhile exercise.

My core argument is that the exclusion of democratic rights from the scope of section 33 helps to justify a particularly expansive understanding of the democratic rights – particularly the right to vote.[5] This thesis draws in part on the notion of the Charter's democratic rights as "structural rights," and Yasmin Dawood's work which argues that the Supreme Court should interpret the right to vote as encompassing more than simply the right to cast a ballot or even the more expansive right to participate meaningfully in an election.[6] Dawood argues that the Charter's democratic rights should be read as "protecting a fair and legitimate democratic process."[7] In this chapter, I agree with this reading of the right to vote and suggest that it is not only supported by some of the existing section 3 jurisprudence, but that an argument grounded in the text and purpose of section 33 also lends it credence. Ultimately, my conclusion is that laws that demonstrably and appreciably impact our democratic structures must be considered beyond the reach of section 33, regardless of whether they would be found to directly infringe the democratic rights in the Charter under a more traditional or constrained understanding of those rights.

II. THE CONTEXT: ONTARIO'S ELECTION FINANCES ACT

a. Getting Comfortable with Section 33

Others in this volume have commented on the lack of agreement among scholars about even some of the most basic facts surrounding the notwithstanding clause – including the number of times it has been invoked. The unique Quebec approach to the Charter generally, and section 33 specifically, has also been addressed in this volume, suggesting that uses outside of Quebec cannot be fairly compared to that province's invocations. I intend to focus on the recent interest in the clause in Ontario by the Conservative provincial government, since it serves as a useful lens through which to view the interaction between the clause, democratic rights, and democratic accountability.

In September 2018, the premier of Ontario threatened to use the clause after a superior court decision found the government's Better Local Government Act[8] unconstitutional. That legislation dramatically reduced the number of wards in Toronto (from forty-seven to twenty-five, essentially doubling the size of the population represented in each ward) in the middle of a municipal election. Belobaba J.'s decision focused on whether the law violated the freedom of expression of candidates and voters and concluded that it did so in a way that could not be justified. He held that, "The Supreme Court has stated time and again that 'preserving the integrity of the electoral process is a pressing and substantial concern in a free and democratic society.' Passing a law that changes the city's electoral districts in the middle of its election and undermines the overall fairness of the election is antithetical to the core principles of our democracy."[9]

Within hours of the Superior Court's decision being released, the government announced that it would invoke the notwithstanding clause in order to carry out its plans to reduce the size of Toronto's city council.[10] The premier's statement to the press following the decision demonstrated a fairly casual attitude about the use of the clause. While Premier Ford stated that he had "a great deal of respect for our judicial system,"[11] he also said that it was the government who would ultimately be held accountable by the electorate, and announced his plan to reintroduce the legislation while invoking section 33. He continued, "I also want to make it clear that we're prepared to use section 33 again in the future. We're taking a stand. If you want to make new laws in Ontario or in Canada, you first must seek a mandate from the people and you have to be elected. Because it is the people who will decide what is in their best interests for this great province."[12]

The government also announced its intention to appeal the decision. The government's request that the Court of Appeal stay the Superior Court decision was granted,[13] and its appeal ultimately succeeded, both before the Court of Appeal[14] and eventually, by a five-judge majority, at the Supreme Court of Canada.[15] As a result, the legislature never had to move forward with passing a new Better Local Government Act in which section 33 was invoked.

The Ontario premier's comfort with invoking the clause,[16] despite facing significant criticism and in the absence of any provincial precedent for doing so, marked an important shift and foreshadowed what was to come. When provisions of another piece of election legislation (this time related to *provincial* elections) were struck down by the court in 2021, the Ontario government decided not to bother with an appeal. It simply re-enacted the law that had been struck out and invoked section 33 to immunize it from further review. This serves as the most instructive case study for examining how section 33's democratic accountability objective might be compromised when the clause is invoked in a law of democracy context.

b. Challenging Third Party Advertising Restrictions

In the *Working Families* case,[17] a group of unions and individuals under the banner of Working Families Ontario sought to challenge changes made to Ontario's Election Finances Act. This act was amended by the Liberal government in 2017[18] so that, for the first time, third-party election advertising was subject to spending limits in the six months leading up to the issuance of an election writ. Since many Canadian jurisdictions have adopted fixed election dates, there have been attempts to adjust spending rules so that they are not easily evaded in the lead up to the election period. Perhaps more significantly, the 2017 amendments did not only alter the time period in which restrictions operated, they also amended the meaning of election advertising so that it included not only advertising with the purpose of promoting or opposing a party, leader, or candidate, but also any advertising that "takes a position on an issue that can reasonably be regarded as closely associated with a registered party or its leader or a registered candidate."[19]

This extension to issue-based advertising significantly widens the scope of restricted political expression. Moreover, it can be difficult to assess which issues are "reasonably ... regarded as closely associated" with a party or candidate when an election is still more than a year off. Concerns about the breadth of the third-party advertising restrictions were raised when a legislative committee studied the bill. There was also precedent from another jurisdiction that called the constitutionality of the provisions into question.

When the initial amendments were made creating a six-month prewrit period, Ontario's chief electoral officer, Greg Essensa, addressed the legislative committee considering the bill. Essensa took the view that third-party advertising should be regulated at all times, regardless of proximity to an election. However, he also clearly preferred a definition of political advertising that steered clear of issue-based advertising, stating, "Between elections, issue-based advertising should not be regulated. I do not think it is helpful in the non-writ period to use the measure of whether or not the advertising is associated with a candidate or a party. Rather, I propose that third-party political advertising that is subject to regulation and reporting is solely limited to advertising that directly depicts leaders and their parties, and specifically advocates that citizens support or oppose them when they are next at the ballot box."[20]

The British Columbia Court of Appeal had also previously considered regulation of third-party advertising during a pre-writ period in an election law that included a broad definition of political advertising. That court twice struck down restrictions on the basis that they were unjustified limits on freedom of expression. In the first case, limits imposed in a sixty-day pre-election period were struck down.[21] The sequel litigation involved a forty-day pre-election period which the court also struck down.[22] The breadth of the definition of political advertising was a significant factor. The Court of Appeal worried that the definition captured "any public communication on government action."[23] Finding that this had little to do with electoral fairness, the provisions were found to be of no force or effect.

The chief electoral officer's recommendation and the BC Court of Appeal's decisions were not heeded by Ontario's lawmakers. Thus, as a result of the 2017 amendments, Ontario's scheme restricted third-party advertising (broadly defined) for six months prior to the start of an election. The Working Families group issued a Notice of Application to challenge the constitutionality of the law on the basis that it unreasonably restricted freedom of expression. The government responded to the application with their own evidence, including expert reports and affidavits that sought to justify the six-month spending limit as necessary and reasonable to ensuring "a fair and proper election process."[24]

Before the *Working Families* case made it to a hearing, the provincial government (now led by the Progressive Conservatives) introduced new amendments to the Election Finances Act in 2021.[25] While Bill 254 maintained the same monetary limit on third-party election advertising spending in the pre-writ period, the amendments doubled the period itself, from six months to a year. Now third parties would be restricted in their spending on political ads (including issue-based ones) for an entire twelve months before a writ was dropped. It is also worth noting that while the bill placed more restrictions on third parties, it doubled the allowable donations to political parties[26] and also increased the annual per-vote funding for parties.[27] Further, changes had been made by the prior government which substantially reduced the auditor general's power to meaningfully review government ads and determine if they included partisan content.[28]

Putting these elements together certainly appeared to provide the incumbent governing party with a major advantage, and could reasonably be said to silence, or at least muffle, the third-party voices that were critical of government. Moreover, although the legislation lays out some criteria[29] by which the chief electoral officer may determine whether an ad constitutes "political advertising," the line between acceptable issue ads and unacceptable political ads will often be blurry.[30] The bill received royal assent about a month before the pre-writ period was set to begin, so those who wished to challenge the rules (and avoid having to comply with them) had very little time in which to do so.

Working Families amended their application and challenged Bill 254 in court. Justice Morgan at Ontario's Superior Court of Justice easily determined that there was a violation of section 2(b) of the Charter, and that the violation was not justified under section 1.[31] The case was in some ways an easy victory because the government's own evidence had initially indicated that a six-month period of restricted pre-writ activity was reasonable. When they amended the law and it was challenged, some of the same government experts swore affidavits that a twelve-month period was also reasonable. This clearly self-serving evidence made it very difficult for the government to credibly argue that its measures were the least restrictive ones necessary under section 1 of the Charter. As the court noted, "Without meaning to stress the obvious, it is hard to see how 12 months is minimal if 6 months will do the trick ... The more the restriction on their political expression, the more the Applicants' rights are limited. When compared with a twelve-month impairment, a six-month impairment will always be the more minimal one."[32]

The court struck down the impugned provisions with immediate effect and the Ontario government immediately announced its intention to re-introduce the changes while invoking section 33. Bill 307 did just that and was challenged once again by *Working Families*, this time on the grounds that it violated section 3 of the Charter. Some of the parties also raised challenges to the use of the clause more generally. Morgan J. once again heard the case at first instance, but this time he found no violation of section 3. Justice Morgan articulated the view that there were no substantive requirements that limited the operation of section 33, echoing the Supreme Court's analysis in *Ford*.[33] Significantly, Justice Morgan recognized the role that section 33 plays as a tool of democratic accountability: "Section 33 was originally conceived not as an anti-democratic instrument but as a democracy-fostering mechanism. It was included in the Charter as a counterbalance to what were perceived as anti-majoritarian, judicially enforced Charter norms. That is, it was, and is, a means of bringing Charter matters to the electorate where they otherwise would not go. In that respect, it allows for 'accountable public discussion of rights issues.'"[34]

He also noted that given the government's capacity (and sometimes desire) to limit the franchise, section 33 had to be handled with care in the context of voting rights.[35] Although Justice Morgan agreed with much that the appellants and interveners had to say about the expansive scope of the right to vote,[36] he nevertheless found that it was not implicated by the changes to third-party election advertising rules. The case was heard by the Ontario Court of Appeal in June 2022 and a decision rendered in March 2023.[37] The Court of Appeal found that the right to vote in section 3 of the Charter was infringed and that the infringement could not be justified under section 1. It struck down the spending restrictions but suspended the declaration of invalidity for twelve months to allow the province to fashion Charter-compliant legislation.

III. DEMOCRATIC RIGHTS AS STRUCTURAL RIGHTS

a. Supreme Court's Approach to the Right to Vote

The Supreme Court of Canada, and the country's superior and appellate courts as well, have often been asked to weigh in on the nature of the democratic rights that are protected by the Charter. There is a compelling argument that the courts already have a relatively expansive understanding of the right to vote, or, at least, the rights arising from the principle of democracy. Yasmin Dawood has

argued that the Supreme Court has recognized at least four democratic rights in its election law jurisprudence: 1) the right to effective
representation; 2) the right to meaningful participation; 3) the right
to equal participation; and 4) the right to a free and informed vote.[38]
Some of these rights emanate directly from section 3 of the Charter,
while others appear to be supported by the broader principle of
democracy, which is said to be an unwritten constitutional principle
undergirding the Charter as a whole.[39]

It is not uncommon to see governments alter the electoral rules
of the game to their benefit. In a 2012 article in the *University of
Toronto Law Journal*,[40] Yasmin Dawood described this problem of
"partisan self-dealing" as a central challenge for democratic governance. Dawood is interested in how we should conceive of the
democratic rights protections contained in the Charter and their
capacity to address this perennial problem. She notes, "Electoral
rules that govern voting, political parties, electoral boundaries,
apportionment, the administration of elections, and campaign
finance are often designed to achieve partisan objectives. By manipu-
lating these rules, elected representatives stifle political competition,
thereby reducing democratic accountability."[41]

The Charter's democratic rights create the space for judicial oversight of the democratic process in a manner that could help to limit
partisan or incumbent self-entrenchment. Dawood argues that the
Supreme Court should interpret the right to vote as encompassing
a new democratic right: the right to a fair and legitimate democratic process. She suggests that we can conceptualize this right as
"structural" in nature, structural rights being "individual rights that
take into account the broader institutional framework within which
rights are defined, held, and exercised."[42] According to Dawood, the
right to vote presupposes an institutional framework which includes
elections, candidates, political parties, and constituencies. The right
to vote cannot be exercised without these institutions.[43]

Although the court has not articulated the right to vote as including
the right to a fair and legitimate democratic process, existing case law
on the right to vote does support a relatively broad understanding of
what the right entails. It also supports the notion that courts should
closely and carefully scrutinize measures put in place by elected representatives that interfere with fundamental democratic rights (including
the right to vote) as well as those that might amount to an alteration
in the "rules of the game" of electoral politics.[44]

In *Sauvé v. Canada*, the Supreme Court considered the constitutionality of a provision of the Canada Elections Act which rendered a person in a correctional institution serving a sentence of two years or more as ineligible to vote. The decision was split 5–4, with Chief Justice McLachlin (as she then was) pointing out a key distinction between the majority and dissenting views:

> My colleague Justice Gonthier proposes a deferential approach to infringement and justification. He argues that there is no reason to accord special importance to the right to vote, and that we should thus defer to Parliament's choice among a range of reasonable alternatives. He further argues that in justifying limits on the right to vote under s. 1, we owe deference to Parliament because we are dealing with "philosophical, political and social considerations," because of the abstract and symbolic nature of the government's stated goals, and because the law at issue represents a step in a dialogue between Parliament and the courts.
>
> I must, with respect, demur. The right to vote is fundamental to our democracy and the rule of law and cannot be lightly set aside. Limits on it require not deference, but careful examination. This is not a matter of substituting the Court's philosophical preference for that of the legislature, but of ensuring that the legislature's proffered justification is supported by logic and common sense.[45]

A more recent case dealing with voting eligibility took a similarly stringent approach to justification under section 1. In *Frank v. Canada*, the court considered a challenge to provisions of the federal election legislation that said that Canadians residing abroad for five years or more were ineligible to vote. The majority of the court once again pointed to the fundamental nature of the right to vote and said that while all infringements must be evaluated under section 1 on a balance of probabilities standard, "Reviewing courts must examine the government's proffered justification carefully and rigorously in this context rather than adopting a deferential attitude. Deference may be appropriate in the case of a complex regulatory response or a decision involving competing social and political policies, but it is not the appropriate posture for a court reviewing an absolute prohibition of a core democratic right."[46]

Although the court has been more deferential in some cases dealing with the electoral model Canada chooses to follow, its broad understanding of the nature of democratic rights remains evident throughout. In *Figueroa v. Canada (Attorney General)*,[47] for example, the Supreme Court considered provisions of Canada's federal election legislation that required a political party to nominate candidates in at least fifty electoral districts in order to benefit from registered party status.[48] The majority examined some of the court's prior statements on the nature of the right to vote, acknowledging that the right was about more than simply casting a ballot, and that it included a right to effective representation. In the *Figueroa* case, the court went further still, stating that the right to vote also encompasses "the right of each citizen to play a meaningful role in the electoral process."[49] The majority also concluded that the right to vote "imposes on Parliament an obligation not to interfere with the right of each citizen to participate in a *fair* election."[50] Citing *Libman*,[51] the majority found that the political equality of citizens – entrenched in the Constitution – underlies the principle of electoral fairness, stating that "elections are fair and equitable only if all citizens are reasonably informed of all the possible choices and if parties and candidates are given a reasonable opportunity to present their positions."[52]

Given the broader "institutional framework" in which the right to vote is situated, the meaningful participation will be largely elusive if the democratic process generally, and the electoral structures in particular, are not widely viewed as fair, legitimate, and equitable. Although not the basis for the Court of Appeal's decision in *Working Families 2*, this line of reasoning supports the finding that the right to vote can be impacted by third-party advertising restrictions. These restrictions impact the ability of voters to be reasonably informed and to receive information from a variety of sources (and not exclusively those running for elected office). The government's purported objectives in restricting third-party advertising spending in the pre-election period are not relevant at this stage, but will come into the analysis when considering whether the limitation on the right to vote is reasonably justified under section 1 of the Charter. The arguments that can be made on this issue are beyond the scope of this chapter.

b. The Notwithstanding Clause as Interpretive Tool

The court's democracy jurisprudence has also referenced the fact of the democratic rights' exclusion from the scope of section 33 as an important interpretive clue. In *Sauvé*, the court noted that the

Charter's framers "signalled the special importance of this right [to vote] not only by its broad, untrammelled language, but by exempting it from legislative override under s. 33's notwithstanding clause."[53] This passage was also quoted by the majority in *Frank*.[54]

The five-year sunset clause included in section 33(3) was placed there precisely to ensure that a government that invoked the clause would have to be accountable to the electorate for doing so. There is clearly a special relationship between the democratic rights and the notwithstanding clause – hinged on the principle of democratic accountability – even if the full scope and import of that relationship remain unclear.

To take the most extreme example, we could return to Bill 307 but imagine that in addition to the restrictions on third-party advertising, the bill also included a total prohibition of any discussion of the government's use of section 33. This would clearly violate section 2(b), but given its impact on the ability of the electorate to hold the government accountable, there is an equally strong argument that democratic rights are directly engaged and that such a law could and should be struck down despite the use of section 33. Allowing governments to manipulate the rules of the electoral game and then insulate themselves from review by invoking section 33 is not in keeping with the spirit or purpose of the notwithstanding clause.[55]

IV. CONCLUDING THOUGHTS: THE CLAUSE AS A FORCE FOR GOOD?

At the outset of this chapter, I noted that many comments on the notwithstanding clause come from a place of discomfort with its existence and use in ways that appear to undermine rights. I share this discomfort, but also recognize that, at least for the time being, the clause is a part of our Charter. What I have tried to sketch out here is a means of using the clause not as a shield by governments wishing to override constitutional rights, but as a sword by the electorate, ensuring that the clause fulfills its function as a meaningful tool of democratic accountability. To do this, we should understand the democratic rights in the Charter expansively and ensure that the clause is not used to interfere with or undermine the electoral systems that form the foundation for our democracy.

Elsewhere in this volume, Newman has described the carve outs from section 33 as protecting rights of voice and rights of exit.[56]

Legislation that clearly touches on those rights of voice cannot and should not be touched by section 33. Although our democratic structures don't always work in a way that amplifies the voices that are otherwise silenced, surely allowing governments to manipulate the rules for their own benefit is not what was intended by excluding these rights from the scope of the notwithstanding clause. There is a strong argument to be made for disallowing the use of section 33 in any case where the purpose or effect of the legislation at issue is to appreciably impact our democratic structures. Giving our democratic rights a generous interpretation enhances not only their breadth in our ongoing democratic experiment, but also helps to support section 33 in doing its democratic accountability work.

NOTES

This piece is written in my personal capacity and the views expressed in this chapter do not necessarily reflect the views of my employer.

1 *Ford v. Quebec* [1998] 2 SCR 712.
2 Tsvi Kahana, this volume, chapter 13, makes the argument that some uses of the clause are tyrannical, when motivated by a desire to disadvantage minorities, silence opposition, or when it results in exceptionally severe rights violations.
3 Dwight Newman, this volume, chapter 3.
4 Quebec's use of the notwithstanding clause in relation to Bill 21, which prohibits some public servants from wearing religious symbols, is a prime example of using the clause to undermine the protection the Charter offers to minority rights. In Ontario, in addition to the circumstance discussed in this chapter, the government adopted legislation invoking section 33 to address a threatened labour strike by educational workers. While the labour protections that Canadian courts have read into section 2(d) of the Charter are not without controversy, the government's willingness to so quickly and casually invoke the clause was widely viewed as a serious threat to all labour rights throughout the province. The Ontario labour movement mobilized quickly and, as a result, the government ultimately agreed to repeal the legislation and head back to the bargaining table.
5 See also Jamie Cameron, this volume, chapter 17. Cameron and I make similar arguments about the relationship between sections 3 and 33 of the Charter. In Cameron's view, the jurisprudence under section 3 is already well placed to address the concerns raised in the *Working Families* 2 case discussed herein. I find her argument persuasive and compelling, but have

attempted here to argue that, to the extent section 3 does not already protect against the kind of interference at issue in *Working Families 2*, the
right to vote should be interpreted more expansively to address the
democratic accountability deficit that would otherwise result.

6 Yasmin Dawood, "Electoral Fairness and the Law of Democracy:
A Structural Rights Approach to Judicial Review," *University of Toronto
Law Journal* 62, no. 4 (2012): 499.

7 Ibid., 504.

8 Better Local Government Act, 2018, S.O. 2018, c. 11 – Bill 5.

9 *City of Toronto et al. v. Ontario (Attorney General)*, 2018 ONSC 5151 at
para 73.

10 See, for example, John Rieti, "Premier Doug Ford to Use Notwithstanding
Clause to Cut Size of Toronto City Council," CBC News, 18 June 2004,
https://www.cbc.ca/news/canada/toronto/judge-ruling-city-council-bill-
election-1.4816664.

11 CTV News, "Doug Ford to Use Notwithstanding Clause to Force Toronto
City Council Cuts," 10 September 2018, https://www.youtube.com/
watch?v=apzahAUEcsQ.

12 CTV News.

13 *Toronto (City) v. Ontario (Attorney General)*, 2018 ONCA 761.

14 *Toronto (City) v. Ontario (Attorney General)*, 2019 ONCA 732.

15 *Toronto (City) v. Ontario (Attorney General)*, 2021 SCC 34.

16 In one television interview, Ford said, "I don't call it the nuclear option,
I call it the will of the people's option." Global News, "Doug Ford
Explains Why He's Not Using Notwithstanding Clause to Slash Toronto
City Council," https://www.youtube.com/watch?v=msEoFbN4-jM. As
noted above (note 3), the premier's casual resort to section 33 in the
labour relations context in November 2022 was met with fierce resistance
and threatened to lead to nationwide protests. The democratic accountability function of section 33 was in full view with these events. The government ultimately realized the price of invoking the clause was too high,
and not one it was willing to bear.

17 As laid out in more detail above, this case has been through several itera-
tions. The case challenging the law on the basis of section 2(b) of the
Charter is *Working Families Ontario v. Ontario*, 2021 ONSC 4076
[*Working Families 1*]. The case challenging the law on the basis of section
3 of the Charter is *Working Families Ontario v. Ontario*, 2021 ONSC
7697 [*Working Families 2 (ONSC)*] and *Working Families Coalition
(Canada) Inc. v. Ontario (Attorney General)*, 2023 ONCA 139 [*Working

Families 2 (ONCA): leave to appeal granted, SCC File No. 40725 (9 November 2023)].

18 Election Finances Statute Law Amendment Act, S.O. 2016, c. 22.

19 Election Finances Act, R.S.O. 1990, c. E.7, s. 1(1) "political advertising."

20 *Official Report of Debates (Hansard)*, Legislative Assembly of Ontario, 6 June 2016, https://www.ola.org/sites/default/files/node-files/hansard/document/pdf/2016/2016-06/committee-transcript-1-EN-06-JUN-2016_G056.pdf.

21 *British Columbia Teachers' Federation v. British Columbia (Attorney General)*, 2011 BCCA 408.

22 *Reference re Election Act (BC)*, 2012 BCCA 394.

23 See *Reference re Election Act (BC)*, 2012 BCCA 394 at para. 20. In assessing the constitutionality of Ontario's provisions in the *Working Families 1*, Morgan J. distinguished the Ontario legislation from BC's, stating that "the guidance and context provided by the EFA effectively limit the application of the term 'political advertisement' to election-oriented communications ... The very fact that what is and what is not a 'political advertisement' can be coherently debated in terms of the EFA's own guidelines saves it from the kind of stark indeterminacy that the rule of law eschews. It is not mathematically precise, but it is also not so vague as to make either compliance or regulatory decision-making incoherent or unknowable." *Working Families 1*, paras 43, 45.

24 *Working Families 1* at para. 6.

25 Protecting Ontario Elections Act, S.O. 2021, c. 5.

26 Bill 254, Protecting Ontario Elections Act, 2021, 1st Sess, 42nd Parl, 2021, clause 7.

27 *British Columbia Teachers' Federation v. British Columbia (Attorney General)*, clause 12(1).

28 Amendments were made to Ontario's Government Advertising Act in 2015 which imposed a specific and narrow definition of "partisan." As noted in AG's report in 2020/21: "When significant amendments to the Act were introduced by the government in 2015, we cautioned that these would weaken the Act and open the door to publicly funded partisan and self-congratulatory government advertisements on television and radio, in print and online. These amendments imposed a specific and narrow definition of 'partisan' as the only measure we could use in our reviews. Essentially, as long as the government avoids using the name, voice or image of an elected official or the logo of a political party, directly identifying and criticizing a recognized party or a member of the assembly or including, to a significant degree, a colour associated with the government

party in an advertisement, the Auditor General cannot find it partisan under the Act. Our approval is still required under the amended Act before an advertisement can run; however this approval is almost always automatic." *Review of Government Advertising* (Office of the Auditor General of Ontario, December 2021), 2–3, https://www.auditor.on.ca/en/content/annualreports/arreports/en21/AR_GAA_en21.pdf.

29 Election Finances Act, R.S.O. 1990, c. E.7, s. 37.0.1 states: "In determining whether an advertisement is a political advertisement, the Chief Electoral Officer shall consider, in addition to any other relevant factors, (a) whether it is reasonable to conclude that the advertising was specifically planned to coincide with the period referred to in section 37.10.1; (b) whether the formatting or branding of the advertisement is similar to a registered political party's or registered candidate's formatting or branding or election material; (c) whether the advertising makes reference to the election, election day, voting day, or similar terms; (d) whether the advertisement makes reference to a registered political party or registered candidate either directly or indirectly; (e) whether there is a material increase in the normal volume of advertising conducted by the person, organization, or entity; (f) whether the advertising has historically occurred during the relevant time of the year; (g) whether the advertising is consistent with previous advertising conducted by the person, organization, or entity; (h) whether the advertising is within the normal parameters of promotion of a specific program or activity; and (i) whether the content of the advertisement is similar to the political advertising of a party, constituency association, nomination contestant, candidate or leadership contestant registered under this Act."

30 In the *Working Families* case, the Ontario English Catholic Teachers' Association (OECTA) put forward evidence of how it had been chilled in expressing itself during a labour dispute with the government because of the proximity in time to a by-election. Out of an abundance of caution, and out of fear of being found to have violated the third-party advertising rules, OECTA pulled some ads in certain geographic areas.

31 *Working Families 1*.

32 Ibid., para 66.

33 *Working Families 2*, para 15.

34 Ibid., para 16.

35 Ibid., para 17.

36 Ibid., paras 56, 96.

37 *Working Families 3*.

38 Yasmin Dawood, "Democracy and the Right to Vote: Rethinking

Democratic Rights under the Charter," *Osgoode Hall Law Journal* 51, no. 1 (2013): 251. In *Working Families 2* (ONCA), a majority of the Ontario Court of Appeal found that the spending restrictions infringe the informational component of the voter's section 3 right to meaningful participation in the electoral process. This chapter was written prior to the Ontario Court of Appeal rendering its decision in *Working Families 3*. It has been updated to reflect the fact of the court's decision but does not purport to engage in a thorough analysis of the decision or its impact on the interpretation of sections 3 and 33 of the Charter.

39 Dawood, 255 and *Reference re Secession of Quebec* [1998] 2 SCR 217.

40 Dawood.

41 Ibid., 500.

42 Ibid., 503.

43 Dawood, "Right to Vote," 264.

44 The majority decision in *Working Families 2* (ONCA) does not accept that the government was engaged in partisan self-dealing in enacting the impugned spending restrictions but does accept a broad understanding of the right to vote and the need for close judicial scrutiny of measures that impact democratic rights. The majority finds (at para. 85) that a violation of section 3 will be established if it can be shown that the spending restrictions limit information to voters in "such a way as to undermine the right of citizens to meaningfully participate in the political process and to be effectively represented." The majority uses two "proxies" or methods of ascertaining whether the restriction is constitutionally offside, namely whether the restriction is "carefully tailored to ensure that candidates, political parties and third parties are able to convey their information voters," and whether the restrictions allow for a modest informational campaign to be carried out.

45 *Sauvé v. Canada (Chief Electoral Officer)*, 2002 SCC 68 at paras 8–9. The majority further noted (at para 15) that, "The Charter charges courts with upholding and maintaining an inclusive, participatory democratic framework within which citizens can explore and pursue different conceptions of the good. While a posture of judicial deference to legislative decisions about social policy may be appropriate in some cases, the legislation at issue does not fall into this category. To the contrary, it is precisely when legislative choices threaten to undermine the foundations of the participatory democracy guaranteed by the Charter that courts must be vigilant in fulfilling their constitutional duty to protect the integrity of this system."

46 *Frank v. Canada*, 2019 SCC 1 at para 43 [*Frank*].

47 2003 SCC 37 [*Figueroa*].

48 Candidates from registered parties can issue tax receipts for donations made outside the election period, list their party affiliation on the ballot, and transfer unspent election funds to the party.

49 *Figueroa*, para 25.

50 2003 SCC 37 at 51 (emphasis added).

51 *Libman v. Quebec (Attorney General)* [1997] 3 SCR 569 [*Libman*].

52 Citing *Libman*, para 47.

53 *Sauvé*, para 11.

54 It is worth noting that the dissent in *Frank* also explicitly referenced section 33, holding that, "The majority's point that s. 3 cannot be overridden by s. 33's notwithstanding clause should not, in our respectful view, be taken as conferring judicial license to strike down legislation on the basis of disagreement with Parliament's policy objectives in legislating on the exercise of the right to vote. Rather, it should encourage judicial restraint in considering those objectives, knowing that a finding of constitutional invalidity would absolutely foreclose Parliament from pursuing them." *Frank*, 141.

55 I recognize that incorporating aspects of expressive freedom into the understanding of the section 3 right to vote may have unintended consequences and that there may be a slippery slope that leads to incorporating aspects of other rights into section 3 in order to avoid the operation of the notwithstanding clause. If the clause is intended as a measure of democratic accountability, too much judicial creativity to avoid its use will be problematic. At the same time, I maintain the view that using the clause in the realm of electoral law presents special problems that require unique solutions.

56 Dwight Newman, this volume, chapter 3.

17

The Text and the Ballot Box: Section 3, Section 33, and the Right to Cast an Informed Vote

Jamie Cameron

Since its enactment in 1982, expectations and apprehensions about how the Charter might change us – for better or for worse – have had time to settle. While constitutional rights will ever spark controversy, Canada is for the most part content with, and proud of, its Charter of Rights and Freedoms.[1]

As always, the override stands watch over the Charter's guarantees, its presence a constant and implacable warning that rights are subject to legislative recall. Section 33's "notwithstanding" mechanism acts as a brake on rights, empowering legislatures to override constitutional guarantees and immunize laws from Charter review.[2] Without it, constitutional rights would have failed, because a textual caveat preserving a role for legislative supremacy was a non-negotiable condition of the Charter's adoption.[3] Since its inception, section 33 has ruled from the background, placing a constant and unpredictable burden on the Charter's rights and freedoms.

Always a provocation, the override stirs controversy even when quiescent. It can easily be forgotten that constitutional rights were initiated amid profound uncertainty about section 33 and its impact on the Charter. To some, planting an override in a document purporting to constitutionalize rights was incoherent because it legitimized derogations and encouraged legislatures to negate Charter entitlements.[4] In allaying those concerns, the leaders of Canada's constitutional patriation described section 33 as a failsafe that would remain dormant in all but rare or exceptional circumstances.[5] Little in the provision supports that view because the textual constraints are modest, and legislatures have constitutional permission to override the Charter's rights and freedoms, essentially at will.

Once the text's architectural see-saw of rights and their override was set in motion, the Charter's guarantees initially co-existed in relative peace with section 33.[6] While not dormant, the override was used sparingly and, albeit with exceptions, did not corrode the Charter's core protections.[7] Over the years, section 33 was feted in academic scholarship praising the override as part of dialogue theory, an innovative feature of rights constitutionalism, and the inspiration for the "Commonwealth" model of rights protection.[8]

Recently, the override has resurfaced more ominously than before, and fears that section 33 will be invoked with increasing regularity to emasculate the Charter's essential promises are now real. Those concerns arise principally in Quebec and Ontario, where provincial governments have relied on section 33 to enact legislation promoting majoritarian dominance and suppressing electoral rights of democratic participation.[9]

The override's ascent as a rights-negating mechanism has prompted renewal in the scholarship and a quest to carve out a residual role for judicial review of section 33 legislation. Emergent theories challenge the long-standing assumption that the override is a "no go" zone, maintaining instead that section 33 does not disable it, but accepts and even requires a form of constitutional review. Though there are variations, these proposals maintain that, short of invalidating it, courts can play an active role in interpreting section 33 legislation.[10] The suggestion has provoked responses from others who reject claims that the override is amenable to review, dismissing this as a form of constitutional heresy.[11] These exchanges are a continuation of 1982's threshold debate, and represent the current generation's theorizing about the contradiction that defines the Charter and has dogged its evolution in the first forty years. At this time, the discussion is no longer abstract, but arises in settings where section 33 legislation has endangered the central foundations of rights protection under the Charter.

A fresh issue stirred by recent section 33 legislation concerns the untouchable rights that cannot be overridden. Only three in number, these guarantees comprise the Charter's democratic rights (sections 3–5), mobility rights (section 6), and minority language rights (section 23).[12] As *Hak v. Quebec* demonstrates, setting these rights apart and insulating them from section 33 can lead to seeming anomalies. There, the Quebec Superior Court selectively invalidated provisions that violate section 3's right to vote and section 23's minority language guarantee, but found that Bill 21's override pre-empted challenges to Quebec's mandatory secularism law under sections 2 and 7 to 15 of the Charter.[13] Those carve-outs from section 33 in sections 3 and 23 provided vital relief from Bill 21's ban on wearing religious symbols to give or receive certain public services, but only in those domains.

Meanwhile, the province of Ontario enacted Bill 307 and relied on section 33 to reinstate Bill 254 and its unconstitutional restrictions on third-party political advertising.[14] In brief, Bill 254 violated section 2(b)'s guarantee of expressive freedom because it extended restrictions on third-party political advertising from six to twelve months in the period prior to a fixed date election. Though both bills breach section 2(b), the question is whether Bill 307 – which overrides sections 2 and 7 to 15 – also violates section 3's democratic rights. Such a conclusion would essentially negate the province's reliance on section 33. In addition, it invokes the relationship between the Charter's democratic rights and section 33, drawing the override directly into an analysis of Bill 307's constitutionality.[15] Though section 3 is not subject to section 33, the override plays a central role in the interpretation of the Charter's democratic rights.

Working Families v. Ontario (*Working Families 2*) marks the first time override legislation forms the backdrop to an interpretation of section 3's democratic rights.[16] Bill 307's use of the override places the relationship between section 33 and the right to vote in sharp relief, exposing a symbiotic relationship between the two that informs the Charter's democratic rights. Democratic accountability, a principle that grounds the underlying assumptions of both, establishes a critical bond between these provisions of the Charter. That bond requires vigorous enforcement of the right to vote, not only to protect section 3's democratic rights, but also to legitimize section 33's legislative override. Put simply, the legitimacy of section 33 and its theory of democratic accountability are contingent on an interpretation of section 3 that prohibits interference with the democratic process. As explained below, Bill 307 violates section 3 because it interferes with that process and undermines the voter's right to cast an informed vote.

Not only does it inform the constitutionality of Bill 307, the symbiosis between sections 3 and 33 has broad implications for

Canada's system of democratic constitutionalism. A finding that Bill 307 breaches section 3 reinforces established principles of interpretation that anchor democratic accountability in the Charter's text and architecture. *Working Families* 2 therefore marks a turning point in the evolution of the override because it calls on the courts to protect the Charter's democratic rights, especially and *a fortiori* when section 33 legislation places significant restrictions on vital avenues of participation in pre-electoral public discourse.

This brief chapter develops a revelatory interpretation of sections 3 and 33. The next section analyzes the textual relationship between these provisions, showing how deeply the accountability principle is embedded in each. That principle informs the legitimacy of section 33 and plays a key role in defining the scope of section 3's entitlements. From there, the discussion turns to section 3, explaining how legislation that violates the section 2(b) rights of third-party political advertisers also offends and undermines the section 3 rights of citizen voters. Throughout, the analysis draws on unwritten constitutional principles – specifically, the democratic principle and its corollaries of accountability and unfettered and free public discussion – to inform the interpretation of section 3.

On that point, the Supreme Court's recent decision in *City of Toronto v. Ontario* emphasized the primacy of the text in constitutional adjudication and directed a relatively narrow interpretive role for unwritten principles.[17] Notably, the majority opinion stated that protection from perceived injustices cannot be found in "amorphous" underlying principles, but rests, instead, "in the text of the Constitution and the ballot box."[18] That, in short, is precisely and exactly the point of this article: that the texts of sections 3 and 33, informed by the principle of democratic accountability, guarantee the integrity of the ballot box and the entitlements that safeguard the democratic rights of the electorate.

While section 33 empowers legislatures to override section 2(b)'s rights of democratic participation, its carve-out for section 3 expresses textual intolerance for derogations from ballot-box rights that are guaranteed by the Charter. As explained below, the accountability principle requires vigilant scrutiny and enforcement of these entitlements, which include the right of meaningful participation and access to information that can influence the vote, both during and outside the period of the election writ.

SECTIONS 3 AND 33: CONSTITUTIONAL TEXT AND THE PRINCIPLE OF DEMOCRATIC ACCOUNTABILITY

The constitutionality of Bill 307's restrictions on pre-writ third-party political advertising pivots on the texts of sections 3 and 33, and their symbiotic connection to the principle of democratic accountability. That principle aligns these provisions, creating a textual and interpretive bond between the two and the democratic imperative that is the foundation of Canada's system of constitutionalism. In complement, these provisions of the Charter serve this unassailable function mutually and symbiotically with each other.

Accountability is a constituent element of the democratic principle and one of the Constitution's primordial values. In the *Secession Reference*, the Supreme Court linked accountability to the consent of the governed and the legitimacy of democratic institutions that "must allow for the participation of, and accountability to, the people, through public institutions."[19] The court bolstered the point, drawing a link between a functioning democracy and a continuous process of discussion, stating that the Constitution mandates government by democratic legislatures, and an executive accountable to them.[20]

As a matter of text, sections 3 and 33 are explicitly linked to the principle of democratic accountability. For instance, in guaranteeing the citizen's right to vote and requiring a general election to be held not less than once every five years, sections 3 and 4 clearly and purposively serve the democratic principle and its objective of democratic accountability.[21] Moreover, excluding sections 3 and 4 from the override highlights the sacrosanct status of these entitlements and prohibits legislatures from interfering with or corrupting the democratic process.[22] These points are insistently confirmed and entrenched in the section 3 jurisprudence.[23]

Meanwhile, section 33 serves democratic purposes somewhat differently, empowering legislatures to override Charter guarantees and shield statutory provisions from Charter review. Democratic accountability is the fundamental condition of section 33, because that is what makes it legitimate for legislatures to override the Charter's rights and freedoms. For that reason, the text promotes accountability by hedging section 33's democratic prerogative in important ways. First, a legislature that chooses to engage the override must provide a "sufficiently express declaration of override" to meet section 33(1)'s requirement of form.[24] Albeit far from onerous, this requirement is designed to draw attention to the override, promoting an informed and reasoned debate in the legislature and public discourse about the decision to invoke section 33. Accountability is contingent on a concept of transparency that requires governments to disclose the essential elements of section 33 legislation and engage a process of wide public discussion.[25]

Second, section 33(3)'s "sunset clause" textualizes the principle of accountability by automatically expiring override legislation five years after its enactment. It is no accident that section 33's five-year lifespan cross-references section 4's equivalent lifespan for the mandate of federal and provincial governments. To pause and emphasize this critical point, section 33's sunset clause is precisely in tempo with section 4's requirement of a general election within the same interval.[26] Separately and together, the five-year limit on an electoral mandate and lifespan of section 33 legislation entrench mechanisms of democratic accountability. Just as democratically elected governments are subject to accountability through section 4's five-year electoral interval, section 33 demands accountability five years after any section 33 legislation's enactment.

The principle of democratic accountability is valuable to constitutional interpretation in this context because it aligns sections 3 and 33. Specifically, section 33's underlying principle of accountability – and the legitimacy of asserting this power – cannot be satisfied unless the Charter's democratic rights are vigorously protected. The sunset clause and its objective of calling governments to account for enacting section 33 legislation can only work where section 3's rights are protected from partisan and other forms of interference. The result may seem paradoxical – even subversive – because it requires section 3's voting rights to be enforced against section 33 legislation in order to defend the override's own democratic purposes. Few objectives are as close to the heart of the Charter as this.

At its inception, section 33 was grounded in and contingent on these principles of accountability and transparency. In reflecting on the override, Jean Chrétien explained that section 33's requirements of a notwithstanding declaration and five-year lifespan were intended to discourage governments from using the override. In particular, the sunset clause would require periodic public debate about the legitimacy of overriding the Charter and discourage the "ill-considered" use of section 33.[27] Roy McMurtry, another prominent leader during the patriation negotiations, declared that "political *accountability* is the best safeguard against any improper use of the 'override clause' by any parliament in the future."[28] Civil liberties leader Alan Borovoy called the override a "red flag" for the opposition parties and press, predicting that it would be politically difficult for a legislature to override the Charter, and concluding that "political difficulty is a reasonable safeguard for the Charter."[29]

These views are also reflected in the academic commentary. Weiler, who proposed and defended the override, explained that "representative democracy implies a structural core consisting of periodic elections" and a public that has been educated about the issues "through vigorous public commentary, especially by an uninhibited press."[30] Though it gives the people a say after the fact, the five-year sunset mechanism requires legislatures and the electorate to think the problem through again and again.[31] Russell is another influential scholar who supported it because the override would provoke a process of "wide public discussion so that the politically active citizenry participate in and share responsibility for the outcome."[32] At the same time, he cautioned that though it provides an opportunity for "responsible and *accountable* public discussion of rights issues," that purpose could be "seriously undermined" if legislatures were free to use the override without discussion and deliberation.[33]

Exempting the Charter's democratic rights from section 33 confirms that the legitimacy of the override is contingent on a process of democratic accountability. Legislatures can only be called to account for overriding Charter rights when the sanctity of the democratic process is preserved by prohibiting governments from violating sections 3 and 4. Put another way, the theory of the override requires sections 3 and 4 to be excluded, because empowering legislatures to negate these guarantees would defeat section 33's embedded principle of accountability. The alternative is ominous, because including democratic rights in section 33's override would compromise the provision's legitimacy and threaten the Constitution's system of democratic constitutionalism.

Theories for the renewal of section 33 support this conception through a functional approach to section 33 and its underlying principle of accountability. As Leckey and Mendelsohn argue, the electorate cannot fully perform its duty to hold legislatures accountable without access to information about the constitutionality of section 33 legislation. Accordingly, they maintain that the judiciary can and should support the public's "constitutional role," making declarations that enable the electorate to assess section 33 legislation and decide whether or how to hold the legislature accountable for enacting it. Though it does not rest on a textual link to section 3, and addresses the status of rights that are subject to section 33 legislation, this conception of review complements and is consistent with the proposition that the override's legitimacy depends on the efficacy of mechanisms of accountability. That point is especially compelling when section 33 legislation overrides section 2(b) in circumstances that place section 3's non-derogable democratic rights at stake.[34]

Another contribution to this volume draws attention to the opportunity – and risk – of a government altering the electoral rules to restrict other voices and create advantages for the incumbent party and its candidates. In "section 33, the Right to Vote and Democratic Accounability," Zwibel maintains that governments cannot be allowed to "manipulate the rules for their own benefit," and treats section 33 as a sword the electorate can assert to enforce its democratic entitlements, not a shield that protects legislation from review.[35]

Though section 3 should receive a robust and generous interpretation in all cases, Bill 307 presents a distinctive and unprecedented challenge to the Charter's democratic rights. Where section 33 legislation eliminates other guarantees like section 2(b), courts must be vigilant in thwarting any threat to the integrity of the democratic process. As explained, democratic accountability is as essential to the legitimacy of section 33 as it is to section 3's democratic rights. Where override legislation undercuts rights of democratic participation during a lengthy pre-writ period, section 33 and its concept of democratic accountability inform the interpretation of section 3. As such, section 33's underlying assumption of accountability aligns with section 3's role in protecting and preserving the Charter's concept of democratic constitutionalism.

Another aspect of the democratic principle that cannot be forgotten is the role of participation as a core element of a functioning democracy. That principle is also embedded in the architecture of the Charter's democratic rights, and a constitutional jurisprudence that identifies free, unfettered discussion and access to information as the sine qua non of a functioning democracy. As explained in the next section, these values inflect and infuse section 3's democratic rights.

THE TEXT, THE BALLOT BOX, AND
THE RIGHT TO CAST AN INFORMED VOTE

Bill 307's override pushed section 2(b) aside and brought the Charter's democratic rights to the forefront, drawing attention to core
questions about the relationship between section 3 and section
33. Under section 3, the right to vote is tantamount to inviolate:
the entitlement cannot be overridden and any infringements are
subject to an exacting standard of justification under section 1. In
interpreting this guarantee, the Supreme Court has been unequivocal that section 3 demands robust and vigilant protection from
interference by the state.[36] That conception of section 3 incorporates a basic and non-negotiable postulate of democratic accountability. A second postulate of accountability extends the scope of
section 3 beyond the concrete right to vote and includes functional
components such as the right to play a meaningful role in electoral
discourse, the right to cast an informed vote, and the right to effective representation.[37]

The democratic principle and democratic accountability require a
functional approach that includes entitlements that make the right to
vote meaningful. In recognition of that, the section 3 jurisprudence
interprets the right to vote generously and inclusively of meaningful
participation and a right of access to information that could influence an informed vote. Notably, these entitlements are not confined
to the election, but extend beyond and throughout the pre-writ
period. In developing a conception of democratic rights under the
Charter, the court's landmark decision in *Figueroa v. Canada* proposed a standard for breach that asks whether legislative measures
undermine section 3's bundle of entitlements.[38] The question in
Working Families 2 is whether Bill 307's restrictions on third-party
participation in political discourse undermined voters and their
rights to participate in a meaningful way and cast an informed vote.

In *Figueroa*, the federal tax scheme created advantages for
larger political parties vis-à-vis smaller parties that did not meet
a fifty-candidate threshold. It is critical to note, in the context of
Bill 307's year-long restrictions in the pre-writ period, that the
advantages and disparities at issue in *Figueroa* were not limited to
an electoral period, but were of general application.[39] The Supreme
Court held that different treatment under the tax regulations violated the rights of members and supporters of parties below the

threshold, because it diminished their capacity to engage in meaningful participation by introducing their ideas and opinions into the
open dialogue and debate the election process engenders.[40]

In addition, *Figueroa* found that that the disparities for smaller
parties had a "more general adverse effect" on the section 3 rights of
voters.[41] As Iacobucci J. explained, the impact of the regulations on
those parties had larger implications in undermining the right of each
citizen to information that might influence their exercise of the vote.
In finding a breach of section 3, he emphasized that a citizen cannot
vote in a way that "accurately reflects" their preferences without
access to information that enables them to assess the strengths and
weakness of the political parties and their candidates.[42]

There are compelling parallels between *Figueroa* and *Working
Families 2*. While *Figueroa*'s disparate tax rules disadvantaged smaller
political parties, Bill 307's advertising restrictions dilute the voices
of third-party political participants, to the point of effectively preventing them from exercising rights of democratic participation for
a prolonged period prior to an election. One difference is that the
disparity in Bill 307 is not between political parties – which are not
subject to the twelve-month restrictions – but between political parties
and third-party participants.[43] For purposes of section 3, that is not
a principled difference. It matters little whether the restrictions are
aimed at smaller political parties, as in *Figueroa*, or at third-party
speakers exercising their democratic rights under section 2(b): in both
instances, the rights of voters are at stake. Bill 307's limits on third-
party participation seriously undermine voter access to information
that could influence the ballot. Though limits on third-party political
advertising that violate section 3 might be justifiable, that is a section 1 issue and does not arise in determining the threshold question
of breach. In addressing that issue, the question under *Figueroa* is
whether Bill 307's twelve-month restrictions on third-party political
advertising undermine the rights of voters under section 3.

A conception of section 3 that valorizes these entitlements is
fortified by the democratic principle and its corollary of a right to
participate in the free discussion of public affairs. As noted above,
City of Toronto accepted this principle and its status as one of the
Constitution's unwritten principles that legitimately informs the
interpretation of section 3. There, the Supreme Court described it as
a principle by which the Constitution is "to be understood and interpreted," and one that includes the right of citizens to participate in

the process of representative and responsible government.[44] In particular, the court reaffirmed that the democratic principle is "relevant as a guide to the interpretation of the constitutional text," because it supports "an understanding of free expression as including political expression in furtherance of a political campaign."[45] The same principle is yet more indispensable to the interpretation of section 3.

The principle of free and open discourse has deep pedigree in the constitutional jurisprudence, tracing its pre-Charter lineage from the *Alberta Press Case* to *Switzman v. Elbling*, and from there to the Charter.[46] In the *Alberta Press Case*, Chief Justice Duff famously stated that democratic institutions derive their efficacy from the free public discussion of affairs, and that citizens have a "fundamental right to express freely [their] untrammelled opinion about government policies and discuss matters of public concern."[47] While his conception of democracy would demand "the freest and fullest analysis and examination from every point of view of political proposals," Cannon J. endorsed "the right of the people" for access to information on questions of public interest, "from sources independent of the government."[48] The *Alberta Press Case* was followed many years later by *Boucher v. the King*, in which Rand J. explicitly confirmed the principle of accountability in stating that, "The administrators of what we call democratic government have come to be looked upon as servants, bound to carry out their duties *accountably* to the public."[49] In *Switzman v. Elbling*, Rand J. deepened his theory of democratic participation, speaking of the "free public opinion of an open society" and the "condition of a virtually unobstructed access to and diffusion of ideas."[50] These quotes are representative, but not exhaustive, of the degree to which accountability is linked in the jurisprudence to a process of open and unfettered public discourse. *City of Toronto* contemplates that this legacy can inform the interpretation of section 3, and in principle it must.

Nor are these views about the vital role of unobstructed access to ideas outdated. Rather, the *Secession Reference* incorporated a pre-Charter conception of democratic engagement and the bonds between accountability and a free and open democratic process. As the court explained, the democratic principle predates the modern Constitution and is a "baseline against which the framers of our Constitution, and subsequently, our elected representatives under it, have always operated."[51] The *Secession Reference* went on to state that this principle is fundamentally connected to the Charter's

promotion of self-government, as reflected in the guarantees protected by sections 3 and 4 of the Charter.[52] As the court stated,
section 4's exemption from section 33's legislative override affirms
the democratic principle "with particular clarity."[53]

The significance of these unwritten principles to section 3 and
Working Families 2 is this: Bill 307's use of the override against section
2(b) also and additionally undermines citizen access to information
that is the sine qua non of democratic participation and accountability.
The affront to section 3 is not minor, but severe, all but insulating the
incumbent government and other political parties from a discourse of
accountability in the pre-writ period. Bill 307 violated the section 2(b)
rights of third parties by placing severe restrictions on their freedom
to participate in the democratic process. In addition, it undermined
the democratic rights of the electorate, who were denied the benefit
of unfettered debate on the merits of a government – as well as other
parties and their candidates – that was standing for election. By sub-
ordinating democratic participation to the goal of protecting political
incumbents, Bill 307 impoverished the electoral process and its foundation in principles of transparency and accountability.

The democratic principle and democratic accountability are a
vital adjunct to the interpretation of sections 3 and 33, and fall
squarely within the *City of Toronto*'s directions for their use in decision-making. As explained, sections 3 and 33 are textually bound
by a synchronous and immutable five-year interval of democratic
accountability. In principle, preserving rights of meaningful participation and access to information about the electoral process is as
central to section 33 as it is to section 3.

Section 33 is an integral part of the Charter that interacts with
and must be interpreted alongside other provisions which not only
include, but point directly at, the Charter's democratic rights. That
is why the democratic principle and democratic accountability are
fundamentally implicated when section 33 engages section 3's entitlements. In such circumstances, section 33's underlying assumption
of democratic accountability inflects the interpretation of section
3's entitlements and the role they play in protecting the integrity
of the democratic process. Override legislation that undermines the
integrity of the democratic process – by stifling voter access to information on issues of public interest from sources independent of the
government – cannot comply with section 33's principle of democratic accountability.

CONCLUSION

In *Quebec (AG) v. 9147-0732* and *City of Toronto*, the Supreme Court addressed models of constitutional interpretation, pushing back against interpretive principles and sources not proximate to the text.[54] In *City of Toronto*, the court accepted that the text is not an exclusive interpretive tool and expressly agreed that unwritten principles play a valuable role in purposive interpretation.[55] As the analysis above demonstrates, the constitutionality of Bill 307 under section 3 raises issues that fall squarely within the court's conception of unwritten constitutional principles and their role in interpretation. In this, the text and the ballot box are conceptually and structurally integrated. The *texts* of sections 3 and 33 address and safeguard the accountability of the *ballot box*, and in doing so reinforce the primacy of the democratic principle and its requirement of accountability. Put shortly, a theory of purposive interpretation is at work, demonstrating how the text works seamlessly with the democratic principle and democratic accountability to protect the integrity of the ballot box. Section 33's foundation in the ballot box demands a generous interpretation of section 3, and a conclusion that Bill 307's use of the override to defeat the section 2(b)'s rights of third-party speakers violated the democratic rights of citizen voters.

Bill 307 could override section 2(b)'s guarantee of expressive freedom, but not the rights of the voter under section 3 of the Charter. The legislature's restrictions on third-party political advertising undermine voter access to information – including opinions, perspectives, and points of view – that could influence the minds of voters in deciding how to cast their ballot. The breach of section 3 in this instance is informed by the scope and extent of the infringement, which applied for a full twelve months prior to the writ period and targeted the voices of third-party participants, but not political parties. As explained above, section 3's entitlements are not confined to the election per se, but, in the interest of accountability, must extend into the pre-writ period. In the circumstances, it is less difficult to imagine that the restrictions had a substantial and even crucial impact on the section 3 rights of voters than to assume that the lack of discourse arising from Bills 254 and 307 made no difference to the electorate.

It is telling that voter turnout in Ontario's provincial election on 3 June 2022 was the lowest on record.[56] Though voter apathy may be a multifactorial phenomenon, both generally and in this election, it is not far-fetched to conclude that the Ontario government dampened voter engagement by doubling down on rights of democratic participation. First, Bill 254 prevented third-party political advertisers from robust engagement in the pre-election discourse for a prolonged period of twelve months, and violated their rights under section 2(b) in doing so. Then, after Bill 254 was declared unconstitutional, the government further undermined democratic accountability by invoking section 33 to all but negate the violation and effectively insulate itself from criticism for overriding sections 2 and 7 to 15 of the Charter.

More recently, following the June 2022 provincial election, Ontario invoked section 33 against labour unions. On 3 November 2022, the government enacted Bill 28, the Keeping Students in School Act, relying on section 33 pre-emptively as a shield to protect legislation that unconstitutionally imposed a collective agreement on public sector education workers.[57] Faced with an uprising from labour unions acting in solidarity, the government promised to repeal the legislation in exchange for an agreement that workers would return to their jobs. It is striking that while the use of section 33 in Bill 28 was rapidly challenged, Bill 307 was not as controversial as it should have been. Whether it would have made a difference is speculative, but the effect of Bill 307 was to emasculate voices, like those of the *Working Families* 2 litigants – public sector unions representing public sector employees – and prevent them from participating in the election in a meaningful way and informing the vote of the electorate.

The Charter's democratic rights loom larger when section 33 legislation negates section 2(b)'s rights of democratic participation. Wisely, section 3 was excluded from section 33 to ensure that governments could not use the override to break the line of accountability that is the foundation of Canada's system of democratic constitutionalism. Interpreting section 3 to protect access to information and the principle of accountability links to and reinforces the conditions under which it is legitimate for a legislature to rely on the override. Bill 307 and *Working Families* 2 demonstrate that the legislature cannot invoke section 33 to override section 2(b)'s rights of democratic participation and simultaneously undermine the democratic rights of voters under section 3. Somewhat paradoxically, it is necessary to invalidate Bill 307 under section 3 to protect the principle of accountability and legitimacy of the override under section 33.

ADDENDUM

Almost nine months after the appeal was heard, the Ontario Court of Appeal rendered its decision in *Working Families 2* on 6 March 2023.[58] This addendum reports, briefly, that the majority opinion by Justices Zarnett and Sossin allowed the appeal (Justice Benotto, dissenting), declared the twelve-month spending limit provision invalid, and suspended the declaration of invalidity for twelve months.[59] The government of Ontario has indicated that it intends to seek leave to appeal at the Supreme Court, though first the court must address written submissions on the further question whether other provisions of the legislation should also be declared invalid.

The court's conclusion that unconstitutional section 2(b) legislation protected by the override also violated section 3 of the Charter is a consequential victory for rights of democratic participation and the voters' right to cast an informed vote. That said, the majority opinion's section 3 analysis is questionable and must be revisited on further appeal. In short, Justices Zarnett and Sossin fashioned a test from *Harper v. Canada*'s section 3 analysis that requires the claimant to establish an absence of careful tailoring in the government's interference with the right to vote, and an inability to mount a "modest informational campaign."[60] The court's "proxies" for breach under section 3 are faulty because in combination they set an onerous standard that runs contrary to authority, including *Figueroa v. Canada*. Specifically, *Working Families 2*'s proxies require the claimant to prove two negatives. The first element, placing the onus to address the absence of legislative tailoring on the applicant, confuses the functions of breach and justification; on this, Benotto J.A. is surely correct. Meanwhile, the second element does not consider the nature of the interference with the voter's right of access to information, but focuses instead on third parties, requiring them also to prove a negative – that the legislation prohibits even a "modest informational campaign."

The proxies the court grafted onto the *Figueroa* test reflect a restrictive conception of section 3 and set a strict standard of breach. In doing so, *Working Families 2* places inappropriate reliance on *Harper v. Canada*'s section 3 analysis and does not improve on *Figueroa*'s less cumbersome test, which simply asks whether the governmental interference undermines section 3's rights of meaningful participation and access to information. The focus is on the nature of the governmental interference with access to information about the vote, and not on legislative tailoring and whether a modest informational campaign can be conducted. Moreover, it is seriously open to question whether access to modest levels of information is sufficient to protect the voter's right of meaningful participation, including the right to cast an informed vote.

NOTES

I thank Peter Biro and Nathalie Desrosiers for inviting me to speak at "The NWS Clause at 40: Canadian Constitutional Democracy at a Crossroads." Note that I represented the Centre for Free Expression, one of the intervenors in *Working Families v. Ontario* (*Working Families 2*), 2021 ONSC 4076 (with Christopher Bredt). This article offers an academic analysis and does not represent the views of the CFE or of co-counsel.

1 Part 1 of the Constitution Act, 1982, being Schedule B to the Canada Act 1982 (UK), 1982, c.11.
2 Section 33, which in this article is referred to as the override, empowers legislatures to enact laws "notwithstanding" section 2 and sections 7 to 15 of the Charter (s. 33(1) and 2), requires an express declaration to activate the override (s. 33(1)), places a five-year limit on section 33 legislation (s. 33(3)), and provides for the override's renewal (s. 33(4)).
3 In the words of then-Prime Minister Trudeau, "It is a regressive Section but it was necessary to reach a compromise ... because some Premiers did not want the full Charter," *House of Commons Debates*, 20 September 1983, at 27292.
4 As Maxwell Cohen stated, "It is simply not possible to say, in the same breath, let us have a doctrine of supremacy of Parliament, let us have a supremacy of Charter regime." "Colliding Visions: The Debate over the *Charter of Rights and Freedoms*, 1980-81" in *Litigating the Values of a Nation*, ed. Joseph M. Weiler and Robin M. Elliot (Toronto: Carswell Co. Ltd, 1986), 24.
5 Jean Chrétien, "Bringing the Constitution Home," in *Towards a Just Society: The Trudeau Years*, ed. Thomas Axworthy and Pierre E. Trudeau (ON: Viking Press, 1990), 306 (stating that the override would "only be used in the most extreme and compelling circumstances").
6 In 2000, Howard Leeson described the override as a compromise that "leaves no one happy, but no one hurt." "Section 33, the

Notwithstanding Clause: A Paper Tiger?" in *Judicial Power and Canadian Democracy*, ed. Paul Howe and Peter H. Russell (Montreal-Kingston: McGill-Queen's University Press, 2001).

7 The government of Quebec passed omnibus legislation overriding the Charter following the Constitution's 1982 patriation. An Act Respecting the Constitution Act, 1982, C.Q.L.R., c-L-4.2. The province also used the override in response to *Ford v. Quebec* [1988] 2 S.C.R. 712. An Act to Amend the Charter of the French Language, 1988, c.54.

8 See generally, Stephen Gardbaum, *The New Commonwealth Model of Constitutionalism: Theory and Practice* (UK: Cambridge University Press, 2013). For a comment on this phenomenon, see Jamie Cameron, "Collateral Thoughts on Dialogue's Legacy as Metaphor and Theory," *University of Queensland Law Journal* 35, no. 1 (2016): 157.

9 See An Act Respecting the Laicity of the State, S.Q. 2019, c.12 (Bill 21), and An Act Respecting French, the Official and Common Language of Quebec, S.Q. 2022, c.14 (Bill 96). In Ontario, see The Protecting Elections and Defending Democracy Act, 2021, S.O. 2021, c.31 (Bill 307).

10 See, for example: Grégoire Webber, Eric Mendelsohn, and Robert Leckey, "The Faulty Received Wisdom around the Notwithstanding Clause," *Policy Options*, 10 May 2019, policyoptions.irpp.org/magazines/may-2019/faulty-wisdom-notwithstanding-clause; Robert Leckey and Eric Mendelsohn, "The Notwithstanding Clause: Legislatures, Courts, and the Electorate," *University of Toronto Law Journal* 72, no. 2 (2022): 189; Grégoire Webber, "Notwithstanding Rights, Review, or Remedy? On the Notwithstanding Clause on the Operation of Legislation," *University of Toronto Law Journal* 71 (2021). See also Robert Leckey, this volume, chapter 5.

11 See, for example, Maxime St-Hilaire and Xaiver Foccroulle Ménard, "Nothing to Declare: A Response to Grégoire Webber, Eric Mendelsohn, Robert Leckey, and Léonid Sirota on the Effects of the Notwithstanding Clause," *Constitutional Forum* 29, no. 1 (2020): 38–9 (stating that their arguments constitute a "creative but ultimately erroneous development in legal thought on s. 33"). See also: Guillaume Rousseau and François Côté, "A Distinctive Quebec Theory and Practice of the Notwithstanding Clause: When Collective Interests Outweigh Individual Rights," *Revue générale de droit* 47 (2017): 237; Dwight Newman, "Canada's Notwithstanding Clause, Dialogue, and Constitutional Identities," in *Constitutional Dialogue: Rights, Democracy, Institutions*, ed. Geoffrey Sigalet, Gregoire Webber, and Rosalind Dixon (Cambridge: Cambridge University Press, 2019), 209.

12 Section 33(1) explicitly states that section 2 and sections 7 to 15 of the Charter are subject to the legislative override; other guarantees that are not specifically included in its scope are excluded.

13 2021 QCSC 1466.

14 After *Working Families Ontario v. Ontario*, 2021 ONSC 4076 (*Working Families 1*) declared Bill 254 invalid on 8 June 2021, the Ontario legislation responding by enacting Bill 307 less than one week later. The legislation was introduced, debated, and enacted, receiving royal assent by 14 June 2021.

15 Bill 254 amended the Election Finances Act, R.S.O. 1990, c.E7, which for the first time introduced pre-writ restrictions on third-party political advertising. Among other things, Bill 254 – The Protecting Ontario Elections Act, 2021 – doubled the pre-election restrictions to twelve months, but retained the third-party global spending amount of $600,000. Bill 254's twelve-month period of restrictions was declared unconstitutional, and Bill 307, which re-enacted the same restrictions, is also unconstitutional under section 2(b), but protected by the override.

16 2021 ONSC 4076 (upholding Bill 307), *Working Families Coalition (Canada) Inc v Ontario*, 2023 ONCA 139 [*Working Families 2*] (ONCA) (allowing the appeal), leave to appeal granted, SCC File No 40725 (9 November 2023).

17 *City of Toronto v. Ontario*, 2021 SCC 34, at para. 73 (citing *British Columbia v. Imperial Tobacco Canada Ltd.* [2005] 2 S.C.R. 473).

18 *City of Toronto v. Ontario*, para. 59 (citing *Imperial Tobacco*).

19 *Reference re Secession of Quebec* [1998] 2 SCR 217, para. 67.

20 Ibid., para. 68.

21 Section 3 guarantees every citizen the right to vote in provincial and federal, but not municipal or other elections, and section 4 places a five-year limit on a legislature's electoral mandate.

22 See *Reference re Secession of Quebec*, para. 65 (stating that the democratic principle is affirmed with particular clarity in that section 4 is not subject to section 33). See also Paul C. Weiler, "Rights and Judges in a Democracy: A New Canadian Version," *University of Michigan Journal of Law Reform* 18, no. 1 (1984): 51–80 (describing the "full entrenchment" of democratic rights as "insurance against the remote possibility of a government's attempt to perpetuate itself by denying basic rights of participation").

23 See note 36. See also *Thomson Newspapers v. Canada (AG)* [1998] 1 S.C.R. 877, para. 79 (stating that although the override is rarely invoked,

"the fact that s. 3 is immune from such power clearly places it at the heart of our constitutional democracy").

24 *Ford v Quebec* [1988] 2 SCR 712, para. 33.

25 See Weiler, "Rights and Judges," 81 (stating that to use section 33, a government would have to "use a formula" designed to draw the proposal to the attention of the opposition, the press, and the general public).

26 Symmetrically, section 4 provides that no federal government or legislative assembly shall continue for longer than five years, and section 33(4) states that a section 33(1) declaration invoking the override power ceases to have effect five years after it comes into force. Charter, sections 4 and 33(3).

27 Jean Chrétien, "Bringing the Constitution Home," 305.

28 Roy McMurtry, "The Search for a Constitutional Accord – A Personal Memoir," *Queen's Law Journal* 8 (1982): 65 (emphasis added).

29 Quoted in Dickson, "Alberta and the Notwithstanding Clause," *LawNow* (2000): 41.

30 Ibid., 67.

31 Weiler, "Rights and Judges," 82, n99.

32 Peter H. Russell, "Standing Up for Notwithstanding," *Alberta Law Review* 29, no. 2 (1991): 299.

33 Ibid. (emphasis added).

34 Leckey and Mendelsohn, "The Notwithstanding Clause," 198-9 (discussing the electorate and legislative accountability).

35 Cara F. Zwibel, this volume, chapter 16.

36 See, for example: *Sauvé v. Canada* [2002] 2 S.C.R. 519, at para. 15 (stating that "it is precisely when legislative choices threaten to undermine the foundations of the participatory democracy guaranteed by the Charter that courts must be diligent in fulfilling their constitutional duty to protect the integrity of this system"); *Frank v. Canada* [2019] 1 S.C.R. 3 at para. 44 (confirming that any intrusions on section 3's "core democratic right" must be reviewed under a "stringent" justification standard that "carefully and rigorously" reviews the government's "preferred" justification for the violation).

37 *Figueroa v. Canada* [2003] 1 S.C.R. 913, paras. 19–32 and 53–4 (explaining these entitlements).

38 *Figueroa v. Canada*, paras. 54, 57, 58 (establishing that the question in every case is whether a measure *undermines* any of the voter's entitlements under section 3).

39 *Figueroa v. Canada*, para. 47 (explaining that the regulations relating to parties below the statutory threshold applied outside the writ period).

40 Ibid., para. 53.

41 Ibid., para. 54.

42 Ibid. See also para. 57 (explaining how the regulations undermined the right to exercise the vote in a manner that "accurately reflects" the voter's preference).

43 In leaving Bill 254's six-month period for restrictions on political spending intact, Bill 307 created a significant disparity between those parties and section 2(b)'s third-party political advertisers.

44 *City of Toronto v. Ontario*, para. 77.

45 Ibid., paras. 77, 78.

46 The most celebrated pre-Charter decisions are: *Reference: Re Alberta Legislation* [1938], S.C.R. 100 (the *"Alberta Press Case"*); *R. v. Boucher* [1951] S.C.R. 265; *Saumur v. Quebec (City)* [1953], 2 S.C.R. 299; and *Switzman v. Elbling* [1957] S.C.R. 285. For a recent discussion of the formative role of these pre-Charter decisions, see Jamie Cameron, "Resetting the Foundations: Renewing Freedom of Expression under s. 2(b) of the *Charter*," in *The Forgotten Foundations of the Canadian Constitution*, eds. Brian Bird and Derek Ross (Toronto: LexisNexis, 2022).

47 *Alberta Press Case*, 148.

48 *Alberta Press Case*, 148, 106.

49 *Boucher*, 680 (emphasis added).

50 *Switzman*, 305, 306.

51 *Reference re Secession of Quebec*, para 62.

52 Ibid., para. 65.

53 Ibid.

54 2020 SCC 32 (addressing the status of international and comparative law in constitutional interpretation), and *City of Toronto v. Ontario* (addressing the status of unwritten constitutional principles).

55 *City of Toronto v. Ontario*, para. 55.

56 4.6 million of 10.7 million eligible voters cast a vote. See "Elections Results," *Elections Ontario*, https://www.elections.on.ca/en/resource-centre/elections-results.html.

57 Section 13, S.O. 2022, c.19.

58 2023 ONC 139.

59 Ibid., paras. 142, 143.

60 Ibid., paras. 85–94.

18

Notwithstanding Minority Rights: Rethinking Canada's Notwithstanding Clause

Caitlin Salvino

I. INTRODUCTION

When the notwithstanding clause[1] was included in the final draft of the Canadian Charter of Rights and Freedoms (Charter), it was regarded as a measure of last resort that would rarely be used by legislatures except in "non-controversial circumstances" or to "correct absurd situations."[2] This characterization of the notwithstanding clause has been largely reflected in its forty-year existence. Between 1982 and 2022, the notwithstanding clause has only been tabled in twenty-six bills.[3] The federal government has never tabled a bill invoking section 33. The provincial and territorial legislatures that have tabled notwithstanding clause bills are Alberta,[4] New Brunswick,[5] Ontario,[6] Quebec,[7] Saskatchewan,[8] and the Yukon.[9] Of these twenty-six tabled notwithstanding clause bills, only eighteen invocations were promulgated and effective.[10]

In its first forty years of existence, the academic literature on the notwithstanding clause has focused primarily on its role as a dialogic tool within the relationship between the courts and the legislatures. I argue, however, that the academic commentary's focus on the notwithstanding clause as a dialogic tool has overlooked the unique vulnerability of minority groups to its application. To address this literature gap, I argue that the process-oriented approach to section 33 is ill-suited in the context of minority groups. The political risk associated with embedded section 33 democratic safeguards provide inadequate protection for the interests of minority groups and may make them more vulnerable to targeting through the notwithstanding clause.

My analysis is two-fold. First, I review the existing notwithstanding clause literature and argue that there is a paucity in the academic commentary on the relationship between minority groups and section 33. Second, I argue that minority groups are uniquely vulnerable to section 33. I present that the drafters of the notwithstanding clause adopted a process-oriented approach to section 33. The process-oriented approach was achieved through the embedding of two safeguards within the structure of section 33: (1) democratic accountability through the legislative process; and (2) democratic accountability through the electoral process. I then apply John Hart Ely's critique of process-oriented approaches to judicial review to argue that the section 33 accountability safeguards are ill-suited for the unique vulnerability of minority groups.

II. SCHOLARSHIP RESPONSES TO THE NOTWITHSTANDING CLAUSE

Since the adoption of the Charter, the notwithstanding clause has been a central focus of Canadian scholars who considered its role as a possible solution to the counter-majoritarian dilemma. The early notwithstanding clause literature celebrated section 33 as an ingenious legislative invention.[11] Other scholars, however, were more critical of its design and suggested reforms to increase its ability to resolve the perceived dilemma of judicial supremacy.

For example, Peter Russell supports the continued availability of the notwithstanding clause on both substantive and procedural grounds. On substantive grounds he argues that no judge is infallible, nor is any right absolute. Thus, constitutional democracies need processes, such as the notwithstanding clause, that facilitate discussing and possibly rejecting a court's judgment.[12] On procedural grounds, he argues that the notwithstanding clause facilitates good governance by encouraging government transparency.[13] To ensure that the notwithstanding clause can better fulfill its substantive and procedural role within Canadian democracy, Russell argues that section 33 must be reformed to bar omnibus application and require renewal after elections.[14] He argues that his suggested reforms create opportunities for accountable discussions of rights issues and achieve meaningful reflection on the use of section 33 after an "election cooling off period."[15]

Tvsi Kahana theorizes that two factors impact public deliberation on section 33 uses: visibility and accessibility.[16] First, a notwithstanding clause use is invisible when the legislature applies it to an issue not on the public agenda. Second, a notwithstanding clause use is inaccessible when it is invoked to respond to complex policy questions not easily understood by the public.[17] To him, the invisibility and inaccessibility of notwithstanding clause uses hinder its ability to be a tool that is accountable to democratic processes through extensive public discussions over its invocation. To increase the visibility and accessibility of section 33 uses, Kahana suggests that the notwithstanding clause be limited to Supreme Court of Canada (SCC) decision responses, which has the effect of elevating any responsive section 33 use to the national agenda.[18]

Finally, Scott Reid's "democratic override" theory proposes referendums for section 33 invocations to "democratize" its use. He argues that the notwithstanding clause is facing a crisis of legitimacy whereby the public does not trust legislatures more than the judiciary to be the final decision-maker on rights. To increase its legitimacy, Reid argues that the decision to invoke the notwithstanding clause must be invested in the people through a democratic referendum.[19]

This review of the early section 33 literature reveals its focus on the role of the notwithstanding clause as a dialogic tool. Both by celebrating its design and suggesting reforms, scholars analyzed its impact on the relationship between the courts and the legislatures. I argue that this literature has thus far overlooked the intersection of minority groups and the notwithstanding clause. The next section seeks to add to the existing literature by addressing this gap and analyzing the unique vulnerability of minority groups to the notwithstanding clause.

III. UNIQUE VULNERABILITY OF MINORITY RIGHTS TO SECTION 33

I argue that minority groups[20] are uniquely vulnerable to the notwithstanding clause. Specifically, the process-oriented approach that underlies the structural design of section 33 is insufficient to ensure protection for the rights of minorities. Minority groups are vulnerable to targeting through the notwithstanding clause because the democratic accountability processes embedded in section 33 cannot safeguard their interests. Consequently, the political risk linked to the notwithstanding clause is a weak deterrent when minority groups are the target.

In the following section, I analyze the process-oriented approach adopted in the design of the notwithstanding clause. I begin by presenting the process-oriented approach, its leading critiques by John Hart Ely, and its relationship with section 33. Through a structural analysis of section 33, I identify two democratic accountability safeguards in the legislative process and the electoral process. I argue that these section 33 embedded democratic accountability safeguards mirror a process-oriented approach to judicial review. I then apply Ely's critiques of process-oriented approaches to argue that the notwithstanding clause democratic accountability safeguards are ill-suited for the unique vulnerability of minority groups.

i. Process-Oriented Approaches to Judicial Review and John Hart Ely

Through the Charter, Canada adopted an entrenched set of rights and fundamentally transformed the enforcement role of the courts. Prior to the Charter, Canada's model of constitutional judicial review was limited to the division of powers.[21] The statutory Canadian Bill of Rights was not entrenched, and the courts were hesitant to apply it to remedy government rights violations.[22] Further, the interpretive approach of an "implied bill of rights" within the 1867 Constitution Act, first introduced by Chief Justice Lyman Duff in *Reference Re Alberta Legislation*, was never recognized by the majority of the SCC before the adoption of the Charter.[23]

When the Charter was adopted, the previously limited role of the courts was transformed through the creation of entrenched rights and meaningful enforcement mechanisms. The Charter drafters explicitly rejected a process-oriented approach to judicial review, instead entrenching both procedural and substantive constitutional rights. The adoption of a substantive approach to judicial review was criticized by proponents of a process-oriented approach, most notably Patrick Monahan.[24] Monahan argues that the Charter now provides courts with the authority to make political decisions on matters of public policy masked as objective legal decisions.[25] To him, the rights guaranteed in the Charter are not based on objective standards dealt with by the courts only on legal grounds.[26] Rather, Monahan asserts that many Charter provisions are vague and invite the courts to make political decisions balancing the interests of society against individual rights.[27] He regards the section 1 *Oakes* test as proof of the political character of judicial review because it requires an inherently normative assessment.[28] He argues that it is not the role of the judiciary to make such normative assessments on the substantive outcomes of public policy based on their own assessment about what is right or good.[29] Such an approach results in the judiciary overstepping its appropriate constitutional role by making substantive choice values on public policy.[30]

As a response to the perceived politicization of the judiciary, Monahan proposes that the courts take on a more limited and circumscribed form of judicial review that focuses largely on upholding the integrity of political processes. His process-oriented approach is based on the principle of equal access to and participation in a political system. The role of the courts should be to advance democracy by removing barriers limiting public debate and accessing political processes.[31] He views this limited approach to judicial review as a way for constitutional adjudication to act in aid of democracy, rather than its current form which he perceives is a derogation from it.[32]

Monahan's critique of substantive approaches to judicial review mirrors that proposed by the American legal scholar Jeremy Waldron.[33] To Waldron, modern liberal society is characterized by what he considers "rights disagreements."[34] He asserts that these rights disagreements are best dealt with by the legislatures, as they are democratically elected with the freedom to debate the moral and other implications of the final decision over the scope of certain rights.[35] Similar to Monahan, Waldron proposes limiting judicial review to safeguarding democratic processes that guarantee access to the political systems.[36] He argues that it is politically and democratically illegitimate to privilege the decision-making role of a small group of unelected and unaccountable judges over the wills of a democratic legislature representative of the people.[37]

In responses to proponents of process-oriented approaches to judicial review, the American legal scholar John Hart Ely put forward a strong defence of substantive approaches to judicial review in constitutional democracies. Ely criticizes the process-oriented approach by arguing that democracy within a constitutional system requires more than "a voice and a vote" for minority groups.[38] Ely was influenced by the 1938 decision of Chief Justice Harlan Fiske Stone in *United States v. Carolene Products Co.* and its well-known footnote number four. In *Carolene Products*, the United States Supreme Court recognized that although the courts must maintain a presumption of constitutionality and deference to government leg-islation, in some instances they may need to intervene in cases that curtail individual rights.[39] In footnote number four, Justice Stone acknowledged that legislation that creates barriers to accessing polit-ical processes or discriminates against already vulnerable "discrete and insular minorities" should undergo more judicial scrutiny under the Fourteenth Amendment.[40]

Ely built on *Carolene Products* by arguing that the role of the courts should not be limited to guaranteeing access to political pro-cesses. He argues that process-oriented approaches to judicial review ignore how the majority continuously ignores the needs and rights of minorities who lack political representation. He writes that, "No matter how open the process, those with the most of the votes are in a position to vote themselves advantages at the expense of oth-ers, or otherwise refuse to take their interests into account."[41] He uses the examples of legislative discrimination against non-citizens, the impoverished, and members of the LGBTQ2S+[42] community as demonstrative of the vulnerability of minority groups to the major-ity electorate who maintain legislative control and enact policies that either ignore their interests or are directly harmful to them.[43]

The academic debates on process-oriented approaches to judicial review are particularly relevant in the context of the notwithstand-ing clause. Although the Charter explicitly adopted a substantive approach to judicial review, the notwithstanding clause through its democratic accountability safeguards was designed from a pro-cess-oriented approach. In the next section, I discuss the two identified democratic accountability safeguards and apply Ely's critique of the process-oriented approach to the notwithstanding clause.

ii. Democratic Accountability Mechanisms Embedded in Section 33

I argue that the notwithstanding clause drafters[44] embedded dem-ocratic accountability safeguards within section 33 that mirror a process-oriented approach to judicial review. Through a structural analysis of section 33, I identify two democratic accountability safeguards: (1) democratic accountability through the legislative process; and (2) democratic accountability through the electoral process. I argue that the design of the notwithstanding clause mirrors a process-oriented approach because the two embedded section 33 safeguards are only aimed at ensuring access to political processes through the legislature and elections. After identifying the two democratic accountability safeguards, I apply Ely's critique of process-oriented approaches to judicial review. I argue that minority groups are uniquely vulnerable to these two democratic accountability safeguards that focus on preserving democratic processes to potentially remove governments that invoke the notwithstanding clause. Consequently, based on the structural design of section 33, minority groups are more vulnerable to being targeted through its invocation.

a. Democratic Accountability through the Legislative Process

Any notwithstanding clause invocation requires the legislature to "expressly declare in an Act of Parliament or of the legislature ... that the Act or a provision thereof shall operate notwithstanding a provision included in section 2 or sections 7 to 15 of this Charter."[45] Per section 33(1), a valid notwithstanding clause act must be passed by a simple majority in the legislature, undergoing all the reading and committee stages of a bill's consideration.[46] Unlike the Emergencies Act, which can be enacted by the executive before tabling in the legislature,[47] the notwithstanding clause cannot be unilaterally invoked by the executive.

This legislative process requirement of an express notwithstanding clause declaration passed by the legislative branch adds an element of transparency to notwithstanding clause invocations. The legislative process requirement notifies other legislators, the media, and the public of the intended notwithstanding clause invocation and enables them to respond in various ways. As argued by Meghan Campbell, the legislative process requirement fosters dialogue by not only requiring the government to publicly state its intent to override the rights of its constituents, but by indirectly requiring them to justify their decision.[48]

In practice, the section 33 legislative process requirement embedded within section 33 has seemingly had little effect on the practice of invoking the notwithstanding clause. A review of the past uses of the notwithstanding clause reveals that often the legislative process requirement results in little to no deliberation or consideration of the use of the notwithstanding clause. For example, in 1998 Quebec successfully invoked the notwithstanding clause in An Act to Amend the Charter of the French Language.[49] The notwithstanding clause bill was introduced in response to the SCC's decision in *Ford v Quebec*, finding that the legislative requirement of unilingual outdoor commercial signs unjustifiably infringed freedom of expression under section 2(b) of the Charter.[50] The responsive notwithstanding clause bill was passed less than a week following the *Ford* decision and was passed without any debate in the legislature.[51] This example demonstrates that the notwithstanding clause legislative process requirement may not in practice cause the deliberative and transparency impacts its purported to have – especially when a government with a legislative majority is the one tabling the notwithstanding clause bill.

Despite the practical challenges identified with the legislative process requirement, I argue that the purported visibility and transparency benefits for the public at large has limited application in the context of minority groups. Minority groups are uniquely vulnerable to legislative processes where their interests are not a priority of elected legislatures.

Ely's critique of process-oriented approaches is particularly relevant to the section 33 legislative process requirement. He argues that elected legislators often ignore the rights of minorities who lack political representation and are not required as a voting bloc for their re-election.[52] The notwithstanding clause legislative process requirement does not sufficiently protect minority groups as it is influenced by similar structural flaws raised by Ely. As highlighted by Ely, many issues for minority groups are not a concern of the majority and are often unpopular among voters. To elected representatives, who are statistically often not members of a minority group, there could be little concern for the interests or rights of minority groups.

Furthermore, the legislature primarily represents the interests of the majority, who may be apathetic to, or actively support, the targeting of minority groups. These instances create situations in which governments can invoke the notwithstanding clause to target minority groups with little opposition in the legislature or need for a fulsome deliberation. Canadian Charter case law demonstrates that often the rights of minorities are related to issues that can be controversial and steeped in stigma.[53] The controversial nature of many of the minority groups rights can result in the public being outwardly supportive of the limitation of their rights through the notwithstanding clause. Throughout Canadian history, there are countless examples of popular support for discriminatory policies, such as Japanese internment camps[54] and the creation of residential schools for Indigenous children.[55]

In the contemporary era, one need not look further than Quebec's 2019 notwithstanding clause invocation in An Act Respecting the Laicity of the State.[56] In Quebec, the Coalition Avénir Quebec (CAQ) party made limiting minority religious rights a central part of their election campaign by committing to bar public servants from wearing religious symbols. In spite of, or potentially because of, CAQ's commitment to ban religious symbols in the public service, they won the election in a landslide.[57] Further polling conducted in March 2019 confirmed the popularity of the policy in Quebec with 74 per cent of those polled saying they supported the ban being applied to judges, prosecutors, police, and prison guards, and 69 per cent saying they supported the ban being applied to teachers.[58] In 2022, the Quebec government was re-elected again in a majority landslide.[59] The recent experiences in Quebec reveal the shortcomings of the section 33 legislative process requirement when it comes to minority groups.

Before moving to the second embedded democratic accountability safeguard, I will make a final point about Quebec. The province of Quebec illustrates the complex relationship between minority groups and the notwithstanding clause that requires further exploration. Quebec's uses of the notwithstanding clause demonstrates that section 33 can be used simultaneously as a tool to target and promote minority group interests.[60] Quebec is both a minority linguistic population within Canada and a majority linguistic population within its provincial boundaries. Quebec's past use of the notwithstanding clause demonstrates multiple instances where the national minority, but regional majority, francophone population has supported the application of the notwithstanding clause to directly or indirectly suspend the rights of regional minorities, such as anglophones[61] and religious minorities.[62]

Although a full analysis of this complex intersection between Quebec, minority rights, and the notwithstanding clause falls outside the scope of this chapter, my critique of the process-oriented approach embedded within section 33 remains applicable. I argue that minority groups are uniquely vulnerable to the notwithstanding clause. The process-oriented democratic accountability safeguards are ill suited to respond to the needs of minority groups when they lack representation in legislative and electoral processes. For example, if the federal government uses the notwithstanding clause within their sphere of authority to undermine the interests of Quebec's francophone population, my identified shortcomings in the section 33 process-oriented approach are relevant. Quebec's francophone population would lack legislative and electoral representation at the federal level and the majority national anglophone population could be apathetic or actively support the temporary suspension of their rights. Thus, although Quebec has a unique status as both a regional majority and national minority population, my critique of the notwithstanding clause process-oriented approach remains applicable.

b. Democratic Accountability through the Electoral Process

Democratic accountability through the electoral process was structurally embedded in the notwithstanding clause to limit its unfettered use. These electoral democratic accountability mechanisms are two-fold. First, section 33(3) of the Charter creates a five-year sunset clause for the notwithstanding clause. In 1982, acknowledging the vast override powers of section 33, the drafters of the notwithstanding clause agreed to place a temporal restriction on its application. Any notwithstanding clause invocation will automatically expire five years after its coming into force.[63] The intended purpose of the five-year sunset clause was to limit the unchecked powers of the legislature to set aside constitutionally entrenched rights. Through review and renewal requirements on five-year intervals, democratic elections act as a check on section 33 by ensuring that it is reviewed every election cycle – making it subject to removal or expiration through the election of different political parties.[64]

The sunset clause cyclically increases the visibility of any active notwithstanding clause invocations. In theory, although not always in practice, the required renewal of the notwithstanding clause results in a resurrection and reconsideration of its necessity. In many instances governments have allowed the notwithstanding clause to expire, ultimately avoiding a renewed debate on the merits of its invocation.[65] The inclusion of a five-year expiration period intrinsically ties the use of the notwithstanding clause to elections, so that its renewal must be considered by each successive government during their mandate. This electoral accountability requirement can have the indirect impact of increasing the visibility of the notwithstanding clause during elections, elevating it as a key issue to be considered by voters.

Second, democratic Charter rights are excluded from the scope of the notwithstanding clause. Per section 33(1), the notwithstanding clause can only be applied to sections 2 and 7 to 15 of the Charter.[66] The notwithstanding clause explicitly excludes democratic rights enumerated in sections 3, 4, and 5 of the Charter. These democratic rights guarantee the right of every Canadian citizen to vote in elections and requires federal and provincial legislative bodies to hold elections every five years. Legislatures may not employ the notwithstanding clause to limit constituents' access to elections or to delay the elections beyond their five-year terms.

The drafter's purposeful exclusion of democratic rights from the notwithstanding clause sought to elevate democratic processes as an accountability mechanism on section 33. Through elections, citizens can hold governments accountable for uses of the notwithstanding clause. Central to the design of the notwithstanding clause is the risk of political consequences. This design of political risk assumes that an unjustified invocation of the notwithstanding clause will be viewed unfavourably by the electorate who value individual constitutional rights.

Taken together, democratic accountability through the electoral process consists of two elements: the sunset clause and the exclusion of democratic rights. The combined effect of these two structural elements seeks to give the final say on the notwithstanding clause to the electorate.

Although the electoral process democratic accountability mechanism is a powerful limit on the unfettered use of the notwithstanding clause, it has significant shortcomings in the context of minority groups. First, by definition, minority groups have minimal impact through the ballot box. Second, many minority groups face barriers to voting, including minority groups who experience higher rates of poverty and homelessness, lack of identification, election dates on religious holidays, or an inability to physically access voting stations. Third, there are minority groups that have no ability to participate in elections due to their status as children or non-citizens. Minority group members without legal voting status have limited or no ability to directly influence elections. Based on these identified issues of demographics, access, or an inability to vote because of legal status, minorities groups are often unable to meaningfully influence elections.

Recognizing the existing demographic and electoral barriers, minority groups are often required to rely on the public to take an interest in their rights. In the context of the notwithstanding clause, minority groups face the same dilemma they experience with the legislative process requirement. The political costs of the notwithstanding clause are inadequate when the public is either apathetic or actively supportive of the temporary curtailment of their rights. For example, Quebec's invocation of section 33 targeting religious minorities through An Act Respecting the Laicity of the State has broad popular support across the province. The popular support for An Act Respecting the Laicity of the State demonstrates the vulnerability of minority groups to rely on the majority to protect their interests.

On a more fundamental level, the creation of a constitutional tool where the public can indirectly vote on the limitation of minority rights is antithetical to the purpose of constitutional rights entrenchment. This is a view articulated by Ely, who argues that minority groups require more than access to political processes to have their rights respected. He argues that minority groups are vulnerable to the majority who continuously out-vote them to maintain legislative control and enact policies that either ignore minority interests or are directly harmful to them.[67] Through the creation of the Charter, political leaders at the time affirmed that there are fundamental rights that require constitutional protection from federal and provincial legislatures – and by extension the electorate. There was a conscious decision to place these rights within an entrenched Constitution and provide courts judicial review enforcement mechanisms to ensure that these rights are respected by the legislative and executive branches. In the years since the entrenchment of the Charter, minority groups have repeatedly turned to the courts seeking protections for their fundamental Charter rights from government infringement.[68] The adoption of a substantive approach to Charter judicial review has been central to the maintenance of continued respect for the rights of minorities.

The paradox of the notwithstanding clause is that when minority groups are most in need of judicial review protections from government rights infringements, section 33 can be invoked to circumvent this process. The legislature's ability to use the notwithstanding clause to immunize themselves pre-emptively or reactively from the Charter reduces constitutional minority rights protections to a symbolic nature that are ultimately unenforceable. The creation of democratic accountability mechanisms through the electoral process, although well-intentioned, is ill-suited for minority groups who face numerous demographic and access barriers in voting. Minority groups are then vulnerable to the wills and interests of the majority, who may be apathetic to their situation or actively support the limitation of their rights.

IV. CONCLUSION

There is a need for further consideration and reflection on the intersection of minority groups and the notwithstanding clause. I argued that the notwithstanding clause process-oriented approach is ill-suited for the unique vulnerability of minority groups. The structural design of section 33 may create a situation where one of the only notwithstanding clause uses that do not incur significant political consequences is the targeting of minority rights. This lack of political consequences for the application of the notwithstanding clause to minority groups may have enhanced repercussions in an age of rising populism. The unique vulnerability of minority groups to the notwithstanding clause should be considered in future discussions on judicial interpretation, reform, and abolishment of the notwithstanding clause.

NOTES

I am grateful to my MPhil and DPhil supervisor Professor Kate O'Regan whose support and guidance was invaluable throughout my graduate research, part of which led to this chapter. Many thanks to Peter Biro and Nathalie Des Rosiers for hosting the conference that led to this collection, as well as the other conference participants and the anonymous referees for their very helpful feedback. Special thanks to Peter Biro for leading the development of this collection – bringing together leading Canadian constitutional scholars at a crossroads moment for the notwithstanding clause.

1 Entrenched under section 33 of the Charter, the notwithstanding clause is a constitutional tool that permits federal, territorial, and provincial legislatures to temporarily pre-empt judicial review or overrides judicial decisions that concern sections 2 and 7 to 15 of the Charter. See Canadian

Charter of Rights and Freedoms, s. 33, Part 1 of the Constitution Act, 1982, being Schedule B to the Canada Act, 1982 (UK),1982 c 11 [Canadian Charter].

2 *House of Commons Debates*, 32-1 (20 November 1981) at 13042–3.

3 See my article documenting the notwithstanding clause political uses from 1982 to 2021. In this chapter, I have added the recent Quebec (2022), Ontario (2022), and Saskatchewan (2023) section 33 uses that have occurred since the article's publication. See Caitlin Salvino, "A Tool of Last Resort: A Comprehensive Account of the Notwithstanding Clause Political Uses 1982–2021," *Journal of Parliamentary and Political Law* 16, no. 1 (2022). See also: An Act Respecting French, the Official and Common Language of Québec, sq 2022, c 14; Keeping Students in Class Act, 2022, SO 2022, c 19; Bill 137, The Education (Parents' Bill of Rights) Amendment Act, 3rd Sess, 29th Leg, Saskatchewan, 2023.

4 Bill 26, Institutional Confinement and Sexual Sterilization Act, 2nd Sess, 24th Leg, Alberta, 1998; Marriage Amendment Act, RSA 2000, c 3.

5 Bill 11, An Act Respecting Proof of Immunization, 3rd Sess, 59th Leg, New Brunswick, 2019.

6 Bill 31, The Efficient Local Government Act, 1st Sess, 42nd Leg, Ontario, 2018; Protecting Ontario Elections Act, SO 2021, c 5; Keeping Students in Class Act, SO 2022, c 19.

7 Quebec has passed sixteen notwithstanding clause acts, including an omnibus act applying the notwithstanding clause to all existing statutes, five pension-related acts, six education-related acts, one agriculture-related act, and three miscellaneous acts. See Salvino, "Tool of Last Resort."

8 An Act to Provide for Settlement of a Certain Labour-Management Dispute Between the Government of Saskatchewan and the Saskatchewan Governments' Employees Union, SS 1984-85-86, c 111; The School Choice Protection Act, SS 2018, c 39; Bill 137, The Education (Parents' Bill of Rights) Amendment Act, 3rd Sess, 29th Leg, Saskatchewan, 2023.

9 Bill 16, The Land Planning and Development Act, 2nd Sess, 42nd Leg, Yukon, 1982.

10 Saskatchewan and Alberta passed promulgated but not effective legislation. Both Saskatchewan's 1987 and Alberta's 2000 notwithstanding clause acts were later declared moot by the SCC. See Salvino, "Tool of Last Resort."

11 Lorraine Weinrib argued that the notwithstanding clause "frees Canada from the crisis of judicial legitimacy that mars other rights protecting systems." See Lorraine Eisenstat Weinrib, "Learning to Live with the Override," *McGill Law Journal* 35 (1990): 571. Kent Roach argued that

the notwithstanding clause is "far from a dead letter" as it plays an influential role in keeping the both the judiciary and legislature accountable.
See Kent Roach, *The Supreme Court on Trial: Judicial Activism or
Democratic Dialogue* (Toronto: Irwin Law, 2001), 78. Paul Weiler characterized the notwithstanding clause as an intrinsically sound solution to the
dilemma of legislatures and courts by masterfully combining the systems
of British parliamentary supremacy and American judicial supremacy.
See Paul C. Weiler, "Rights and Judges in a Democracy: A New Canadian
Version," *University of Michigan Journal of Law Reform* 18, no. 1
(1984): 51–80.

12 Peter H. Russell, "Standing Up for Notwithstanding," *Alberta Law
    Review* 29, no. 2 (1991): 293–309, https://doi.org/10.29173/alr1563.

13 Ibid., 299.

14 Ibid., 301.

15 Ibid., 302.

16 Tsvi Kahana, "The Notwithstanding Mechanism and Public Discussion:
    Lessons from the Ignored Practices of Section 33 of the Charter,"
    Canadian Public Administration 44, no. 3 (September 2001): 255.

17 Ibid., 257.

18 Ibid., 278.

19 Russell, "Standing Up for Notwithstanding," 204.

20 My analysis relies on the definition of minority group by sociologist Louis
    Wirth: "Any group of people who, because of their physical or cultural
    characteristics, are singled out from the others in the society in which they
    live for differential and unequal treatment, and who therefore regard
    themselves as objects of collective discrimination." See Louis Wirth, "The
    Problem of Minority Groups," in *The Science of Man in the World Crisis*,
    ed. Ralph Linton (New York: Columbia University Press, 1945), 347.

21 See, for example, cases where Canadian courts upheld discriminatory legis-
    lation finding no ground to intervene under the 1867 Constitution, includ-
    ing the SCC upholding the disenfranchisement of Canadians of Asian origin
    in British Columbia (*Cunningham v Homma* [1902] UKPC 60, [1903] 9 AC
    151); racial segregation of restaurants, taverns, and theatres (*Franklin v
    Evans* [1924] 55 OLR 349); *Christie v York Corporation* [1940] SCR 139, 1
    DLR 81; *Loew's Theatres v Reynolds* [1921] QR 30 BR 459); and barring
    individuals of Chinese origin from hiring white women in Saskatchewan
    (*Quong-Wing v Regina* [1914] 49 SCR 440, 18 DLR 121).

22 In the thirty-five Canadian Bill of Rights cases heard by the SCC between
    1960 and 1982, only one resulted in a law being declared having no force
    or effect. See *The Queen v Drybones* [1970] SCR 282, 9 DLR (3d) 473. See

also Michael Mandel and Stephane Kirkland, *The Charter of Rights and the Legalization of Politics in Canada* (Toronto: Thompson Educational, 1994), 14–15.

23 *Reference Re Alberta Legislation* [1938] SCR 100, 2 DLR 81.

24 Patrick Monahan, "Judicial Review and Democracy: A Theory of Judicial Review," UBC *Law Review* 21, no. 1 (1987): 87.

25 Ibid., 88.

26 Robert Sharpe and Kent Roach, *The Charter of Rights and Freedoms*, 5th ed. (Toronto: Irwin Law, 2013), 28.

27 Monahan, "Judicial Review," 88.

28 Ibid., 106–15.

29 Ibid., 114–15.

30 Ibid.

31 Ibid., 89.

32 In 2006, Monahan conducted an empirical study of constitutional cases that led him to conclude that the courts, through judicial review under the Charter, have taken an appropriate approach to judicial review by operating as a "meaningful and substantive limit on the authority of government while avoiding many of the pitfalls made by critics." See Patrick Monahan, *Constitutional law*, 3rd ed. (Toronto: Irwin Law, 2006), 390–3.

33 Jeremy Waldron, "The Core of the Case Against Judicial Review," *Yale Law Journal* 115 (2006): 1346.

34 Ibid., 1353.

35 Ibid., 1381.

36 Ibid., 1372.

37 Ibid., 1353.

38 John Hart Ely, *Democracy and Distrust: A Theory of Judicial Review* (Cambridge: Harvard University Press, 1980).

39 *United States v Carolene Products Co.*, 304 U.S. 144 (1938) at footnote 4.

40 *United States v Carolene Products Co.*

41 Ely, *Democracy and Distrust*, 135.

42 LGTBQ+ refers to Lesbian, Gay, Transgender, Bisexual, Queer or Questioning, and Two-Spirit.

43 Ely, *Democracy and Distrust*, 161–2.

44 "Drafters of the notwithstanding clause" refers to the representatives that participated in the final 1981 November Accord. By using this language, I do not dismiss the important role of the Canadian public and civil society organizations in shaping the Charter draft through the 1981 Special Joint Committee on the Constitution. See Adam M. Dodek, *The Charter*

Debates: *The Special Joint Committee on the Constitution and the Making of the Canadian Charter of Rights and Freedoms* (Toronto: University of Toronto Press, 2018).

45 Canadian Charter, s. 33(1).
46 Ibid.
47 The Emergencies Act, RSC 1988, c C-29.
48 Meghan Campbell, "Reigniting the Dialogue: The Latest Use of the Notwithstanding Clause in Canada" (2018) 1 Public L 1 at 2.
49 An Act to Amend the Charter of the French Language, RSQ 1988, c 54.
50 *Ford v Quebec (Attorney General)* [1988] 2 SCR 712; 54 DLR (4th) 577 at para 60.
51 Robert Yalden, "Liberalism and Language in Quebec: Bill 101, the Courts, and Bill 178," *University of Toronto Faculty of Law Review* 47 (1989): 973.
52 Ely, *Democracy and Distrust*, 135.
53 See for example *Suresh*, where the SCC considered the section 7 right of non-Canadian citizen accused of terrorism and at risk of harm if deported. This case occurred right after the terrorist attacks of 11 September 2001, at a period where Muslim men accused of terrorism were not regarded favourably by the public. See *Suresh v Canada (Minister of Citizenship and Immigration)*, 2002 SCC 1.
54 Tom Sando, *Wild Daisies in the Sand* (Edmonton: NeWest Press, 2002).
55 "Honouring the Truth, Reconciling for the Future: Summary of the Final Report of the Truth and Reconciliation Commission of Canada," *Truth and Reconciliation Commission of Canada*, 2015, https://publications. gc.ca/site/eng/9.800288/publication.html.
56 An Act Respecting the Laicity of the State, CLQR 2019, c 12.
57 "Results of October 1st, 2018 General Election," *élections Québec*, 2018, www.electionsquebec.qc.ca/provinciales/en/results_2018.php.
58 Presse canadienne, "Religious symbols: Quebecers back ban and notwith-standing clause, poll says," *Montreal Gazette*, 29 March 2019, montreal-gazette.com/news/local-news/religious-symbols-quebecers-back-ban-and-notwithstanding-clause-poll-says.
59 "Results of October 1st, 2018," *élections Québec*.
60 Because of Quebec's unique status as a minority population within Canada at large, scholars Guillaume Rousseau and François Côté argue that it is "simply false" to suggest that Quebec's recent secularism and French language notwithstanding clause acts "promote only the human rights of the majority to the detriment of the minorities." See

a Distinctive Québec Theory of the Notwithstanding Clause: A Distinct Approach for a Distinct Society and a Distinct Legal Tradition," this volume, chapter 10.

61 See, for example, An Act to Amend the Charter of the French Language; An Act Respecting French, the Official and Common Language of Québec, SQ 2022, c 14.

62 An Act Respecting the Laicity of the State.

63 Canadian Charter, s. 33(3).

64 Peter Hogg, *Constitutional Law of Canada*, student ed. (Scarborough: Carswell, 2006), 881.

65 I discuss the notwithstanding clause invocations that were permitted to expire in Salvino, "Tool of Last Resort."

66 Canadian Charter, ss. 2, 7–15.

67 Ely, *Democracy and Distrust*, 161–2.

68 See, for example: *Syndicat Northcrest v Amselem*, 2004 SCC 47; *Multani v Marguerite-Bourgeoys (Commission scolaire)*, 2006 SCC 6; *Vriend v Alberta* [1998] 1 SCR 493 [1998] ACS 29; *Sauvé v Canada* [1993] 2 SCR 438, 64 OAC 124.

19

Detoxing Democracy:
Exploring Motivation, Authority, and Power

Sabreena Delhon

The Notwithstanding Clause at 40: Canadian Constitutional Democracy at a Crossroads brought together legal academics, legal practitioners, journalists, and civil society representatives to mark the fortieth anniversary of section 33 of the Canadian Charter of Rights and Freedoms by examining its impacts on Canadian democracy. Our conversations focused on questions related to the courts' treatment of section 33, including whether it strikes the right balance between judicial and executive dialogue, and whether its deployment by provincial and territorial governments has resulted in greater public engagement in debates about rights and freedoms. These are valuable and important avenues for exploration and reflection. However, many of these conversations made a critical assumption: that the electorate is equipped to actively participate in the political discourse.

As the chief executive officer of the Samara Centre for Democracy, a non-partisan civil society organization dedicated to strengthening Canada's democracy, my contribution to the program consisted of illuminating the contemporary challenges to democratic engagement, and asking if the electorate is sufficiently enabled to play its role in holding governments accountable, especially in situations related to our rights and freedoms. If our electorate is unable to express its will through voting and/or participate in debates about the use of the notwithstanding clause, we risk generating conditions for uses of section 33 that compromise the health of our democracy.

Leckey and Mendelsohn note that section 33 "assigns to the electorate an important role in assessing the legitimacy and justifiability of a protected law's impact on rights."[1] Here, I explore how the threat of democratic backsliding, distrust in the justice system, and online toxicity impact electoral engagement and more broadly the future of democratic revitalization in Canada.

A UNIQUELY CANADIAN COMPROMISE

Section 33 of the Canadian Charter of Rights and Freedoms, known colloquially as "the notwithstanding clause," allows for Parliament or a legislature to expressly declare, in an act of Parliament or of the legislature, that such act or legislation shall operate notwithstanding the existence of certain other rights in the Charter.[2] It is a uniquely Canadian compromise, allowing a government to override certain sections of the Charter for reasons of public policy.

To appreciate the implications of section 33 on contemporary Canadian democracy, we need to understand the historical and political context in which it was created. In the early 1980s, Prime Minister Pierre Elliot Trudeau included the notwithstanding clause to win the support of hesitant provinces in the creation of the Charter. It theoretically allowed provinces to retain their legislative power regardless of Charter infringements. Then-Justice Minister Jean Chrétien characterized the clause as a "safety valve," something that would be used rarely and in non-controversial situations to "provide the flexibility required to ensure that legislatures rather than judges have the final say on important matters of public policy."[3]

Those involved in its drafting were cautiously optimistic that any prospective use of section 33 would be subject to vigorous political debate and civic participation, thus resulting in political accountability. At the time of its inception, Manitoba's attorney general lauded section 33 as exemplifying "the right to use the authority of Parliament and the elected legislatures to identify, define, protect, enhance and extend the rights and freedoms Canadians enjoy."[4] The ability to shape political discourse through democratic participation was seen as essential to section 33, implying that not only governments but, crucially, the electorate would serve as an authority on the rights and freedoms of Canadians. Similarly, it was assumed that the necessary re-enactment of the override power every five years allowed voters to issue their own referendum on a government's use of the power and, where applicable, result in a change of government.[5]

Section 33 assumes a third party in the perpetual dialogue between the courts and legislatures in Canada, that being an active, informed, and empowered electorate. Yet dialogue is an imprecise word, subject to different interpretations and contexts. There remains no clear process to ensure accessible participation in this critical dialogue or an understanding of how to measure outcomes. For example, in his inquiry into dialogic constitutionalism, Gargarella critiques the dialogue that is meant to ensue from the invocation of the notwithstanding clause in Canada, insisting that dialogue should not be reduced to an exchange of arguments between the branches, nor should it reproduce the inequalities that may exist between the participants.[6] He questions whether authentic public discussion has ever ensued from the invocation of the notwithstanding clause, and argues that, "The existence of severe social inequalities and ... the prevalence of institutions that are not well prepared for the promotion of an inclusive dialogue seem to seriously conspire against the potentials of an egalitarian, dialogic practice."[7]

Taking my cue from Gargarella, I suggest that Canada be very specific when we refer to the electorate's participation in any dialogue about the use of section 33. How have provincial and territorial governments invited the participation of their constituents into debate about a particular use of the notwithstanding clause? What type of information was shared with the electorate to prompt their participation? What kind of assurances were offered to make that participation safe, equitable, and accessible to all? And most importantly, what resulted from the electorate's participation in such debates?

Some legal scholars endorse adding procedural requirements to the usage of section 33 in order to ensure greater public participation. MacLean and Froc envision three safeguards to inform future uses of the notwithstanding clause:

1 Governments must give broad public notice of their intention to invoke Section 33 to pass a law violating one or more Charter guarantees, and they must clearly spell out those guarantees;
2 Governments must facilitate meaningful public deliberation of the merits of their proposed laws and their reasons for violating – potentially or actually – one or more Charter guarantees;

3   When an individual or group goes to court to challenge the
    validity of a law shielded from Charter scrutiny, the govern-
    ment must not pass the law until the process is complete.[8]

Similarly, the Canadian Bar Association has endorsed the creation
of new federal and provincial guidelines for "meaningful and transparent public consultation" for the usage of the notwithstanding
clause.[9] These perspectives argue that the usage of section 33 in contemporary Canada requires meaningful public participation – and I
agree. Without express dialogue between the electorate and its elected
government about the use of the notwithstanding clause, we are left
with an entrenched status quo that can hinder advances for inclusion
and engagement. This is a worrying circumstance, particularly in a
period where our political climate is displaying many frailties.

DEMOCRATIC BACKSLIDING

Recent years have seen what scholars describe as a global democratic recession.[10] This entails an "erosion of checks and balances,
hollowing out institutions of accountability," and a shrinking space
for civil society.[11] The International Institute for Democracy and
Electoral Assistance has identified a range of drivers for democratic
backsliding, including social and political polarization, a rise of
populist parties in government, and the spread of disinformation.[12]
While Canada enjoys a strong reputation for its democracy interna-
tionally, it must remain steadfast in ensuring a robust and resilient
culture of civic engagement.[13]

Low public trust in elected officials,[14] the spread of misinformation through social media,[15] and signs of social polarization[16]
are all variables that are readily challenging Canada's democracy. A study by McGill University-based think tank the "Digital
Democracy Project" found that Canadians associate negative
feelings with others merely because they share opposing partisan perspectives.[17] Their study suggests that this is concerning
for Canadian democracy because it demonstrates that "polarization does not just influence people's opinions about the parties,
but also how they view ordinary Canadians."[18] In addition, the
Consortium on Electoral Democracy has found that 92 per cent of
Canadians feel that politicians are willing to lie to get elected, even
though 80 per cent report being satisfied with their democracy.[19]

These findings indicate that Canada should not be complacent. Over the course of the COVID-19 pandemic, "partisan identities [have shaped] our willingness to get vaccinated and follow public health measures" such as wearing a mask.[20] In addition, during this extended emergency we have seen a rise in polarization and acts of violence against Asian communities.[21]

We must also pay attention to the polarization that occurs within our media institutions. While we assume that they can drive independent debate about the notwithstanding clause, a recent empirical research project found that the ideological orientation of various news outlets is strongly associated with how section 33 is portrayed.[22] In this period of global democratic backsliding, we face urgent and complex challenges related to trust, risk, and knowledge. Much of the historical debate around section 33 assumes that the political sphere is open and inviting to all Canadians – but there are many indicators that this is increasingly not the case.

DISTRUST IN PUBLIC INSTITUTIONS

These indicators relate to many factors, including disengagement and disenfranchisement from public institutions, such as the justice system. In 2021, Statistics Canada conducted the Canadian Legal Problems Study to gain a better understanding of access to justice challenges and resolution methods.[23] They found that 18 per cent of Canadians experienced at least one dispute or problem they considered "serious" or "difficult to fix" in the past three years. Socio-economic factors including income and ability increased the likelihood of experiencing a serious issue.[24] A 2016 study measuring how Ontarians perceived the justice system found that the majority of respondents described it as oppressive (54 per cent), not representative of all Ontarians (63 per cent), and intimidating (71 per cent).[25] Furthermore, four out of ten Ontarians saw the justice system as unfair, regardless of their race, gender, age, or income.[26] It is unlikely that views of the justice system have improved over the course of the pandemic, which has seen marginalized and middle-income individuals navigating a surge in legal problems related to domestic violence,[27] family breakdown,[28] hate crimes,[29] and employment issues.[30] In addition, the 2021 *Race and Criminal Injustice* report found a perception of bias in the criminal court system, with Black and Asian participants most likely to hold this view.[31]

It is important to note that within this justice context, COVID-19 has had a disproportionate impact on low-income and racialized communities,[32] long-term care home residents,[33] frontline workers,[34] and incarcerated individuals.[35] Across these categories, women are bearing the brunt of adverse outcomes.[36] These groups are also most likely to face barriers to casting a ballot.[37] Understanding how Canadians experience interactions with public institutions like the justice system provides an indication of their capability and motivation to engage with democracy more broadly. Public institutions are meant to serve and be accountable to their constituents. Concerted, continuous efforts are required to secure trust and maintain a strong civic connection with the electorate.

ONLINE TOXICITY

This feeling of alienation and disengagement is further emphasized when people go online.[38] Online platforms amplify harmful content in a way that is out of proportion to its prevalence in the real world, distorting our public sphere as well as our social norms.[39] This calls for a level of responsiveness to how technology is shaping our current democratic context.

This circumstance is what inspired the Samara Centre's SAMbot project, which uses a machine learning bot to track abusive tweets received by candidates in Canadian elections. In addition to counting the number of tweets, text is analyzed for toxicity attributes to determine sentiment. The purpose of this initiative is to examine how the amplification and abundance of abuse online is a barrier to civic engagement.

For the 2021 federal election, SAMbot analyzed over 2.5 million tweets received by 298 candidate accounts over the course of five weeks. Approximately 20 per cent of the tracked tweets were abusive, meaning that the text was likely to be considered uncivil, insulting, hostile, and may even be threatening or profane.[40] Over 140,000 tweets contained sexually explicit content, much of which was misogynistic and largely directed at just eighty-eight female candidates. In addition, our analysis found 212,059 tweets containing identity attacks and 291,393 containing threats.[41]

These findings illuminate the scale and intensity of harm in Canada's political discourse within our digital public square. Online toxicity is a key reason for why people leave politics, do not enter politics, or simply avoid the political conversation altogether.[42] Abundant online harm, the very limited trust in the justice system, and the adverse experiences of the pandemic make for urgent problems that can have serious consequences for one's civic connection.

Considering this context, it is apparent that Canadians are in need of supported opportunities to enhance their capability to robustly engage and participate in their democracy. If the expectation is that the electorate play a critical role in assessing the use of section 33, then we as a society need to ensure they are sufficiently enabled to do so. What can be done to ensure the electorate can effectively play their part?

SUPPORTING DEMOCRATIC REVITALIZATION

To enable and expand the electorate's capacity for democratic engagement, we need to champion democratic revitalization in Canada. Han provides important insights on how to foster and encourage contemporary active citizenship and civic participation. She observed that, "The challenge of democracy in the 21st century comes from a society that has neglected the challenge of enabling people's power."[43] To meet this challenge head on, Han argues that we need to cultivate a new kind of leader in civil society, one that has the ability to respond with agility on shifting terrain.[44] For Han, "Either those who have the motivation to make change lack the authority or capacity to act, or those who have the authority lack the motivation. Solving problems of power, then, requires bringing motivation and authority into alignment."[45]

Therefore, to drive change, contemporary leaders must be able to balance tensions – to move with ease from the top-down and bottom-up – and to adeptly navigate both constituency and institutional demands. New leadership must be representative, inclusive and diverse, as well as able to understand the role of power in democratic life. Han argues that this goes beyond asking people to merely express their choice and requires the electorate to be invited into "structures or venues that enable them to negotiate power."[46] This observation resonates and aligns with the three recommendations set out earlier by Froc and MacLean in the context of the notwithstanding clause in Canada.

Canadians want a greater say in decisions affecting their lives.[47] Public participation such as citizen assemblies or reference panels provide key ways to respond to this call. These approaches fall under the broader practice of deliberative democracy which, when properly implemented, can strengthen the civic capacity of the public, enhance trust of democratic institutions, and produce informed solutions to complex problems.[48] They also offer tangible avenues for civil society leaders to "consider the ways they are creating opportunities for people to learn and negotiate power with each other and with people in positions of authority."[49]

A notable example of this model is the Canadian Commission on Democratic Expression, an initiative led by the Public Policy Forum from April 2020 to March 2023, that reviews the state of Canadian democracy and how it can be strengthened. The commission hosted a small, representative citizens assembly tasked with examining available and original research to assess solutions to online harms. They released annual reports detailing their findings to the federal government and the Canadian public. In their most recent report, the assembly tackled misinformation and endorsed twenty-seven recommendations to support democracy while reducing misinformation online.[50] From this example, we can see the value of meaningful public discourse in determining solutions to pressing public challenges. Drawing from the world of deliberative democracy does not make for a perfect solution, but it does broaden and diversify means of civic engagement that enable the electorate to play their role in assessing the legitimate and justifiable use of section 33. In addition, this kind of shift in engagement puts citizens at the centre, which can bolster against the threat of democratic backsliding by repairing the relationship between the electorate and their institutions.

As we begin to emerge from the pandemic, we have a crucial opportunity to shape new norms along with practical and innovative approaches to strengthening civic participation.[51] COVID-19 public health measures have intersected with restrictions on civil liberties.[52] This is particularly important in the context of the notwithstanding clause, which can create opportunities for misuses of power and distort the role of courts in our democracy. The increasing centralization of power in leaders' offices and the enormous authority of majority governments in a first-past-the-post voting system can create a circumstance where courts become the only form of substantive opposition. This can hinder the electorate's sense of agency and should be of serious concern for "partisans of all stripes."[53]

For Des Rosiers, section 33 is a dangerous tool that can undermine the edifice of the Charter and international approaches to human rights.[54] She asserts that civil society should do more to raise the political cost for the use of section 33 by demanding a high standard of accountability from elected officials. Failure to react in this manner could result in section 33 being employed as a tool of authority and method to advance populism. The activation of civil society to hold power to account is linked to safeguarding the advancement of minority rights that the Charter has accumulated over the last four decades.

Civil society also plays a mediating function, for, as Salvino notes, the current majoritarian approach that is meant to bring democratic accountability to the use of section 33 has serious limitations.[55] There is no requirement for legislative debate and there is no recognition that the majority can be apathetic and discriminatory. We cannot assume that voters support minority rights and we must be mindful of the potential for the inappropriate use of section 33 to advance populist ends. These circumstances underscore the task of civil society to bring forth political consequences for the use of the notwithstanding clause as a tool of authority and to protect the health of our democratic culture.

CONCLUSION

We are facing a critical opportunity to evolve how we approach civic engagement and enable the electorate to play their role in holding power to account. Failure to do so risks generating conditions for use of the notwithstanding clause that can compromise our democratic culture.

To make change, we must be responsive to challenges and barriers to participation related to the threat of democratic backsliding, trust in our institutions, and technology's influence on our democracy. Canada needs to advance how it develops new leaders and fosters civic skills in order to support an engaged citizenry for the twenty-first century.

The absence of meaningful civic engagement opportunities for the electorate creates a climate ripe for misuse of section 33. We must be proactive by providing opportunities for increased transparency, accountability, and engagement through public deliberation. By strengthening civic connection, the electorate will be better equipped to actively participate in dialogue around fundamental issues of rights and freedoms, including the invocation of the notwithstanding clause. The fortieth anniversary of the Charter offers an ideal opportunity for reflection on the current democratic culture in Canada. It is important to remember our history and learn from it, but we must not be nostalgic –·for as one golden age ends we can set about realizing the next one. Together, we can broaden our democratic imagination to develop meaningful and responsive support for the electorate.

NOTES

My thanks to Karin Galldin for comments on an earlier draft and to Braelyn Guppy for her research assistance.

1 Robert Leckey and Eric Mendelsohn, "The Notwithstanding Clause: Legislatures, Courts, and the Electorate," *University of Toronto Law Journal* 72, no. 2 (2022): 189.
2 The rights which can be subsumed under such an override are those in sections 2 (Fundamental Freedoms), 7–14 (Legal Rights), and 15 (Equality Rights). Canadian Charter of Rights and Freedoms, s. 33, Part I of the Constitution Act, 1982, being Schedule B to the Canada Act, 1982 (UK), 1982, c 11.
3 As cited by Peter Biro, "Introduction – Chekhov's Gun Inverted," 11 April 2022, 05:40 to 06:21, www.youtube.com/watch?v=v3ce22wWY4w.
4 G.W.J. Mercier, former attorney general of Manitoba, as quoted in "The Notwithstanding Clause of the Charter," ed. David Johansen and Philip Rosen (Library of Parliament & Law and Government Division, 2013), 4.
5 Peter Hogg, "A Comparison of the Bill of Rights and the Charter," in *The Canadian Charter of Rights and Freedoms: Commentary*, ed. Walter Tarnopolsky and Gérald-A. Beaudoin (Toronto: Carswell, 1982).
6 Roberto Gargarella, "Why Do We Care about Dialogue?: 'Notwithstanding Clause,' 'Meaningful Engagement' and Public Hearings: A Sympathetic but Critical Analysis" in *The Future of Economic and Social Right*, ed. Katherine Young (Cambridge: Cambridge University Press, 2019), 212–32.
7 Gargarella, 232.
8 Jason MacLean and Kerri Froc, "Notwithstanding the Notwithstanding Clause, the Charter is Everyone's Business," *The Conversation*, 26 July 2021,theconversation.com/notwithstanding-the-notwithstanding-clause-the-charter-is-everyones-business-163143.
9 "Guidelines on Use of the Notwithstanding Clause of the Charter of

Rights and Freedoms," *The Canadian Bar Association*, 19 February 2020, www.cba.org/Our-Work/Resolutions /Resolutions/2020/Guidelines-on-Use-of-the-Notwithstanding-Clause-of.

10 Larry Diamond, "Facing Up to the Democratic Recession," *Journal of Democracy* 26, no. 1 (2015): 141.

11 Ibid., 149.

12 *Global State of Democracy Report 2021: Building Resilience in a Pandemic Era* (Stockholm: International Institute for Democracy and Electoral Assistance, 2021), doi.org/10.31752/idea.2021.100.

13 "Freedom in the World 2021: Canada," *Freedom House*, 2021, reedomhouse.org/country /canada/freedom-world/2021.

14 Allison Harell, Laura B. Stephenson, Daniel Rubenson, and Peter John Loewen, *Democracy Checkup 2021* (London, ON: Consortium on Electoral Democracy, 2021), c-dem.ca/wp-content/uploads/2021/12 / DC-2021-Codebook-Dec-2021-Draft.pdf.

15 Karine Garneau and Clémence Zossou, "Misinformation during the COVID-19 Pandemic," *Statistics Canada*, 2 February 2021.

16 Sanjay Ruparelia, "The Rising Threats to Democracies," *Policy Options*, 7 September 2022, policyoptions.irpp.org/magazines/septembe-2021/ the-rising-threats-to-democracies/.

17 Taylor Owen et al., "Research Memo #3 Polarization and its Discontents," *Digital Democracy Project*, 2019, 3–4, www.mcgill.ca/max bellschool/files/maxbellschool/ddp-research-memo-3-sept2019.pdf.

18 Ibid., 8.

19 Sabreena Delhon, "It's Time for a Digital Democracy Detox," *Policy Options*, 15 September 2021, policyoptions.irpp.org/magazines/ septembe-2021/its-time-for-a-digital-democracy-detox/.

20 Owen, "Research Memo #3."

21 Vanessa Balintech, "2 Years into the Pandemic, Anti-Asian Hate Is Still on the Rise in Canada, Report Shows," CBC News, 3 April 2022, www.cbc. ca/news/canada/toronto/2-years-into-the-pandemic-anti-asian-hate-is-still-on-the-rise-in-canada-report-shows-1.6404034.

22 Eleni Nicolaides and David Snow, "A Paper Tiger No More? The Media Portrayal of the Notwithstanding Clause in Saskatchewan and Ontario," *Canadian Journal of Political Science* 54, no. 1 (2021): 61.

23 Laura Savage and Susan McDonald, "Experiences of Serious Problems or Disputes in the Canadian Provinces, 2021," *Statistics Canada*, 20 January 2022, www150.statcan.gc.ca/n1/pub/85-002-x/2022001/arti-cle/00001-eng.htm.

24 Ibid.

25 David Coletto, *Public Perceptions of Access to Justice in Ontario* (The Action Group on Access to Justice, 2016), 1, lawsocietyontario.azureedge. net/media/lso/media/tag/resources/abacus_tag_release_oct14.pdf.

26 Ibid.

27 Megan L. Evans, Margo Lindauer, and Maureen E. Farrell, "A Pandemic within a Pandemic: Intimate Partner Violence during COVID-19," *New England Journal of Medicine* 383 (2020), doi:10.1056 /NEJMp2024046.

28 Perlita Stroh, "Pandemic 'Pressure Cooker' Is Driving More Couples to Seek Advice about Separation, Divorce," CBC News, 18 November 2020, www.cbc.ca/news/canada/covid-19-panemic-divorce-rates -1.5795625.

29 Nicolaides and Snow, "A Paper Tiger No More?"

30 Aidan Macnab, "No Area of Law More Affected by COVID-19 than Employment Law, Says Lawyer," *Canadian Lawyer*, 13 May 2020, www. canadianlawyermag.com/practice-areas/labour-and- employment/ no-area-of-law-more-affected-by-covid-19-than-employment-law-says-lawyer/329592.

31 Scot Wortley, Akwasi Owusu-Bempah, and Huibin Lin, *Race and Criminal Injustice: An Examination of Public Perceptions on, and Experiences with, the Criminal Justice System Among Residents of the Greater Toronto Area* (Ryerson University Faculty of Law, 2021), 7, cabl. ca/wp-content/uploads/2021/02/CABL-Report-Race-and-Criminal-Injustice-Feb-10-2021.pdf.

32 Astrid Guttmann et al., COVID-19 *in Immigrants, Refugees and Other Newcomers in Ontario: Characteristics of Those Tested and Those Confirmed Positive, as of June 13, 2020* (Toronto, ON: ICES, 2020), 4.

33 Ryan Rocca, "A Look at What Has Gone Wrong in the Ontario Long-Term Care amid the Coronavirus Pandemic," Global News, 24 November 2020, globalnews.ca/news/7471775/what-went-wrong-ontario-long-term-care-coronavirus/.

34 James T. Brophy, Margaret M. Keith, Michael Hurley, and Jane E. McArthur, "Sacrificed: Ontario Healthcare Workers in the Time of COVID-19," *New Solutions* 30, no. 4 (2020): 267–81.

35 Martha Paynter and Linda Mussell, "Worsening Conditions in Prisons during COVID-19 Further Marginalize Criminal Women," Dal News, 19 October 2020, www.dal.ca/news/2020/10/19/ worsening-conditions-in-prisons-during-covid-19-further-marginal.html.

36 Marilyn Gladu, *Impacts of COVID-19 Pandemic on Women: Report of the Standing Committee on the Status of Women* (House of Commons, March 2021), https://publications.gc.ca/collections/collection_2021/parl/xc71-1/ XC71-1-1-432-6-eng.pdf.

37 Livianna Tossutti, *The Electoral Participation of Ethnocultural Communities* (Ottawa, ON: Elections Canada, 2007); Amira Elghawaby, "Why Immigrant, Newcomer and Racialized Communities Still Face Barriers to Voting in Canada," *PressProgress*, 14 September 2021, pressprogress.ca/why-immigrant-newcomer-and-racialize d-communities-still-face-barriers-to-voting-in-canada/.

38 Michael Morden, *The Samara Centre's Field Guide to Online Political Conversations* (Toronto: The Samara Centre for Democracy, 2019).

39 Renee Diresta, "Free Speech Is Not the Same As Free Reach," WIRED, 30 August 2018, www.wired.com/story/free-speech-is-not-the-same-as-free-reach/.

40 SAMbot, *Samara Centre for Democracy*, July 2022, https://www.samaracentre.ca/project/sambot.

41 SAMbot 2021 Federal Election Report, *Samara Centre for Democracy*, August 2022, https://www.samaracentre.ca/articles/sambot-2021-federal-election-snapshot.

42 SAMbot 2021 Federal Election Report.

43 Hahrie Han, "Problems of Power," *Stanford Social Innovation Review* 18, no. 1 (2019): 6, ssir.org/articles/entry/fixing_democracy_demands_the_building_and_aligning_of_peoples_motivation_and_authority_to_act#.

44 Hahrie Han, "Practicing Democracy: A Conversation with Professor Hahrie Han," 00:06:10, 17 June 2020, www.youtube.com/watch?v=bz DXXZHQaJc.

45 Ibid.

46 Hahrie Han and Jae Yeon Kim, "Civil Society Realized: Equipping the Mass Public to Express Choice and Negotiate Power," *The ANNALS of the American Academy of Political and Social Science* 699, no. 1 (2022): 179, //doi.org/10.1177/00027162221077471.

47 Michael Morden and José Ramón Martí, "Canada Can Prove it's a Leader in Deliberative Democracy," *Policy Options*, 27 November 2020, policyoptions.irpp.org/magazines/november-2020/canada-can- prove-its-a-leader-in-deliberative-democracy/.

48 OECD, *Innovative Citizen Participation and New Democratic Institutions: Catching the Deliberative Wave*, June 2020, doi.org/10.1787/339306da-en.

49 Morden and Ramón Martí, "Canada Can Prove," 181.

50 *Canadian Commission for Democratic Expression* (Ottawa, ON: Public Policy Forum, 2022), ppforum.ca /wp-content/uploads/2022/05/DemX-2-English-May-4-1.pdf.

51 Sanjay Ruperlia, "Joe Biden's Summit for Democracy Creates an Opportunity to Rethink our Current Political Path," *Globe and Mail*,

December 2021, www.theglobeandmail.com/opinion/article-joe-bidens-summit-for-democracy-creates-an-opportunity-to-rethink-our/.

52 *Stay Off the Grass:* COVID-19 *Law Enforcement in Canada* (Toronto, ON: Canadian Civil Liberties Association, June 2020), ccla.org/wp-content/uploads/2021/06/ 2020-06-24-Stay-Off-the-Grass-COVID19-and-Law-Enforcement-in-Canada1.pdf.

53 Ben Woodfinden, "Doug Ford's Notwithstanding Decision is a Symptom of a Problem with Canada's Democracy," *Maclean's*, September 2018, https://www.macleans.ca/opinion/doug-fords-notwithstanding-decision-is-a-symptom-of-a-problem-with-canadas-democracy/.

54 Nathalie Des Rosiers, "The Dialogue Theory: Key Elements and the Argument Against Pre-emptive Use of Section 33," 11 April 2022, 00h:44:15, www.youtube.com/watch?v=W6A-BN AJEOA&list=PLZPXYnb596cbuBGZcrJ9WVep8VzrD6eJp&index=3.

55 Caitlin Salvino, "Notwithstanding Minority Rights: Re-Thinking Canada's Notwithstanding Clause," 12 April 2022, 00h:04:00, www.youtube.com/watch?v=DiXe7vRzf8w&list=PLZPXYnb596c buBGZcrJ9 WVep8VzrD6eJp&index=6&t=1263s.

Contributors

THOMAS S. AXWORTHY is Massey College Public Policy chair, senior fellow at the Munk School of Global Affairs, and secretary general of the InterAction Council, and is a former principal secretary to Prime Minister Pierre Trudeau.

PETER L. BIRO is a lawyer and the founder of Section 1 (www.section1.ca), a democracy and civics education think-tank. He is a senior fellow of Massey College, a centre associate of the University of British Columbia Centre for Constitutional Law and Legal Studies, a fellow of the Royal Society of Arts (FRSA), and chair emeritus and past chair of the Jane Goodall Institute. He is the editor of *Constitutional Democracy Under Stress – A Time for Heroic Citizenship* (Mosaic Press).

GREGORY B. BORDAN is counsel at Norton Rose Fulbright in Montreal. He has extensive experience in the areas of regulatory law, product liability, constitutional law, including Charter of Rights issues, and in matters related to the Charter of the French Language. He is also secretary of the Legal Committee of the Coalition Inclusion Quebec, one of the plaintiffs challenging Quebec's Bill 21, Quebec's ban on religious symbols.

JAMIE CAMERON is professor emerita, having retired from Osgoode Hall Law School in January 2020. Over the years, she has taught and written on constitutional and public law issues, including the Charter of Rights and Freedoms, freedom of expression and the press, academic freedom, US constitutional law, judicial biography, and criminal law. She has recently appeared before the courts, including the Supreme Court of Canada, in Charter cases.

FRANÇOIS CÔTÉ holds a bachelor's degree in civil law
(U. Sherbrooke), master's degrees in common law (U. Sherbrooke)
and international law (U. Montpellier), and completed his doctorate degree (U. Laval and U. Sherbrooke) on the contrast-
ing epistemics of the civilian and common law legal traditions
regarding fundamental rights. He is a lawyer and lecturer practicing and teaching in Montreal and Sherbrooke, specialized in civil
law, fundamental rights, comparative law, and linguistic rights.

SABREENA DELHON is the chief executive officer of the Samara
Centre for Democracy, a non-partisan registered charity with a
mission to realize a resilient democracy with an engaged public
and responsive institutions. For over a decade, she has directed
multi-stakeholder research and outreach initiatives that have made
an impact across justice, academic, and non-profit sectors. Sabreena has appeared as an expert witness before parliamentary committees on matters relating to political participation and frequently
provides commentary about democratic engagement for various
media outlets. She holds a BA in sociology from the University of
Alberta, an MA in sociology from Dalhousie University, and is a
senior fellow at Massey College.

ANTOINE DUTRISAC is an articling student at Davies, Ward,
Phillips & Vineberg. He received his LL.B, J.D, and LL.M from
Université de Sherbrooke.

MARY EBERTS is a senior fellow at Massey College with a national
litigation practice focused on equality rights and Indigenous rights.
She represented the Canadian Advisory Council on the Status of
Women during the drafting of the Charter of Rights, with par-
ticular focus on section 15; the Ad Hoc Committee of Canadian
Women on the Constitution as counsel in the Secession Reference
and during the hearings on the Meech Lake Accord; and the Native
Women's Association of Canada with respect to the Charlottetown
Accord. She has been counsel in matters before the Supreme Court
of Canada, the Federal Court and Court of Appeal, the Ontario
Supreme Court and Court of Appeal, the Quebec Superior Court
and Courts of Appeal in Yukon, British Columbia, Prince Edward
Island, and Alberta. She has held the Henderson Chair in Human

Rights at the University of Ottawa and the Ariel Sallows Chair in Human Rights at the College of Law, University of Saskatchewan, and is an officer of the Order of Canada.

XAVIER FOCCROULLE MÉNARD holds a B.C.L. and an LL.B./ JD from the McGill University Faculty of Law and an LL.M. in legal theory from the University of Toronto, as well as being a Runnymede Society alumnus. He practices as a banking and finance lawyer at Norton Rose Fulbright Canada LLP in Montréal and he is a centre associate to the UBC Centre for Constitutional Law and Legal Studies. He regularly publishes on legal theory, banking and finance law, and constitutional law.

TSVI KAHANA is professor of law at Ono Academic College, Israel. He writes in the fields of constitutional law, constitutional theory, and comparative constitutional law, and has written extensively both about section 33 of the Canadian Charter of Rights and Freedoms and about the notwithstanding clause in the Constitution of Israel.

KRISTOPHER E.G. KINSINGER is the national director of the Runnymede Society and an adjunct lecturer in law at Redeemer University in Hamilton, Ontario. He received his Bachelor of Arts (Honours) from the University of Waterloo in 2016 and his Juris Doctor from Osgoode Hall Law School in 2019, where he was awarded the Bora Laskin Prize for writing the best paper in his year on the topic of law, religion, and society. He was called to the Ontario bar in 2021 and completed his Master of Laws at McGill University in 2021 on a Joseph Armand Bombardier Canada Graduate Scholarship and as the recipient of the Pilarczyk Graduate Award in Law.

ROBERT LECKEY teaches and researches in family law, constitutional law, and comparative law at the McGill Faculty of Law, where since 2016 he has been dean and Samuel Gale Professor. His books include *Bills of Rights in the Common Law* (Cambridge University Press, 2015). A former clerk for Justice Michel Bastarache at the Supreme Court of Canada, he is a member of the Law Society of Ontario and an advocate emeritus of the Barreau du Québec.

CHRISTOPHER MANFREDI has served as provost and vice-principal (academic) at McGill University since 1 July 2015. His research interests include judicial politics, constitutional design, constitutional theory, law and politics, and legal mobilization. He has published extensively in academic and professional journals, has authored or edited seven books, and is a highly regarded political and legal commentator.

JONATHAN MONTPETIT is a senior investigative journalist for CBC News. He covered Quebec politics for many years and has written extensively about the Laicity Act (Bill 21) and secularism debates in the province. He holds graduate degrees in political science from the London School of Economics and McGill University. He spent the 2021–22 academic year as the St Clair Balfour Fellow at Massey College.

DWIGHT NEWMAN, KC, is professor of law at the University of Saskatchewan where he was also the 2013–23 Canada Research Chair in Indigenous Rights in Constitutional and International Law. He has published over 150 articles or chapters and fifteen books, and his work has been cited at all levels of courts.

BENOÎT PELLETIER is a lawyer, doctor of laws, and university professor. As a constitutionalist, he is frequently invited by the media to comment on current events. He was a member of Quebec's National Assembly and a minister in the Charest government. His ministerial responsibilities included Canadian intergovernmental relations, Indigenous affairs, the reform of democratic institutions, the Canadian francophonie, access to information, and internal trade. He is a member of the Order of Canada and an officer in the National Order of Quebec.

GUILLAUME ROUSSEAU completed his doctoral studies in law at l'Université Paris I Panthéon-Sorbonne. He is full professor and the director of the Graduate Applied State Law and Policy programs at the Université de Sherbrooke and associate professor at the Université Laval. He teaches and researches in the field of constitutional law. Professor Rousseau is also a lawyer who acted as legal counsel to the government of Quebec during the preparation and hearings leading to the adoption of the Act Respecting the Laicity of the State.

CAITLIN SALVINO received an MPhil and DPhil in law from the University of Oxford where she studied as a Rhodes Scholar (Ontario, 2018). Her graduate research at the University of Oxford focused on Canada's notwithstanding clause and was supervised by Professor Kate O'Regan. She is an active community advocate and in 2022 was awarded the Governor General Award in Commemoration of the Persons Case for outstanding contributions to gender equality in Canada.

MARION SANDILANDS is a partner at Conway Baxter Wilson LLP. After her call to the bar, she served as a law clerk to the Honourable Andromache Karakatsanis at the Supreme Court of Canada. She has also served as a law clerk and as counsel at the Federal Court. Marion acts for civil society organizations, school boards, parliamentarians, and Indigenous clients. Marion also holds an MA in international affairs and has worked in the field of international development. Marion has appeared before the Supreme Court of Canada on matters of constitutional law and teaches Canadian Federalism Law at the University of Ottawa.

GEOFFREY SIGALET is assistant professor of political science at UBC's Okanagan Campus. He has held fellowships at McGill's Research Group for Constitutional Studies, the Queen's Faculty of Law, and Stanford Law School. He earned his PhD from Princeton University in 2018.

MAXIME ST-HILAIRE holds a doctorate in law (LLD) from Laval University and is professor at the Faculty of Law at Université de Sherbrooke, where he teaches constitutional law and legal philosophy. In 2021, he won this university's research and creation award, in the human sciences category, for his book titled *Les Positivismes juridiques au XXe siècle. Normativismes, sociologismes, réalismes* (PUL, 2020). In 2014, he won the "Prix Minerve 2014" award for his book titled, *La lutte pour la pleine reconnaissance des droits ancestraux: problématique juridique et enquête philosophique* (Yvon Blais, 2015). While a doctoral student, he served as a law clerk to the Honourable Marie Deschamps J., at the Supreme Court of Canada (2009–10), after an internship at the Venice Commission (2007–08).

GRÉGOIRE WEBBER is Canada Research Chair in Public Law and Philosophy of Law at Queen's University and joint founder and executive director of the Supreme Court Advocacy Institute, which provides free advocacy advice to counsel appearing before the Supreme Court of Canada. He was previously senior policy advisor with the Privy Council Office and legal affairs advisor to the attorney general of Canada and minister of justice.

CARA FAITH ZWIBEL is legal counsel at Ontario's Office of the Information and Privacy Commissioner (IPC) where she provides advice and legal counsel on issues related to Ontario's access to information and privacy laws. Prior to joining the IPC, Cara was director of the Fundamental Freedoms Program at the Canadian Civil Liberties Association (CCLA) for over a decade. Her role at the CCLA involved managing litigation, representing CCLA before the courts, appearing before legislative committees, and public education and media work. Cara clerked for the Honourable Justice Ian Binnie at the Supreme Court of Canada. She completed her undergraduate studies in political science at McGill University, graduated from Osgoode Hall Law School in 2004, and was called to the bar of Ontario in 2005. Cara has a master of laws degree from New York University.

Index

principles, 100–1, 157. *See also*
constitutional structure
human rights. *See* bills of rights;
rights
Hunter v. Southam (1984), 255

identities, diverse. *See* diversity;
minority groups
immunization act (New Brunswick,
2019), 117, 128n45
Indigenous peoples: overview,
84–5, 211; criminal justice practices, 85, 92n56; *Dickson v.
Vuntut Gwitchin* (2021), 84,
91n54; gender equality (s. 35(4)),
340–1, 363n103; NWC not to
apply, 211; reform proposals,
84–5; rights (s. 25), 84–5,
91nn53–4; rights (s. 35), 33, 42,
84, 340–1, 363n103; TRC call to
action, 85, 92n56; Yukon, equality rights (1982), 82, 225n5
informed electorate. *See* electorate,
informed
inspections. *See* search and seizure
(s. 8)
interculturalism, 222–3
interjurisdictional immunity, 214
interpreter, right to (s. 14), 229n72
Irwin Toy Ltd. v. A.G. Quebec
(1989), 211

Jolin-Barrette, Simon, 271, 278,
280, 330n8, 337n71
judicial branch: activism, 197–8;
balance of legislative-judicial
supremacy, 49–54, 61n24, 75,
86n1, 197–8; Charter and
increased authority of, 44;
comparative law, 152–3;

constitutional supremacy, 54,
110, 192, 197–8; coordinate
interpretation, 8–9, 12, 54, 59,
76; court curbing, 89n27, 169,
175, 177, 179–80, 226n17;
court-packing, 180, 226n17,
321; courts as political actors,
8–9, 110, 175–80, 185–91, 208–
9; framers' intents, 155–8; institutional constraints and
strategies, 186, 199n10; judicial
decision-making, 185–91; judicial independence, 168, 177,
180, 199n10, 226n17; judicial
independence (Quebec), 280;
jurisdictional boundary, 12;
legitimacy of authority, 52–3;
local knowledge weaknesses, 80,
179; normative legitimacy,
49–54, 62n45, 405; "passive virtues," 104, 171; policy objectives, 185–91, 404–5; protection
of rights, 412; "reading in" as
remedy, 178; strategic behaviour,
196, 199n10; strong-form
review, 153; value of judicial
declarations, 119–20
judicial review: overview, 55–6, 94,
109–10, 125n11, 126n26, 132–3,
158–60; absence of terminology
in NWC, 55, 94, 113, 114,
124n10, 125n11, 134; declaratory
relief, 55–8, 134–5, 137, 152,
195, 333n28; educational function, 17, 55, 58, 94, 104, 113,
115–16, 119–20, 157–8, 317–18,
334n33; *Ford* (1988), 56,
126n26, 126n28, 136–7, 148–51;
judicial duty to review, 104,
131n79, 152, 158, 171; legal case

or targeted choices, 111–12,
116–21; constitutional supremacy, 54, 110, 192, 197–8; coordinate interpretation with judges,
8–9, 12, 54, 59, 76; empirical
review of debates on NWC, 78;
framers' intents, 121; jurisdictional boundaries, 12; legitimacy
of authority, 52–3; normative
legitimacy, 49–54, 62n45, 405;
parliamentary debate choices,
118–20; parliamentary supremacy, 6–7, 10, 41, 61n24, 71,
76–9, 135, 137–8, 139–40, 272–
3; public trust in elected officials,
16, 422; quality of legislative
debates, 78, 121, 358n30, 408,
427; reform proposals, 193,
358n30; respect for judiciary and
rights, 120; role in interpreting
Constitution, 228; timing
choices, 118, 120. *See also*
Quebec, distinctive Quebec
theory
legitimacy of authority: overview,
52–3, 208; constitutional
supremacy, 54, 110, 192, 197–8;
democratic support, 114; normative legitimacy, 49–54, 62n45;
popular support, 208; respect for
order, 208; rule of just law, 53
Letsas, George, 90n43
Lévesque, René, 30–3, 38, 43, 215,
264, 275
liberal constitutionalism: overview,
16–17, 191–4, 272–6, 280–1;
checks and balances, 74, 274,
279–80, 321; constitutional
supremacy, 110, 197–8; democratic backsliding, 3–4, 11–12,

14, 16, 276–81, 422–3; living
tree doctrine, 193, 344; paradox
of judicial power, 110; pluralistic
nationalism, 276; Quebec rise
and fall, 14, 272–81; reform proposal of NWC amendments,
192–4
Libman v. Quebec (1997), 373
life, liberty, and security of person
(s. 7): *Khadr* (2010), 55, 63n60,
134–5, 137, 151–2, 159;
Morgentaler (1988), 177–9,
188–9; non-Canadian citizens,
417n53; NWC to apply, 206–7,
211; remedy, 134–5, 137; *Suresh*
(2002), 417n53
limitations clause (s. 1): overview,
9, 76, 101, 220–1, 292, 320–7;
analysis in two steps, 14–15,
322–7, 335n58, 336n67; balance
of probabilities, 372; collective
and individual rights, 215–17,
220; constitutional structure, 76,
325–6; judicial review, 112–13,
316–18, 327; justification, 212,
213, 320, 322; "least restrictive," 369; necessity test, 212–
13; NWC's uses, 211, 216; *Oakes*
test overview, 187–8, 323–5;
patriation history, 348; purpose
test, 320–4; Quebec context,
215–17, 220–1, 292, 330n12;
"reasonable limits," 101, 320,
326; reform proposals, 287, 316,
323–9, 336n67; rights as existing
prior to legal enactment, 317,
319–20, 325–6; right to vote,
373; Supreme Court's narrow
application, 220–1; text of, 320;
threshold test, 287, 316, 323–9,

367–9, 383, 388–9, 392–4;
informed electorate, 389–96;
legitimacy of NWC and enforcement of voting rights, 383–4,
386–7; meaningful participation,
389–96; normalization of uses,
315–16, 388; NWC's legitimacy
and s. 3 rights, 383–4, 392;
NWC's symbiotic relationship
with s. 3, 383–5; response to
judicial decision, 315–16, 383,
394, 398n15, 400n43; similar to
Quebec uses, 270n60, 316; timing choices, 118, 194–5, 315–16;
unwritten principles, 392; as violation of s. 3's democratic rights,
383, 392
Ontario, Bill 307 Protecting
Elections and Defending
Democracy Act (2021), *Working
Families* challenges: overview,
288, 367–70, 376n17, 378n38,
383–9, 392–6; Bill 254 challenge, 369, 383, 393–4, 398n15;
Bill 307 challenge, 369–70, 383–
9, 398n16; democratic right to
vote (s. 3), 370, 383–8, 395–6;
Figueroa (2003), 390, 395–6;
freedom of expression (s. 2(b)),
358n29, 369, 395–6; *Working
Families*, 358n29; *Working
Families 1* (s. 2(b)), 376n17,
377n23; *Working Families 2* (s.
3), 375n5, 376n17, 378n38,
379n44, 383–9, 392–6, 398n16;
Working Families 3 (s. 3),
378n38
Ontario (AG) v. G (2020), 149,
164n71, 208–9
O'Regan, Seamus, 39

Pal, Michael, 90nn41, 42
pandemic impacts, 281, 423, 425,
426
paramountcy doctrine: Charter of
the French Language, 254;
hierarchy of laws, 138, 171–2;
Quebec charter (notwithstanding
clause), 253; Quebec Charter of
Human Rights (1975), 274
Paris, Erna, 11–12
Parizeau, Jacques, 276
parliament. *See* legislative branch
patriation history: overview, 25–6,
207; Aboriginal and treaty
rights, 33, 42, 84–5, 341;
amending formula, 27–8, 30–8,
42–3, 83, 130n64, 155–8;
Charlottetown referendum
(1992), 35–6, 263, 265; Charter
as nation-building, 262–3; compromise, as concept, 26–30, 37,
42; compromises, 28, 31–8,
42–3, 70, 130n64, 155–8, 321–
2; conference (1980), 30; continuity with bills of rights, 13–14,
62n39, 75–6; framers' intents,
6–7, 19n15, 121, 136, 163n64,
325, 342–3, 386–7; Gang of
Eight, 30–2, 34, 36, 38; gender
equality, 33; historical approach
to interpretation, 70–2, 146,
155–7; historical context, 30–1,
42–3, 62n39, 75–6; Joint
Committee (1981), 33, 345–9,
361n58, 361n71, 416n44;
Kitchen Accord, 25–6, 342,
357nn22, 23; Lévesque's role,
30–3, 38, 43, 275; media cover-
age, 33; Meech Lake Accord, 35,
263, 265, 266, 275; minority